THE BERKOWITZ EDITION

REBBE
NACHMAN'S
TORAH

BRESLOV INSIGHTS INTO
THE WEEKLY TORAH READING

COMPILED BY
CHAIM KRₐ

EDITED ᴮ
Y. HALₗ

בראשית
GENESIS

Published by
Breslov Research Institute
Jerusalem/NY

With great thanks to HaShem
I dedicate this first volume of
The Berkowitz Edition
of the Breslov Chumash
to my parents of blessed memory

Rose and Hymie Berkowitz

May the study of
this commentary on the Torah
uplift all souls
and may it be a great blessing
to the Jewish people

May this volume kindle the eternal flame
that burns within us all
and may it hasten the coming of Mashiach
that he should come in our days,
reuniting the nation of HaShem
and bringing us to Zion!
Amen!

Ira Berkowitz

Breslov Research Institute
extends its heartfelt thanks to

Alvin and Elaine Gordon

and the

Lowenstein Foundation

for initiating this project,
for their continuous encouragement,
and for their munificent support
in bringing this work to fruition

This publication is dedicated
in memory of our dear parents

ר' אליעזר בן ר' יצחק הלוי
Leonard Reich

ר' יהושע בן ר' אברהם
George Korot

הא' עליזה בת ר' יהודה הכהן
Frieda Korot

.ת.נ.צ.ב.ה.

May their memory be for a blessing

Dedicated through the generosity of

ר' זאב בן ר' אליעזר הלוי
Steve Reich

וזוגתו הא' ברכה בת ר' יהושע
Beryl Korot Reich

ר' עזרה בן ר' זאב הלוי
Ezra Reich

אורה בת ר' עזרה הלוי
Orah Reich

This publication is dedicated
to my dear grandfather

Rabbi Daniel Shapiro

who I never knew
but whom I've always known

since it was his life
that inspired me
to always strive
for greater heights

Diana Korzenik

"

This publication is dedicated
in honor of my dear parents
and children

ר' יעקב בן פיגא
וזוגתו
הא' עלקא בת חנה

ובני
אליעזר משה בן חוה
לאה רבקה בת חוה
חנה שרה בת חוה

Dedicated in honor of
and to the merit of

Yaakov ben Feiga
Elka bat Chana

Eliezer Moshe ben Chavah
Leah Rivka bat Chavah
Chana Sara bat Chavah

The Steinberg Family of Toronto

"

"

In loving honor
and gratitude to
my dear parents

Edward and Ann Menaged

for giving me a wonderful education
in Torah and in life

May HaShem bless them

David E. Menaged

"

This book is dedicated

in memory of a wonderful wife,

mother, daughter,

sister, sister-in-law and aunt

Anita Dougherty

May HaShem bless her soul

in the Garden of Eden

and may she merit to see only

nachas and *simchas* from all of her family

With deepest love,

James Dougherty, Lindsay and Carly Dougherty
Marlene Knopf, Mel Knopf
Fern Akrish, Jonathan Akrish
Stefanie, Lisa and David Akrish
Jay Knopf, Lisa Shulman
Robbie and Emily Knopf

Contents

Foreword

"This is *the* book of the generations of man" (Genesis 5:1).

The Five Books of Moses, known as the *ChuMaSh* (חומש, from the Hebrew word *ChaMeiSh* [חמש, five]), span nearly 2,500 years. The opening chapters of the Book of Genesis cover the 2,000 years from Adam until Abraham, with the remaining chapters of Genesis encompassing just over 300 years from Abraham until the passing of Joseph. The first two chapters of the Book of Exodus speak of the 210 years of bondage in Egypt, and the remainder of the *Chumash* covers the forty years from the Exodus until the passing of Moses.

So much for a "history" book which is much more than history.

The Five Books of Moses are also known as the Torah. *ToRaH* (תורה) comes from the root word *hoRaH* (הורה, teach or guide), for the Torah is *the* teacher and *the* guide. Out of His great love for us, God gave us the Torah as His gift, to be our guide for all times and in all situations. Through its stories and laws, the Torah aims to define for us what is right and what is wrong, what is good and what is evil, and how to cultivate a constant awareness of the One Who created it all.

But how are we to learn from the Torah's presentation? How can we live like the Patriarchs and Moses? Are we condemned to the family squabbles of Ishmael and Isaac, Jacob and Esau, and Joseph and his brothers? How do we internalize the bondage in Egypt, the Exodus, the Splitting of the Sea, and the travails of the Jewish people in their journey through the "desert"? What is the Tabernacle? Where is our manna? What of Balaam's curses, and who are the "spies" among us? And what do all the many Torah laws mean to our 21st-century way of thinking?

In truth, the Torah is a closed book and its terse structure discloses little of what it is really all about. The stories it relates about the lives of the founders of Judaism do not tell us how to live our own lives. For this, we must turn to our Sages, who offer extensive commentary on the Mishnah, Talmud, Midrash and Kabbalah, as well as the writings of commentators throughout the ages, to get a better feel for the Torah's messages to us.

"Shema Yisrael—Hear, Israel! God is our Lord. God is One" (Deuteronomy 6:4).

Perhaps the greatest message that the Torah conveys is encapsulated in *Shema Yisrael*, the verse that expresses our belief in God and our willingness to follow His directives. When we recite *Shema Yisrael*, we announce to all that God is One—the One God Who created everything. Notwithstanding the many parts of Creation, everything emanated from the One God. Therefore everything in the world—yes, *everything*—has some presence of Godliness in it. This means that everyone and everything has the ability to connect with God, for he, she or it is already a part of God.

It also means that everything in life can reflect God. Every thought, word or deed can be the bearer of a message from God, telling us to become more aware of our Creator. Nowhere is this message clearer than in the Torah, which proclaims the Unity of God. This can be understood with the following.

It is well known that the Torah contains 613 *mitzvot* (commandments) *(Makkot 23b)*. The word *mitZVah* (מצוה) comes from the root word *tZeVet* (צות, join, attach). When we perform a mitzvah, we join ourselves and the world around us to God.

The 613 *mitzvot* are divided into 248 positive commandments and 365 prohibitions. These commandments encompass every aspect of our relationship with God, with our fellow human beings, and with all existence. Through these commandments, God provided every necessary tool with which man could connect to Him and bring all of creation to its ultimate perfection. The human body also has 248 limbs (listed in *Ohalot* 1:8), corresponding to the positive commandments of the Torah, and 365 connective tissues, veins and sinews, corresponding to the 365 prohibitions of the Torah *(Zohar* I, 170b). Thus, man was fashioned in the pattern of the Torah—not only his soul, but his body as well. The Torah is the link that allows man to experience and feel the Godliness vested in him.

The *Zohar* (III, 73a) teaches: "God, the Torah and Israel are one." When we recite *Shema Yisrael*, we announce God's Unity. When we study the Torah, we do the same: we proclaim that God and His

Torah are one, we acknowledge God's presence in our lives, and we begin to develop a personal relationship with our Creator.

》》

The messages that the Torah sends us, and the import of those messages for a successful life, are best explained in the teachings of Rebbe Nachman of Breslov (1772-1810) and his main disciple, Reb Noson (1780-1844). The way they develop their discourses, revealing God's presence in every aspect of life, helps us understand and apply the Torah's messages to our own lives. After studying Breslov teachings for even a little while, one gets the feeling that God is with him on each page and is calling out to him, "Come! I am here for you!" This has been my personal experience and that of many of my friends and colleagues.

Both Rebbe Nachman and Reb Noson imbue us with the feeling that we can be active participants in Creation, and that each of us can make the world a better place through our thoughts, words and deeds. They make us feel that we are Adam and Eve in the Garden of Eden, embarking on a new beginning. We are standing by the Tree of Life and the Tree of Knowledge of Good and Evil, armed with the choice to either succumb to the enticements of the Serpent or draw nourishment from the Tree of Life. What we choose will impact the future of mankind and the world.

》》

Since the Torah contains much advice for living, we can gain the most benefit by studying it under the guidance of the tzaddikim, whose lessons afford the best counsel (cf. *Likutey Halakhot, Birkhot HaPeirot* 5:17). Reb Noson notes that the best and most important commentary with which we should study the Torah is that of Rashi, who sticks to the simple meaning of the verses while directing us to our Sages' teachings rather than engaging in philosophical discussions (*Likutey Halakhot, Tefilah* 4:7). For this reason, the present work primarily quotes Rashi's interpretation of the verse where it adds depth and reason to the Breslov commentary, rather than citing the original source in the Talmud or Midrash. The few words used by Rashi in his insights are known to contain pages of commentary unto themselves, and Rebbe Nachman and Reb Noson are fond of quoting them and developing them into remarkable counsel.

This work is not intended as a "true" translation of the *Chumash*. In the many translations and commentaries already on the market, we see the variety of ways that each verse can be translated, along with dozens of interpretations. For readers who seek a straightforward translation, we recommend *The Living Torah* (translated by Rabbi Aryeh Kaplan and published by Moznaim Publishers of Brooklyn, N.Y.) and the *Gutnick Chumash* (compiled by Rabbi Chaim Miller from Chabad teachings and published by Kol Menachem of Brooklyn, N.Y.). There are also several informative editions published by ArtScroll, including the *Stone Chumash* and the *Rashi Chumash*. Here we provide a translation that fits closely with the simple meaning of the verse yet lends itself to the commentary of Rebbe Nachman and Reb Noson.

It is our heartfelt wish that readers will gain an appreciation of the personal relationship they can have with God and the levels they can attain through these lofty teachings. May God grant us the wisdom to understand His messages and apply them in the proper way. Then we will merit to see the Coming of Mashiach, the Rebuilding of the Temple, and the Ingathering of the Exiles, speedily in our days. Amen.

Chaim Kramer
Iyar 5771
May 2011

Acknowledgements

> Rebbe Nachman taught: "You should always be grateful to the person who gives you something" (*The Aleph Bet Book, Charity* A:13).

To begin to thank all the people who helped bring this book to fruition might take as many years as it took to prepare the book itself. Instead, we ask forgiveness from the many while we limit our acknowledgements to those who have been the primary supporters of *Rebbe Nachman's Torah* from its beginnings until the present day.

First and foremost, we acknowledge Alvin and Elaine Gordon, who set the whole project in motion with the innocent question "Does Rebbe Nachman offer commentary on the weekly Torah readings?" We had just begun to collect the material on the Bible and weren't sure where to go with it. Their question galvanized us into organizing the material and presenting it *parashah* by *parashah*, verse by verse, giving readers a "handbook" of Breslov thought to enhance their weekly learning and discussions at the Shabbat table.

As word got out that we were doing a *Chumash* project, several people came aboard to help with the financing. In addition to the Gordons and the Lowenstein Foundation, we were blessed with assistance from Steve and Beryl Reich, Jay and Lisa Knopf, and David Menaged. Others, too, from a long list of worthy donors, gave of their time, effort and money to keep this effort going. Noteworthy among them are Diana Korzenik and the Steinberg Family of Toronto, who have been solid pillars of support for this and many other Breslov Research Institute projects. Considering the time and costs involved in this lengthy project, we were blessed even more recently by Ira Berkowitz, who, like a knight in shining armor, came across with a considerable contribution in memory of his dear mother, may she rest in peace.

Our deepest appreciation goes to R' Yaacov Dovid Shulman, who made sense, in English, of the profound insights from Rebbe Nachman's *Likutey Moharan*. And "were all the seas ink, and all the reeds quills," they would not suffice to thank Y. Hall for the excellent rendering of Reb Noson's *Likutey Halakhot* into a language understandable even to the layman. We also commend B. Aber for the superb graphic design.

Thanks are also due to our staff, whose input helped with the flow of this work, and to my wife for putting up with me. I bought a magnet for our refrigerator that says it all: "I do not suffer from stress, but I am a carrier." And she still puts up with me.

May God help us see this project and many others through to completion, and may we all be worthy of seeing the Coming of Mashiach, the Rebuilding of the Temple and the Ingathering of the Exiles, speedily in our days. Amen.

C. K.

A General Overview

Those who are familiar with Rebbe Nachman's lessons know that he begins with a certain premise and develops it using biblical proof-texts as well as Talmud, Midrash, Kabbalah, *Zohar* and other teachings. Building and adding more ideas, he weaves an incredibly beautiful tapestry as the sum of his lesson. Reb Noson follows the same pattern in his discourses. For the student of Breslov, these lessons combine a profound commentary on biblical verses with a wealth of common-sense advice. But for the editor seeking to isolate each teaching verse by verse, the gems of counsel on specific verses are not readily seen. One must plumb the writings of Rebbe Nachman and Reb Noson to find these golden nuggets, as they are intricately woven into their discourses in a most exquisite manner.

Thus, the compilation of this work called for extracting virtually each teaching "out of context" and developing it as a stand-alone unit. For the most part, Rebbe Nachman's and Reb Noson's comments do stand on their own, but several are best understood in their original context. Therefore we present the following as a general overview of *Rebbe Nachman's Torah*.

Several basic, recurring themes are found throughout Breslov teachings, among them: faith, truth, morality, guarding the covenant of Abraham, the central place of the tzaddik in Judaism, giving charity or acting charitably, joy and happiness, guarding and/or controlling one's thoughts, and the primacy of Torah study and prayer. Since these ideas are central to Jewish thought, they are approached again and again in Rebbe Nachman's teachings, and always from a different viewpoint. The three which stand out more than the others are faith, the covenant, and the tzaddik.

❯ *Faith*

As Rebbe Nachman explains: "Fortunate are we that Moses gave us the Torah which begins with "In the beginning God created Heaven and earth." We are commanded to believe in God through faith alone and not enter into speculation (*Rabbi Nachman's Wisdom* #5). This is because faith is built into the Act of Creation, as it is written, "All His works are with faith" (Psalms 33:4).

Reb Noson further explains that in four areas, faith is an absolute necessity. These are: faith in God, faith in the Torah as God's gift to us, faith in the righteous leaders (e.g., Moses, King David, and all the true tzaddikim and leaders of the Jewish nation throughout the ages), and perhaps the most important faith of all, faith in one's self—that one is important in God's eyes, that no matter how far he feels from God, he can always turn to Him, that he has a purpose in life, that he has the faith and the self-confidence necessary to deal with others, and that he has the inner strength to change his habits and better his life (cf. *Likutey Halakhot, Masa u-Matan* 3:6).

Also included in the concept of faith are truth and honesty, since faith implies faithfulness and the ability to trust others, a situation that is made possible only with trustworthiness.

〉 *The Covenant*

The theme of morality and guarding the covenant refers to the Covenant of Abraham, the *brit milah* (covenant of circumcision). *Brit milah* is not a religious ceremony that can be celebrated one day and forgotten the next. It is the eternal bond between God and the Jewish people. The removal of the foreskin of the sexual organ symbolizes the removal of all that is impure from a person's life; with purity of mind and heart, he can then use his organ of procreation to become a partner with God in the ongoing creation of the world. It is unthinkable that one should abuse this power of procreation for lustful purposes, for this pollutes the world with ever-increasing and degrading desires. When a person guards his covenant by elevating his moral thoughts and intentions, he raises himself and, indeed, many others to a heightened awareness of honesty, decency and purity. In Rebbe Nachman's words: "The main way to come close to God is through the guarding and rectification of the covenant" (*Likutey Moharan* I, 29:4).

〉 *The Tzaddik*

The tzaddik is perhaps the most discussed yet least-understood concept in Rebbe Nachman's teachings. This concept is first mentioned in a Talmudic dictum:

> Rabbi Elazar said: For even one tzaddik, the entire world was created. We learn this from the verse "God saw that the light was

good" (Genesis 1:4). "Good" is none other than the tzaddik, as it is written, "Say of the tzaddik, it is good" (Isaiah 3:10). Rabbi Chiya said in the name of Rabbi Yochanan: For even the sake of one tzaddik, the world will be sustained, as it is written, "The tzaddik is the foundation of the world" (Proverbs 10:25) (*Yoma* 38b).

It is axiomatic that the tzaddik is central to Judaism. His tenaciousness to serve God against all odds—witness Abraham's ostracism by the rest of the world for rejecting idolatry and preaching belief in God—and his complete self-nullification before God when serving as the nation's leader—as Moses was willing to "erase" himself if God would not forgive the people's rebelliousness (Exodus 32:32)—has saved the Jewish people time and again during our long history. This is because the tzaddik transcends this material world; he has a grasp of the spiritual even as he exists on the physical plane. As such, he is a sort of bridge between us and God. Of course, no Jew needs an intermediary between himself and God. God certainly does not need anyone to act on His behalf, and neither do we, for we can always search for and seek out God, and we can find Him. But the tzaddik has already found God, and therefore, to put it simply, he knows the way to find God. This means he is the ideal one to teach us whatever we must know in order to draw close to God.

Yet the tzaddik is much more than a teacher who gives us a Godly viewpoint. The tzaddik is on such a high plane that he is truly God's emissary to bring us God's message. Only Moses could bring us the Torah as we know it, and only the very great tzaddikim in each generation—the prophets, the righteous kings, the leading Sages, *Geonim*, Codifiers, and the like—are able to transmit God's instruction, the Torah, to us. (In his classic work, the *Mishnah Torah*, Maimonides lists the leaders of each generation from Moses until the end of the Talmudic era.) And the tzaddikim are given the power from Above to teach the Torah as they see fit—for example, the Talmudic Sages introduced many new laws and guidelines to preserve Torah observance. So too, in each generation, the tzaddikim wield a "God-like power" to direct the nation according to their understanding of the Torah and the generation they live in.

This is a very bold concept, yet not a new one at all. We learn that the tzaddik has this power from the Torah itself. Throughout

Scripture, we find the verse "*Vayedaber YHVH el Moshe leimor*—God spoke to Moses, saying" (Exodus 13:1; 14:1; 25:1; 30:11, et al.). *VayeDaBeR* (וידבר, He spoke) comes from the same root as *DaBaR* (דבר, leader) (Rashi on Deuteronomy 31:7; see *Sanhedrin* 8a). Reb Noson explains that when God spoke to Moses, not only did He speak to him and give him direction, He also passed on that direction and leadership to Moses himself. With each *Vayedaber*, God handed over leadership and direction to Moses, for him to implement the teachings as he saw fit (*Likutey Halakhot, Milah* 2:8).

Understanding the greatness of the tzaddik is crucial to our understanding of the Torah. The Talmud, Midrash, *Zohar* and Kabbalah, and virtually all Chassidic teachings, are replete with statements regarding the greatness of the tzaddik and his central role in Judaism. As Rebbe Nachman emphasizes in his major teaching of *hitbodedut*, each person must develop his own direct connection to God (*Likutey Moharan* I, 52; ibid. II, 25). But the tzaddik is a tzaddik, a leader who gives of himself for others without ever seeking any remuneration, and who will continuously give of himself until his end.

Everyone understands the importance of having qualified leaders—witness the outpouring of emotion and determination on Election Day when people run to the polls to vote for the most mediocre politicians! But Rebbe Nachman looks at leadership from a different viewpoint. His observation of leadership views the likes of Abraham, Moses, King David and Rabbi Akiva, people who gave their lives for others without any regard for themselves. For this reason, the Torah ends with the passing of Moses, for once we bond with such a tzaddik, we are on the right path.

But the Torah does not end. It begins again and again. And this is why we will find many teachings in *Rebbe Nachman's Torah* that are explained with the understanding of the role of the tzaddik in our lives.

Beginnings ⟩

Beginnings

❧ **This is the book of the generations of man** (Genesis 5:1)

Each year we repeat the cycle of weekly Torah readings. Each reading is divided into seven portions, one for each day of the week. Though we repeat the Torah each year, it is a new book each time, as it reflects each person's unique situation and gives him understanding and inspiration to navigate life's challenges and adversities. The Torah contains allusions to each and every person; it is the story of each individual's life. Every person can find himself in the Torah reading of that day and week, and draw inspiration from it (*Likutey Halakhot* I, p. 196a-392).

❧ **The Torah**

The Torah is called a "testimony"—it is a testimony to the reality and Unity of God. The entire Torah, with all its laws and bylaws, the Books of the Prophets and the Writings, as well as the Talmud, Midrash, *Zohar*, Kabbalah, and all the commentaries that accompany these works fit together with incredible precision and perfection. Even a little awareness of the Torah and its contents shows that it is not a man-made presentation, but testimony to our Creator Who gave the Torah to us. Thus, it is written, "The Tablets are the work of God, and the writing is the writing of God" (Exodus 32:16) (*Likutey Halakhot* VII, p. 30-16a).

❧ **The Torah was given after twenty-six generations**

Before God gave the Torah, there had to be a revelation of the desire for Torah and Godliness on the part of mankind. Thus, the Giving of the Torah was delayed for twenty-six generations (Adam to Noah, ten generations; Noah to Abraham, ten generations; Isaac, Jacob, Levi, Kehot, Amran, Moses, six generations [*Chagigah* 13b]), until all the good desires and longings of the tzaddikim in those generations had filled the world with good desires. Then the Torah was given (*Likutey Halakhot* IV, p. 74).

❧ **The reading of the Haphtarah and Maphtir**

The *Maphtir* is the last passage read from the Torah during the Shabbat and Festival services; the *Haphtarah* is a passage read from the writings of the Prophets, whose theme relates to that week's Torah reading. The custom of reading the *Maphtir* and the *Haphtarah* was instituted in Talmudic times during a period of decrees that prohibited the public reading of the Torah. At that time, the Sages instituted the custom of reading a passage from the Books of the Prophets in place of the Torah reading. Today, this *Haphtarah* is recited after the regular Torah reading.

The prophets generally speak of the consolation of the Jewish nation at the end of time—thus, the word *maPhTiR* (מפטיר) alludes to *PaTuR* (פטור, exempt), or an end to suffering, in the merit of upholding the Torah. The *haPhTaRah* (הפטרה) also represents a beginning, as in *PeTeR chamor* (פטר חמור), a firstborn donkey that *PoTeR* (פוטר, exempts) the womb from another firstborn birth (see Rashi on Exodus 13:2). By beginning anew, we can refresh ourselves and our attitude towards serving God, and we will merit to see the end of suffering (*Likutey Halakhot* I, p. 452).

▶ Studying with Rashi

By far, the best commentary with which to study the Torah is that of Rashi, who keeps to the simple meaning of the Torah while directing the reader to our Sages' teachings rather than to philosophical discussions (*Likutey Halakhot* I, p. 348).

A number of people were once praising Rashi's commentaries in Rebbe Nachman's presence. The gist of the conversation was that for a straightforward commentary on the Bible, one need only use Rashi's commentary, as many of the others follow the philosophers (*Tzaddik* #410). The Rebbe remarked, "You may not realize it, but Rashi is like the Torah's brother. Every Jew, from childhood on, studies both the Written and Oral Torah with Rashi's commentary. Think of this and you will understand Rashi's unique greatness" (*Rabbi Nachman's Wisdom* #223).

From Beginning to End

The holiday of Simchat Torah encapsulates the idea that the Torah has no beginning, middle or end. On that day, when we finish the annual cycle of Torah readings with the last section of Deuteronomy, we immediately return to the beginning with a reading from the first section of Genesis. These teachings underscore the link between the end of the *Chumash* and its beginning.

》 *Bereishit...before the eyes of all Israel*

The Torah begins with the letter *Bet* (ב) of *Bereishit* (בראשית) and ends with the letter *Lamed* (ל) of *YisraeL* (ישראל) (Deuteronomy 34:12). Together these letters spell *LeV* (לב, heart). Man's spirit resides in his heart, always motivating him to greater heights (*Likutey Moharan* I, 10:7).

Furthermore, the Torah represents the heart, the dwelling place of the spirit (*Likutey Moharan* I, 10:7). The more we align ourselves with the Torah, the more fully we can develop our spirit.

Thus, we find that God's Holy Name *Elohim* appears thirty-two times in the account of Creation, corresponding to the numerical value of the word *LeV* (לב, heart) (*Likutey Moharan* I, 19:9). This teaches that when we attune our hearts to God, we are able to perceive Him through every facet of Creation.

》 *Bereishit...before the eyes of all Israel*

The Torah itself epitomizes the idea of what Torah is meant to be. It begins with *Bereishit*, the "Concealed Saying"—implying that God is hidden from us and we have no idea what He is all about. It concludes with "what Moses did before the eyes of all Israel" (Deuteronomy 34:12)—implying that the Torah is now revealed to everyone. The Torah teaches us that on the one hand, God is ineffable and one can never know Him; yet at the same time the world is filled with His glory, and His glory is constantly before our eyes (*Likutey Halakhot* V, p. 60a).

》 *Bereishit...before the eyes of all Israel*

The word *BeREiShIT* (בראשית) contains the words *RaShEi* (ראשי) and *BaT* (בת). These refer to four levels: the *Rashei*, which are three "leaders" or "heads" (Chesed, Gevurah, Tiferet), and *Bat* (Malkhut). These four levels correspond to the four colors of the eye (white/sclera, red/muscle, color/iris and black/pupil). Thus, the first word of the Torah speaks about sight—i.e., Divine Providence (*Likutey Halakhot* II, p. 4a).

Divine Providence is drawn from *reishit,* from the very beginning point of Creation, directly from God Himself. A person must draw that Divine Providence into his own sight and "before the eyes of all Israel," so that everyone can constantly perceive God's presence and the Divine Providence that directs all our lives (*Likutey Halakhot* II, p. 10).

⟩ Simchat Torah and Bereishit

The Festival of Sukkot corresponds to the *sefirah* of Binah (Understanding). Fulfilling the mitzvah of sukkah makes it possible for a person to build a house. This is as is written, "With wisdom, a house is built, and with understanding, it will stand" (Proverbs 24:3). Also, observing the Festival of Sukkot is beneficial for the protection of one's flocks. The reason is as follows:

Binah corresponds to the heart. Human beings are unique in that, as babies, they draw nourishment from breasts that are next to the mother's heart—in contrast to animals, which draw nourishment from dugs that are near the mother's waste organs. The same idea applies in a spiritual sense. When a person behaves properly, he draws nourishment from Binah, the heart. Otherwise, he descends to the level of an animal and draws nourishment from the "waste." In the latter case, he takes the nourishment that should rightfully go to animals, preventing the animals from gaining proper sustenance on a spiritual level.

On Sukkot, such a person reconnects to Binah—the heart— and thereby makes it possible for animals to receive their proper sustenance. Furthermore, on Sukkot (more precisely, on Simchat Torah), we complete the cycle of Torah readings and begin the Torah anew. The Torah corresponds to Ze'er Anpin, which is rooted in Binah. Thus, we make a fresh start in our relationship to the Torah by beginning the Torah reading anew right after Sukkot (*Likutey Moharan* I, 266).

Genesis 〉 *Bereishit*

Parashat Bereishit

1:1   בְּרֵאשִׁית בָּרָא אֱלֹהִים אֵת הַשָּׁמַיִם וְאֵת הָאָרֶץ

In the beginning God created Heaven and earth.

⟫ In the beginning God created Heaven and earth

Moses did us a great favor by beginning the Torah with the simple words "In the beginning God created Heaven and earth." In this way, he provided us with a model of faith that involves no sophistication or philosophy (*Rabbi Nachman's Wisdom* #219).

⟫ In the beginning God created Heaven and earth

The world was created principally for the sake of testing people's faith. Once, a follower of Rebbe Nachman was experiencing doubts. The Rebbe told him that all of creation came into being because God saw that there would be people who would cling to faith despite being plagued by confusion. God saw that these people would overcome their questions and remain strong in their beliefs, and for them, He created the world (*Rabbi Nachman's Wisdom* #222).

⟫ In the beginning

The Torah specifically begins with the account of Creation to instill in us the faith that God created the entire world *ex nihilo*. This is *the* foundation of faith (*Likutey Halakhot* II, p. 250).

⟫ Bereishit–God created

The word *BeREiShIT* (בראשית) has the same letters as *Beit REiShIT* (בית ראשית, the home comes first), referring to a person's home. The person himself reflects the Torah, as in "This is the Torah, man" (Numbers 19:14). The walls of each private home demarcate it as individual property—this refers to The Individual, the One God, Whose house it really is (*Likutey Halakhot* III, p. 414). Thus, the beginning of the Torah tells us how to prepare ourselves to live a life of Torah: by dedicating our homes to God.

〉 *Bereishit*

The word *BeREiShIT* (בראשית) may be written as *BeiT REiShIT* (בית ראשית). The word *BeiT* (בית) may itself be read as the word *BaYiT* (בית, home), and the word *reishit* (beginning) can be understood as referring to the Torah (*Vayikra Rabbah* 36:4). Thus, the word *Bereishit—bayit reishit—*teaches us that a person who builds his life on Torah principles brings benefit to his home. This is reflected in the fact that when we return to our homes following the holiday of Sukkot, we begin reading the Torah again from *Bereishit* (*Likutey Moharan* I, 266).

〉 *Bereishit*

Challah (the kneaded dough given to the Kohen), *Bikkurim* (first fruits) and *Terumah* (tithes) are called "first." In the merit of performing these *mitzvot*, the world was created (*Bereishit Rabbah* 1:4).

This Midrash teaches that charity is the first and foremost pillar of Creation. Before a person performs any creative act, he would be wise to give charity (*Likutey Halakhot* III, p. 216a).

〉 *Bereishit—The blueprint of the world*

I was with Him as a nursling (Proverbs 8:30).

Do not read *AMoN* (אמון, nursling), but *UMaN* (אומן, blueprint) (*Bereishit Rabbah* 1:1).

The Torah is the blueprint of the world. Everything is sustained by combinations of letters in the Torah (*Likutey Moharan* I, 33:3). Therefore one can always find the Torah, which provides a pathway to God, in whatever exists in creation.

〉 *Bereishit*

The word *Bereishit* can also be translated as "for the sake of the head." The world was created for the sake of Israel, which is its head (*Vayikra Rabbah* 36:4).

When God created the world, He anticipated the pride and joy that He would derive from the good deeds of His nation, Israel. Therefore He created everything in the world in accordance with how it would reflect that pride and joy (*Likutey Moharan* I, 17:1). Some people might reflect the beauty of the Swiss Alps; others, the beauty of the Amazon rainforest or even the Sahara Desert. Every

Jew must be aware of how important he is in God's eyes, and know that in one way or another, he reflects the beauty of Creation.

❱ Bereishit

The beginning of wisdom is the fear of God (Psalms 111:10).

The letters of the word *BeREiShYT* (בראשית) can be transposed to form the phrases *YaREi BoSheT* (ירא-בשת, awe-humility) and *YaREi ShaBbaT* (ירא-שבת, awe-Shabbat). *ShaBbaT* (שבת) is associated with repentance, for it contains the same letters as *TaShuV* (תשב, you will repent).

Thus, with the word *Bereishit*, the Torah indicates the importance of striving for awe of God. With this awe, a person can attain great levels of humility before God, so that even if he falls, he can always return to Him (*Likutey Moharan* II, 72; ibid., I, 38). Furthermore, *YaREi BoSheT* (awe-humility) indicates that a person's humility—which is due to his understanding of the awesomeness of God—inspires him to fear God (*Likutey Moharan* I, 22:10).

❱ Bereishit

The letters of the word *BeREiShYT* (בראשית) can be transposed to spell *YaREi ShaBbaT* (ירא שבת, Shabbat-observer). In the merit of keeping Shabbat, a person merits to fear of God (*Likutey Halakhot* III, p. 1a).

❱ Bereishit

The word *BeREiShYT* (בראשית) has the same letters as *YaREi ShaBbaT* (ירא שבת, Shabbat-observer) (*Tikkuney Zohar* #9, p. 24b). Shabbat is equal to the entire Torah (*Yerushalmi, Shabbat* 1:8).

The Torah preceded the creation of the world by 2,000 years (*Bereishit Rabbah* 8:2). Since Shabbat is compared to the entire Torah, we can say that Shabbat also preceded the world by 2,000 years. These 2,000 years are represented by the boundary of 2,000 *amot* (cubits) outside the city limits, up to which a person may walk on Shabbat. This boundary also corresponds to the boundary of the mind, which imposes limitations on what we can understand, what is beyond us, and where we must strengthen our faith. Thanks to these boundaries, we can draw the intellects of Torah and the sanctity of Shabbat to recognize Creation as God's handiwork (*Likutey Halakhot* III, p. 102).

⟩ *Bereishit bara Elohim*

> Our Sages teach that the Egyptian king Ptolemy ordered the seventy elders of Israel to translate the Torah into Greek. As they did so, the elders altered the translation of several verses in order to avoid misinterpretation. They changed the verse "*Bereishit bara Elohim*—In the beginning God created" to "*Elohim bara bereishit*—God created in the beginning." Otherwise, Ptolemy was liable to have read the verse as "[An entity called] In The Beginning created God" (*Megillah* 9a).

Rebbe Nachman teaches that the elders had to alter the verse because, in its pure form, the Torah is so intense that a person who is distant from God cannot properly understand it. For the same reason, the Torah contains narratives, and the Talmud and Midrash are replete with stories—these are vehicles through which the light of Torah can be transmitted to relatively simple or unknowledgeable people. The Rebbe adds that this explains why many tzaddikim converse on mundane topics with their followers. They do so in order to transmit Torah concepts in a simple format that their followers can grasp (*Likutey Moharan* II, 91).

⟩ *Bereishit*–The Concealed Saying

> The world was created with Ten Sayings ("God said…"). Yet only nine times does the Torah record the words "God said." This teaches that *Bereishit* is a Concealed Saying (*Rosh HaShanah* 32a).

Just as *Bereishit* is a Concealed Saying, God's presence is concealed in Creation. When the Torah states: "The earth was formless and empty, with darkness upon the face of the depths, and the spirit of God hovered above the surface of the waters" (Genesis 1:2), it gives us hope for our own lives. Despite everything that can overwhelm a person and upset his life, God is with him and can take him out of his confusion and chaos (*Likutey Halakhot* III, p. 213a). This point is made even clearer by the fact that the Torah never mentions the creation of the waters, only that the spirit of God "hovered above the surface of the waters." Though certain things in Creation conceal Godliness, we should always know that God is present (ibid., p. 430).

⟩ *Bereishit—The Concealed Saying*

Repentance was created prior to the world (*Pesachim* 54a).

The Concealed Saying of *Bereishit* alludes to the Hidden Torah, which sustained the world prior to the Revelation at Sinai. The Hidden Torah is the root of Creation, from which all else developed. Each succeeding Saying revealed more and more of God's glory, until the entire world was filled with His glory.

The Concealed Saying of *Bereishit* is loftier than the Torah, for when a person sins, the Torah demands punishment for the wrongful deed that has been committed. Theoretically, repentance shouldn't help—but it does, because repentance is rooted in *Bereishit*, in the Hidden Torah. This also explains why the recital of Kaddish can bring merit to a deceased parent. Ostensibly, whatever a person accomplished during his lifetime remains on his record as a credit or demerit. How can the efforts of another person change the record? But in the Kaddish prayer we say, "Who is exalted beyond all blessings and praises"—this refers to the Concealed Saying, the root of everything, which connects directly to repentance and rectification (*Likutey Halakhot* V, p. 88-45a).

⟩ *Bereishit—The Concealed Saying*

Why must one of the Ten Sayings be concealed?

There are three ways in which God's voice is conveyed: through a direct sound, through a reflected sound, and through an admixture of the two. The direct sound is that of God speaking to us—to our souls—sending us messages and giving us directions to serve Him. Were we to hear this voice directly, however, we would not have free choice. The Midrash relates that the Jews at Sinai gave up their souls each time they heard God's voice directly, because it was too intense for them (*Shemot Rabbah* 29:4).

The reflected sound is similar to an echo, as if God's voice hits the material world and bounces back off it. This voice is easier to hear, but it is tainted by the materialism which it contacts. One must not make the mistake of thinking it is only God's voice, lest the materialism within the reflected sound overwhelms him and leads him to error and even atheism. Instead, he should strive to identify God's voice within the reflected sound.

The Concealed Saying is God's direct voice. The other Sayings are an admixture containing the potential of the direct sound together with the reflected sound. It is this third type of sound that we are able to hear and react to positively (*Likutey Halakhot* VI, p. 18a).

❱ *Bereishit*

The world was created with Ten Sayings (*Avot* 5:1).

The first of these Sayings is the word *Bereishit*. This is a Concealed Saying, in that nothing is actually said—in contrast to the following nine Revealed Sayings, each one of which is introduced by the phrase *Vayomer Elohim* (God said).

As a whole, these Ten Sayings correspond to the Ten Commandments, indicating that the might of Creation can be found in the Torah. The nine Revealed Sayings correspond to the Revealed Torah. With its commandments, rewards and punishments, the Revealed Torah represents the realm of justice, which is a manifestation of God's kindness in that it shows us the path He wants us to follow. The Concealed Saying, *Bereishit*, corresponds to the Hidden Torah, which contains the mysteries of the Kabbalah and the mysteries of Creation. This Hidden Torah includes provisions for a concealed level of kindness, known as the Treasury of Unearned Gifts, which God created to delay the application of justice and give a person the chance to repent (see *Likutey Halakhot* VIII, p. 221b).

❱ *Bereishit*

Rabbi Eliezer states that the world was created in the month of Tishrei. Rabbi Yehoshua claims that it was created in Nisan (*Rosh HaShanah* 10b).

Repentance was created prior to the world (*Pesachim* 54a).

The word *BeREiShIT* (בראשית) alludes to these two views. The first letter, *Bet* (ב), which has a numerical value of 2, is followed by the word *REiShIT* (ראשית, beginning). *Bet reishit* indicates "two beginnings"—i.e., Tishrei and Nisan (*Likutey Moharan* I, 49:6). Because these months represent new beginnings, they are both propitious for repentance.

Bereishit

The letters of the word *BeREiShYT* (בראשית) can be rearranged to form the phrase *ROSh BaYiT* (ראש בית, head of the house). The "head" refers to the tzaddik and the "house" to the world. A person's first step in drawing close to God should be to seek out the tzaddik (*Likutey Moharan* II, 67).

Bereishit–The Holy Land

Rashi asks why the Torah begins with the account of Creation rather than starting with the commandments, which are its *raison d'etre*. To answer this question, he quotes the verse "The might of His works He told His people, to give them the heritage of the nations" (Psalms 111:6). Rashi explains that because God created the entire world, it belongs to Him and He can give any part of it to whomever He sees fit. Should the nations of the world claim that the Jews wrongfully seized the Holy Land, they can reply that in the beginning, God gave it to the gentiles, but then He took it from them and gave it to the Jews (Rashi on Genesis 1:1).

In the verse cited by Rashi, "The might of His works He told His people," the word *ko'ach* (כח, might) has the numerical value of 28. This corresponds to the number of letters in the first verse of Genesis (*Likutey Moharan* I, 44:1). In this way, the Torah teaches us that when we are cognizant of God's might, we reveal the sanctity of the Holy Land, which God gave specifically to His chosen people (ibid., II, 78).

Reb Noson raises a question regarding Rashi's explanation: What difference does our reply make to the gentiles? Reb Noson states that it may well make no difference to them. But when we proclaim our faith in God and invoke His might, it strengthens our own faith in God and reinforces our belief in our right to possess the Holy Land (cf. *Likutey Halakhot, Shomer Sachar* 4:1).

Bereishit–The Holy Land

Why does the Torah begin with *Bereishit*? If the nations should say, "You are thieves, because you took by force the land that belongs to the seven Canaanite nations," tell them, "The whole world belongs to God, Who created it. He can give the land to whomever He wishes" (Rashi).

And if you tell them, will they listen? The truth of the matter is that the *kelipot*—and by extension, the nations—always claim that everything is theirs. The husk always precedes the fruit; therefore the nations were given control of the Holy Land before the Jews, and thus, they claim that we stole the Land from them. However, when we study and observe the Torah, we reveal God's will in the world. Then the nations are forced to admit to the truth and rescind their claims (*Likutey Halakhot* VIII, p. 155a).

⟩ *Bereishit—The Holy Land*

> Why does the Torah, which details the history of the Jewish people, begin with the Act of Creation? It is a reproof to the nations of the world, who might claim that the Land of Israel belongs to them. We can point to this passage and reply, "God created the entire world and it is His. He gave the Land to you. But then He took it away from you and gave it to us" (Rashi).

God gave us the Holy Land to observe the Torah, as in "He gave you the lands of nations…in order that you observe His laws and Torah" (Psalms 105:44-45). Therefore, when we observe the Torah, the Land is ours. By observing the Torah, everyone will merit to see God's greatness and will believe that He created the entire world. They will thereby come to know Him and acknowledge our rights to the Land. If we do not observe the Torah, we give credence to the claims of the other nations (*Likutey Halakhot* I, p. 237a-474).

⟩ *Bereishit—The Holy Land*

> Why does the Torah begin with *Bereishit*? If the nations should say, "You are thieves, because you took by force the land that belongs to the seven Canaanite nations," tell them, "The whole world belongs to God, Who created it. He can give the Land to whomever He wishes" (Rashi).

The power to convince the world that the Holy Land belongs to us lies in the Torah, which details God's Creation and His ownership of it. Without the Torah, we have no claim to the Land. What sustained the world until the Torah was given? *Matnat Chinam*—God's Lovingkindness, The Treasury of Unearned Gifts.

For us to expound the Torah and claim the Land, we must draw pure Torah; it must be drawn properly from Above. We can access this Torah through prayer, by beseeching God and asking Him to bestow His Lovingkindness upon us—rather than asking for His beneficence by saying we expect our prayers to be answered because we deserve it. The first type of prayer is the one offered by the very great tzaddikim such as Moses (see Rashi on Deuteronomy 3:23). Such a prayer is answered from God's Treasury of Unearned Gifts—the same Treasury that sustained the world until the Torah was given.

As for the second type of prayer, which demands results based on the rewards for our deeds, the person who offers it is comparable to a thief who demands and takes what he wants. To pray in this manner negates the concept of God's Treasury of Unearned Gifts and counters the ideals of a pure Torah received through Lovingkindness. Moreover, since the Treasury of Unearned Gifts is conceptually the Hidden Torah that sustained the world, such a person shows that he does not rely upon the Torah for his sustenance. Thus, the nations that claim the Jews took their land in the manner of thieves have a legitimate grievance. But when we pray to God to reward us from His Treasury of Unearned Gifts, we affirm the Torah that sustains the world, entitling us to the Land (*Likutey Halakhot* VIII, p. 221b).

❱ *Bereishit—The Holy Land*

God created the world to reveal His will. When we find and reveal His will, we can conquer the Holy Land. Moreover, every place that we conquer and transform into a place of holiness, such as a synagogue (cf. *Megillah* 29a), reveals God's will. Thus, building a synagogue or some other foundation of holiness is akin to conquering the Holy Land (*Likutey Halakhot* I, p. 464).

❱ *Bereishit—The Holy Land*

Why does the Torah begin with the account of Creation rather than with the first mitzvah given to the Jews, that of declaring the New Moon? According to Rashi, the account of Creation comes to teach us that the Holy Land belongs to us. In reality, we cannot establish and declare the New Moon without knowing the mysteries of intercalation, which can be attained only through the sanctity of the Holy Land and the ordainment of Sages who can declare the New Moon (*Sanhedrin* 2a). Thus, the Torah had to begin with the account of Creation in order to reveal the sanctity of the Holy Land, so that we can draw that sanctity and ability to declare the New Moon (*Likutey Halakhot* III, p. 232; see below, p. 55).

⟩ *Elohim*

> Jewish tradition teaches that God began to create the universe
> solely with the attribute of judgment, as evidenced by the mention
> of His Holy Name *Elohim* throughout the Creation account. But
> once He started to do so, He "reconsidered," as it were, and
> blended that judgment with compassion (Rashi).

Judgment represents *tzimtzum* (constriction or restraint). That
tzimtzum prepared the way for the creation of the evil inclination
(since the attribute of judgment represents the "left side" [see
Charts, p. 345], from which the forces of the Other Side draw their
sustenance).

Thus, God first created the world with the attribute of judgment,
which corresponds, as it were, to His "evil inclination." He then
"broke" His "evil inclination" by incorporating the attribute of
compassion into His Creation. He did this in order to create the
power of free choice, with which man, too, can break his evil
inclination (*Likutey Moharan* I, 72).

⟩ *Bereishit–Judgment/Compassion*

> In the beginning, it arose in God's First Thought to create the
> world with the attribute of judgment. God saw, however, that man
> would not be able to survive with strict justice, so He blended the
> attribute of compassion with the attribute of judgment (Rashi).

We know that God created the world to show His compassion
(*Etz Chaim* 1:2; see *Likutey Moharan* I, 64:1). If so, why did He approach
Creation using the attribute of judgment? Where does compassion
exist in judgment?

The answer is that God wanted the world to operate according
to a system of strict justice. In such a world, if a person sinned
and deserved punishment, he would immediately recognize God
as the Cause of his suffering and turn to Him for forgiveness. By
nullifying himself to God, he would draw very close to his Creator,
which is the ultimate compassion. However, God perceived that
the vast majority of people would be unable to exist in such a
system. After all, who is truly able to attain such a level of self-
nullification? Therefore He attached compassion to judgment and
used them both to create the world.

This explains the meaning of "the original light that enabled a
person to see all around the world. God saw that the wicked would

misuse it, and hid it for the tzaddikim" (*Chagigah* 12a). This great light, the light of Godliness, allows the one who nullifies himself to God to "see" what the Infinite can see. God hid this light for the tzaddikim, who know how to nullify themselves before God (*Likutey Halakhot* II, p. 237a-474-238a).

Bereishit—Judgment/Compassion

It is known that God created the world in order to reveal His compassion (see *Etz Chaim* 1:2). If so, why did He first decide to create the world with the attribute of judgment?

In truth, God wanted judgment to rule *because of* His great compassion. He wanted man to earn his reward rather than receive it as a gift. (That is, God's compassion becomes aroused because of a person's sin, which He forgives. Then the person does not actually earn his reward on his own merit.) God's attributes are truly beyond comprehension. Even when He performs kindness, there is an element of justice to it, and when He institutes judgments, they are bound together with compassion (*Likutey Halakhot* VIII, p. 20a).

Elohim

Inherent within each new situation is the Divine attribute of judgment. Just as all of Creation came into being only after the *Tzimtzum*, so too, we can attain our own goals only after we face the constraints of each new instance of *tzimtzum*—with its chaos, emptiness and darkness—until we come to the light (cf. *Likutey Moharan* I, 84).

Bereishit bara

The first two words of the Torah are *Bereishit bara* (In the beginning He created). The word *BaRA* (ברא) can be seen as the first half of the word *BeREishit* (בראשית). Thus, we can see *Bereishit* as a whole word and *bara* as half a word.

Bereishit is whole in that it indicates the primal reality prior to Creation, when God alone existed. This level is represented by prayer, when a person merges with His Creator. *Bara* is half a word, insofar as it represents the reality following the Act of Creation; this reality appears to be separate from God (although this is actually not the case). This level is represented by the Torah, where a person studies about his Creator and learns how to pray and to become subsumed in his Creator (*Likutey Moharan* I, 22).

❭ *Bereishit bara Elohim*

The final letters of the words *BereishiT barA ElohiM* (בראשית ברא אלהים), can be rearranged to spell *EMeT* (אמת, truth) (*Tikkuney Zohar*, end).

Truth is God's seal, and the entire world stands upon this foundation (*Likutey Halakhot* I, p. 158).

❭ *Bereishit bara Elohim*

The first three words of the Torah, *BereishiT BarA ElohiM* (בראשית ברא אלהים)—form a double acrostic. The initial letters of these words spell *BaBA* (בבא, Aramaic for "gate"), and the final letters of these words can be rearranged to spell *EMeT* (אמת, truth) (*Tikkuney Zohar*, end). *BaBA* is a reference to the Talmudic tractates of *BaVA Kama* (בבא קמא, First Gate), *BaVA Metzia* (בבא מציעא, Middle Gate) and *BaVA Batra* (בבא בתרא, Last Gate), which address the laws of damages, business and trading, and property and inheritance, respectively.

God created the world with intellect, as the verse states: "All were made with wisdom" (Psalms 104:19). For Creation to continue, man must guard his own intellect. He does so by adhering to truth, which is an inherent part of Creation. Should man fail to guard his intellect, he will fall prey to *BaBA*—to the conflicts and damages that are also inherent in Creation (*Likutey Halakhot* VIII, p. 234b).

1:2   וְהָאָרֶץ הָיְתָה תֹהוּ וָבֹהוּ וְחֹשֶׁךְ עַל־פְּנֵי תְהוֹם
וְרוּחַ אֱלֹהִים מְרַחֶפֶת עַל־פְּנֵי הַמָּיִם

The earth was formless and empty, with darkness upon the face of the depths, and the spirit of God hovered above the surface of the waters.

❭ *Creation of the waters*

The waters were the first creation in the world (see Rashi on Genesis 1:1), referring to *chiddush ha-olam* (renewal of the world). Therefore water is the main means of purification from all impurities, since it symbolizes renewal (*Likutey Halakhot* II, p. 22).

The earth was formless and empty, with darkness...and the spirit of God hovered above the surface of the waters

> God created the world because of the Jews, who are called *reishit* (first) (*Vayikra Rabbah* 36:4).

God created the world in anticipation of the pride He would have in the Jewish nation. Yet immediately after Creation, the earth was "formless and empty, with darkness," since the deeds that take place in this world cover over and conceal the source of that pride. Still, the spirit of God can be found by the "waters"—i.e., in charitable deeds. By engaging in charitable acts, man can elevate himself to the level where God takes pride in him, and thereby reveal that pride—i.e., the spirit of God (*Likutey Halakhot* VII, p. 41a).

Formless and empty, with darkness upon the face of the depths...spirit of God

> "Formless," "empty," "darkness" and "depths" refer to the four exiles (*Bereishit Rabbah* 2:4). The "spirit of God" is the spirit of Mashiach (*Zohar* I, 192b).

God sees the end from the very beginning. In the beginning, He foresaw that there would be exiles and suffering. But also in the beginning, He created the source of consolation from that suffering: Mashiach and Redemption. Moreover, the spirit of God "hovers" above the depths. Even in the midst of suffering, the "spirit of God" hovers right above a person (*Likutey Halakhot* II, p. 236).

Formless and empty

God created an emptiness and void in which His Presence was not manifest. Yet He also made His spirit available, "hovering above the surface of the waters." This means that it is possible for us to counter the emptiness and void and find God in this world.

"Water" is a reference to Torah (cf. Isaiah 55:1), and the "spirit of God" alludes to the spirit of Mashiach (*Zohar* I, 192b), who will ultimately counter the confusions of this world. We arouse the spirit of Mashiach when we translate the Torah that we are learning into our own words—particularly, into our mother tongue. By restating the Torah in our own idiom, we draw its holiness into the mundane world and bring it closer to the Messianic era (*Likutey Moharan* I, 118).

In particular, the "spirit of Mashiach" refers to Mashiach's deep sense of morality. We attach ourselves to that spirit when we ourselves attain a pure and moral attitude—and that makes it possible for us to "hover above the surface of the waters"—i.e., to learn Torah in depth (ibid., II, 32).

⟩ Formless and empty

The earth that is without form, and desolate, represents the evil that can overcome a person. To rectify this evil, one must find its counterpart of good. This ability is found in the "spirit of God"—namely, the spirit of Mashiach, who always finds the good in everything. Thus, the Torah immediately states: "God said, 'Let there be light'"—which corresponds to the good—"and God separated between the light and the darkness"—since by searching for the good, one can separate good from evil (*Likutey Halakhot* I, p. 3a).

⟩ The spirit of God hovered above the surface of the waters

When there is *tohu vavohu*—too much confusion—one cannot see or experience God. Yet he should be aware that God is always "hovering" nearby. At any time, a person can attach himself to God and bring about a revelation of Godliness (*Likutey Halakhot* III, p. 306).

⟩ The spirit of God

The "spirit of God" can be found in the Torah. When we study Torah and generate original Torah ideas, we literally draw God's spirit onto ourselves (*Likutey Moharan* II, 72; ibid., I, 78).

⟩ The spirit of God

A harp hung above King David's bed. At midnight, the northern wind (*ruach tzafon*) blew upon it, and it awoke him to serve God (*Berakhot* 3a).

Ruach (wind) also means "spirit." *TZaFoN* (צפון, northern) is similar to *tZaFuN* (צפון, hidden)—i.e., something hidden in the heart. The northern wind that woke David to serve God is the "spirit of God hovering over the surface of the waters." That spirit is hidden within each individual's heart, and awakens him to serve God (*Likutey Moharan* I, 8:2).

Darkness upon the face of the depths... Let there be light

Why is it that goats precede the sheep in a flock? Just like the Creation: First came darkness, then came light (*Shabbat* 77b). (Goats are generally a darker shade than sheep.)

The seed of a medicinal plant must be nurtured to sprout properly so its healing qualities can take effect. So too, faith must be nurtured for its qualities to be effective. Even more, faith must precede healing. Why? "Just like the Creation: First came darkness, then came light." "Darkness" signifies a lack of advice; "light" represents clear counsel. A person who is surrounded by the "darkness" of indecision must seek counsel from one who can reveal it to him. That one is the tzaddik, whose "deep waters are counsel in the heart of man, and a wise man will draw them forth" (Proverbs 20:5). "Waters"—i.e., counsel—nurture the "seed"—faith—which sprouts into vegetation and herbs that can heal. Thus, first comes darkness, which causes a person to be ill. Then comes "light"—counsel, faith and healing (*Likutey Moharan* II, 5:2-3; *Likutey Halakhot* VIII, p. 86b).

1:3   וַיֹּאמֶר אֱלֹהִים יְהִי אוֹר וַיְהִי־אוֹר

God said, "Let there be light," and there was light.

Creation

On the First Day, everything was created in potential, to be actualized on its own, individual day (Rashi).

The original light created on the First Day was deemed too great for this world, and was hidden away for the tzaddikim in the Future (see *Bereishit Rabbah* 12:6).

Creation demonstrates the process of bringing potentiality into actuality. Right from the beginning, obstacles exist—the chaos, the void, the darkness—representing the impediments that each person faces when he tries to create a spiritual life for himself. One must persevere. Then "God said, 'Let there be light,' and there was light"—meaning, the light that is there in potential will come into existence. It is up to each person to seek out and reveal this light (*Likutey Halakhot* IV, p. 149a-298).

⟩ The creation of light

"Light" refers to what exists after Creation. Prior to Creation, everything is considered "darkness"— i.e., beyond comprehension (*Likutey Halakhot* II, p. 466).

⟩ Bereishit…tohu vavohu…Let there be light

Reishit (the beginning) represents true wisdom. *Tohu vavohu* (chaos and confusion) represent the secular wisdoms that intervene to distance a person from God. Yet "the spirit of God" is always present, "hovering above the surface of the waters." To reveal it, we require the "light"—the teachings and guidance of the tzaddikim (*Likutey Halakhot* VII, p. 282).

⟩ God said, "Let there be light," and there was light

"Let there be light"—this is the right hand. "And there was light"—this is the left hand (*Tikkuney Zohar* #30, p. 74a).

The two hands represent any act of creation, since they are the organs with which we can build, form and construct anything, from the first thoughts of doing to the actual, finished product. Therefore the hands represent definition. The force that effects creation is the spirit of God, but in the beginning of any creative effort, that spirit is cloaked in darkness and confusion. Whenever we want to convert our thoughts and ideas into actual deeds, we must first define what we are attempting. This will help us overcome the challenges and obstacles—the darkness and confusion—that arise to block our path, and draw out the spirit of God to help us succeed (*Likutey Halakhot* II, p. 370).

1:4   וַיַּרְא אֱלֹהִים אֶת־הָאוֹר כִּי־טוֹב וַיַּבְדֵּל אֱלֹהִים
בֵּין הָאוֹר וּבֵין הַחֹשֶׁךְ

God saw that the light was good. God separated between the light and the darkness.

⟩ God saw that the light was good

The original light illuminated so brightly that a person could see the entire globe. God foresaw that the wicked would misuse this light, and hid it for the tzaddikim for the Future (*Bereishit Rabbah* 12:6).

From the very beginning of Creation, God envisioned everything that would take place until the end of time. Similarly, our goal should be to look towards the end of time, to the place beyond our temporal lives, and focus on the World to Come. Thus, "God saw that the light was good"—He saw that it was not for this world, and He hid it for the tzaddikim (ibid., 12:6). A person who desires to see this light must therefore attach himself to the tzaddikim, follow in their paths, and always focus on the ultimate goal (*Likutey Halakhot* I, p. 284).

God saw that the light was good

"God saw that the light was good"—i.e., that it would be good for it to be hidden (*Bereishit Rabbah* 12:6).

The "light" of the Torah refers to its mysteries. A person must delve into Torah in order to attain that light. The light of the tzaddik is similarly hidden (*Likutey Moharan* I, 33:5).

The light was good

God hid the light that He created on the First Day of Creation so that the wicked could not partake of it. This light is so awesome that it must be concealed, or else it will overwhelm the unworthy ones. But the tzaddikim merit to see this light, since although it is hidden, it does illuminate this world. Additionally, the light of the tzaddikim themselves is also hidden from the world, and people do not always merit to see who these tzaddikim are. Still, their light also illuminates this world, and one who seeks the tzaddikim will merit to see this light (*Likutey Halakhot* I, p. 22).

The light was good

God wanted His great light to shine for all mankind. But His light was so great that people would be unable to receive it in good and beneficial measures. Therefore God hid the light so that each person would look within his capabilities and not beyond them (*Likutey Halakhot* II, p. 414).

God saw that the light was good…God called the light "day," and the darkness He called "night"

"Light" is a means by which we can see and comprehend our surroundings. "Good" refers to the Torah (*Avot* 6:3). Thus, the terms "light," "good" and "day" correspond to spiritual awareness. Darkness, on the other hand, represents the constriction of that awareness (*Likutey Moharan* I, 74).

At the time of Creation, darkness preceded light. Similarly, an individual must begin with faith, which functions during the obscurity called "night" when vision and knowledge are limited. Then he must attain counsel, as alluded to in the verse "He reveals depths that were concealed within darkness" (Job 12:22). "Depths" corresponds to counsel, as in the verse "Deep waters are counsel in a man's heart" (ibid., 20:5) (*Likutey Moharan* II, 5:2). Only after one experiences "darkness" can he attain "light"—i.e., proper vision and understanding.

⟩ Let there be light…He separated…one day

Light and darkness cannot serve together. Therefore "He separated" them (Rashi).

Light is *da'at* (knowledge). Darkness is foolishness (*Likutey Halakhot* I, p. 7a). By separating the two, God made each distinct. Once they were distinct, they could then be joined together, since each one knew its place. Thus, "There was evening and there was morning, one day" (*Likutey Halakhot* I, p. 100a).

1:5   וַיִּקְרָא אֱלֹהִים לָאוֹר יוֹם וְלַחֹשֶׁךְ קָרָא לָיְלָה וַיְהִי־
עֶרֶב וַיְהִי־בֹקֶר יוֹם אֶחָד

God called the light "day," and the darkness He called "night." There was evening and there was morning, one day.

⟩ God called the light "day"

Any architect of value will constantly seek to design new and different structures. The Architect of the world certainly creates new things each day. Each day must shine brightly, with added light. We can emulate God by cultivating renewed energy and a fresh approach each day, to add light and goodness to our lives (*Likutey Halakhot* I, p. 123a-246).

》 *God called the light "day"*

The phrase "God called the light 'day'" implies that we must inject intellect and spiritual light into every one of our days (*Likutey Moharan* II, 4:8). That is, each day has to illumine more than the previous day (*Likutey Halakhot* IV, p. 171a). The main light of day is Divine Providence. One who believes that nature is an independent power is entrenched in night and darkness (ibid., I, p. 153a-306).

》 *The darkness He called "night"*

"Darkness" refers to the Babylonian Talmud (see *Sanhedrin* 24a).

The commentaries explain that this is not a description of the Talmud itself, God forbid, but of the difficulty of studying and recalling it.

During our long exile, the Talmud—which embodies the Oral Law—has held us together as a nation. Thus, it can be compared to faith, which also serves us during bleak times (*Likutey Moharan* I, 35:4).

Since the Talmud corresponds to "night," it is particularly propitious to study it (or the Mishnah, its foundation) during the night (ibid., I, 3).

》 *God separated between the light and the darkness*

"Light" refers to stories about the righteous. "Darkness" refers to stories about the wicked (*Bereishit Rabbah* 3:8).

Only a person who can tell the difference between spiritual light and spiritual darkness can differentiate between stories about tzaddikim and stories about wicked people.

The Midrash relates that the tzaddik Phineas was able to fly—but so was the wicked Balaam (see *Bamidbar Rabbah* 22:5). Evil mimics good. While similar stories may be told about tzaddikim and wicked people, one must learn to differentiate between true light and its pale imitation (*Likutey Moharan* I, 234).

Many times these stories appear to be the same. We must learn to differentiate between what is truly light and what is darkness, because the stories by and about tzaddikim bring light into the world, while the stories by and about the wicked bring darkness (*Likutey Halakhot* I, p. 106a).

⟩ *Night and day*

Each day of a person's life contains a night and a day—both ups and downs. Our main mission in life is to combine the two, to understand that even in the darkness, there is light, and that notwithstanding the light and good moments, there could be difficult moments, too. With this understanding, we attain true faith and come to recognize God (*Likutey Halakhot* II, p. 202-102a).

⟩ *There was evening and there was morning*

One can attain "daylight" and intellect only when he acknowledges that there is a "night" and constrictions that precede it (*Likutey Halakhot* I, p. 208a).

⟩ *There was evening and there was morning, one day*

Time itself is a creation spawned by the word *Bereishit* (see *Chagigah* 12a).

This world lies within time and space. It is our mission to transcend time and space, to join "after Creation" with "before Creation" (*Likutey Halakhot* I, p. 40a).

⟩ *Yom Echad*

The verse should have said "the First Day." Instead it is written, "Day One," to indicate that God is One (Rashi).

The term "Day One" indicates that at that time, everything was included in God's Unity (*Likutey Halakhot* V, p. 97a).

⟩ *Creation of the angels*

Angels were created on the Second Day, so that no one would say the angel Michael had stretched [the heavens] to the south while the angel Gabriel had stretched them to the north (*Bereishit Rabbah* 3:8; see Rashi).

God had no need for helpers when He created the world. Nevertheless, He created angels in order to implant the idea of free choice in Creation. Had God ruled openly and exclusively, no one would ever choose to oppose His will. By concealing His authority and assigning messengers to carry out His wishes, God made His authority less obvious and gave people the freedom to decide how they would think and act.

Thus, on the First Day of Creation, God created the world and everything in it. On the Second Day, He created angels to carry out the specifics of each creation. Man can now choose to accept that whatever happens—even if it seems to occur through an intermediary—comes from God Himself (*Likutey Halakhot* VII, p. 207a).

1:6   וַיֹּאמֶר אֱלֹהִים יְהִי רָקִיעַ בְּתוֹךְ הַמָּיִם וִיהִי מַבְדִּיל בֵּין מַיִם לָמָיִם

God said, "Let there be a firmament in the midst of the waters, and it will separate between water and water."

Let there be a firmament in the midst of the waters

At the onset of Creation, everything was a single unity. But on the Second Day, God created the firmament to separate the "lower waters" from the "upper waters." Each of these "waters" desired to be close to God, and they cried and pleaded with Him for that privilege (*Tikkuney Zohar* #5, p. 19b). We see, then, that the firmament keeps the lower waters at a distance from God.

We generally find that the greater the value of our objective, the greater the obstacles that we face in order to attain it. And once we reach a goal, the greater our satisfaction in having done so and in having withstood the challenges along the way.

God created a "firmament" that separates us from our spiritual goal. If we truly desire Godliness and spirituality, we will cry out to God and beg Him to draw us close. Thus, the obstacles we face in our spiritual search are not meant to keep us at a distance, but to *increase* our desire to attain the knowledge of God (*Likutey Moharan* I, 66:4).

It will separate between water and water

When the waters were separated, the lower waters began to cry. Each said, "I want to be before the King!" [Therefore] God made a covenant with the waters that they would be placed upon the Altar [in the Temple, during Sukkot] (*Tikkuney Zohar* #5, p. 19b).

The lower waters "cried" because they didn't know that it was possible to reveal Godliness through them. The firmament represents the tzaddik, who shows those "below" that even they can reveal Godliness (*Likutey Halakhot* II, p. 29a).

1:7   וַיַּעַשׂ אֱלֹהִים אֶת־הָרָקִיעַ וַיַּבְדֵּל בֵּין הַמַּיִם אֲשֶׁר
      מִתַּחַת לָרָקִיעַ וּבֵין הַמַּיִם אֲשֶׁר מֵעַל לָרָקִיעַ
      וַיְהִי־כֵן

God made the firmament. He separated between the waters that were below the firmament and the waters that were above the firmament. So it was.

〉 *He separated between the waters that were below the firmament and the waters that were above the firmament…*
Let the waters below the heavens be gathered to one place

The separation of the waters represents a dispute that was for the benefit of the world (*Bereishit Rabbah* 4:6). Similarly, we find many disputes throughout the Talmud that are for the benefit of the world. This is seen in the verse "Let the waters below the heavens be gathered (יקוו, *yiKaVu*) to one place"—that is, the divided waters should unite. A *miKVah* (מקוה, pool of water used for ritual purification) has the same power to create unity from division. Thus, immersing in a mikvah is propitious for peace and unity (*Likutey Halakhot* VI, p. 7a).

1:9   וַיֹּאמֶר אֱלֹהִים יִקָּווּ הַמַּיִם מִתַּחַת הַשָּׁמַיִם אֶל־
      מָקוֹם אֶחָד וְתֵרָאֶה הַיַּבָּשָׁה וַיְהִי־כֵן

God said, "Let the waters below the heavens be gathered to one place, and let the dry land be seen." So it was.

〉 *Let the waters below the heavens be gathered to one place, and let the dry land be seen*

The "waters" represent *da'at* (knowledge of God), as in "The world will be filled with knowledge of God, as water covers the seabed" (Isaiah 11:9). Our mission in life is to gather as much *da'at* as we can and gather it to the "one" place—in other words, to recognize the One God. As we say in the Shema, "God is our Lord, God is One" (Deuteronomy 6:4). Then "the dry land will be seen," for earth corresponds to faith. When a person uses his intellect to seek God, he attains a level of faith in God (*Likutey Halakhot* III, p. 306).

1:11   וַיֹּאמֶר אֱלֹהִים תַּדְשֵׁא הָאָרֶץ דֶּשֶׁא עֵשֶׂב מַזְרִיעַ
זֶרַע עֵץ פְּרִי עֹשֶׂה פְּרִי לְמִינוֹ אֲשֶׁר זַרְעוֹ־בוֹ עַל־
הָאָרֶץ וַיְהִי־כֵן

God said, "Let the earth sprout vegetation. Plants bearing seeds and fruit trees that produce fruit, each after its own kind, with seeds in it, will be on the earth." So it was.

﴿ *Fruit trees that produce fruit, each after its own kind*

When God commanded the trees to reproduce and yield fruit after their own kind, the grasses drew an inference in regard to themselves: "If the trees, which are large and do not reproduce in close proximity, must bring forth fruit only after their own kind, then how much more does that apply to us, for we are small and do reproduce in close proximity?" Upon hearing this, the ministering angel proclaimed: "May God's glory last forever!" (*Chullin* 60a).

Rebbe Nachman applies this idea to the marital union. "Trees" correspond to tzaddikim, who are great in stature and whose marital relations do not occur in close proximity but are limited to Shabbat (cf. *Ketuvot* 62b). "Grasses" correspond to the average person, who does engage in marital relations in close proximity—i.e., during the week. The fact that the ministering angel proclaimed: "May God's glory last forever!" teaches us that all people must be careful to maintain sanctity in this area of life—even the lofty tzaddikim. Then they do God's will, as do the plants, which reproduce only "after their own kind" (*Likutey Moharan* I, 11:7).

﴿ *Fruit trees that produce fruit*

A person must also become "a tree that produces fruit." Through his study of Torah, he can cull advice on how to draw close to God (*Likutey Halakhot* VIII, p. 149b). Performing good deeds also corresponds to a person being a fruit-bearing tree.

1:16 וַיַּעַשׂ אֱלֹהִים אֶת־שְׁנֵי הַמְּאֹרֹת הַגְּדֹלִים אֶת־הַמָּאוֹר הַגָּדֹל לְמֶמְשֶׁלֶת הַיּוֹם וְאֶת־הַמָּאוֹר הַקָּטֹן לְמֶמְשֶׁלֶת הַלַּיְלָה וְאֵת הַכּוֹכָבִים

God made the two great lights—the greater light to rule the day and the lesser light to rule the night—and the stars.

⟩ *The two great lights*

Originally, God created the sun and moon as equals. But the moon complained, "Can two kings make use of the same crown?" (*Chullin* 60b). In the verse, the Hebrew word for "lights" (מארת, *MeORoT*) is spelled deficiently, without the letter *vav* (מאורות, *MeOROT*), implying that the diminution of the moon was a *MeARah* (מארה, curse) visited upon it for speaking in this fashion (Rashi on Genesis 1:14, 16).

These "two great lights" were intended to be a person's intellect and his faith. That which a person could understand using his intellect, and that which was beyond his capabilities, would be equal in his mind. But the moon (which corresponds to faith) complained, "Can two kings make use of the same crown?" indicating that it wanted to be the greater light. (For through faith, one can attain far greater levels than he could possibly attain through intellect [since faith can reach the Infinite, while intellect cannot]) (*Likutey Halakhot* III, p. 214). God then told the moon, "Go and diminish yourself," for when a person tries to reach levels beyond his abilities, he must be restrained. Though God expects a person to strive for that which is beyond him, he must take care not to extend himself too far beyond his capabilities.

⟩ *The two great lights*

The main creation was for mankind to be exposed to truth. God is truth and His seal is truth. A person who seeks truth will be able to experience God. But not always do we see truth; there are times when we need to believe it exists and seek it from that point of faith.

The sun and the moon refer to truth and faith, respectively. God wanted both to be equal. In this world, however, the light of truth is too great an illumination for most people to bear directly. Of necessity, Godliness must be concealed, so the only way to receive the light of truth is through faith. Therefore the moon was diminished, to show that faith must receive its illumination from the sun, from truth (*Likutey Halakhot* VII, p. 6-4a).

❩ *The two great lights*

The sun and the moon were created of equal size, but afterwards the moon was diminished. By calculating the exact lunar cycle and the reappearance of each New Moon, our Sages bring the solar and lunar cycles into harmony. Therefore, when we observe Rosh Chodesh, we rectify the moon's blemish, towards the day when the "light of the moon will be as the light of the sun" (Isaiah 30:26) (*Likutey Halakhot* II, p. 340).

❩ *The greater light…the lesser light*

The sun—the "greater light"—represents wisdom, which illumines the path a person walks upon and directs him to his goal. The moon—the "lesser light"—represents faith, which guides a person when he cannot understand the circumstances of his life's journey. This is why the moon shines at night, in darkness—for in a person's darkest moments, faith illumines his path (*Likutey Moharan* I, 35:5-6).

Originally, these two lights were created as equals—thus, a person's faith would be as solid as his intellect. However, God then diminished the moon—and so a person must struggle to build his faith, especially when he faces challenges. He must always work on strengthening his faith until, in the words of the prophet, "the light of the moon will be as the light of the sun" (Isaiah 30:26) (*Likutey Moharan* I, 1:2).

❩ *The two great lights, the greater light…the lesser light*

The sun represents clear knowledge; the moon indicates lack of knowledge. They were created equal, for as much as a person knows, he must realize that there is much that he still does not know. The moon protested, however, saying, "Can two kings make use of the same crown [of knowledge and lack thereof—see *Likutey Moharan* I, 24]?" Thus, the moon was diminished—it waxes and wanes, just as a person grows in knowledge yet forgets what he has learned.

Nevertheless, both the sun and the moon—clear knowledge and lack of knowledge—are absolutely essential, for Keter, the highest level of understanding, consists of both "knowing God, yet accepting that He is beyond knowledge." The moon looked beyond its level and lost some of its importance. A person, too, must know when to search for greater knowledge and understanding, and when to desist (*Likutey Halakhot* I, p. 414-208a).

⟫ *The lesser light*

The moon represents the *sefirah* of Malkhut, which corresponds to prayer. This "lesser light" must be elevated to become a "great light"—the *sefirah* of Binah, which corresponds to repentance and knowledge of God (*Likutey Moharan* I, 49:5-6). Praying to God brings a person to true repentance.

⟫ *The two great lights*

Originally, God created the sun and moon as equals. But the moon complained, "Can two kings make use of the same crown?" (*Chullin* 60b). In the verse, the Hebrew word for "lights" (מארת, *MeORoT*) is spelled deficiently, without the letter *vav* (מאורות, *MeOROT*), implying that the diminution of the moon was a *MeARah* (מארה, curse) visited upon it for speaking in this fashion (Rashi on Genesis 1:14, 16).

This diminution is the cause of childhood disease, for a reduction of the light of the lesser light corresponds to a reduction of life force to small children (*Ta'anit* 27b).

The fact that the *vav* is missing indicates the presence of Lilith, an evil force that attacks young children (*Zohar* III, 234a). This force is called *LYLYt* (לילית) because it is always whining (מיללת, *meYaLeLet*) and brings *YeLaLah* (יללה, wailing) into the world, producing songs of lament (*Likutey Moharan* I, 151; ibid. 226).

This also explains why wicked people, who are attached to this *kelipah* of depression, sing sad and mournful tunes (*Likutey Moharan* I, 226).

The moon's diminished light and the energy of Lilith correspond to a weakened capacity to see and choose the proper path in life (see also ibid., I, 205).

⟫ *The stars*

Because it was diminished, the moon was given the stars to accompany it (*Chullin* 60b).

The stars represents the tzaddikim (cf. Daniel 12:3) who find goodness even in the darkest moments and merit even in the most unworthy people. Their actions rectify the diminished moon (*Likutey Halakhot* II, p. 304).

1:20   וַיֹּאמֶר אֱלֹהִים יִשְׁרְצוּ הַמַּיִם שֶׁרֶץ נֶפֶשׁ חַיָּה וְעוֹף יְעוֹפֵף עַל־הָאָרֶץ עַל־פְּנֵי רְקִיעַ הַשָּׁמָיִם

God said, "Let the waters teem with living creatures and let birds fly over the earth, against the face of the firmament of the heavens."

⟩ *Birds*

Birds were created from a combination of the elements of water and earth. They occupy a stratum between the human and the animal, insofar as they possess a modicum of the power of speech (and thus continuously chirp). Speech is a combination of the planes of Heaven (the "upper waters") and earth; therefore, like birds, speech consists of "water" and "earth." Since speech is associated with Heaven and earth, when a person expresses himself properly, he connects Heaven and earth (*Likutey Moharan* I, 11:8).

1:24   וַיֹּאמֶר אֱלֹהִים תּוֹצֵא הָאָרֶץ נֶפֶשׁ חַיָּה לְמִינָהּ בְּהֵמָה וָרֶמֶשׂ וְחַיְתוֹ־אֶרֶץ לְמִינָהּ וַיְהִי־כֵן

God said, "Let the earth bring forth living creatures, each according to its own kind— animals and creeping things and beasts of the earth, each according to its own kind." So it was.

⟩ *Let the earth bring forth living creatures, each according to its own kind*

"Earth" is equivalent to the *sefirah* of Malkhut, which is associated with the earth. Therefore earth—like Malkhut—represents the Oral Law. And the Oral Law is the source of the spirit of every living being, as the verse states: "Let the earth bring forth living creatures, each according to its own kind" (*Likutey Moharan* I, 12:1).

1:26 וַיֹּאמֶר אֱלֹהִים נַעֲשֶׂה אָדָם בְּצַלְמֵנוּ כִּדְמוּתֵנוּ
וְיִרְדּוּ בִדְגַת הַיָּם וּבְעוֹף הַשָּׁמַיִם וּבַבְּהֵמָה
וּבְכָל־הָאָרֶץ וּבְכָל־הָרֶמֶשׂ הָרֹמֵשׂ עַל־הָאָרֶץ

**God said, "Let us make man in our image
and likeness. They will rule over the fish of
the sea, the birds of the sky, the animals and
the entire earth, and every creeping thing
that creeps upon the earth."**

〉 *Let us make man in our image and likeness*

In the Book of Ruth, when Naomi asked Ruth where she received
the wheat that she brought home, Ruth replied, "The name of
the man for whom I did (*asiti*) today is Boaz" (Ruth 2:19). The *Zohar*
teaches that this verse is speaking of charity, which is alluded to
in the word *ASiti* (עשיתי, I did). The root of that word is the same
as the root of the word *na'ASeh* (נעשה, let us make), and thus
recalls the creation of man (*Zohar* I, 13b).

God created man to be charitable and kind (*Likutey Moharan* I,
37:3; ibid., II, 2:4). The "image"—corresponding to man's spiritual
essence—charitably gives its light to the "likeness"—corresponding
to man's body.

The concept of charity also applies to a marriage. Each partner in
a marriage relationship can be either a benefactor or a beneficiary.
As such, husband and wife must always be considerate of one
another. When they are in a relationship of mutual kindness, they
are considered to be complete—a whole "human being" (*Likutey
Moharan* I, 13:5).

〉 *Let us make man*

God created Adam alone so that each individual (a new "Adam")
will say that the world was created for him (*Sanhedrin* 37a).

Therefore each individual has a responsibility to refrain from
sinning, which would damage the world and harm others. Instead,
he must seek to improve the world, particularly by praying for all of
existence—even for the animal, vegetable and mineral kingdoms
(*Likutey Moharan* I, 5:1).

The creation of man

Man was created with the ability to attain two types of intellectual illumination. One consists of the wisdom and knowledge that comes after years of effort; the other is an influx of intellect that comes to a person suddenly and opens his mind. The latter type of intellectual illumination is a gift of God, a holy spirit that a person can attain as a result of sanctifying his eyes, ears, nose and mouth, avoiding immorality, and seeking truth.

The phrase "Back and front have You hemmed me in" (Psalms 139:5) (which refers to the creation of Adam and Eve back-to-back [see below, p. 60]) alludes to these two types of intellect—one coming slowly from the "back" and the other opening up suddenly from the "front" (*Likutey Moharan* I, 21:1).

The creation of man

For two-and-a-half years, the Schools of Shammai and Hillel argued as to whether man should have been created, until they concluded that it would have been better had he not been created (*Eruvin* 13b).

That being the case, why did God create man? The answer is that if one takes into account only man's toil and suffering in this world, then indeed, it would have been better had man not been created. But in the context of man's ability to attain the ultimate goal of the World to Come, it is certainly better that he was created (*Likutey Moharan* II, 39).

Let us make man

The angels claimed, "Do not create man, for he will sin against You." God answered, "Is it for naught that I am called Compassionate?!" (*Pesikta de-Rav Kahana* 24:7).

The angels could not understand how God could derive pleasure from the service of a lowly human being. Only God, Who knows Himself, could create a corporeal being that would bring delight to the highest of levels, to God Himself (*Likutey Halakhot* V, p. 24).

1:27   וַיִּבְרָ֨א אֱלֹהִ֤ים ׀ אֶת־הָֽאָדָם֙ בְּצַלְמ֔וֹ בְּצֶ֥לֶם אֱלֹהִ֖ים
בָּרָ֣א אֹת֑וֹ זָכָ֥ר וּנְקֵבָ֖ה בָּרָ֥א אֹתָֽם

**God created man in His image. In the image
of God, He created him; male and female
He created them.**

〉 *Male and female*

Adam and Eve were originally created back-to-back, after which
God separated them so that they were able to turn to face each
other (*Berakhot* 61a).

So too, in order to turn to God, we must first "cut" ourselves
apart from our attachment to this material world (*Likutey Moharan* I,
108). To keep the metaphor straight: We must first cut ourselves
apart from our alienated relationship with God before we are able
to face Him and relate to Him.

〉 *God created man*

The angels argued with God, "Do not create man, for he will sin
against You" (*Pesikta de-Rav Kahana* 24:7).

But God did create man, for He is compassionate beyond
description. God saw to it that there would be tzaddikim in every
generation who would work to infuse people with the knowledge
of God and who would eventually bring all people back to serve
God (*Likutey Halakhot* III, p. 37a). However, from the accusations of the
angels stem all strife and arguments between people today (*Likutey
Halakhot* II, p. 360).

〉 *Adam was created last*

Shabbat, the day God finished His Creation, represents the
World to Come, the level of "beyond time." Adam was created just
before Shabbat, because man's mission is to elevate everything
from the level of being ruled by time to the level beyond time
(*Likutey Halakhot* III, p. 420).

1:28   וַיְבָרֶךְ אֹתָם אֱלֹהִים וַיֹּאמֶר לָהֶם אֱלֹהִים פְּרוּ וּרְבוּ
       וּמִלְאוּ אֶת־הָאָרֶץ וְכִבְשֻׁהָ וּרְדוּ בִּדְגַת הַיָּם וּבְעוֹף
       הַשָּׁמַיִם וּבְכָל־חַיָּה הָרֹמֶשֶׂת עַל־הָאָרֶץ

God blessed them. God said to them, "Be fruitful and multiply, and fill the earth and conquer it. Rule over the fish of the sea, the birds of the sky, and every living creature that creeps upon the earth."

⟩ *Be fruitful and multiply*

The mitzvah of having children and multiplying one's offspring points to a singular goal. Though there will be many individual minds and intellects, all will agree to unite and serve the One God (*Likutey Halakhot* VIII, p. 69b-70a).

⟩ *Be fruitful and multiply*

Just as a person must be fruitful in the physical sense, he must also be fruitful in the spiritual sense. He must study Torah and develop original thoughts in his learning, thoughts that will "bear fruit" and bring him close to God. In fact, each soul brought to this world represents a new Torah thought (*Likutey Halakhot* VI, p. 156).

⟩ *Be fruitful and multiply*

Although God's Creation is diverse, it is all an extension of God Himself. Therefore the world is really a single unity. In particular, each human being reflects Godliness in one way or another, for all are made "in the image of God." Thus, it is a mitzvah to parent children, for the existence of each child constitutes an additional expression of Godliness (*Likutey Moharan* II, 37).

⟩ *Be fruitful and multiply*

This is the first mitzvah of the Torah and its importance cannot be understated. For this mitzvah represents the guarded covenant. Every person must engage in having children and everyone— tzaddik and simple person alike—is capable of drawing pure souls to the world. Indeed, the holy Rabbi Shimon bar Yochai had ancestors who were simple people, yet from them came a great tzaddik who said he had the power to rectify the entire world

(*Sukkah* 45b). Similarly, from the union of Judah and Tamar (Genesis 38), Mashiach will eventually be born (*Likutey Halakhot* III, p. 26a).

⟩ *Be fruitful and multiply*

One cannot just live his life and then depart this world without leaving his *da'at*, his knowledge of God, behind. One's children can transmit his *da'at* further (*Likutey Halakhot* VI, p. 14). This is the mitzvah of having children, to perpetuate one's life through living descendants who attain knowledge of God. This is because the main purpose of marriage is the propagation of the species. Leaving behind children alludes to the idea of remembering a person forever. This "eternal" memory implies recalling God and the ultimate purpose of Creation: to merit to the World to Come (*Likutey Halakhot* II, p. 364).

⟩ *Be fruitful and multiply*

As long as Adam was alone, there was only one—corresponding to the truth, which is one. As soon as there were two (Adam and Eve), the potential for falsehood came into existence. Falsehood and the evil that derives from falsehood led man astray, to the point that Adam and Eve ate from the Tree of Knowledge against God's express command. Then Cain killed Abel. Then the Generation of the Flood, about whom it is written, "When man *increased* in the world" (Genesis 6:1), turned to atheism and idolatry.

Why, then, does the first mitzvah of the Torah enjoin man to "be fruitful and multiply"? Why would God institute a mitzvah that leads to falsehood, jealousies and all types of sin? The answer is that specifically in this way, man can exercise free choice. From the many, he will search for the One, and embark on his own individual path to recognize God (*Likutey Halakhot* IV, p. 200a-400).

⟩ *Be fruitful and multiply*

Rebbe Nachman once said, "A person should pray to have many children, despite the way they may turn out! For when Mashiach comes, he will rectify the entire world, and everyone—all the way back to Adam—will be rectified" (*Aveneha Barzel* p. 21, #4).

❩ *Multiply and fill the earth*

"Fill the earth"—because "the whole earth is filled with His glory" (Isaiah 6:3). That is, we should fill the earth with people who fill the earth with God's glory (*Likutey Halakhot* I, p. 157a).

1:31   וַיַּרְא אֱלֹהִים אֶת־כָּל־אֲשֶׁר עָשָׂה וְהִנֵּה־טוֹב מְאֹד
        וַיְהִי־עֶרֶב וַיְהִי־בֹקֶר יוֹם הַשִּׁשִּׁי

God saw all that He had made and behold! It was very good. There was evening and there was morning, the Sixth Day.

❩ *It was very good*

"Very good"—this is a reference to the Angel of Death (*Bereishit Rabbah* 9:10).

It is "very good" that death exists, for without the fear of death, people would spend their lives frivolously, always thinking that there will be time later on to accomplish (see *Bereishit Rabbah* 9:6-12).

"The Angel of Death" represents all the evil that exists in the world. The presence of evil makes it possible to choose between good and evil; when a person subdues evil by choosing good, he attains great reward. Moreover, that subdued evil itself becomes the foundation upon which he can build the structure of goodness (*Likutey Moharan* I, 38:7). As a result of death, the soul can ascend to a world that is entirely good. Thus, a person should always look beyond the sufferings of this world and focus on the Future Reward, which makes it possible for him to attain joy (*Likutey Moharan* II, 33).

❩ *It was very good*

"Very good"—this is a reference to the Angel of Death (*Bereishit Rabbah* 9:10).

The phrase "It was very good," which represents the existence of the Angel of Death and evil, appears in the description of the Sixth Day of Creation, the day that God created man. Just as God intended man to recognize and serve Him, so too, each person must attempt to persuade the realm of the Angel of Death to be aware of God (*Likutey Moharan* I, 10:3).

⟩ *It was very good*

As long as a person is clothed in a physical body, he can know God only in a hidden manner. But after death, when he sheds his corporeality, he can know the essence of God. Thus, death is "very good" (*Likutey Halakhot* I, p. 109a).

⟩ *It was very good*

Adam brought death into the world by eating from the Tree of Knowledge. However, death is now a "blessing," since it purifies the body before it rises again in the Resurrection. Therefore "It was very good"—this is death *(Bereishit Rabbah* 9:10) (*Likutey Halakhot* I, p. 134).

⟩ ***There was evening and there was morning, the Sixth Day***

The letters of the word *BeREiShIT* (בראשית) may be rearranged to form the words *BaRA ShIT* (ברא שית, He created six). God created the original Six Days (*Likutey Moharan* I, 63:1), of which the principal was the Sixth. That day corresponds to the sixth of the seven lower *sefirot*, Yesod (Foundation), which implies morality (see Charts, p. 344). On this day, man—the foundation of the world—was created.

⟩ ***The Sixth Day***

"The Sixth Day"—this alludes to the sixth day of Sivan, when the Torah was given (Rashi).

Created on Friday, the eve of Shabbat, man was supposed to usher the entire Creation into a state of Shabbat and rest. It is impossible to enter into Shabbat unless one toils during the preceding six weekdays, and the main effort of preparing for Shabbat takes place on the Friday before. Therefore one who takes his efforts of the week and puts in his toil for Shabbat connects the weekdays to Shabbat, and links this world with the World to Come (since Shabbat is one-sixtieth of the World to Come). Therefore Rashi explains: "'The Sixth Day'—this alludes to the sixth day of Sivan, when the Torah was given"—since the Torah forms the link between these two opposite worlds (*Likutey Halakhot* I, p. 228a).

⟩ ***The Sixth Day***

The earth was unstable until the Torah was given (Rashi).

The Torah was actually present in the world from the time of Creation, for Torah is what sustains the world. However, this refers to the Hidden Torah, which corresponds to God's Lovingkindness which sustains the unworthy. This form of sustenance is not the ideal. Therefore all Creation awaited "*the* Sixth Day"—the sixth day of Sivan, when the Torah was given—so that the world could be sustained by the Torah in its revealed state (*Likutey Halakhot* VIII, p. 3a).

⟩ The Sixth Day

This alludes to the sixth day of Sivan, when the Torah was given (Rashi).

The world was created for the Torah (*Bereishit Rabbah* 1:1).

According to God's original plan, the Torah was to be given in the one-thousandth generation after Creation. But God saw that because of brazenfaced, wicked people who sprang up in each generation, the world could not exist without Torah. So He gave it to mankind in the twenty-sixth generation (Adam to Noah, ten generations; Noah to Abraham, ten generations; Isaac, Jacob, Levi, Kehot, Amram, Moses, six generations) (*Chagigah* 13b-14a; see above, p. 25).

Since the world was created for the Torah, according to the Midrash, why did God give the Torah only in the twenty-sixth generation? How could the world have survived without Torah for that long? And had God waited until the one-thousandth generation, would there have been any tzaddikim to receive it at that late date? And if there were tzaddikim, wouldn't they have deserved it immediately, instead of in the one-thousandth generation?

Indeed, there were tzaddikim who served God even before the Torah was given, such as Abraham (*Kiddushin* 82b) and the other Patriarchs. Furthermore, "Every generation has tzaddikim like Abraham" (*Bereishit Rabbah* 56:7). With the presence of these tzaddikim, the world could have existed without Torah, for these tzaddikim would have taught people how to serve God. Thus, God could delay the Giving of the Torah until the one-thousandth generation to allow the tzaddikim to teach the people and help clarify and purify their powers of imagination, which had been blemished through the sin of Adam. In this way, we could have received the Torah in an absolutely refined and purified state that would inhibit any further desire to sin.

However, in every generation, we find brazenfaced, wicked people who mock the tzaddikim and slander them, making it extremely difficult for their fellow men to benefit from them. Therefore God gave us the Torah much earlier, despite our not being completely worthy of it, since the giving itself caused a cleansing of the imagination, purifying our faith to a certain degree. This purification enables us to overcome the protestations of the wicked (*Likutey Halakhot* II, p. 123a-124a).

⟩ *Yom HaShishi*

The letter *hei* of *Yom HaShishi* (יום הששי, *the* Sixth Day) mirrors the *hei* of *HaMotzi* (המוציא, in the blessing over bread). It is a *hei ha-yediah* (a specific *hei*), teaching us that all our sustenance is rooted in the Act of Creation (*Likutey Halakhot* II, p. 13a-26).

2:2	וַיְכַל אֱלֹהִים בַּיּוֹם הַשְּׁבִיעִי מְלַאכְתּוֹ אֲשֶׁר עָשָׂה
	וַיִּשְׁבֹּת בַּיּוֹם הַשְּׁבִיעִי מִכָּל־מְלַאכְתּוֹ אֲשֶׁר עָשָׂה

With the Seventh Day, God completed His work that He had done. He rested on the Seventh Day from all His work that He had done.

⟩ The Seventh Day

The six days of the week correspond to the Tree of Knowledge of Good and Evil. Shabbat, the seventh day, corresponds to the Tree of Life (cf. *Zohar* I, 27a).

Da'at (Knowledge) consists of three sets of opposing concepts: permitted and forbidden, fit and unfit, pure and impure. The six days of the week represent our sifting through these states of being in order to properly serve God. Therefore they are days of work. If a person repents but then stumbles because he is not in full control of his emotions and intellect, his repentance corresponds to the weekdays, to the Tree of Knowledge in which good and evil are mixed together.

Shabbat, on the other hand, represents the Tree of Life. When a person repents successfully, that corresponds to Shabbat, the "day of rest" from one's evil desires. The letters of the word *ShaBbaT* (שבת) can be rearranged to form the word *TaShuV* (תשב, you will repent). Shabbat represents true repentance (*Likutey Moharan* I, 79).

The Seventh Day

The six days of the week are divided into the three pairs (*Bereishit Rabbah* 11:8). As for Shabbat, it is paired with the Jewish people. A person who observes Shabbat can rejoice with his mate, as it were (*Likutey Moharan* I, 277).

God made the world in six days and rested on Shabbat

"Made the world" represents an "arousal from below," signifying man's efforts to create during the six days of the week. "Rested on Shabbat" represents an "arousal from Above," in that everything is performed by God alone, for He bestows benevolence even if we do not make an arousal from below (*Likutey Halakhot* III, p. 2).

With the Seventh Day, God completed His work…He rested on the Seventh Day

What was the world missing? Rest. Comes Shabbat, and with it comes rest (Rashi).

The rest that was created on Shabbat completed the Act of Creation. For the rest that comes on Shabbat—the focal point of the six weekdays—sustains the world (*Likutey Halakhot* II, p. 109a).

God completed His work

A person should also consider that all of his work is completed on Shabbat (Rashi on Exodus 20:9).

For this reason, we are forbidden to ask God for our mundane needs on Shabbat, since everything should seem complete and perfect at that time (*Likutey Halakhot* III, p. 8a).

Seven Days of Creation…seven weeks of the Omer

Each of the Seven Days of Creation reflects a separate *tzimtzum* (constriction) of time and space, within which the creation of that Day was formed. Similarly, each day that we count in the seven weeks of the Omer reflects a separate *tzimtzum* of constricted intellect. One who reigns in his intellect can focus on faith, through which he can find Godliness in every part of creation, as in "All His works are with faith" (Psalms 33:4). Thus, the Counting of the Omer reflects the greatness of faith, as it allows a person to restrain his intellect and focus on faith. Then he can receive the Torah (see *Likutey Halakhot* III, p. 109a).

2:3 וַיְבָ֤רֶךְ אֱלֹהִים֙ אֶת־י֣וֹם הַשְּׁבִיעִ֔י וַיְקַדֵּ֖שׁ אֹת֑וֹ כִּ֣י ב֤וֹ
שָׁבַת֙ מִכָּל־מְלַאכְתּ֔וֹ אֲשֶׁר־בָּרָ֥א אֱלֹהִ֖ים לַעֲשֽׂוֹת

God blessed the Seventh Day and made it holy, because on it He rested from all His work that God created to do.

⟩ God blessed the Seventh Day

By observing Shabbat as a day of rest, we express our faith that God created the world and rested on the Seventh Day. Thus, Shabbat corresponds to faith, which is the source of all blessing, as indicated in the verse "A man of faith has abundant blessings" (Proverbs 28:20). Therefore "God blessed the Seventh Day"—for, like faith, Shabbat is the source of all blessing for mankind (*Likutey Moharan* I, 31:2).

⟩ God blessed the Seventh Day and made it holy

Blessing always accompanies sanctity. Therefore the Seventh Day—Shabbat—contains blessing.

Sanctity specifically refers to a holy tongue. A person who speaks holy words attains blessing (*Likutey Moharan* II, 2:5).

⟩ Created to do

Why was man created lacking (i.e., without a *milah*)? Everything was created lacking. Wheat requires grinding. Peas require processing… So too, man requires rectification (*Bereishit Rabbah* 11:6).

Every craftsman requires tools to pursue his trade. For example, a goldsmith needs raw gold ore and a blacksmith needs a hammer and anvil, without which they cannot ply their crafts. Who created the first tools that man used to create more tools, if not God? Yet if God can create all the necessary first tools, why did He give man the necessity to work? Why didn't God create everything already prepared for man to enjoy?

The answer is that everything in this world must go through a process of rectification. Wheat must be ground into flour, garments must be woven from fiber, and so on. God created man incomplete so that he would work to attain perfection—for his own sake and for the sake of all creation (*Likutey Moharan* I, 19:end). The main means of purification is morality; hence, man was created requiring circumcision (*Likutey Halakhot* VIII, p. 158a).

Thus, God purposefully created everything lacking in order to give man the responsibility of bringing Creation to the level of perfection. And He gave man the free will to create, build and perfect, or—God forbid—to destroy. The Hebrew word *UMaN* (אומן, craftsman) is similar to the word *EMUNah* (אמונה, faith), for man is entrusted by God to do his part faithfully (ibid., p. 161a).

❯ Because on it He rested from all His work that God created to do

> God began to create demons late Friday afternoon. When Shabbat began, only their spirits had been formed, and there was no time left to make bodies for them (*Zohar* I, 47b).

Rebbe Nachman draws a parallel between this teaching and a person who is led astray by fantasy and illusion. If one does not make preparations for Shabbat, his thoughts are "disembodied" and do not reside within a reliable structure (*Likutey Moharan* I, 54:6).

2:4 אֵלֶּה תוֹלְדוֹת הַשָּׁמַיִם וְהָאָרֶץ בְּהִבָּרְאָם בְּיוֹם
עֲשׂוֹת יְיָ אֱלֹהִים אֶרֶץ וְשָׁמָיִם

These are the generations of Heaven and earth when they were created, on the day that God made earth and Heaven.

❯ Elohim and YHVH

God originally planned to create the world through the attribute of judgment (Rashi on Genesis 1:1). Later, He tempered His Creation with the attribute of compassion, since only very great tzaddikim could survive in a world of strict justice (as we find with the Patriarchs: "*Elohim* [the attribute of judgment] Who shepherded me" [Genesis 48:15]). The attribute of judgment remains in the Vacated Space which was left after God contracted His Presence (the *Tzimtzum*), leaving room for the evil inclination. The evil inclination is rooted in judgment. The strength to break the evil inclination has its roots in compassion and mercy (corresponding to God's Holy Name *YHVH*). Each time that a person conquers his evil inclination, he draws compassion and mercy to this world (*Likutey Halakhot* I, p. 72a-144).

⟩ Behibaram

The word *beHiBaRAM* (בהבראם, when they were created) has the same letters as *ABRaHaM* (אברהם), in whose merit the world was created (*Bereishit Rabbah* 12:9).

Abraham represents the person who seeks God. In the merit of even one person who seeks God, this entire world was created and is sustained (*Likutey Halakhot* IV, p. 272).

⟩ Behibaram

Generally speaking, a person cannot accomplish anything with anger or force. Even if he does achieve something, he would have achieved much more had he used goodness and kindness (*Rebbe Nachman, Breslov oral tradition*).

This idea is alluded to in the word *BeHiBaRAM* (בהבראם, when they were created), whose letters can be rearranged to spell *BeAVRaHaM* (באברהם, in Abraham). Abraham represents the attribute of *chesed* (kindness). This teaches that all new creations are rooted in kindness (*Likutey Moharan* II, 2:3).

The attribute of kindness, which corresponds to Abraham and is alluded to by the word *Behibaram*, is especially necessary in raising children (ibid., I, 67:7).

⟩ Behibaram

Before God began the Creation, the entire world was considered a "possible reality." But after God created Jewish souls, the world became a "necessary reality." That is, the creation of the souls "forced" God, as it were, to create the world for them (see *Likutey Moharan* I, 52). The Torah hints at this relationship in the word *beHiBaRAM* (בהבראם), since it was *ABRaHaM* (אברהם), the progenitor of the Jewish nation, who caused the world to come into existence (*Likutey Halakhot* II, p. 234a).

⟩ God

Trust in God forever, for God (*Yah*) is the Rock of worlds (Isaiah 26:4).

The Divine Name *YaH* (י-ה) is composed of the first two letters of the Tetragrammaton, *YHVH* (י-ה-ו-ה). The letter *yod* (י), which represents the wisdom and intellect of the Torah, corresponds to the *sefirah* of Chokhmah. The letter *hei* (ה), which has the numerical value of 5, corresponds to the Five Books of Moses, as well as to the five classes of consonants that appear in the Torah (guttural, palatal, lingual, dental and labial).

A person who utilizes his three powers of intellect (Chokhmah, Binah and Da'at) and his power of speech to study Torah truly becomes a human being—Adam. *ADaM* has the numerical value of 45, which is equal to the numerical value of *YaH* (15) multiplied by 3 (i.e., the three intellects). Therefore the verse from Isaiah may be understood to mean: "With the Torah, God created all the universes for the sake of Man" (*Likutey Moharan* I, 101).

2:5   וְכֹל שִׂיחַ הַשָּׂדֶה טֶרֶם יִהְיֶה בָאָרֶץ וְכָל־עֵשֶׂב
הַשָּׂדֶה טֶרֶם יִצְמָח כִּי לֹא הִמְטִיר יְיָ אֱלֹהִים עַל־
הָאָרֶץ וְאָדָם אַיִן לַעֲבֹד אֶת־הָאֲדָמָה

All the wild shrubs were not yet on the earth, and all the wild grasses had not yet sprouted, because God had not yet caused it to rain upon the earth, and there was no man to work the land.

❭ *All the wild grasses had not yet sprouted*

The grasses stood at the surface of the earth and waited for Adam to pray for rain (Rashi).

On the Seventh Day of Creation, God "rested from all His work that God created to do" (Genesis 2:3)—meaning, He now gave the world to man to continue working and completing what He had initiated. In this manner, God created the grasses but waited for man to complete the Creation by praying for the rain that would help the grasses grow (*Likutey Halakhot* II, p. 260).

2:7 וַיִּיצֶר יְיָ אֱלֹהִים אֶת־הָאָדָם עָפָר מִן־הָאֲדָמָה
וַיִּפַּח בְּאַפָּיו נִשְׁמַת חַיִּים וַיְהִי הָאָדָם לְנֶפֶשׁ חַיָּה

**God formed the man of dust from the earth.
He breathed into his nostrils a breath of
life, and the man became a living soul.**

⟩ *Vayitzer*

Vayitzer (וייצר, He formed) is spelled with two *yods*, one of them
seemingly superfluous. This indicates that there were two types
of creation: one for good and one for evil (*Zohar* III, 111a); one for
judgment and one for kindness (*Berakhot* 61a) (*Likutey Moharan* I, 48:1).

VaYitZeR comes from the word *YotZeR* (יוצר, create or form), and
is related to the word *YetZeR* (יצר, a person's inner inclination). The
thoughts of a person's *YetZeR HaTov* (good inclination) form good
things, whereas the thoughts of his *YetZeR HaRa* (evil inclination)
form evil things (*Likutey Moharan* I, 49:1).

⟩ *Adam was formed from the earth*

God created *ADaM* (אדם, man) specifically from the *ADaMah*
(אדמה, earth) so that when he reaches out to God from his dense,
material existence, he can experience God's glory, which fills the
earth (*Likutey Halakhot* VII, p. 52a).

⟩ *Adam was formed from the earth*

In one respect, earth represents dense materialism; in another,
it symbolizes humility. Man was created from earth so that he
could subjugate his material desires in an effort to come close
to God. Then earth—dense materialism—transforms to levels of
Nothingness (*Likutey Halakhot* VII, p. 114).

⟩ *Nishmat chaim*

NiShMat (נשמת, breath) is related to *NeShaMah* (נשמה, soul),
rendering this verse as "He breathed into his nostrils a living soul."
The soul is from God Himself. Therefore the soul is supreme and
the body should be subordinate to it (*Likutey Halakhot* I, p. 108a).

⟩ *He breathed into his nostrils a breath of life*

The breath is associated with life. One breathes through the
nose, which represents patience. And this is particularly true of a
long breath—i.e., a sigh (*Likutey Moharan* I, 8:1).

⟩ He breathed into his nostrils a breath of life

> God created man from both Heaven and earth in order to ensure peace in His Creation. For on the First Day, He created Heaven and earth. On the Second Day, He made the firmament; on the Third Day, the earth; on the Fourth Day, the celestial bodies; on the Fifth Day, the fish. Had Adam been created exclusively from the earth, four days of Creation would have been given over to earthly products and only three days to heavenly creations. So God breathed His breath into Adam, making Adam a product of both Heaven and earth, so that jealousy should not exist and peace should reign (Rashi).

The main design of Creation was for peace to reign between all of its segments. Everything—all sparks of holiness, all levels of creation—would be joined together in unison, thus elevating everything to God. And so it would have been, had Adam not eaten from the Tree of Knowledge of Good and Evil. By eating from the Tree, Adam brought hatred and jealousy into the creation. Thus, the snake was cursed, "I will place hatred between your descendants and hers" (Genesis 3:15) (*Likutey Halakhot* IV, p. 223a).

⟩ The man became a living soul

> Animals also are called living souls. But man is greater, for he possesses intellect and the power of speech (Rashi).

Man is called a living soul because he alone has the intellect to seek out God, to understand from all the other parts of creation that God exists, and to communicate that knowledge to others (*Likutey Halakhot* II, p. 175a).

⟩ The man became a living soul

> "A living soul"—a speaking spirit (Targum Onkelos).

Truly becoming a "man" in a spiritual sense means that one attains speech—communication that is linked to an elevated consciousness (*Likutey Moharan* I, 60:8).

2:8   וַיִּטַּע יְיָ אֱלֹהִים גַּן־בְּעֵדֶן מִקֶּדֶם וַיָּשֶׂם שָׁם
אֶת־הָאָדָם אֲשֶׁר יָצָר

God planted a garden in Eden, to the east, and there He placed the man that He had formed.

》 *God placed Adam in the Garden of Eden*

Adam was so great that he entered the Garden of Eden immediately. Had he not sinned, he could have eaten the fruit from the Tree of Life and transcended the constraints of time and space. He could have ascended to the highest of levels, to the Throne of Glory itself (*Likutey Halakhot* I, p. 39a).

2:9   וַיַּצְמַח יְיָ אֱלֹהִים מִן־הָאֲדָמָה כָּל־עֵץ נֶחְמָד
לְמַרְאֶה וְטוֹב לְמַאֲכָל וְעֵץ הַחַיִּים בְּתוֹךְ הַגָּן
וְעֵץ הַדַּעַת טוֹב וָרָע

God caused to sprout from the earth every tree that is pleasing to the sight and good for food. The Tree of Life was in the middle of the garden, and the Tree of Knowledge of Good and Evil.

》 *The Tree of Life*

In Rebbe Nachman's tale of "The Seven Beggars" (*Rabbi Nachman's Stories* #13), the Beggar on the Fifth Day speaks about a Tree that has three roots—faith, awe and humility—and a trunk that is truth. All people are somehow connected to this Tree, for it is the root of all souls. This is an allusion to the Tree of Life.

The four attributes—faith, awe, humility and truth—are the pathway to repentance. They correspond to the four shofar blasts that we hear on Rosh HaShanah—*Tekiah, Shevarim, Teruah* and the final *Tekiah*. These attributes are specifically recalled on Rosh HaShanah because that was the day that Adam was created and the same day that he sinned.

Since Adam was banished from the Garden of Eden, his mission and that of his descendants is to elevate man back to his original, unblemished level in the Garden. He accomplishes this by sounding the shofar, since sound (or voice) acts as an intermediary between the material and the spiritual, between this world and the Garden of Eden.

After Adam ate from the Tree, God called to him. Adam replied, "I heard Your voice in the garden" (Genesis 3:10), since God aroused the concept of the voice to inspire Adam to repent. We, too, can arouse repentance with the sounds of the shofar on Rosh HaShanah, rectifying the sin of Adam that occurred on Rosh HaShanah and meriting to the Tree of Life (*Likutey Halakhot* VII, p. 210a).

⟩ *Eitz HaChaim, Eitz HaDa'at*

The Hebrew word *EitZ* (עץ, tree) comes from same root as the word *EitZah* (עצה, advice). The *Eitz HaChaim* (Tree of Life) and *Eitz HaDa'at* (Tree of Knowledge) represent the advice that a person seeks throughout his life.

Had he eaten from the Tree of Life, Adam would have received the proper counsel for how to live. Then he truly would have lived forever, for he would not have had to face conflicting advice at every turn and would most certainly have attained the World to Come. But because he ate from the Tree of Knowledge of Good and Evil, he brought himself to a situation of always facing a choice between "good" (i.e., good advice) and "evil" (i.e., wrong and bad advice).

All of Adam's descendants must now seek the path back to the Tree of Life. Yet because of Adam's sin, we are confronted with the "revolving sword"—the many choices that prevent us from immediately seeing the real, true and good advice necessary for us to "live forever." Nevertheless, those who attach themselves to the true tzaddikim—the ones who have found the path back to the Garden of Eden—can overcome the "revolving sword," since they will receive proper and good advice from them (*Likutey Halakhot* III, p. 233a; see also ibid., p. 235a).

⟩ *The Tree of Knowledge of Good and Evil*

The Tree of Knowledge of Good and Evil is a medium for both good and evil. It is also called *kelipah nogah* (literally, "a bright husk"), a force that contains both good and evil (as opposed to the other *kelipot*, which are purely evil).

The Tree of Knowledge of Good and Evil represents the Aramaic language, which is a medium between the Holy Tongue (Hebrew) and the other seventy languages. Thus, there are three levels—the sanctified (the Holy Tongue), the mundane (Aramaic), and the unholy (the seventy languages).

Eve corresponds to speech. Therefore the Serpent approached her and sullied her purity by adulterating it with the character of Aramaic, the mundane (*Likutey Moharan* I, 19:4).

2:10   וְנָהָר יֹצֵא מֵעֵדֶן לְהַשְׁקוֹת אֶת־הַגָּן וּמִשָּׁם יִפָּרֵד
וְהָיָה לְאַרְבָּעָה רָאשִׁים

A river flowed out of Eden to water the garden. From there, it separated into four major rivers.

⟩ *The Garden of Eden*

The tzaddik is the Gardener of the Garden of Eden (*Zohar* II, 166b).

Thus, anyone who is close to a true tzaddik can experience the delight of that Garden (*Rabbi Nachman's Wisdom* #252).

⟩ *A river flowed out of Eden to water the garden. From there, it separated into four major rivers*

"A river flowed out of Eden"—this corresponds to prayer. "To water the garden"—this corresponds to Torah. Prayer connotes that which is beyond description—something that a person yearns for but which is distant from him. Torah represents that which he can attain—something that is before him and accessible.

The "river" comes to "water the garden"—that is to say, prayer enables the person to understand and gain access to the Torah. Prayer and Torah assist plants to grow—i.e., they cause souls to grow spiritually.

"From there, it separated"—Torah causes evil to separate and depart from a person.

"Into four major rivers"—this refers to the four letters of the Tetragrammaton, which are the source of everything in the world, and more specifically, the source of the good found in the four elements (*Likutey Moharan* I, 8:7).

〉 *A river flowed out of Eden*

This river represents the source of waters necessary for the mikvah. One who immerses in a mikvah submerses himself in the waters of Eden (*Likutey Halakhot* IV, p. 476; see also *Waters of Eden: The Mystery of the Mikveh* by Rabbi Aryeh Kaplan, NCSY/Orthodox Union, 1982).

〉 *A river flowed out of Eden…it separated into four major rivers…the gold of that land was good*

Our primary goal is to draw Godliness into everything we do, imbuing each thing with life and vitality. Since everything in this world requires something to sustain it, the act of drawing Godliness also draws livelihood and sustenance. Thus, "A river flowed out of Eden"—this indicates that Godliness was being drawn forth into this world and that it was manifest in the sustenance provided by the rivers. There was such abundant Godliness that there was even "gold, good and beneficent gold" (*Likutey Halakhot* VIII, p. 251a).

2:15   וַיִּקַּח יְיָ אֱלֹהִים אֶת־הָאָדָם וַיַּנִּחֵהוּ בְגַן־עֵדֶן
        לְעָבְדָהּ וּלְשָׁמְרָהּ

God took the man and placed him in the Garden of Eden, to work it and to guard it.

〉 *God took the man*

"God took the man"—He removed Adam from the four elements, which correspond to man's base desires (*Zohar* I, 27a).

Only when a person transcends those desires may he truly be called a "man" (*Likutey Moharan* I, 37:3).

When a person repents, God separates him from his base desires and draws him close (ibid., I, 79).

2:16   וַיְצַו יְיָ אֱלֹהִים עַל־הָאָדָם לֵאמֹר מִכֹּל עֵץ־הַגָּן
אָכֹל תֹּאכֵל

**God commanded the man, saying, "From all
the trees of the garden, you should eat."**

⟩ *From all the trees of the garden, you should eat*

Why was Adam commanded to eat from all the trees in the
Garden of Eden, when the main commandment was *not* to eat
from the Tree of Knowledge?

By commanding Adam to eat from the other trees, God revealed
to him the great reward of eating in holiness: it brings man to
perfection. One who eats in holiness is likened to one who ate the
manna, as well as one who eats the food of Shabbat. This type of
eating leads a person to desire Godliness and draw close to God.
Moreover, it reveals Divine will. Conversely, eating from the Tree
of Knowledge of Good and Evil is an act grounded in the realm of
this world and cannot bring a person to perfection. Thus, Adam
was commanded to eat from the other trees, and at the same time
he was instructed *not* to eat from the Tree of Knowledge (*Likutey
Halakhot* II, p. 18-10a).

2:17   וּמֵעֵץ הַדַּעַת טוֹב וָרָע לֹא תֹאכַל מִמֶּנּוּ כִּי בְּיוֹם
אֲכָלְךָ מִמֶּנּוּ מוֹת תָּמוּת

**"But from the Tree of Knowledge of Good
and Evil, you should not eat—for on the day
you eat from it, you will surely die."**

⟩ *But from the Tree of Knowledge of Good and Evil, you should
not eat*

The first mitzvah Adam was commanded was not to eat from the
Tree of Knowledge of Good and Evil. This mitzvah is so important
because by eating in holiness, one can draw Divine will down into
this world and connect this world with all the supernal worlds.
By subverting this mitzvah, Adam drove a separation between this
world and all the others, and polluted his soul.

As punishment, he was cursed with mortality. Mortality separates body from soul, just as Adam separated between the worlds. The Torah is the rectification for man's mortality, since it enables him once again to join the lower world with the supernal worlds (*Likutey Halakhot* II, p. 26-14a). Thus, when the Jewish people received the Torah at Sinai, they ceased to be polluted (*Shabbat* 146a) and they were freed from the rule of the Angel of Death (*Vayikra Rabbah* 18:3).

⟩ *For on the day you eat from it*

Each day has both good and evil in it. One must always seek the good within each day and make sure that the good dominates the evil. One who slackens his attempts "eats from the Tree of Knowledge of Good and Evil" and allows the evil to overcome him (*Likutey Halakhot* VII, p. 64).

2:18 וַיֹּאמֶר יְיָ אֱלֹהִים לֹא־טוֹב הֱיוֹת הָאָדָם לְבַדּוֹ
אֶעֱשֶׂה־לּוֹ עֵזֶר כְּנֶגְדּוֹ

God said, "It is not good for man to be alone. I will make a helper opposite him."

⟩ *I will make a helper opposite him*

Man and woman are rooted in the level of Keter, which represents the ability to think things through and reach accurate decisions. Keter encompasses two opposite functions. There is a tendency of Keter to seek the higher level, and there is a built-in function of the Keter that acts as a restraint, holding back the Keter from advancing beyond the level it is on until it is ready to climb another notch on the spiritual ladder. (Each of the Ten Sefirot in each world is comprised of Ten Sefirot, and there are hundreds upon hundreds of levels and sub-levels. On each level is a Keter that strives to advance to the next higher level [see *Likutey Moharan* I, 24 for a detailed explanation; see also *Anatomy of the Soul*, Chapter 16]).

Thus, the Torah states: "I will make a helper opposite him"—for at their root, these opposite functions work in harmony, serving both to advance and restrain a person. Only through marriage, when man and woman are united, can their Keter function properly (*Likutey Halakhot* VI, p. 36a).

2:19   וַיִּצֶר יְיָ אֱלֹהִים מִן־הָאֲדָמָה כָּל־חַיַּת הַשָּׂדֶה וְאֵת כָּל־
עוֹף הַשָּׁמַיִם וַיָּבֵא אֶל־הָאָדָם לִרְאוֹת מַה־יִּקְרָא־
לוֹ וְכֹל אֲשֶׁר יִקְרָא־לוֹ הָאָדָם נֶפֶשׁ חַיָּה הוּא שְׁמוֹ

**God formed from the earth every wild beast
and every bird of the sky. He brought them
to the man to see what he would name each
one. Whatever the man called each living soul,
that became its name.**

❱ **Whatever the man called each living soul, that became
its name**

God created the world for man to complete, as it is written,
"That God created *to do*" (Genesis 2:3). The way that man completes
Creation is by drawing and revealing the Godliness in everything.
Therefore Adam gave names to all the creatures. A name alludes to a
creature's essence; its source is in God's Name. Whenever that name
is mentioned, it invokes God's greatness (*Likutey Halakhot* III, p. 7a).

❱ **Nefesh chayah hu shemo**

The phrase *nefesh chayah hu shemo* (a living creature, that is its
name) may be interpreted to mean that a creature's living soul is to
be found in its name. In other words, a person's essential life force
and mission in life are associated with his name (*Likutey Moharan* I,
56:3; ibid., II, 66). Some people complete their mission early and
then receive a new mission, and correspondingly, a new name.
Our Sages teach that Moses had many names (*Sanhedrin* 19b), for
he had many tasks in life and required a different name for each
one. For the same reason, it is customary to give a dangerously ill
person a new name. Because he fulfilled the destiny indicated by
his original name, he is granted a new name associated with his
new mission (*Rabbi Nachman's Wisdom* #95).

❱ **Its name**

A person who is willing to give his "name" to God—i.e., to
remain devoted to serving God regardless of how much people
criticize him—is considered to have sacrificed himself for the
Name of God (*Likutey Moharan* I, 260).

⟫ *Its name*

The essence of who a person is may be inferred from a combination of the letters of his name. For example, Rebbe Nachman indicated the essence of his disciple, R' Shimon (שמעון, *ShiMOAN*), by noting that the letters of his name could be rearranged to form the phrase *AvON MaSh* (עון מש, away with sin). Someone else named Shimon would resonate to a different rearrangement of the letters—perhaps even *ShaM AvON* (שם עון, there is sin) (God forbid). From this, we see that a person's name can contain the secret of his existence, even though many people may share that name (*Rabbi Nachman's Wisdom #44*).

⟫ *Its name*

The name of an object corresponds to the ultimate spiritual goal of reality. By knowing the name of something, we can understand its Godly essence and come to the reality of the Messianic age.

This idea is alluded to in the Hebrew word *SheiMOT* (שמות, names), which is an acronym for the phrase *Takhlit Ma'aseh Shamayim Va'aretz* (תכלית מעשה שמים וארץ, the purpose of the work of Heaven and earth) (Friday-night liturgy) (*Likutey Moharan* II, 39).

⟫ *Its name*

A person's name forms a garment for his soul after his death (*Rabbi Nachman's Wisdom #95*). That is, the way the person conducts himself and leaves behind a name for himself, becomes the "garment" of his soul and the way he will be seen in the World to Come.

2:20 וַיִּקְרָא הָאָדָם שֵׁמוֹת לְכָל־הַבְּהֵמָה וּלְעוֹף הַשָּׁמַיִם
וּלְכֹל חַיַּת הַשָּׂדֶה וּלְאָדָם לֹא־מָצָא עֵזֶר כְּנֶגְדּוֹ

The man gave names to all the animals, the birds of the sky, and all the wild beasts. But man did not find a helper opposite him.

⟫ *Adam gave names*

The light of God, which permeates all of creation, may be found in the components of every entity in the world. Those components are mirrored in the letters of its name. Thus, a person can find God in these letters (*Likutey Moharan* I, 19:7).

This is alluded to in the phrase "The man gave names." Adam drew the light of God into each item of creation through the name that he gave it. Through our knowledge of those names, we, too, can recognize God and draw close to Him (see ibid.; *The Aleph-Bet Book*, True Knowledge, B:1-2).

》 *Adam gave names to all*

A name is truly a wonder. With one word, we can describe any item that would otherwise require many sentences to depict. Take, for example, a table. We can call it "a flat wooden surface with four legs attached, which stands on its own and allows people to sit around it and place things on it." Or we can simply say "table." Without descriptive nouns, we would be unable to truly communicate our desires. There would be no business or trade (try selling stock in a nameless corporation!). Try to describe a person. Then say his name, which expresses everything about him in a word.

The same applies to God. Without a Name, how would we ever be able to refer to Him? However, we must take care to know at all times that the Name is merely a description of what God is and what He can do. In truth, it can never describe Him in totality (*Likutey Halakhot* I, p. 112a-113a).

》 *Adam gave names*

From his understanding of this world, Adam was able to name each thing in creation. He was even able to give a Name to God (*Bereishit Rabbah* 17:4), for he attained a certain knowledge of God as well. This knowledge was based on his recognizing the life force that lies behind each thing (*Likutey Halakhot* V, p. 25a). This is because a name embodies the essence of the soul. One can know everything about a person just by mentioning his name. A name also embodies a person's life force. Thus, when Adam gave names to all creatures, he drew their life forces from their source (ibid., II, p. 100).

》 *A helper opposite him*

"Adam" corresponds to a person's voice, "Eve" to its articulation into speech. A person's speech is his "helper." With it, he can reach out to God at all times—even in his darkest moments, when negative forces oppose and constrict him (*Likutey Moharan* I, 19:8).

⟩ Let us make man...a helper opposite him

If he merits it, she will be a helper. If he is not meritorious, she will oppose him (Rashi).

Before creating man, God took counsel with His Heavenly Court ("Let *us* make man"). Kindness said, "Create man, for he will engage in acts of kindness." Truth said, "Do not create man, for he will be full of falsehood." Righteousness said, "Create man, for he will act righteously and be charitable." Peace said, "Do not create man, for he will be argumentative." What did God do? He cast Truth down to the earth, as it is written, "You have cast Truth down to the earth" (Daniel 8:12). The ministering angels asked, "Master of the Universe, Truth is Your seal and insignia. Why do you disdain it?" God then ordered Truth to rise up from the earth, as it is written, "Truth will sprout from the earth" (Psalms 85:12; *Bereishit Rabbah* 8:5).

This Midrash is difficult to understand. Why would God cast His own seal, Truth, to the earth in such a manner that even the angels had to ask Him what He meant by it? Secondly, how can there be an argument between Truth and God, since God Himself is Truth and it was His will to create man (which He eventually did)? How can Truth argue with Truth? And thirdly, why wasn't Peace reprimanded, for it also opposed God's will?

There is truth, and then there is a core of truth—the *emeser emes*, the *real* truth. The truth is that man will be full of falsehood and strife. He will believe that his point of view alone is the true one—as will the next person. For this reason, Truth claimed that man would be false, as each person's perception of truth is limited. Man fails to see that although there are many people with different ideas, there is always only one core of truth. The person who is willing to forgo victory for his own viewpoint will merit to see the *real* truth and find the One God within the diversity of mankind. Therefore God cast to the earth that single-minded truth, the truth that does not allow for other people to air their perceptions of truth, for this is not the real truth.

The earth represents materialism, in which the Truth of God is concealed. Yet within it, a person can attain knowledge of God through faith. Thus, Truth was cast down so that a person could nurture his faith and make the truth sprout forth, and thereby find God.

Eve was created to be a helper opposite Adam. Between the two of them, they should have recognized the need to search for the core of truth, which would have protected them from sin and brought about a manifestation of God and His Truth in the world. This is the deeper meaning of "If he merits it, she will be a helper. If he is not meritorious, she will oppose him." By working together, they can find the real truth. If not, they will experience constant opposition, strife and challenges.

Peace also objected to man's creation, but it was not cast to the earth. This is because the main source of strife lies in a person's perception of truth. Were his perception to be refined so that he recognizes the *real* truth, then peace would reign and strife would no longer exist (*Likutey Halakhot* IV, p. 398-404, 402-202a, 406-207a).

⟫ *Let us make man...a helper opposite him*

If he merits it, she will be a helper. If he is not meritorious, she will oppose him (Rashi).

"*If* he merits"—depending on the person's thoughts and deeds, this can change many times during a single day! (*Rabbi Eliyahu Chaim Rosen*).

⟫ *A helper opposite him...bone from my bone and flesh from my flesh...a man should leave his father and mother and bond with his wife*

Man represents truth. Woman represents faith. Truth is too awesome a light to receive directly. It is impossible to face the absolute truth—i.e., God—and transmit Godliness further in its raw form. A filter must be taken from truth itself, a vessel that can accurately reflect the light of truth and transfer it along to others. Therefore woman was created—"bone from my bone and flesh from my flesh"—this is one's faith.

"Father" and "mother" represent the intellect. One must leave behind his intellect in matters that are beyond his comprehension and bond with his wife, with his faith. Only then can they become "one flesh"—for together, faith and truth can reflect the absolute truth (*Likutey Halakhot* IV, p. 234a-468).

2:21   וַיַּפֵּל יְיָ אֱלֹהִים תַּרְדֵּמָה עַל־הָאָדָם וַיִּישָׁן וַיִּקַּח אַחַת מִצַּלְעֹתָיו וַיִּסְגֹּר בָּשָׂר תַּחְתֶּנָּה

God made the man fall into a deep slumber, and he slept. He took one of his ribs and closed the flesh in its place.

❯ God made the man fall into a deep slumber

The drowsiness that befell Adam was representative of the Tree of Knowledge, which contains both good and evil. A person can sleep either with the goal of refreshing his soul and embarking on a life of spirituality and good deeds, or with the goal of renewing his strength so as to pursue material pleasures.

In the latter case, he will face myriad choices, many of them leading him astray. The numerical value of the word *TaRDeiMaH* (תרדמה, slumber) is equivalent to that of *TaRGUM* (תרגום, Aramaic translation). A person who "sleeps away his life" without striving to realize his spiritual potential is liable to be influenced by the evil found in *Targum*. In particular, "sleep" can refer to unintended sin, when a person's good intentions are entangled with evil deeds (*Likutey Moharan* I, 19:end).

❯ God made the man fall into a deep slumber

"Sleeping" is associated with lust. Sleep implies closed—i.e., blemished—eyes, which act as the messengers to arouse lust in a person. Therefore, each morning upon arising and opening our eyes, we are obligated to begin anew to accept the yoke of Heaven (by reciting the Shema). This way, we cast off our sleep/lust and draw the antidote for lust: the Torah (*Likutey Halakhot* I, p. 152a).

❯ Vayapeil

VaYaPeiL (ויפל, caused to fall) is an acronym for the phrase *Peh La-hem Ve-lo Yedabeiru* (פה להם ולא ידברו, they have a mouth but do not speak) (Psalms 115:5). In order to subdue evil—to "put it to sleep"—one must not speak evil. We also find that Joseph was able to interpret dreams—which come to a person in his sleep—because he transcended the level of sleep (*Likutey Moharan* I, 19:4).

⟩ *He closed the flesh*

The word *vayiSgor* (ויסגר, He closed) marks the first appearance of the Hebrew letter *samekh* (ס) in the Torah. *Samekh* connotes a "support," a means of supporting man in his endeavors. As long as man is alone, he has no support. He must be married.

On a deeper level, Adam reflects the voice and Eve reflects speech. The voice alone is not enough to support a person in his spiritual challenges; he needs speech to articulate and communicate Torah study and prayer.

The letter *samekh* has the numerical value of 60. If a non-kosher ingredient gets mixed up with a kosher food, the admixture can be declared kosher if there is sixty times the amount of kosher versus non-kosher ingredients. In order to be able to overcome adversity, Adam—the voice—needs a *samekh*—a support and a helpmate. This is Eve, who represents articulate and sanctified speech (*Likutey Halakhot* IV, p. 114a).

⟩ *He closed the flesh in its place*

When God separated Eve from Adam, He sealed the flesh in the place of the incision (*Berakhot* 61a). God formed the woman as a "storehouse," wider at the bottom and narrower at the top, so that she would be able to bear children (*Berakhot* 61a).

ChaTaKh (חתך, incision) is similar to *ChiTuKh* (חתוך, articulation). The formation of Eve indicates the creation of holy, articulated speech (*Likutey Moharan* I, 19:3). The word "storehouse" connotes the fear of God, as in the verse "The fear of God is His storehouse" (Isaiah 33:6). Through holy speech (represented by Eve), a person can attain the fear of God (*Likutey Moharan* I, 19:3), and afterwards he can come to a deep understanding of God (ibid., I, 60:3).

2:22   וַיִּבֶן יְיָ אֱלֹהִים אֶת־הַצֵּלָע אֲשֶׁר־לָקַח מִן־הָאָדָם
       לְאִשָּׁה וַיְבִאֶהָ אֶל־הָאָדָם

God built the rib that He had taken from the man into a woman, and He brought her to the man.

⟫ *God built the rib that he had taken from the man into a woman, and He brought her to the man*

> There was the image of a throne, and upon the image of the throne was an image like the appearance of a man upon it (Ezekiel 1:26).

Adam corresponds to the "man upon it," and Eve—"the mother of all life" (Genesis 3:20)—corresponds to the "throne," which is the source of all souls. When Adam and Eve unite, they make it possible for man to rule over all of creation—even over the angels. This is what is meant by the verse "God built the rib that He had taken…into a woman…and He brought her to the man." God took the energy of Eve, the source of all souls, and brought that to human beings. Thus, God gave His awesome authority to man so that man might even be able to rule over angels (*Likutey Moharan* II, 1:2).

More specifically, God gave man the power to overcome his own "angel"—his evil inclination (*Rabbi Eliyahu Chaim Rosen*).

⟫ *Adam and Eve*

> God made man upright, but they sought many accounts (Ecclesiastes 7:29).

> As an individual, man—Adam—was upright. But as soon as Eve was created and there were two humans, *they* sought many accounts (Rashi).

As long as man is alone, he is an individual; he represents truth, absolute truth, because the truth is only one. But as soon as Eve enters the picture, "one" becomes "two." Wherever there is more than one, falsehood can manifest itself. Had he been left alone, Adam would never have succumbed to the Serpent's enticement. But the Serpent was able to entice Eve, for she represents a "second path," a path that allows falsehoods to take root.

Falsehood manifests in Eve because she was created during Adam's "sleep," which represents constricted consciousness (imagination as opposed to intellect). Specifically in imaginations and allusions does falsehood take root (*Likutey Halakhot* IV, p. 193a-386, 196a). The Hebrew word for sleep, *SheINah* (שינה), is similar to *ShINuy* (שינוי, change). The constricted consciousness of sleep allows for falsehood and changes and differences between people (*Likutey Halakhot* IV, p. 195).

2:23   וַיֹּאמֶר הָאָדָם זֹאת הַפַּעַם עֶצֶם מֵעֲצָמַי וּבָשָׂר
מִבְּשָׂרִי לְזֹאת יִקָּרֵא אִשָּׁה כִּי מֵאִישׁ לֻקֳחָה־זֹּאת

The man said, "This time it is bone from my bone and flesh from my flesh. This will be called woman, for she was taken from man."

〗 *This will be called woman, for she was taken from man*

The language is similar (Rashi).

From this verse, we see that the world was created with the Holy Tongue. Adam called the woman *IShah* (אשה), which is similar to the word *ISh* (איש, man). In Rashi's words, "*Lashon nofel al lashon*—The language is similar," or more literally, "Language falls upon language."

"This" refers to speech, as in the verse "*This* is what their father said to them" (Genesis 49:28) (*Likutey Moharan* I, 34:1; ibid., 19:3). Eve—woman—corresponds to perfected speech. When a person engages in holy speech, he subdues evil speech. Thus, Rashi's comment can be read as teaching that "unholy language falls due to holy language" (*Likutey Moharan* I, 19:3).

2:24   עַל־כֵּן יַעֲזָב־אִישׁ אֶת־אָבִיו וְאֶת־אִמּוֹ וְדָבַק
        בְּאִשְׁתּוֹ וְהָיוּ לְבָשָׂר אֶחָד

**Therefore a man should leave his father
and mother and bond with his wife, and
they will become one flesh.**

❯ *Therefore a man should leave his father and mother and bond with his wife*

By means of a holy spirit, God conveyed the message to Adam
and Eve that promiscuity is forbidden (Rashi).

From this, we may infer that when a person attains a holy
spirit, he can subdue his lust (*Likutey Moharan* I, 19:3).

Rebbe Nachman also taught: "Just do good and work on your
devotions honestly. If you are persistent, the good will stay and the
bad will automatically disappear" (*Tzaddik* #447).

❯ *They will become one flesh*

One should unite his flesh with his speech—represented by
Eve—so that his flesh is indeed nullified to his holy speech. In other
words, the material merges with the spiritual (*Likutey Moharan* I, 75).

2:25   וַיִּהְיוּ שְׁנֵיהֶם עֲרוּמִּים הָאָדָם וְאִשְׁתּוֹ וְלֹא יִתְבֹּשָׁשׁוּ

**The man and his wife were both naked, but
they were not ashamed.**

❯ *The man and his wife were both naked*

In the Garden of Eden, garments were unnecessary. Then, a
person could attain knowledge of God without needing to clothe
that knowledge in a "garment." After Adam's sin, garments became
necessary to attain knowledge of God, because the light is too great
for us to receive directly. This is why Adam was originally clothed
in garments of *ohr* (אור, light) (*Likutey Halakhot* I, p. 46a-92).

❯ *The man and his wife were both naked*

There was no humility before the sin, so clothes were unnecessary. Since sinning elicits humiliation, Adam and his wife became

embarrassed to walk about naked after they ate from the Tree. Clothing also represents fear, because "fear is humility" (*Nedarim* 20a), and humility leads to fear of God. This fear is the rectification of sin (*Likutey Halakhot* I, p. 89a).

⟩ *They were not ashamed*

Prior to eating from the Tree of Knowledge of Good and Evil, Adam and Eve were pure and without lust, and therefore they felt no shame. Shame results from vice (*Likutey Moharan* I, 19:3).

⟩ *They were not ashamed*

Before they sinned, Adam and Eve had no reason to feel embarrassed, as their minds were completely pure. They also did not fear the evil eye (which represents jealousies, lusts, and evil intent in the minds of other people towards them). However, they fell victim to the Serpent's evil eye when he persuaded them to eat of the forbidden tree, saying, "Your eyes will be opened" (Genesis 3:4).

After they sinned, God made them clothing. One who has fallen victim to the evil eye must learn to conceal himself from it, to "clothe himself" for protection (*Likutey Halakhot* III, p. 261a-522). Wearing *tzitzit* on one's clothing rectifies the evil eye, as the verse "Do not stray after your heart and after your eyes" (Numbers 15:39) is found in the passage of *tzitzit* (*Likutey Halakhot* III, p. 522).

3:1   וְהַנָּחָשׁ הָיָה עָרוּם מִכֹּל חַיַּת הַשָּׂדֶה אֲשֶׁר עָשָׂה יי׳ אֱלֹהִים וַיֹּאמֶר אֶל־הָאִשָּׁה אַף כִּי־אָמַר אֱלֹהִים לֹא תֹאכְלוּ מִכֹּל עֵץ הַגָּן

The Serpent was the most cunning of any of the wild beasts that God had made. He said to the woman, "Did God really say that you shouldn't eat from any of the trees of the garden?"

⟩ *The Serpent was the most cunning*

This refers to people whose evil and heretical words cause tremendous damage (*Likutey Moharan* I, 63) and cunningly use philosophies to entrap others (*Likutey Halakhot* III, p. 32).

》 *The Serpent was the most cunning*

The Serpent draws its strength from cunning, from *da'at* (*Likutey Halakhot* II, p. 113a). This cunning refers to atheism. Being too clever can mislead a person away from God (*Likutey Halakhot* II, p. 11a).

》 *The Serpent was the most cunning*

The reason why people must struggle with their thoughts and consciences is due to the Serpent's "cleverness," which brought death upon mankind. Sleep, a form of constricted consciousness, also stems from the Serpent. A person must work to shed his slumber—his constricted consciousness—and the questions and evil thoughts that invade and pervade his mind, limiting his awareness of God (*Likutey Halakhot* I, p. 15a-15b; see also *Likutey Moharan* I, 117).

》 *The Serpent*

Conceptually, the confusions that man faces are called *zuhamot ha-nachash* (the pollution of the Serpent), which is related to the *kelipah* of *nogah*. The Prophet Ezekiel speaks of the existence of three totally evil forces and a fourth force, *nogah*, which is comprised of both good and evil (see Ezekiel 1). All confusions, doubts and difficulties—in faith as well as in life—stem from this *kelipah* (see *Likutey Halakhot* II, p. 116a-232).

》 *The trees of the garden*

One must be careful not to exceed the limitations of his intellect, but to rely upon pure, simple faith. Going beyond one's intellect is sometimes measured by the stringencies a person accepts upon himself.

The Serpent goaded Eve by asking which trees she and Adam could eat from. Contained in this question was the subtle accusation "When serving God, how can you even think of eating? It doesn't behoove a person to eat material food when he wishes to devote his life to spirituality." Desiring to prove her own degree of piety, Eve replied, "God told us only not to eat from the Tree of Knowledge. In addition, we shouldn't even touch it!" (Genesis 3:3). By adding a stringency of her own making, she precipitated her downfall (*Likutey Halakhot* V, p. 10-6a).

3:3 וּמִפְּרִי הָעֵץ אֲשֶׁר בְּתוֹךְ־הַגָּן אָמַר אֱלֹהִים לֹא
תֹאכְלוּ מִמֶּנּוּ וְלֹא תִגְּעוּ בּוֹ פֶּן־תְּמֻתוּן

"And from the fruit of the tree that is in the middle of the garden, God said, 'Do not eat from it or touch it, or else you will die.'"

〉 The Tree of Knowledge

There is a concept of things which are good, and there is a concept of things which are evil. There is also something which forms somewhat of a bridge between the two distinct opposites. The Tree of Knowledge of Good and Evil represents that bridge, for it contains both good and evil.

Similarly, we find the Holy Tongue—words of spirituality— counterposed by evil speech—words of profanity, slander, falsehood and the like. The *Targum* (literally, "translation," referring to the Aramaic translation of the *Chumash* [i.e., Targum Onkelos]) forms the bridge between these two types of speech. (For this reason, the Talmud and *Zohar* are written in Aramaic, as is the Kaddish prayer). The language of *Targum* represents our mundane speech. By taking our everyday speech and conversations and using them for good, we convert the mundane to spirituality. Kaddish transcends all the levels and breaks through all the Gates of Iron that remain shut to our prayers, for it brings even the mundane into the realm of the sanctified. Thus, the Kaddish—i.e., the power of *Targum*—can elevate everything to the highest levels (*Likutey Halakhot* I, p. 81a).

〉 The Tree of Knowledge

The Tree was a grapevine (*Sanhedrin* 70a).

The wine of grapes promotes sleep, since wine is one-sixtieth of death. As the Tree brought death, wine brings sleep. Conversely, drinking wine at the times designated for sanctity—such as on Shabbat and Festivals—promotes life, causing a deep arousal and awakening within the person for great spiritual heights (*Likutey Halakhot* I, p. 92a).

❯ *Do not touch it*

> The Serpent pushed Eve against the Tree and said, "Just as there
> is no death by touching it, there is no death from eating of its
> fruits" (Rashi).

Adam and Eve added another injunction to the prohibition
of eating from the Tree due to incorrect Torah study. They fell
victim to the Serpent's didactics and allowed him to mislead
them in discussions that led to false Torah interpretations and
unnecessary restrictions (*chumrot*). As a result, they embellished
the single mitzvah God had commanded him by formulating
another commandment: "We are not allowed to touch the Tree."
This caused their downfall (*Likutey Halakhot* II, p. 164).

❯ *Do not eat from it or touch it, or else you will die*

The Serpent knew that the Tree of Knowledge of Good and Evil
corresponds to the *kelipah* of *nogah*, which contains both good and
evil. Therefore he told Eve, "If the Tree were totally impure, one
would be defiled even by touching it." In this way, he convinced
Adam and Eve that they would be able to draw from the good of
the Tree and not be tainted by the evil therein (*Likutey Halakhot* III,
p. 54). Just as their eating in sin caused all the blemishes, eating in
holiness rectifies that sin. Therefore the rectification of Adam's sin
can be attained by eating on Shabbat (ibid.).

3:5   כִּי יֹדֵעַ אֱלֹהִים כִּי בְּיוֹם אֲכָלְכֶם מִמֶּנּוּ וְנִפְקְחוּ
             עֵינֵיכֶם וִהְיִיתֶם כֵּאלֹהִים יֹדְעֵי טוֹב וָרָע

> **"For God knows that on the day you eat
> from it, your eyes will be opened. You will
> be like God, knowing good and evil."**

❯ *You will be like God*

> The Serpent told Eve, "God ate from this Tree and created the
> world!" (Rashi).

When Adam ate from the Tree of Knowledge, he blemished
the act of eating by giving primacy to physical consumption over
spiritual sustenance. Adam and Eve were misled by the Serpent,

who implied that the world was not created *ex nihilo* (*yeish me-ayin*, something from nothing), but that a specific mechanism—the fruit of the Tree—brought the world into existence. The pursuit of material sustenance leads to a denial of God's role in Creation. A person who does not believe that God can provide for him will suffer the curse of toiling for his sustenance. The rectification for Adam's sin begins with the willingness to listen to and hear God's voice (*Likutey Halakhot* II, p. 11a).

》 *You will be like God*

The Serpent told Eve, "God ate from this Tree and created the world!" (Rashi).

The Serpent tried to cause the material to be ascendant. But God preceded Creation, creating the world *ex nihilo*. There was no Tree for Him to "eat from" prior to Creation—there was nothing but God! Having faith in God and in *chiddush ha-olam* (the daily renewal of Creation) protects a person from atheism (*Likutey Halakhot* I, p. 148).

》 *Adam, Tree*

Any falsehood that does not begin with truth will not be accepted (Rashi on Numbers 13:27; *Sotah* 35a).

The Serpent lied to Eve, saying that if she ate from the Tree, she would not die. He enticed and convinced Eve of the "truth" of his words until he caused her and Adam to sin.

How can falsehood be so convincing? It must be rooted in truth or else it doesn't have any chance of being accepted. What is this truth? At their root, all things are one. There is no difference between gold, silver, copper, and so on. There is no difference between one, one hundred, or one thousand, because at their root, all things are one—the One God. Only when they devolve into this world do they become different. In this way, falsehood, which begins with truth, masquerades as the truth (*Likutey Halakhot* IV, p. 104-53a).

》 *You will be like God*

The Serpent claimed that God Himself had eaten from the Tree of Knowledge, giving Him the power to create worlds. This claim brought Adam to arrogance, thinking that he, too, would become great and all-powerful. Had he remained humble, he would have lived forever. Instead, he was chased out of the Garden of Eden and became mortal. Yet by dying and returning to dust, he returns to humility. Thus, he merits the Resurrection (*Likutey Halakhot* I, p. 83a).

❯ You will be like God

The Serpent's enticement caused Eve to waver, thinking that she might be able to gain Godly wisdom in order to understand the reasoning behind God's decrees and laws. Even today, one who insists upon knowing and understanding God's reasons before he performs a mitzvah, as did Eve, "eats" from the Tree of Knowledge of Good and Evil. Instead, one must show absolute faith in God, even if he does not know or understand God's reasons. Having faith is a rectification for "eating from the Tree" (*Likutey Halakhot* I, p. 205a-410).

3:6   וַתֵּרֶא הָאִשָּׁה כִּי טוֹב הָעֵץ לְמַאֲכָל וְכִי תַאֲוָה־הוּא
לָעֵינַיִם וְנֶחְמָד הָעֵץ לְהַשְׂכִּיל וַתִּקַּח מִפִּרְיוֹ וַתֹּאכַל
וַתִּתֵּן גַּם־לְאִישָׁהּ עִמָּהּ וַיֹּאכַל

The woman saw that the tree was good to eat, appealing to the eyes and desirable for attaining wisdom. She took some of its fruit and ate, and she also gave to her husband, and he ate.

❯ Good to eat, appealing to the eyes and desirable for attaining wisdom

These three descriptions of the Tree refer to the three main lusts. "Good to eat" refers to gluttony. "Appealing to the eyes" refers to immorality. "Desirable" refers to avarice. The blemish of the Tree of Knowledge impacted all three lusts (*Likutey Halakhot* V, p. 328).

❯ The woman saw…appealing to the eyes and desirable for attaining wisdom

The main blemish of Adam and Eve was in sight. This blemish was caused by the evil eye of the Serpent, who caused them to sin. Only after they ate from the Tree did Adam and Eve realize they were naked and needed clothing to conceal them from another's sight, from an evil eye (*Likutey Halakhot* II, p. 182a). Their eating from the Tree blemished their eyes and their intellect! Now man must avert his gaze from anything that arouses lust, and rectify his intellect (*Likutey Halakhot* III, p. 8a).

} *Appealing to the eyes*

Adam looked where he wasn't supposed to, reaching beyond his field of vision and understanding and rationalizing what God would want him to do. The "revolving sword" that was posted at the entrance to the Garden of Eden (Genesis 3:24) represents Adam's swaying emotions and his ultimate succumbing to gluttony when he rationalized that he could eat from the Tree. Sin is the result for all those who rationalize about God's commandments (*Likutey Halakhot* II, p. 314).

} *And he ate*

Adam blemished his faith in the Sages by having blemished faith in himself and in his ability to believe that he could rise to great spiritual heights. He did not respect himself enough to avoid taking the advice of the Serpent and eating from the Tree (*Likutey Halakhot* III, p. 240).

} *Adam ate from the Tree of Knowledge*

A person can reach the level of knowledge that everything is from God, both the good and the bad. With this knowledge, he can recognize the Unity of God and perceive God in both the good and the bad.

Adam was commanded not to eat from the Tree of Knowledge of Good and Evil so that he would not be exposed to "good and evil," but rather remain with his knowledge of God's Unity. By eating from the Tree, he became cognizant of "bad" as a separate entity. This was his curse, for now he must work hard to nullify himself before God again in order to regain that knowledge of God's Unity (*Likutey Halakhot* V, p. 184a-368).

} *Adam ate from the Tree of Knowledge*

Adam sinned by eating from the Tree of Knowledge of Good and Evil. His sin produced an admixture of good and evil, mixing up two separate entities. Had Adam eaten from the Tree of Life, his eating would have brought him greater strength and vitality. But eating from the Tree of Knowledge of Good and Evil led him to gaze into things beyond his comprehension. He could no longer look at each thing separately, and tried to attain the unattainable (*Likutey Halakhot* IV, p. 204).

▷ *Adam's sin*

How could Adam have sinned if he did not yet possess an evil inclination to sin?

Prior to Creation, there was only God, a perfect state of holiness. As soon as Creation came into being, a state of purity also came into existence. But within that state of purity, one could move towards holiness or towards impurity. Even in a state of purity, impurity exists in potential.

Adam had to purify himself to the point that he could enter the realm of holiness. But the Serpent saw that Adam was vulnerable, and attacked him before he entered that state. This plunged Adam and the entire world into impurity and falsehood (*Likutey Halakhot* IV, p. 196a). Thus, man should act quickly to attain sanctity and protect himself lest he fall prey to his vulnerabilities.

▷ *Adam's sin*

After Adam ate from the Tree, he separated from his wife and spilt seed for 130 years. This sin caused the exile of the Jews to Egypt (*Ari, Sha'ar HaPesukim, Shemot*; see *Eruvin* 18b).

But it would seem that the Exodus from Egypt rectified the sin of immorality, signaling an end to all exiles. However, there exists another cause for immorality and a blemished covenant: improper justice. Until justice becomes perfected, unworthy judges who administer faulty judgments are the prime cause of immorality and exile (*Likutey Halakhot* III, p. 110a).

3:7 וַתִּפָּקַחְנָה עֵינֵי שְׁנֵיהֶם וַיֵּדְעוּ כִּי עֵירֻמִּם הֵם וַיִּתְפְּרוּ
עֲלֵה תְאֵנָה וַיַּעֲשׂוּ לָהֶם חֲגֹרֹת

**The eyes of both of them were opened and
they realized that they were naked. They
sewed together fig leaves and made
themselves loincloths.**

) The eyes of both of them were opened

This means that they understood (Rashi).

Opening one's eyes to understanding is like sunrise, when
the light is bright. Closing one's eyes to understanding can be
compared to sunset (*Likutey Moharan* I, 16).

The eyes are messengers of the intellect. How a person looks at
something determines his understanding of it (ibid., I, 21:2).

To grow spiritually, a person must open the eyes of his intellect
in order to perceive greater levels of being (ibid., I, 74).

When a person develops his trust, he looks up to God to provide
him with his daily needs. Thus, by opening his eyes, a person is
able to see Divine Providence (ibid., I, 76; ibid., I, 225).

3:8 וַיִּשְׁמְעוּ אֶת־קוֹל יְיָ אֱלֹהִים מִתְהַלֵּךְ בַּגָּן לְרוּחַ
הַיּוֹם וַיִּתְחַבֵּא הָאָדָם וְאִשְׁתּוֹ מִפְּנֵי יְיָ אֱלֹהִים
בְּתוֹךְ עֵץ הַגָּן

**They heard God's voice moving about in
the garden in the cool of the day. The man
and his wife hid themselves from God
among the trees of the garden.**

) They heard God's voice

Adam was given one mitzvah: not to eat from the Tree of
Knowledge. Yet he had a deep, burning desire to recognize God, and
acting on that desire, he went beyond his limitations and sinned.
When he heard God's voice coming towards him in the cool of the

day—the time when constrictions are present in the world—he recognized his error of stepping beyond his parameters. Then he merited to repent before God (*Likutey Halakhot* II, p. 456).

3:11 וַיֹּאמֶר מִי הִגִּיד לְךָ כִּי עֵירֹם אָתָּה הֲמִן־הָעֵץ אֲשֶׁר
צִוִּיתִיךָ לְבִלְתִּי אֲכָל־מִמֶּנּוּ אָכָלְתָּ

"Who told you that you are naked?" He said. "Have you eaten from the Tree of which I commanded you not to eat?"

Have you eaten from the Tree

Where do we find *HaMaN* (המן) in the Torah? *HaMiN haEitz* (המן העץ, Have you eaten from the Tree?) (*Chullin* 139).

One who does not eat in holiness recalls the sin of Adam, who ate from the Tree of Knowledge of Good and Evil. This type of eating invokes the power of Haman (*Likutey Halakhot* II, p. 113a).

HaMin haEitz

The word *HaMiN* is spelled the same as *HaMaN*. Eating the "forbidden fruit" leads to a Haman, the apex of arrogance and self-worship (*Likutey Halakhot* I, p. 178).

HaMin haEitz

The Tree was watered by the river, which represents the voice of rebuke. Haman tried to suppress that rebuke. In contrast, tzaddikim merit to hear the voice of rebuke and water the Tree so that it is beneficial (*Likutey Halakhot* I, p. 98).

HaMin haEitz

Not only is Haman alluded to in the Torah, he actually comes from the Torah—from the sin of Adam eating from the Tree of Knowledge of Good and Evil. The Tree represents the Torah. When Adam ate from the Tree, causing good and evil to become mixed together, the letter-combinations of the Torah also became jumbled. If a person is not careful in his Torah study to reach the proper conclusions—that is, he does not separate right from wrong or understand the correct advice that he must follow—then he can actually be misled by the Torah itself! (see *Yoma* 72) (*Likutey Halakhot* V, p. 178a).

》 *Adam ate from the Tree*

To Adam, God's command not to eat from the Tree of Knowledge was a matter of faith: Adam was to believe that he had the power to hear and obey the commandment. To Eve, the prohibition was conveyed through Adam, and as such, represented "faith in the tzaddikim." When she allowed herself to be misled by the Serpent, Eve blemished her faith in the tzaddik, Adam. And when she persuaded Adam to sin, she caused him to lose his faith, too.

In a sense, Adam also demonstrated a blemish of faith in the tzaddikim, for he knew he was formed directly by God and that his soul comprised all the souls of humanity. Recognizing his greatness, he should have withstood temptation. The same idea applies to each one of us. If we were only cognizant of the greatness of our souls, we would never commit a sin or even a blemish. By safeguarding our faith in the tzaddikim—as well as in the "tzaddik within us"—we can merit to spiritual sustenance (*Likutey Halakhot* VIII, p. 137a-137b).

》 *Adam ate from the Tree*

Adam's impatience caused him to sin, bringing about the curse of earning a living, which itself challenges man's patience daily. The Midrash calls impatience "anger" (cf. *Bamidbar Rabbah* 19:9).

Only by practicing patience can a person build a protective wall to guard his wealth. One who gets angry loses his wealth. Moreover, Adam's anger blemished wealth itself, causing it to descend to a place of exile. Thus, we find that all the wealth of the world was brought down to Egypt, the Jewish place of exile, during the famine. At the time of the Exodus, the Jewish nation, which awaited its redemption with great patience, merited to take out that great wealth (*Likutey Halakhot* VII, p. 210).

》 *Adam ate from the Tree*

There is a force which draws a person to God, and an opposing force which draws him to the Other Side. Eating can represent either force. Adam's eating from the Tree was a deed which led to death. At the opposite extreme stands holy eating, which rectifies that sin and leads to life (*Likutey Halakhot* VII, p. 137a).

❧ Adam ate from the Tree

When Adam ate from the Tree, he caused sparks of holiness to scatter throughout the world. Now everything must be rectified and purified to return to the realm of holiness (*Likutey Halakhot* II, p. 56a).

❧ Adam, Eitz HaDa'at

Both Adam's sin of eating from the Tree of Knowledge of Good and Evil and the sin of the Generation of the Flood led to the same result: the mixing of good and evil. (During the Generation of the Flood, each person destroyed his own path, thus mixing up good and evil.) To rectify one's blemishes—which are the result of mixing good and evil—one must eat in holiness and offer prayer to God. Eating in holiness rectifies the sin of eating from the Tree. Prayer recalls the Act of Creation, the sanctity of the Holy Land (see above, p. 37). During Noah's time, the Flood did not enter the Holy Land. Thus, prayer is the means to avoid the floodwaters and the overwhelming confusions brought about by our blemishes (*Likutey Halakhot* II, p. 16).

❧ Adam's blemish of eating

Adam's sin lay in seeking the material sweetness of food rather than its spiritual nourishment. On the day of Rosh HaShanah (the Sixth Day of Creation, the day Adam and Eve were created and sinned), he fell prey to the cunning Serpent and became a victim of his philosophies. We rectify Adam's sin by dipping our bread in honey on Rosh HaShanah, implying that we seek the spiritual sweetness of our food and desire to direct ourselves to God (*Likutey Halakhot* II, p. 82).

❧ Adam, the Tree

The ability to remember the World to Come in this world depends on a person's vision. If he continually looks ahead and sees beyond his vistas, he will remember the ultimate goal. But Adam and Eve blemished sight ("She *saw* that the tree was good to eat"), which blemished their memory of the World to Come.

As punishment for their sin, death came into the world. Death is actually a blessing, for it forces a person to recognize that he must look beyond this world and towards the future, the World to Come. The rectification for a blemished memory lies in Torah, for Torah brings one to life—the real life of the Future (*Likutey Halakhot* VIII, p. 177a-177b).

3:13 וַיֹּאמֶר יְיָ אֱלֹהִים לָאִשָּׁה מַה־זֹּאת עָשִׂית
וַתֹּאמֶר הָאִשָּׁה הַנָּחָשׁ הִשִּׁיאַנִי וָאֹכֵל

God said to the woman, "What is this that you have done?" The woman replied, "The Serpent advised me, and I ate."

》 *The Serpent advised me*

The Serpent was able to gain control over Eve through cunning words, and she succumbed because of her folly. As our Sages teach: "A person does not sin unless he is overcome by a spirit of folly" (*Sotah* 2a) (*Likutey Moharan* I, 19:3).

》 *The Serpent advised me*

HiShIanI (השיאני, he advised me) is similar to *niSUiN* (נשואין, marriage). Receiving advice from someone can be compared to a woman receiving seed from her husband. Just as it takes time for the seed to become a child and grow to maturity, so too, advice takes time to bear fruit.

Eve wished to receive advice that would result in immediate gratification; therefore she was subsequently polluted by it. Ultimately, all of mankind was polluted; only the Jews (at the Revelation at Sinai) attained temporary purification (see *Shabbat* 146a). When a person seeks advice, he must go to true tzaddikim who are knowledgeable in Torah and have attained truth (*Likutey Moharan* I, 7:3).

3:14   וַיֹּאמֶר יְיָ אֱלֹהִים אֶל־הַנָּחָשׁ כִּי עָשִׂיתָ זֹּאת
אָרוּר אַתָּה מִכָּל־הַבְּהֵמָה וּמִכֹּל חַיַּת הַשָּׂדֶה
עַל־גְּחֹנְךָ תֵלֵךְ וְעָפָר תֹּאכַל כָּל־יְמֵי חַיֶּיךָ

God said to the Serpent, "Because you did this, you are cursed more than all the animals and all the wild beasts. You will crawl upon your belly and eat dust all the days of your life."

❯ *You are cursed*

> The Serpent brought thirty-nine curses into the world (ten for Adam, ten for Eve, ten for the Serpent, and nine for the earth) (*Tikkuney Zohar* #48, p. 85).

> Our Sages list thirty-nine categories of work prohibited on Shabbat (*Shabbat* 73a), corresponding to these thirty-nine curses.

If a person falls prey to the Serpent's curse, he assumes the yoke of toiling for his livelihood. However, one who accepts the yoke of God attains "Shabbat" in that his toil is mitigated (*Likutey Moharan* I, 38:7). Then his work parallels the way in which these thirty-nine categories of work were applied to build and maintain the holy Tabernacle (cf. ibid., I, 11:4).

❯ *You are cursed*

> The word "cursed" is associated with both the Serpent and Canaan, who was cursed to be a slave (see Genesis 9:25).

The Serpent brought death into the world by persuading Eve to eat from the Tree of Knowledge. Sleep is one-sixtieth of death (*Berakhot* 57b). Thus, the curse of the Serpent causes a lethargy—or "slave mentality"—associated with lack of purpose (*Likutey Moharan* I, 117). One must try to transcend that curse of the Serpent and fill his days with vitality.

❯ *You will crawl upon your belly*

The Serpent, whose speech was toxic, was deprived of his legs. "Legs" represent holy speech, which Kabbalistically corresponds to the *sefirah* of Malkhut (see Charts, p. 347). In general, a person who lacks holy speech has no "legs" to support him.

The Jews who received the Torah were cleansed of the pollution of the Serpent; therefore the Torah describes them as having "stood" at Sinai (Exodus 19:17) (*Likutey Moharan* I, 38:6).

⟩ *You will eat dust all the days of your life*

The Serpent was condemned to "eat dust." This is "dust of gold" (Job 28:6) —i.e., money.

The phrase "You will eat dust all the days of your life" may be homiletically translated: "Dust will consume all the days of your life," for one who mortgages his life for financial gain will be consumed by monetary concerns. This leads to sadness and depression (*Likutey Moharan* I, 23:6). Similarly, we find that the main toxin of the Serpent is laziness and depression (alluded to in "earth" and "dust") (ibid., I, 189).

3:16   אֶל־הָאִשָּׁה אָמַר הַרְבָּה אַרְבֶּה עִצְּבוֹנֵךְ וְהֵרֹנֵךְ בְּעֶצֶב תֵּלְדִי בָנִים וְאֶל־אִישֵׁךְ תְּשׁוּקָתֵךְ וְהוּא יִמְשָׁל־בָּךְ

He said to the woman, "I will greatly increase your suffering and your pregnancy. You will give birth in pain. Your desire will be towards your husband, and he will rule over you."

⟩ *You will give birth in pain*

The physical travails of childbirth apply in a spiritual sense to "giving birth" to new intellect. The suffering of pregnancy and childbirth corresponds to the difficulties of understanding new studies and comprehending Godliness. Just as a woman in labor cries out from her pains, so too, a person must cry out to God from his pain of not understanding sought-after wisdom. This anguish helps him "give birth" to new understanding. And just as an infant cries, signaling his growing mental capacity, so too, an adult must continually cry out and ask for God's help to grow spiritually (*Likutey Halakhot* IV, p. 240a).

3:17 וּלְאָדָם אָמַר כִּי־שָׁמַעְתָּ לְקוֹל אִשְׁתֶּךָ וַתֹּאכַל מִן־
הָעֵץ אֲשֶׁר צִוִּיתִיךָ לֵאמֹר לֹא תֹאכַל מִמֶּנּוּ אֲרוּרָה
הָאֲדָמָה בַּעֲבוּרֶךָ בְּעִצָּבוֹן תֹּאכֲלֶנָּה כֹּל יְמֵי חַיֶּיךָ

**He said to Adam, "Because you listened
to your wife and ate from the tree about
which I commanded you, saying, 'Do not
eat from it,' the earth will be cursed
because of you. In sadness you will eat
from it all the days of your life."**

》 The earth will be cursed because of you

Though the earth was cursed because of Adam's sin, the ten
mitzvot that we perform before partaking of the earth's bounty
remove that curse. These *mitzvot* are:

1) Not to harness two different types of animals when plowing
   a field;

2) Not to plant different types of seeds together;

3) Not to muzzle the ox while it plows the field;

4) To leave behind a small amount of the harvest for the poor
   (*leket*);

5) To leave behind forgotten sheaves during the harvesting
   (*shikchah*);

6) To leave a corner of the field unharvested for the poor
   (*pei'ah*);

7) To set aside *terumah* (first gift, about 1/100th of the produce)
   for the Kohen;

8) To set aside *ma'aser* (10% of the produce) for the Levite;

9) To set aside *ma'aser sheini* (second tithe, also 10%), to be
   eaten by the field owner in Jerusalem or given to the poor,
   depending on the year;

10) To set aside *challah* (a small amount of the dough before
    baking) for the Kohen (*Orach Chaim* 167).

The number 10 corresponds to the letter *yod* (י), which represents holiness. By performing these ten *mitzvot*, we draw holiness
into the earth and then the earth returns to us bounty and blessing
(*Likutey Halakhot* VIII, p. 184a).

⟩ *In sadness you will eat*

This curse also hangs over our own lives, as we must struggle for a livelihood. It stems from Adam's eating from the Tree—i.e., blemishing proper advice as to the way in which one must earn his living. The rectification for this sin is faith in the tzaddikim, who have perfected their counsel and can bring satisfaction and joy into our lives (see *Likutey Halakhot* III, p. 234a-468).

⟩ *In sadness you will eat*

One who does not believe that he attains his sustenance through Divine Providence will derive his livelihood through sadness and worry. A person must have faith that God provides—and with that, he may transcend the curse of Adam (*Likutey Moharan* I, 23:1).

⟩ *In sadness you will eat from it*

Originally God intended that man's food would grow ready to eat. But because of Adam's sin, all foods now contain an admixture of good and evil, and must be "purified" before consumption. The curse of toiling for one's bread—such as the need to remove the chaff from the wheat, or to prune vines to grow grapes—signifies the process of purifying good from evil. Similarly, a person must purify his faith, removing falsehoods and foolishness so that his faith remains pure (*Likutey Halakhot* II, p. 16a).

⟩ *In sadness you will eat*

Lack of knowledge is the greatest poverty. When Adam ate from the Tree, he blemished his knowledge—his awareness of Divine Providence—and was therefore cursed to eat with sadness and suffering. This alludes to exerting great strength to search for one's livelihood and not being able to seek one's livelihood directly through Divine Providence (*Likutey Halakhot* I, p. 44).

⟩ *In sadness you will eat*

Had Adam not sinned, we would not have had to work hard. All our needs would have been provided through prayer. Now great effort must be expended, both in work and in prayer, to invoke the blessings of God that prevailed in the Garden of Eden (*Likutey Halakhot* III, p. 14).

⟫ In sadness you will eat

The curse of the Serpent leads to toil—the thirty-nine categories of work. This results in depression, which manifests itself in a sluggish pulse. Sighing and deep breathing can alleviate a sluggish pulse and lead a person to joy (*Likutey Moharan* I, 56:9).

⟫ The earth will be cursed...in sadness you will eat

Rebbe Nachman taught:

For certain sins, the punishment is debt. One who is punished for such a sin is constantly in debt. All the merit in the world does not erase his punishment. ...These sins can even cause others to fall into debt. When such transgressions become commonplace, there are many debtors in the world.

The remedy is to repent in general for all your sins. Even though you do not know which sin is causing the debts, repent in general and ask God to save you from that particular sin as well. The time for such repentance is when you are in a state of expanded consciousness.

A debtor is in a state of constricted consciousness. The Sages teach: "Ten measures of sleep came down to the world. Nine were taken by slaves" (*Kiddushin* 49b). Sleep is a state of constricted consciousness and a debtor is a slave, as the verse states: "A borrower is a slave to the lender" (Proverbs 22:7). The nine measures of sleep taken by slaves are the measures of constricted consciousness of the debtor. Therefore one must repent for this sin when he is in a state of expanded consciousness (*Rabbi Nachman's Wisdom* #112).

Rebbe Nachman did not reveal which sin causes debt. An oral tradition among Breslover chassidim maintains that it is a blemish of the covenant, most likely masturbation (*Rabbi Eliyahu Chaim Rosen*). This sin is associated with Adam, who wasted seed for 130 years (*Eruvin* 18b). And, as the verse states: "For a harlot, a man is made to go searching for a loaf of bread" (Proverbs 6:26).

Reb Noson explains that the curse of earning a livelihood, which Adam brought about because of his sin, forces many people to go into debt in order to sustain themselves. Thus, all sins resulting from debt come from Adam's sin. Moreover, most loans require property for collateral, since the *land* was cursed along with mankind (*Likutey Halakhot* VII, p. 48a).

3:18   וְקוֹץ וְדַרְדַּר תַּצְמִיחַ לָךְ וְאָכַלְתָּ אֶת־עֵשֶׂב הַשָּׂדֶה
"It will sprout for you thorns and thistles, and you will eat the grass of the field."

❱ *You will eat the grass of the field...By the sweat of your brow you will eat bread*

> When Adam heard that he would have to eat grass, he trembled. "Will I and my donkey eat from the same trough?" he cried. God replied, "By the sweat of your brow you will eat bread" (*Avot de-Rabbi Natan* 1:7).

If a person eats in an animalistic fashion, he can be stricken with fever until his body trembles. The cure for fever is sweating.

When Adam heard that he would be condemned to eat grass, he was afraid that he would be eating like an animal. He trembled and prayed that he wouldn't fall prey to animalistic tendencies. God told him how he might protect himself: "By the sweat." Which sweat is that? "Of your brow." That is to say, a person must invoke his intellect (his "brow") to seek a higher life as a human being. Then he will eat in a manner fit for a human being (*Likutey Moharan* I, 263).

❱ *You will eat the grass of the field...you will eat bread*

> When Adam heard that he would have to eat grass, he trembled. "Will I and my donkey eat from the same trough?" he cried. God replied, "By the sweat of your brow you will eat bread" (*Avot de-Rabbi Natan* 1:7).

Adam was created as a human being with intellect. When he ate from the Tree, he blemished his intellect and descended to the level of an animal. When God told him he would now eat grass, he trembled and cried, "Does that mean I am beyond hope? Will I always be like an animal?" God answered, "By the sweat of your brow..." Referring to that topmost feature of the human form (the forehead—i.e., the intellect), God hinted that if he was willing to work hard to rectify his sin, he could rise above his lowly state and regain the status of a human being (*Likutey Halakhot* VII, p. 234a-468).

❭ *You will eat the grass of the field…you will eat bread*

Adam's limbs shook when he heard he would have to eat grass—i.e., animal food. When God saw his trembling, He told Adam, "You will eat bread." Fear and one's honest efforts rectify one's food (*Likutey Halakhot* II, p. 36).

❭ *Grass…bread*

At the Pesach Seder, we first eat *karpas* to remind us of the "grass" we are meant to eat if we do not rectify our lives. However, if we are willing to sweat and put effort into our service of God, conducting ourselves in the proper manner and order (i.e., *Seder*), then we merit to eat bread (matzah) and other foods fit for human consumption (*Likutey Halakhot* II, p. 40).

3:19 בְּזֵעַת אַפֶּיךָ תֹּאכַל לֶחֶם עַד שׁוּבְךָ אֶל־הָאֲדָמָה כִּי מִמֶּנָּה לֻקָּחְתָּ כִּי־עָפָר אַתָּה וְאֶל־עָפָר תָּשׁוּב

"By the sweat of your brow you will eat bread, until you return to the earth, for from it you were taken. For you are dust, and to dust you will return."

❭ *By the sweat of your brow you will eat*

Be-zei'at apekha (by the sweat of your brow) literally means "by the sweat of your nose." Why the nose? Because a person breathes through the nose, and that breath expresses his inner desires, whether for good or bad. Furthermore, this breath surrounds and envelops him, creating a good or bad environment in which he will live. Evil thoughts and desires pollute his surroundings, causing him great difficulties. One who wishes to elevate mundane activities like working and eating into levels of holiness must breathe holiness and think good thoughts. In this way, he can "eat by the sweat of his nose" (*Likutey Halakhot* VIII, p. 170a).

❭ *By the sweat of your brow*

The Prophet Isaiah speaks of dew, which refers to the "dew of Torah" (Isaiah 26:19; see *Ketuvot* 111b). *TaL* (טל, dew) has the numerical value of 39. This means that a person who toils in Torah will be spared the travail of the thirty-nine categories of work. Conversely, a person who distances himself from Torah will find that the blessing of the "dew of Torah" will turn into the "sweat of his brow," and he will have to toil in order to support himself (*Likutey Moharan* I, 159).

》 *By the sweat of your brow you will eat bread*

The initial letters of the words *Be-zei'at Apekha Tochal Lechem* (בזעת אפיך תאכל לחם, by the sweat of your brow you will eat bread) have the combined numerical value of 437 (plus four units for the four letters themselves), which is the same as the numerical value of *AL HaSheChITaH* (על השחיטה, in regard to animal slaughter) in the blessing "Who commanded us in regard to animal slaughter." The bitterness of earning a living can be sweetened by eating kosher meat that has been properly slaughtered, and by reciting the proper blessings over food (*Likutey Moharan* I, 37:6).

3:20   וַיִּקְרָא הָאָדָם שֵׁם אִשְׁתּוֹ חַוָּה כִּי הִוא הָיְתָה אֵם כָּל־חָי

The man named his wife Eve because she was the mother of all life.

》 *Chavah*

Eve represents speech. Her name, *ChaVaH* (חוה), is an acronym for the phrase *Ha-me'atreichi Chesed Ve-rachamim* (המעטרכי חסד ורחמים, Who encircles you with kindness and compassion) (*Psalms* 103:4). One who attains proper speech will be the recipient of God's kindness and compassion (*Likutey Moharan* II, 16).

》 *The mother of all life*

Most people believe that man is powerless in the face of "Mother Nature." But we Jews know that our prayers can transcend nature. Rebbe Nachman explains that Eve represents speech—i.e., words of prayer and supplication. The name *ChaVaH* (חוה, Eve) has the numerical value of 18, one more than the word *ChaI* (חי, life). Thus, Eve—prayer—is "the mother of all life," since she transcends all of nature. Our prayers transcend "Mother Nature" and can cause miracles to occur (*Likutey Moharan* I, 216).

⟩ The mother of all life

There is a state of being called "honor" or "glory." This is the "mother of all life," for it is the source of all souls. When the soul passes away, it is taken up into honor, its source. One must be very cautious when some new honor comes his way, for it may have come to take his soul with it back to its source. However, in the majority of cases, honor comes to someone in order to bring him a new spirit and elevate him to new heights here on earth (*Likutey Moharan* I, 67:1).

⟩ Adam and Chavah

ADaM (אדם) represents order, as the letters of his name are written in the order of the Hebrew alphabet (*aleph, dalet, mem*). *Chavah* (חוה, Eve) represents disorder, as the letters of her name appear backwards according to the Hebrew alphabet (*chet, vav, hei*). Order corresponds to daylight and knowledge; disorder represents night and lack of knowledge. We generally sleep at night because that is the time that judgments, constrictions and lack of order reign. When we sleep, we conceptually give ourselves over to God for the period of time that things are going against us, in order to bring things back to "normal," to order (*Likutey Halakhot* I, p. 46).

The Serpent caused Eve to sin by playing on disorder. The evil inclination attacks when a person is confused. Had Adam and Eve joined together in a holy union, they would have created order even from a disorderly situation. But the temptations were great. The Serpent convinced Eve that God was withholding greatness from man, "for He ate from this Tree and created the world. You, too, can be like God…God knows you'll be like Him, and every craftsman hates his competitors" (Rashi on Genesis 3:5). In her confusion, Eve felt that she, too, could rectify problems by herself, without turning to God. This was haughtiness, for Who created both order and disorder in the first place? Therefore Adam and Eve were cursed with fields that grow thorns (Genesis 3:18)—a disorderly life that must now be rectified through sweat and toil (*Likutey Halakhot* I, p. 25a-50-26a).

3:21 וַיַּעַשׂ יְיָ אֱלֹהִים לְאָדָם וּלְאִשְׁתּוֹ כָּתְנוֹת עוֹר וַיַּלְבִּשֵׁם

God made leather garments for Adam and his wife, and He clothed them.

》 Garments of light

Originally, Adam wore garments of *ohr* (אור, light—spelled *aleph, vav, reish*). After he sinned, he had to wear garments of *ohr* (עור, leather—spelled *ayin, vav, reish*) (*Tikkuney Zohar* #58, p. 92b; see also *Bereishit Rabbah* 20:12).

The original "skin" of man was translucent, like fingernails, reflecting light. Man must strive to transform his skin into that nail-like matter. During the Havdalah ceremony which marks the end of Shabbat, we customarily look at the light of the candle reflected on our fingernails. This custom implies to us that we must learn to discern skin from nails, as well as right from wrong and good from evil. We must learn to purify our bodies to reflect the light of the soul (*Likutey Halakhot* I, p. 100a). In fact, had Adam not sinned, he could have transformed his body into a soul! (*Likutey Halakhot* I, p. 216-109a).

》 Garments of light, garments of leather

The Torah is a great light. Created 2,000 years prior to Creation (*Bereishit Rabbah* 8:2), the Torah illumines thousands of worlds and thousands of levels. It is divided into weekly portions, verses, words and letters in order to contain and filter its light in small measures.

Kabbalistically, the *sefirah* of Chokhmah represents "thousands." (Binah represents "hundreds," Ze'er Anpin represents "tens," and Malkhut corresponds to "ones.") It is known that Chokhmah is too great a light to be received without filters. Had Adam not eaten from the Tree of Knowledge, he would have been able to receive that great light of Chokhmah and to perceive God through the light of Torah, which illumines thousands of worlds. He would have been able to "wear" garments of light and live forever (see Genesis 3:22).

But because Adam sinned, he must now wear garments of leather. These correspond to the *tefilin*, which are made of leather (*Tikkuney Zohar* #69, p. 105). *Tefilin* represent great intellect which is filtered and contained. And although Adam was destined to live

1,000 years, he had to pass away before then, since he had lost the ability to attain Chokhmah, the "thousands" (*Likutey Halakhot* VII, p. 16a-32).

Leather garments

These garments represent the *tefilin* (which are made from leather), which the Kabbalah associates with higher levels of consciousness. Such garments represent the attainment of the knowledge of God. This knowledge makes a person humble and inspires him to repent. Then he can rectify his past and return to Eden.

Tefilin represent life (*Menachot* 44b) and correspond to the Tree of Life, not the Tree of Knowledge of Good and Evil. When we don *tefilin*, we draw life onto ourselves (*Likutey Moharan* I, 38:6).

God made garments for Adam and his wife

Before his sin, Adam had no need for "clothing"—meaning, he had no need for Godliness to be enclothed for him, since he was able to attain perceptions of God directly. His sin diminished his intellect, so that afterwards he could receive Godliness only through filters and "garments." Thus, "God made garments for Adam and his wife," so they could attain perceptions of Godliness (*Likutey Halakhot* VII, p. 219a).

God made garments for Adam and his wife…the cherubim

Originally, Adam and Eve were clothed in garments of *ohr* (אור, light)—the light of Godliness. After the sin, clothing made of *ohr* (עור, leather) became necessary. Originally, man was designed to benefit from God's light directly, but now this light comes to him "dressed up" and concealed within "garments." These garments are represented by the cherubim stationed at the entrance to the Garden of Eden. Now man must somehow get past these cherubim in order to regain the Garden of Eden, the light of God.

From the beginning, clothes were sewn from wool or flax. Wool refers to the great light of God; flax refers to judgments and constrictions (i.e., garments). The Torah prohibits the wearing of *sha'atnez* (a combination of wool and flax/linen in the same garment), for such a garment obscures rather than reveals the light of God (see also Deuteronomy 22:11) (*Likutey Halakhot* I, p. 58).

3:23 וַיְשַׁלְּחֵהוּ יְיָ אֱלֹהִים מִגַּן־עֵדֶן לַעֲבֹד אֶת־הָאֲדָמָה
אֲשֶׁר לֻקַּח מִשָּׁם

**God banished him from the Garden of Eden,
to work the earth from which he was taken.**

》 *God banished him from the Garden of Eden*

Adam repented for his sin and brought a sacrifice to God. The animal he sacrificed had one horn (*Chullin* 60a).

KeReN (קרן, horn) is similar to *KaRaN* (קרן, shone). That shining corresponds to the spiritual light of *tefilin*. In order to repent, Adam sacrificed his animalistic, materialistic desires. As a result, he attained the illumination of a great awareness of Godliness, which corresponds to wearing *tefilin* (*Likutey Moharan* I, 38:6).

》 *God banished him from the Garden of Eden*

Adam's expulsion from the Garden of Eden should have taken place on Friday, the day that he sinned. However, Shabbat protected him and he was banished only after its conclusion (*Zohar* II, 138a).

The letters of the word *ShaBbaT* (שבת) can be rearranged to form the word *TaShuV* (תשב, you will repent). Because Adam repented, he was able to invoke the merit of Shabbat, which protected him (*Likutey Moharan* I, 79).

Similarly, the letters of *ShaBbaT* (שבת) may be rearranged to form the word *BoSheT* (בשת, humility). When a person attains humility, he can invoke the merit and protection of Shabbat (ibid., I, 38:7).

》 *God banished him from the Garden of Eden…He chased out the man*

This "chasing" is the banishment from a tranquil life. Now man must travel about and be in constant motion to earn a livelihood. And just as Shabbat protected Adam, allowing him to remain in the Garden of Eden for an extra day after his sin, so too, Shabbat protects each person from this "chasing" for at least one day a week (*Likutey Halakhot* III, p. 106).

Adam was banished...the revolving sword

He was banished after Shabbat, for Shabbat protected him
(*Zohar* II, 138a).

One who tries to do any holy act will face obstacles and
confusions. The only way a person can spare himself from
these confusions is by remaining steadfast in his faith—which,
conceptually, is Shabbat (since by observing Shabbat, we proclaim
our faith in God) (*Likutey Halakhot* III, p. 6a-12).

Adam's reprieve over Shabbat

Adam's sin of eating from the Tree of Knowledge represents
all possible types of sin. But, as we have seen, Shabbat protected
him. Therefore Shabbat-observance represents the protection
from—and rectification of—all sin (*Likutey Halakhot* III, p. 74a).

Adam, Shabbat

After Shabbat, God granted Adam the intellect to strike two stones
together to make fire (*Midrash Tehillim* 92).

God gave Adam this knowledge specifically after Shabbat,
in order to show him how to draw the light of Shabbat into the
weekdays (*Likutey Halakhot* III, p. 189a-378).

3:24 וַיְגָרֶשׁ אֶת־הָאָדָם וַיַּשְׁכֵּן מִקֶּדֶם לְגַן־עֵדֶן אֶת־
הַכְּרֻבִים וְאֵת לַהַט הַחֶרֶב הַמִּתְהַפֶּכֶת לִשְׁמֹר
אֶת־דֶּרֶךְ עֵץ הַחַיִּים

**He chased out the man, and He stationed the
cherubim at the east of the Garden of Eden,
along with the flame of the revolving sword,
to guard the path to the Tree of Life.**

The revolving sword to guard the path to the Tree of Life

The revolving sword refers to arguments and strife. Each person
puts forth his view as the correct path to follow. This causes
confusion about which path is the right one for approaching the
Torah, the Tree of Life (*Likutey Halakhot* V, p. 228).

⟩ *The revolving sword*

The revolving sword corresponds to the evil inclination, which continually changes shape and appears in different guises to the one who is viewing it. The evil inclination is especially adept at convincing a person that certain deeds are so important, they are worthy of being *mitzvot*. In this way, it traps a person in a cycle of deeds which, though they may be good deeds, eventually lead him to evil. This phenomenon especially manifests itself among learned people who take a certain position and then quarrel and cause strife because of their ideas (*Likutey Halakhot* IV, p. 163a-326). The trap set by the evil inclination is a root cause for all strife and arguments between Jews today (*Likutey Halakhot* IV, p. 166a).

⟩ *The revolving sword*

The revolving sword represents the Chambers of Exchanges in which everything in this world is continually exchanged (cf. "Evil to good and good to evil...darkness to light and light to darkness" [Isaiah 5:20]). Abraham married his wife Sarah's maidservant and fathered Ishmael. Though Sarah later gave birth to Isaac, Ishmael claims prominence. Similarly, Isaac had two sons, Jacob and Esau. Though their mother Rebecca was told in a prophecy that the elder would serve the younger (Genesis 25:23), Esau, the firstborn, claims supremacy. The same applies to each individual. All doubts and confusion that besiege a person stem from Adam's sin and from the revolving sword, which puts primacy on the material world and suppresses and conceals the spiritual world (*Likutey Halakhot* I, p. 206-104a).

4:1　　וְהָאָדָם יָדַע אֶת־חַוָּה אִשְׁתּוֹ וַתַּהַר וַתֵּלֶד אֶת־קַיִן
וַתֹּאמֶר קָנִיתִי אִישׁ אֶת־יְהוָה

The man knew his wife Eve. She conceived and gave birth to Cain, saying, "I have acquired a man with God."

❯ *The man knew his wife Eve*

"Knew"—this implies the marital union (Rashi).

This same concept parallels the union between the *sefirot* of Chokhmah (corresponding to Adam) and Binah (corresponding to Eve), which is brought about by the *sefirah* of Da'at (Knowledge). (*Likutey Moharan* I, 15:6).

A relationship might begin on an emotional basis; however, it can develop properly only on the basis of "knowledge"—i.e., intellect. When "knowledge" is present, unity can exist. Conversely, when "knowledge" is absent, there can be no unity (ibid., I, 43).

❯ *The man knew his wife Eve*

"Knew"—this implies the marital union (Rashi).

When a couple unite with love and respect, this is reflected in the quality of their children (*Likutey Moharan* I, 53).

❯ *The man knew his wife Eve, and she conceived*

One who does not have children is considered as one who is dead (*Nedarim* 64b).

The sin of Adam and Eve brought death into the world. The rectification of this sin is an ongoing process that will conclude only with the coming of Mashiach. Until then, the rectification takes place in every generation through the birth of children. How does this work?

The main blemish of eating from the Tree of Knowledge is a blemish in faith in tzaddikim. Tzaddikim are the ones who clarify the law; without them, we are left confused, mired in good and evil, and lack clarification of the Torah. The average person is too challenged to clarify what is right and what is wrong. Faith in the tzaddikim, in their teachings and guidance, helps us focus, because the tzaddikim know how to clarify the law and bring peace. A child is born out of a union, which indicates peace. Thus, the birth of a child represents a rectification of the blemish of faith in the tzaddikim and, by extension, the sin of eating from the Tree of Knowledge (*Likutey Halakhot* VI, p. 158-80a).

4:3   וַיְהִי מִקֵּץ יָמִים וַיָּבֵא קַיִן מִפְּרִי הָאֲדָמָה
מִנְחָה לַיי

A while later, Cain brought some of the fruits of the earth as an offering to God.

⟫ *Cain brought some of the fruits of the earth*

He brought cheap flax as a sacrifice (Rashi).

Flax is an insignificant crop for a sacrifice to God. That Cain brought his offering from flax indicates his negative attitude, and therefore characterizes one who looks for the bad in others (*Likutey Halakhot* VIII, p. 181b).

4:4   וְהֶבֶל הֵבִיא גַם־הוּא מִבְּכֹרוֹת צֹאנוֹ וּמֵחֶלְבֵהֶן
וַיִּשַׁע יְיָ אֶל־הֶבֶל וְאֶל־מִנְחָתוֹ

Abel also brought from the firstlings of his flock and from their choice parts. God showed favor to Abel and his offering.

⟫ *Cain and Abel*

Cain brought flax, an inferior offering. Abel brought wool, a prime offering. Flax corresponds to judgments; Cain represents those who judge others with a critical eye. When Cain saw that his meager offering was rejected, he became angry. This caused the judgments to become stronger and to take control of him, prompting him to kill his brother Abel (*Likutey Halakhot* I, p. 30a-60).

4:6   וַיֹּאמֶר יְיָ אֶל־קַיִן לָמָּה חָרָה לָךְ וְלָמָּה
נָפְלוּ פָנֶיךָ

**God said to Cain, "Why are you angry?
Why has your face fallen?"**

〉 Why has your face fallen

A person's Godly image is inscribed on his face. When his face "falls"—for instance, by displaying anger—he loses that Godly image (*Likutey Moharan* I, 57:6).

4:7   הֲלוֹא אִם־תֵּיטִיב שְׂאֵת וְאִם לֹא תֵיטִיב לַפֶּתַח
חַטָּאת רֹבֵץ וְאֵלֶיךָ תְּשׁוּקָתוֹ וְאַתָּה תִּמְשָׁל־בּוֹ

**"If you do good, will there not be an
elevation? And if you do not do good,
sin crouches at the door. Its desire is
towards you, but you can overcome it."**

〉 If you do good, will there not be an elevation

Se'EiT (שאת, there will be an elevation) is an acronym for the phrase *Sefat Emet Tikon* (שפת אמת תכון, The tongue of truth will endure) (Proverbs 12:19). When a person speaks truth, he elevates reality, bringing about an enduring revelation of Godliness. Conversely, one who does not speak truth conceals Godliness (*Likutey Moharan* I, 48).

〉 Sin crouches at the door

Petach (door) literally means "opening." This "opening" refers to the mouth, as in the verse "Guard the opening of your mouth" (Micah 7:5). When a person speaks improperly, sin can gain preeminence over him (*Likutey Moharan* I, 19:3, 38:2).

"Opening" can also be a reference to the imagination. If one does not control his imagination, he opens himself up to various types of impurity (ibid., I, 25:end).

》 Sin crouches at the door

Petach (door) literally means "opening." This opening represents the Vacated Space, which to us seems devoid of Godliness. Any time a person allows himself to become distanced from God, he creates a Vacated Space and allows sin to enter (*Likutey Halakhot* VIII, p. 122b).

》 Sin crouches at the door

The Other Side stands near the "door," waiting for an opening to enter into a person's life. Therefore we place at the door a mezuzah, containing the Holy Name of God, to prevent the Other Side from entering (*Likutey Halakhot* III, p. 484). Similarly, by drawing ourselves closer to God, we draw God to us, placing near us a "mezuzah"—a means of protection—to shield us from the Other Side.

》 Its desire is towards you, but you can overcome it

If you want, you will be able to overpower it (Rashi)

Rebbe Nachman once said that no one is ever given an evil inclination that he cannot overcome. If a person could not overcome an inclination, God would never have given it to him (see *Likutey Moharan* II, 46; *Likutey Halakhot* II, p. 222).

4:8   וַיֹּאמֶר קַיִן אֶל־הֶבֶל אָחִיו וַיְהִי בִּהְיוֹתָם בַּשָּׂדֶה
וַיָּקָם קַיִן אֶל־הֶבֶל אָחִיו וַיַּהַרְגֵהוּ

Cain spoke to his brother Abel. When they were in the field, Cain rose up against his brother Abel and killed him.

》 Cain killed Abel

The whole world wasn't big enough for Cain—he was jealous of his brother's portion, too. The same jealousies fester within families today. Despite all that parents do to provide for their children, if the children are not satisfied with their portions and allow envy and avarice to control their lives, bitter fighting can break out between siblings even before the inheritance is divided (*Likutey Halakhot* II, p. 127a).

〕 *Cain spoke to his brother Abel*

When Adam blemished himself by eating from the Tree, he also drew blemish and conflict into his seed. Thus, immediately afterwards, Cain and Abel began to argue between themselves. This argument was the forerunner of all strife and conflict to come, especially the opposition directed against the tzaddikim. The conflict between Cain and Abel spawned the conflict between Korach and Moses, as well as all the other conflicts against the tzaddikim, such as those directed against the Ari, the Baal Shem Tov, Rebbe Nachman, and so on (*Likutey Halakhot* III, p. 248).

4:12   כִּי תַעֲבֹד אֶת־הָאֲדָמָה לֹא־תֹסֵף תֵּת־כֹּחָהּ לָךְ
נָע וָנָד תִּהְיֶה בָאָרֶץ

"When you work the earth, it will no longer give its strength to you. You will be a wanderer on earth."

〕 *It will no longer give its strength to you*

When there is bloodshed, the earth does not give forth its produce, and that leads to inflation (*Likutey Moharan* II, 60).

〕 *A wanderer*

Because he sinned, Cain fell under the constraints of space. He had no place at all and had to wander all the time. Wherever he desired to live or work, he could not gain security or rest (*Likutey Halakhot* I, p. 78).

4:14   הֵן גֵּרַשְׁתָּ אֹתִי הַיּוֹם מֵעַל פְּנֵי הָאֲדָמָה וּמִפָּנֶיךָ אֶסָּתֵר וְהָיִיתִי נָע וָנָד בָּאָרֶץ וְהָיָה כָל־ מֹצְאִי יַהַרְגֵנִי

"Behold! Today You have chased me away from the face of the earth, and I am to be hidden from Your Face. I am to be a wanderer on earth, and whoever finds me will kill me."

》 *Today You have chased me away from the face of the earth, and I am to be hidden from Your Face*

The whole earth is filled with His glory (Isaiah 6:3).

When a person commits a sin, he distances himself from God, from His glory that fills the whole earth. It is as if he turns the earth back into *tohu vavohu* (formlessness and emptiness), bereft of God's presence. Therefore Cain said, "You have chased me away from the face of the earth," because he no longer had any place; his world was destroyed.

Cain understood that he had committed a terrible sin by killing Abel, and sought to return to God. He said, "I am so distant from God," and began to look for where God was. He called out, *"Ayeh? Where are You?"* Because Cain repented, God made him a sign that he was accepted: a horn on his forehead. This horn represents the shofar that we blow on Rosh HaShanah, recalling the ram at the Binding of Isaac, when Isaac said, "Where (*Ayeh*) is the ram for a sacrifice?" (Genesis 22:7). That question, *"Ayeh?"* reveals where God is concealed (*Likutey Halakhot* IV, p. 160-162).

4:20　　וַתֵּלֶד עָדָה אֶת־יָבָל הוּא הָיָה אֲבִי יֹשֵׁב אֹהֶל וּמִקְנֶה

Adah gave birth to Jabal; he was the father of all who dwell in tents and tend flocks.

⟩ *He was the father of all who dwell in tents and tend flocks…His brother…was the father of all who play the harp and flute*

With the emergence of the first shepherd, musical instruments came into being. What is the connection between the two?

Firstly, song is so powerful that it can elevate a person to God. Thus, when a shepherd plays music, he keeps himself from descending into animalistic behavior, even though he lives among animals.

Additionally, every blade of grass has its own melody with which it praises God. A field of grass contains many melodies, each field with its own tunes. This accounts for the variety of music found throughout the entire world; in particular, it explains why shepherds from different lands sing different songs. The shepherd who knows the melodies of the field can nurture the grasses by singing the appropriate songs in order to feed his flock.

The Patriarchs and King David were shepherds. They were also the shepherds of their people—their "flocks." By studying the music of their environment, they were able to nourish their people spiritually and bring them close to God (*Likutey Moharan* II, 63).

4:21　　וְשֵׁם אָחִיו יוּבָל הוּא הָיָה אֲבִי כָּל־תֹּפֵשׂ כִּנּוֹר וְעוּגָב

His brother's name was Jubal; he was the father of all who play the harp and flute.

⟩ *The harp and flute…work implements*

Making music entails the separation of good sounds from bad sounds, which corresponds to man's mission of separating good and holy sparks from the realm of evil. To make music, a musician places his hands on the instrument in such a way that different sounds emerge, creating a melody. Similarly, a person who deals honestly in business—e.g., paying his workers on time and not charging interest—elevates the hidden sparks of good from the realm of evil. Thus, song and work accomplish the same rectification (*Likutey Halakhot* VIII, p. 186b).

4:26   וּלְשֵׁת גַּם־הוּא יֻלַּד־בֵּן וַיִּקְרָא אֶת־שְׁמוֹ אֱנוֹשׁ אָז
               הוּחַל לִקְרֹא בְּשֵׁם יְיָ

A son was also born to Seth, and he named him Enosh. Then it became common to call in God's Name.

》 *Then it became common to call in God's Name*

Idolatry became rampant and commonplace (Rashi).

The essence of atheism and idolatry lies in the denial of God's Name. God's Name implies His eternity: the letters of the Tetragrammaton, *YHVH* (י-ה-ו-ה) stand for *HaYaH* (היה, He was), *HoVeH* (הוה, He is) and *YiHeyeH* (יהיה, He will be). Instead, idolatries ascribe supernatural powers to man-made deities. Thus, the prohibition "Do not mention the *names* of other gods" (Exodus 23:13) (*Likutey Halakhot* I, p. 228).

》 *Then it became common to call in God's Name*

Whoever observes Shabbat, even if he serves idols as happened in the generation of Enosh, will have his sins forgiven (*Shabbat* 118b).

Shabbat represents God's Name (*Zohar* II, 88b). A person who does not keep Shabbat blemishes God's Name, which is equivalent to idolatry. But one who observes Shabbat honors God's Name, and this honor, revealing God, has the power to effect forgiveness for all sins, even if the person has served idols (*Likutey Halakhot* III, p. 9a).

5:2 זָכָר וּנְקֵבָה בְּרָאָם וַיְבָרֶךְ אֹתָם וַיִּקְרָא אֶת־שְׁמָם
     אָדָם בְּיוֹם הִבָּרְאָם

**Male and female He created them. He
blessed them and named them Adam on
the day they were created.**

〗 *He named them Adam*

The appellation of "Adam" can be given only when man and
woman are united. When they unite in harmony, they are worthy
of being called *Adam*, human (*Likutey Halakhot* V, p. 197a).

5:28 וַיְחִי־לֶמֶךְ שְׁתַּיִם וּשְׁמֹנִים שָׁנָה וּמְאַת שָׁנָה
      וַיּוֹלֶד בֵּן

**Lemekh lived one hundred and eighty-two
years, and he had a son.**

〗 *He had a son…He named him Noah*

The preceding verses describe how people were given their
names at birth. But Noah was not given a name when he was born.
At that time, severe Divine judgments prevailed against the world.
As long as Noah did not have a name, he was not exposed to these
judgments. We learn from this that in times of suffering, a person
must conceal himself (*Likutey Moharan* I, 174).

5:29 וַיִּקְרָא אֶת־שְׁמוֹ נֹחַ לֵאמֹר זֶה יְנַחֲמֵנוּ מִמַּעֲשֵׂנוּ
      וּמֵעִצְּבוֹן יָדֵינוּ מִן־הָאֲדָמָה אֲשֶׁר אֵרְרָהּ יְיָ

**He named him Noah, saying, "This one
will console us from our toil and the
sadness of our hands, from the earth that
God has cursed."**

〗 *This one will console us from our toil*

NoaCh (נח) was so named because he brought mankind
NeChamah (נחמה, consolation) in the work of one's hands. The

main depression and suffering that people experience centers
around earning a livelihood—i.e., "the sadness of our hands"
(*Likutey Halakhot* II, p. 9a).

⟫ This one will console us from our toil

The tzaddik [through his teachings] brings consolation for all
suffering (*Likutey Halakhot* I, p. 198). Additionally, "toil" refers to the six
weekdays. Shabbat, like Noah, brings relief from that toil (*Likutey
Moharan* II, 2:5).

⟫ The sadness of our hands

When a person feels sad, his pulse—measured on the wrist
near the hands—is depressed and sluggish (*Likutey Moharan* I, 56:9).
One must rest and regain joy in order to revitalize his blood flow.

6:4   הַנְּפִלִים הָיוּ בָאָרֶץ בַּיָּמִים הָהֵם וְגַם אַחֲרֵי־כֵן אֲשֶׁר
יָבֹאוּ בְּנֵי הָאֱלֹהִים אֶל־בְּנוֹת הָאָדָם וְיָלְדוּ לָהֶם הֵמָּה
הַגִּבֹּרִים אֲשֶׁר מֵעוֹלָם אַנְשֵׁי הַשֵּׁם

**The giants were on the earth in those days—
and also afterwards, when the sons of rulers
would come to the daughters of man, and
they would bear children to them. They were
the mighty ones who were men of renown
from old.**

⟫ The giants were on the earth in those days

NeFiLIM (giants) literally means "fallen ones." These were fallen
angels (*Yalkut Shimoni, Bereishit* 6, #47).

Because angels are incapable of withstanding and overcoming
the evil inclination, they succumbed to the lures of the material
world (*Likutey Moharan* I, 244). The soul of a human being, however, is
rooted in a realm higher than that of the angels; therefore man has
the power to overcome his evil inclination. (Angels are resident in
the World of Yetzirah. But the human soul is from God's Throne of
Glory, in the World of Beriah [see Charts, p. 347].)

6:5 וַיַּרְא יְיָ כִּי רַבָּה רָעַת הָאָדָם בָּאָרֶץ וְכָל־יֵצֶר
מַחְשְׁבֹת לִבּוֹ רַק רַע כָּל־הַיּוֹם

God saw that the evil of man was great upon the earth, and every inclination of the thoughts of his heart were only evil all day long.

》 *Only evil all day long*

The final letters of *raK rA koL ha-yoM* (**רק רע כל היום**, only evil all day long) spell the word *AMaLeK* (עמלק). Amalek represents the forces of evil that direct a person to think evil thoughts. Therefore we are commanded: "*Remember* what Amalek did to you" (Deuteronomy 25:17)—be aware of his attempts and attacks in order to overcome him (*Likutey Halakhot* II, p. 205a).

6:6 וַיִּנָּחֶם יְיָ כִּי־עָשָׂה אֶת־הָאָדָם בָּאָרֶץ וַיִּתְעַצֵּב
אֶל־לִבּוֹ

God regretted that He had made man upon the earth, and He was saddened in His heart.

》 *He was saddened in His heart*

The heart is the locus of joy and sadness. When sadness rules the heart, a "flood" of suffering and judgments sets in (*Likutey Moharan* I, 24:2).

》 *He was saddened in His heart*

Nothing causes sadness like the perpetration of sins. The Divine Presence, which is called the "heart," is saddened by sin. When we perform *mitzvot*, especially with joy, we rectify that sadness (*Likutey Halakhot* I, p. 199a).

》 *He was saddened in His heart*

God always seeks ways to give bounty to the world. When people perform good deeds, He is joyous and bestows His beneficence to all of mankind. But when people rebel against God, His joy decreases, and that makes it possible for judgments to affect the world (*Likutey Moharan* I, 5:2).

6:8   וְנֹחַ מָצָא חֵן בְּעֵינֵי יְיָ

But Noah found favor in God's eyes.

⟩ *Noah found favor in God's eyes*

"God's eyes" refers to Divine Providence. The eyes have four colors: the white of the sclera, the red of the muscle, the color of the iris and the black of the pupil. These four colors correspond to the *sefirot* of Chesed, Gevurah, Tiferet and Malkhut.

Money, too, has colors that correspond to the *sefirot*, such as gold and silver (as well as the assorted colors of printed money).

When a person gives money to charity, the colors in the money arouse the corresponding *sefirot*—these are the "eyes" of God which manifest as God's Providence. Then this person attains favor in God's eyes, and he causes their beautiful colors—which also manifest as God's glory—to be revealed in the world for all to see.

Because Noah performed charitable acts, he found favor in God's eyes (*Likutey Moharan* I, 25:4).

Parashat Noach

6:9   אֵלֶּה תּוֹלְדֹת נֹחַ נֹחַ אִישׁ צַדִּיק תָּמִים הָיָה בְּדֹרֹתָיו
          אֶת־הָאֱלֹהִים הִתְהַלֶּךְ־נֹחַ

**These are the generations of Noah:
Noah was a tzaddik, he was perfect in his
generation. Noah walked with God.**

》 *These are the generations of Noah*

Because a tzaddik is the leader of the generation, all of his
contemporaries are associated with, and called by, his name (*Likutey
Moharan* II, 67).

》 *These are the generations of Noah: Noah*

Noah's name is repeated to reflect the fact that each tzaddik
has two spirits: one in this world and one in the World to Come
(*Zohar* I, 59b).

When a tzaddik experiences an ascent—whether because he
is growing spiritually or because his time to leave this world has
come—the higher spirit descends in order to draw the lower spirit
higher, so that they may unite. At that time, a close disciple of the
tzaddik can benefit from the tzaddik's ascent and even receive a
double portion of Godly revelation (*Likutey Moharan* I, 66:1).

》 *These are the generations of Noah...Noah walked with God*

The Torah speaks as if Noah were dying (he "walked with God"),
leaving behind his contemporaries.

When a tzaddik passes away, that is no loss to him, for he is
great and respected in the World to Come—there, he is "walking
with God." But those who are left behind suffer a great loss (i.e., a
"Flood") (*Likutey Moharan* II, 67).

》 *Noach...Elohim*

NoaCh (נח, Noah) symbolizes peace, as his name shares the
same root as the word *NaCh* (נח, rest). *Elohim*, the Holy Name of
God, refers to judgments. Noah represents the perfect tzaddik in

every generation who continuously seeks to mitigate and sweeten the judgments of God (*Likutey Halakhot* VIII, p. 27a).

6:12   וַיַּרְא אֱלֹהִים אֶת־הָאָרֶץ וְהִנֵּה נִשְׁחָתָה כִּי־הִשְׁחִית כָּל־בָּשָׂר אֶת־דַּרְכּוֹ עַל־הָאָרֶץ

God saw the earth and behold! It had been corrupted. For all flesh had corrupted its way upon the earth.

〉 *For all flesh had corrupted its way upon the earth*

"Flesh" refers to sexuality. When people grow debauched, they "corrupt their way" in the sense of harming themselves. Thus, the Generation of the Flood brought about its own demise (*Likutey Moharan* I, 31:4).

6:13   וַיֹּאמֶר אֱלֹהִים לְנֹחַ קֵץ כָּל־בָּשָׂר בָּא לְפָנַי כִּי־מָלְאָה הָאָרֶץ חָמָס מִפְּנֵיהֶם וְהִנְנִי מַשְׁחִיתָם אֶת־הָאָרֶץ

God said to Noah, "The end of all flesh has come before Me, for the earth is filled with robbery because of them. I will destroy them with the earth."

〉 *The end of all flesh*

The "end of all flesh" refers to those who disparage others, always looking for their negative points and seeking to destroy them—i.e., to put an "end to all flesh" (*Likutey Moharan* I, 38:2).

〉 *Filled with robbery*

Although the generation was steeped in idolatry and immorality, its final decree was issued because of theft (Rashi).

The Torah is the mainstay of the world. However, God did not give the Torah until Year 2448 from Creation. The Flood took place some 800 years prior to that. If there was no Torah to sustain the world and show people the right path, why were they punished?

The answer is that the Torah *was* present, albeit in a concealed manner. It manifested itself in commerce and in the way people acted towards each other, falling under the category of *derekh eretz* (literally, "the way of the land"—i.e., respect for others). By stealing from each other, the Generation of the Flood showed that it couldn't care less about *derekh eretz*. Its decree was sealed on that account (*Likutey Halakhot* VIII, p. 219b-220a).

◊ Filled with robbery

Although the generation was steeped in idolatry and immorality, its final decree was issued because of theft (Rashi).

There are two types of immorality: the kind that issues from man's evil desires, and the kind that stems from corrupt judgment (both in the courts and in a person's own life choices). Though a person can descend to deep levels of impurity because of immoral desires, he can be helped out of his predicament. It is much more difficult to repair the immorality of one who has a perverted sense of justice.

This explains why the decree against the Generation of the Flood was not sealed until people began stealing from each other. When they stooped to the lowest levels of immorality by perverting justice, the decree was sealed against them (*Likutey Halakhot* VII, p. 24).

6:14   עֲשֵׂה לְךָ תֵּבַת עֲצֵי־גֹפֶר קִנִּים תַּעֲשֶׂה אֶת־הַתֵּבָה
וְכָפַרְתָּ אֹתָהּ מִבַּיִת וּמִחוּץ בַּכֹּפֶר

"Make for yourself an ark of cypress wood. Make the ark with compartments, and cover it inside and outside with pitch."

◊ Make for yourself an ark

Teivah (ark) also means "word." The "waters" of the Flood refer to the Sea of Wisdom—i.e., the wisdom of the Torah. The Torah requires vessels within which to receive it. Those who defiled the covenant and wasted their seed destroyed their vessels. This caused the waters to turn into a Flood, since there was no place within which to contain those waters of the Sea of Wisdom at that time. Therefore the floodwaters gained the upper hand and rose to cover the entire earth.

Noah was a tzaddik who was able to draw Torah to himself (Noah studied Torah [Rashi on Genesis 7:2]). Therefore his *teivah*, his words of Torah, became his protection against the floodwaters that engulfed the rest of mankind that had rejected God. Yet Noah's *teivah* was not capable of saving others. In contrast, Moses also entered an "ark" (when his mother placed him in the river as a baby) (Exodus 2:3). Since Moses was destined to receive the Torah and bring it down for all mankind, his *teivah*—his words of Torah—was great enough to save everyone (*Likutey Halakhot* I, p. 382).

⟩ Make the ark with compartments

> *KiNim* (קנים, compartments) is similar to *KeiN* (קן, bird's nest) (*Bereishit Rabbah* 31:9).

> The Talmud teaches that the disease *tzara'at* (often mistranslated as "leprosy") is a punishment for evil speech (*Erakhin* 16). In order to be purified of *tzara'at*, a person must bring a sacrifice of birds—for, as our Sages state: "Let the chattering birds come and effect forgiveness for the chattering person" (*Vayikra Rabbah* 16:7).

Teivah (ark) also means "word." A person's "ark," his refuge from the floodwaters of negativity that overwhelm him, consists of his rectifying his every "word."

Thus, our Sages associate the ark's compartments with bird's nests—which are reminiscent of the bird sacrifices that one brings in the course of rectifying his speech. And when a person attains exemplary speech, that creates purity and eventually leads to peace and unity (*Likutey Moharan* I, 14:9).

6:16   צֹהַר תַּעֲשֶׂה לַתֵּבָה וְאֶל־אַמָּה תְּכַלֶּנָּה מִלְמַעְלָה
וּפֶתַח הַתֵּבָה בְּצִדָּהּ תָּשִׂים תַּחְתִּיִּם שְׁנִיִּם
וּשְׁלִשִׁים תַּעֲשֶׂהָ

**"Make a light for the ark, and finish it to a
cubit from above. Put the door of the ark
in its side. Make it with lower, middle and
upper decks."**

❭ *Make a light for the ark*

What was this "light"? Some say a window, some say a precious
stone (Rashi).

The conceptual difference between the two is that a precious
stone glows from within, whereas a window is a medium through
which another light shines.

Rashi's comment may be interpreted as follows: "Some say a
precious stone"—the words that some people speak come from
within. They are absolute truth. "Some say a window"—other
people speak words that come from outside themselves. Truth
from elsewhere must shine into them (*Likutey Moharan* I, 112).

❭ *A light*

Noah was commanded to construct the ark with a sloped roof
that had a light at its summit. A person must learn to look upwards,
beyond this material world, to Heaven, and nullify himself to God.
Had Noah been able to attain a complete self-nullification, he
would have effected forgiveness for his generation, much as Moses
did for his generation. But since Noah attained only a partial self-
nullification, God, in His kindness, enabled Noah to enter the ark
to at least "close himself off" from the world and protect himself
and his family (*Likutey Halakhot* II, p. 482).

❭ *Finish it to a cubit from above*

The initial letters of the words *Amah Tekhalenah Mi-lema'alah*
(אמה **ת**כלנה **מ**למעלה, finish it to a cubit from above) spell *EMeT* (אמת,
truth). A person's words must be true especially when viewed from
the Heavenly aspect—"from Above."

AMaH (אמה, cubit) indicates speech. The first two letters of this word, *Aleph* (א) and *Mem* (מ), stand for *Eish* (אש, fire or heat) and *Mayim* (מים, water or fluids), with which a person produces speech. The letter *hei* (ה) has the numerical value of 5 and indicates the five phonetic sounds (guttural, palatal, lingual, dental and labial) (*Likutey Moharan* I, 112).

》 *Put the door of the ark in its side*

Petach (door) literally means "opening." Words of truth create an opening so that other people may see how to emerge from their darkness (*Likutey Moharan* I, 112).

》 *Make it with lower, middle and upper decks*

When we utter words of prayer with truth, they sustain all levels of existence (*Likutey Moharan* I, 112).

6:17   וַאֲנִי הִנְנִי מֵבִיא אֶת־הַמַּבּוּל מַיִם עַל־הָאָרֶץ לְשַׁחֵת כָּל־בָּשָׂר אֲשֶׁר־בּוֹ רוּחַ חַיִּים מִתַּחַת הַשָּׁמָיִם כֹּל אֲשֶׁר־בָּאָרֶץ יִגְוָע

"As for Me, I am about to bring the floodwaters upon the earth to destroy all flesh in which there is a spirit of life from under the heavens. Everything that is on the earth shall perish."

》 *The Flood*

Until the Revelation at Sinai, when the continuation of the world became contingent upon the Jews' acceptance of the Torah, mankind was sustained through God's kindness. Nevertheless, punishment was meted out in this world (e.g., the Flood, the Tower of Babel, the destruction of Sodom and Gomorrah). The reason for this seeming dichotomy is that God desires *chesed* (kindness) and is willing to grant a stay of punishment if people are cognizant of His kindness, even in a distant sort of way. Such recognition gives them the merit to have a vessel with which to receive His kindness. But if people deny God completely, they destroy their vessel and can no longer receive His kindness. Thus, suffering could exist even in a world sustained by kindness.

When the evil peaked during the Generation of the Flood, only Noah was saved through God's kindness. As our Sages teach: "Even Noah was included in the decree to be wiped out in the Flood, but he found favor in God's eyes" (*Sanhedrin* 108a). Ten generations later, Abraham became known as the "man of *chesed* (kindness)" and his deeds brought stability to the world. Thus, Abraham merited to be the first to reveal the Holy Land, because he aroused the purpose of Creation: God's desire to do kindness for His creatures and to reveal His might. This might is manifest when the Jews merit to receive the Holy Land by quieting the claims to it by the other nations (*Likutey Halakhot* I, p. 490-246a).

⟩ *The Flood*

The main lesson of the Flood points to the overwhelming "flood" of disturbing thoughts that a person experiences throughout his life. The most powerful of these disturbances are thoughts of immorality, which brought on the Flood in Noah's time (see Rashi on Genesis 6:12).

Though the Flood engulfed the entire planet, it did not enter the Holy Land (*Zevachim* 116b). However, a few drops did make their way into the Land. Thus, the "flood" of disturbing thoughts threatens to engulf each and every person, even those who try to maintain some level of sanctity in their lives. One's only hope is to flee to the Holy Land—to sanctify one's "borders" as a protection against disturbing thoughts.

This can be accomplished by attaching oneself to the tzaddikim. For "Tzaddikim will inherit the Land" (Psalms 37:29)—the sanctity of the Holy Land is revealed to us by the tzaddikim, and their teachings and direction can help us find refuge from the floodwaters. Therefore it is written, "God remembered Noah [who is called a tzaddik]" (Genesis 8:1), and shortly afterwards, "God told Abram, 'Go…to the Land'" (ibid., 12:1), since the revelation of the Holy Land begins with the tzaddikim (*Likutey Halakhot* I, p. 482-242a).

⟩ *Mabul*

MaBUL (מבול, Flood) is similar to *bilBUL* (בלבול, confusion) (*Likutey Halakhot* II, p. 16). Confusing thoughts are like a flood which deluges a person during his prayers.

The Talmud teaches that the Flood did not inundate the Holy Land (*Zevachim* 113b). When we arouse the merit of the Holy Land, those confusing thoughts cannot overwhelm us (*Likutey Moharan* I, 44).

⟩ The floodwaters

The "floodwaters" are akin to the "many waters" (Rashi on Song of Songs 8:7).

The "floodwaters" refers to the many nations that seek to overwhelm and destroy the Jewish people. They also refer to a person's love and fear of things in this world, dissociated from the love and fear of God. When a person feels humble before God, he experiences an intense sense of shame before Him, as if his blood (comparable to the waters of the Flood) is being shed. Then the Divine Presence protects him from the "floodwaters" that overwhelm him (*Likutey Moharan* II, 83).

7:8   מִן־הַבְּהֵמָה הַטְּהוֹרָה וּמִן־הַבְּהֵמָה אֲשֶׁר אֵינֶנָּה טְהֹרָה וּמִן־הָעוֹף וְכֹל אֲשֶׁר־רֹמֵשׂ עַל־הָאֲדָמָה

From the clean animals and from the animals that are not clean, and from the birds and all that creeps upon the earth.

⟩ The animals that are not clean

The Torah could have said more succinctly "the unclean animals." But it uses this circumlocution to teach us the importance of avoiding vulgar speech (*Pesachim* 3a).

At times a person is deluged with such a flood of troubles that he cannot speak straight. The solution is to enter the *teivah*, which means both "ark" and "word." Just as Noah entered the *teivah* to escape the Flood, one must enter into holy words to escape his troubles. To access these holy words, he must use a roundabout means of speech (*Likutey Moharan* I, 38:3).

7:19   וְהַמַּיִם גָּבְרוּ מְאֹד מְאֹד עַל־הָאָרֶץ וַיְכֻסּוּ כָּל־
הֶהָרִים הַגְּבֹהִים אֲשֶׁר־תַּחַת כָּל־הַשָּׁמָיִם

**The waters rose upon the earth, and all
the high mountains under all the heavens
were covered.**

> ### The waters rose…and all the high mountains…were covered

The sin of the Generation of the Flood was masturbation (*Niddah* 13a).

The story of the Flood begins with "The end of all flesh has come before Me" (Genesis 6:13). This "end of all flesh" refers to wasted seed [which contains live sperm]. The sin of wasting seed is so severe because the soul that is created from the emission lacks a body in which to reside, similar to demons who have a soul but no body. This leads to "demonic" behavior. Without a body, a soul cannot perform *mitzvot*; therefore it can never reach a state of rectification. The sin of Adam and Eve is also described in these terms: "They were both naked" (ibid., 2:25)—i.e., they had no "clothing," they lacked a garb for their souls.

The blemish of masturbation is so great that it affects the mind as well. "The waters rose"—i.e., the seed was expelled. "All the high mountains…were covered"—this refers to the intellect, the highest place in the body. Since the seed was deemed by the person to be "extraneous" and he wasted it, it ascends to his mind to clog it with extraneous matter that is unimportant to his life. As a result, his thoughts become fragmented and he cannot find proper advice. (The *Zohar* teaches that the seed originates in the mind; thus, wasted seed leads to a wasted mind [*Zohar Chadash* 15a]).

To rectify this sin, one must toil in Torah and produce new interpretations of his learning, thereby increasing the writings of Torah. The 600,000 letters of the Torah correspond to the 600,000 root-souls of Israel. By providing new "bodies" for the letters of Torah, one creates parallel bodies for the corresponding souls of those letters, many of which are naked souls created via masturbation. Thus, it is written, "Make many [Torah] books without end (*KeitZ*)" (Ecclesiastes 12:12)—for these books rectify the *KeitZ kol basar* (the end of all flesh), the sin of wasted seed (*Likutey Halakhot* VI, p. 10-6a-12).

Elsewhere, Reb Noson writes that financing the printing of Torah books is also considered an integral part of the rectification for the sin of masturbation (see *Likutey Halakhot, Birkhot HaShachar* 5:33). And, of course, the main rectification for this sin is the *Tikkun HaKlali*, Rebbe Nachman's General Remedy, which involves the recital of Ten Psalms in this order: 16, 32, 41, 42, 59, 77, 90, 105, 137, 150 (see *Rabbi Nachman's Tikkun*, published by the Breslov Research Institute).

7:22   כֹּל אֲשֶׁר נִשְׁמַת־רוּחַ חַיִּים בְּאַפָּיו מִכֹּל אֲשֶׁר בֶּחָרָבָה מֵתוּ

All that had the breath of life in their nostrils, of everything that was on dry land, died.

〗 *All that had the breath of life in their nostrils…died*

Our speech is not the only thing that makes an impact on other people; even the breath we breathe can affect others. God commanded Noah to closet himself in an ark to escape the punishment of the wicked, for the breath of those evildoers was enough to sway him to sin. The Torah states: "All that had the breath of life in their nostrils…died," for it was their evil breath that contaminated the air and caused Noah to flee. Furthermore, the Talmud teaches that the Flood did not enter the Holy Land (*Zevachim* 113b). So how did the evil people who were living there die during the Flood? The Talmud answers that they died from the *hevel*, from the air! (*Likutey Halakhot* VIII, p. 164a).

8:11 וַתָּבֹא אֵלָיו הַיּוֹנָה לְעֵת עֶרֶב וְהִנֵּה עֲלֵה־זַיִת טָרָף
בְּפִיהָ וַיֵּדַע נֹחַ כִּי־קַלּוּ הַמַּיִם מֵעַל הָאָרֶץ

**The dove came to him towards evening, and
behold! It had plucked an olive branch with
its bill. So Noah knew that the waters had
subsided from upon the earth.**

〉 An olive branch

The olive branch alludes to the oil that would be lit in the
Menorah in the Temple. This light would be able to illumine even
the darkness of life—the floodwaters that threaten to engulf a
person (*Likutey Halakhot* I, p. 262-132a).

8:16 צֵא מִן־הַתֵּבָה אַתָּה וְאִשְׁתְּךָ וּבָנֶיךָ וּנְשֵׁי־בָנֶיךָ אִתָּךְ

**"Leave the ark—you along with your wife, your
sons, and your sons' wives."**

〉 Leave the ark

Noah had to be commanded to enter and exit the ark because
he was unsure of his ability to save himself, let alone the entire
world, through his prayers. To save himself, he had to hide within
the ark—that is, to "hide" in a place of prayer and Torah study. He
also had to be commanded to leave the ark, since he did not know
what to do upon leaving the house of study.

It is God's will that we live in a materialistic world where
we must search for Godliness. We cannot always exist within
the confines of the "ark," wrapped up in our prayers. Therefore,
despite the safety of the ark, we must "go out" and experience the
challenges of life, its ups and downs (*Likutey Halakhot* III, p. 48a).

8:18 וַיֵּצֵא־נֹחַ וּבָנָיו וְאִשְׁתּוֹ וּנְשֵׁי־בָנָיו אִתּוֹ

So Noah left, along with his sons, his wife, and his sons' wives.

》 Noah leaves the ark

When Noah left the ark and saw that the world was destroyed, he began to pray. "Foolish shepherd!" God reprimanded him. "Why didn't you pray for mercy for your generation before the Flood struck?" Moses, in contrast, was a true shepherd, for he prayed for and was willing to give up his life for his flock (Zohar I, 106a).

Noah's error lay in not knowing the value and power of prayer. He was commanded to build an ark of specific proportions to ensure the survival of every type of creature and vegetation in the world. *Teivah* (ark) also means "word," for Noah's ark can be measured by any person in the way he prays to God. Thus, it is written, "The ark rested in the seventh month" (Genesis 8:4)—this alludes to the month of Tishrei and to our prayers that we offer on Yom Kippur. That is, the ark represents the prayers and supplications offered on Yom Kippur (*Likutey Halakhot* III, p. 48a).

8:20 וַיִּבֶן נֹחַ מִזְבֵּחַ לַיָי וַיִּקַּח מִכֹּל הַבְּהֵמָה הַטְּהֹרָה וּמִכֹּל הָעוֹף הַטָּהוֹר וַיַּעַל עֹלֹת בַּמִּזְבֵּחַ

Noah built an altar to God. He took some of the clean animals and some of the clean birds and offered burnt-offerings upon the altar.

》 Noah brought sacrifices

Noah represents the tzaddik of the generation. By bringing sacrifices from the pure animals, Noah was able to elevate them. That is, he subdued the gross materialism represented by their flesh and enabled all mankind to partake of meat (*Likutey Halakhot* IV, p. 95a).

8:21   וַיָּ֣רַח יְיָ֮ אֶת־רֵ֣יחַ הַנִּיחֹחַ֒ וַיֹּ֨אמֶר יְיָ֜ אֶל־לִבּ֗וֹ לֹֽא־אֹ֠סִף
לְקַלֵּ֨ל ע֤וֹד אֶת־הָֽאֲדָמָה֙ בַּֽעֲב֣וּר הָֽאָדָ֔ם כִּ֠י יֵ֣צֶר לֵ֧ב
הָֽאָדָ֛ם רַ֖ע מִנְּעֻרָ֑יו וְלֹֽא־אֹסִ֥ף ע֛וֹד לְהַכּ֥וֹת אֶת־כָּל־
חַ֖י כַּֽאֲשֶׁ֥ר עָשִֽׂיתִי

**God smelled the appeasing fragrance, and
God said to His heart, "I will not continue
to curse the earth because of man, for the
inclination of man's heart is evil from his
youth. Never again will I strike down all life,
as I have done."**

⟫ God said to His heart, "I will not continue to curse"

The *sefirah* of Binah corresponds to the heart. There, Divine
judgments are mitigated at their source (*Likutey Moharan* I, 49:7). God
decreed the onset of the Flood because He felt sadness in His heart
regarding the behavior of humanity. The phrase "God said to His
heart" means that He was bringing that decree to His heart—the
sefirah of Binah—and thereby mitigating it. From this verse, we
also learn that in order to overcome sadness, a person must bring
his heart to joy.

⟫ The inclination of man's heart is evil from his youth

Righteous people control their hearts, whereas wicked people
are controlled by their hearts (*Bereishit Rabbah* 34:10).

In order for a person to gain control over his heart—the seat
of emotions—he must bind it to his intellect so that the latter will
rule (*Likutey Moharan* I, 33:7).

8:22   עֹד כָּל־יְמֵי הָאָרֶץ זֶרַע וְקָצִיר וְקֹר וָחֹם וְקַיִץ וָחֹרֶף
וְיוֹם וָלַיְלָה לֹא יִשְׁבֹּתוּ

"As long as the earth lasts, seedtime and harvest, cold and heat, summer and winter, and day and night will not cease."

〗 *Seedtime and harvest, cold and heat, summer and winter, and day and night*

Everything that exists within time and space is inherently dissimilar. Seedtime and harvest, summer and winter, and day and night represent disparities in time. Warm climates and cold climates reflect disparities in space. All these variations point to the greatness of God, Who used one mold to create widely disparate things. God's greatness is manifest when there is peace, which unites all differences. Torah brings peace because it unites body and soul, and joins time and space with the levels that transcend time and space (see *Likutey Halakhot* II, p. 168a).

9:2   וּמוֹרַאֲכֶם וְחִתְּכֶם יִהְיֶה עַל כָּל־חַיַּת הָאָרֶץ וְעַל כָּל־
עוֹף הַשָּׁמָיִם בְּכֹל אֲשֶׁר תִּרְמֹשׂ הָאֲדָמָה וּבְכָל־דְּגֵי
הַיָּם בְּיֶדְכֶם נִתָּנוּ

"The fear and dread of you will be upon all the wild beasts of the earth and upon all the birds of the sky, in everything that creeps upon the ground and in all the fish of the ocean—they have been given into your hand."

〗 *The fear and dread of you will be upon all creatures*

When a person possesses the "image of God," other creatures fear him. When he grows angry, however, that "image of God" leaves him (*Likutey Moharan* I, 57:6).

9:3   כָּל־רֶמֶשׂ אֲשֶׁר הוּא־חַי לָכֶם יִהְיֶה לְאָכְלָה כְּיֶרֶק
עֵשֶׂב נָתַתִּי לָכֶם אֶת־כֹּל

"Every moving thing that lives will be food for you. Like the vegetation, I have given you everything."

》 *Every moving thing that lives will be food for you*

The ritual slaughter and consumption of animal meat elevates the animal's soul and effects rectification for the world. Before Adam sinned, however, everything in the world was already in a pure state and did not require any rectification. Therefore the consumption of animal meat was prohibited. When Adam ate from the Tree of Knowledge, all the animals ate from it, too (*Bereishit Rabbah* 19:5). At that point, everything descended to such low levels that mankind was unable to rectify animals by consuming their flesh. Mankind descended even further: by the generation of Noah, people were committing the worst sins, and even animals committed licentious acts that caused them to be destroyed in the Flood. Whatever life was worthy of being saved was gathered into the ark.

After Noah left the ark, the world began its process of rectification. Since those animals that remained alive would now contribute to the restoration of the world, they were considered worthy of being elevated. Thus, from Noah's time onwards, mankind was permitted to eat animal meat—as long as the animal had undergone kosher slaughter, which brings about a rectification. Only fish do not require slaughter, for they remained pure since the beginning of time (*Likutey Halakhot* IV, p. 26a-52).

9:4   אַךְ־בָּשָׂר בְּנַפְשׁוֹ דָמוֹ לֹא תֹאכֵלוּ

"Only do not eat flesh of a creature that is still alive."

》 *Do not eat flesh of a creature that is still alive…but of your blood I will demand an accounting*

The commandment not to eat flesh from a live animal is specifically placed next to the commandment that forbids murder

(Genesis 9:5), since they are literally the same concept. Animals contain souls and sparks of holiness that must be elevated via kosher slaughter. One who removes and eats the flesh from a living animal prevents the soul and sparks from being elevated. This constitutes "murder" of that soul and spark. Therefore the Torah juxtaposes these two commandments (*Likutey Halakhot* IV, p. 21a).

9:16   וְהָיְתָה הַקֶּשֶׁת בֶּעָנָן וּרְאִיתִיהָ לִזְכֹּר בְּרִית עוֹלָם
בֵּין אֱלֹהִים וּבֵין כָּל־נֶפֶשׁ חַיָּה בְּכָל־בָּשָׂר אֲשֶׁר
עַל־הָאָרֶץ

"The rainbow will be in the clouds, and I will see it to remember the eternal covenant between God and every living soul in all flesh that is upon the earth."

⟩ The eternal covenant

A person who guards the covenant—i.e., his sexual purity—is considered to be a tzaddik (*Zohar* I, 59b).

Noah was called a tzaddik (Genesis 6:9) because in a generation steeped in sexual immorality, he maintained the highest standards of personal purity. Since all tzaddikim maintain such standards, they are associated with the rainbow-covenant that God made with Noah. Thus, they can arouse the brilliant illumination of the rainbow; this illumination parallels the revelation of Torah mysteries (*Likutey Moharan* I, 42).

⟩ The rainbow will be in the clouds, and I will see it to remember

The rainbow has three primary colors, corresponding to the Patriarchs, who in turn represent the *sefirot* of Chesed, Gevurah and Tiferet.

These *sefirot* also correspond to the elements of fire, air and water. Since these three elements combine to bring forth song (via the "fire" or warmth of the throat, the "water" or fluids of the mouth, and the "air" expelled from the lungs), when we sing before God in prayer, we arouse the merit of the rainbow-covenant that God made with mankind as well as the merit of the Patriarchs.

Thus, singing before God in prayer mitigates strict judgments (*Likutey Moharan* I, 42).

9:18   וַיִּהְיוּ בְנֵי־נֹחַ הַיֹּצְאִים מִן־הַתֵּבָה שֵׁם וְחָם וָיָפֶת וְחָם הוּא אֲבִי כְנָעַן

The sons of Noah who came out of the Ark were Shem, Cham and Japhet. Cham was the father of Canaan.

❯ *Cham*

The word *ChaM* literally means "hot." *ChaM* represents a defiled covenant, the demeanor of one who "warms" himself up to sin (*Likutey Halakhot* I, p. 95a). Furthermore, the numerical value of the name *ChaM* is 48. A person's burning desires in this world can be countered by the forty-eight ways with which the Torah is acquired (*Avot* 6:6) (*Likutey Halakhot* I, p. 134a).

9:21   וַיֵּשְׁתְּ מִן־הַיַּיִן וַיִּשְׁכָּר וַיִּתְגַּל בְּתוֹךְ אָהֳלֹה

He drank some of the wine and became drunk. He uncovered himself in his tent.

❯ *He drank some of the wine and became drunk. He uncovered himself in his tent*

When a person attains full *da'at*, he attains true compassion and understands the importance of extending one's self in self-sacrifice for others (*Likutey Moharan* II, 8:3). Noah showed his weakness by drinking wine, symbolizing constricted *da'at*. Though he was a great tzaddik, Noah did not pray for his fellow man with a readiness for self-sacrifice, as Moses did for the Jewish nation. Because Noah lacked that full *da'at* to rectify Adam's sin and stop the Flood, he fell down naked, like Adam (Genesis 2:25), without garments (*Likutey Halakhot* I, p. 92-47a).

9:22   וַיַּרְא חָם אֲבִי כְנַעַן אֵת עֶרְוַת אָבִיו וַיַּגֵּד לִשְׁנֵי־
       אֶחָיו בַּחוּץ

**Cham, the father of Canaan, saw his father's
nakedness and told his two brothers outside.**

〉 *Cham, the father of Canaan, saw his father's nakedness*

Cham, the father of Canaan, exposed Noah's nakedness, but
Shem and Japhet used garments (i.e., *tzitzit*) to cover their father's
shame. *ChaM* (literally, "hot") represents the evil inclination, which
tries to entice a person (i.e., "warm" his body) to sin. By arousing
a person's imagination and desires, the evil inclination overpowers
him. This is why Cham's descendants, the Canaanites, possessed the
Holy Land for many centuries: the Evil One overpowered the forces
of holiness and wrested it away for itself. But the faith instilled in
the Jewish nation by Moses overpowered Canaan. The Jews believed
God's promise and merited to reconquer the Land (*Likutey Halakhot* I,
p. 48a).

9:23   וַיִּקַּח שֵׁם וָיֶפֶת אֶת־הַשִּׂמְלָה וַיָּשִׂימוּ עַל־שְׁכֶם
       שְׁנֵיהֶם וַיֵּלְכוּ אֲחֹרַנִּית וַיְכַסּוּ אֵת עֶרְוַת אֲבִיהֶם
       וּפְנֵיהֶם אֲחֹרַנִּית וְעֶרְוַת אֲבִיהֶם לֹא רָאוּ

**Shem and Japhet took the cloak and put
it on both of their shoulders. They walked
backwards and covered their father's
nakedness. Their faces were turned away and
they did not see their father's nakedness.**

〉 *Shem and Japhet took the cloak…Cursed is Canaan*

The "cloak" is a reference to *tzitzit*, which protect a person
against the immorality that was inherent in Canaan's abuse of his
grandfather Noah. Canaan was cursed for his behavior. He is comparable to the Serpent, which was also cursed (*Likutey Moharan* I, 7:4;
ibid., II, 1:10).

9:25   וַיֹּאמֶר אָרוּר כְּנָעַן עֶבֶד עֲבָדִים יִהְיֶה לְאֶחָיו

"Cursed is Canaan," he said. "He will be a
slave's slave to his brothers."

〉 A slave's slave

Canaan was cursed like the Serpent, condemned to slothfulness
and laziness (*Likutey Moharan* I, 117).

11:4   וַיֹּאמְרוּ הָבָה נִבְנֶה־לָּנוּ עִיר וּמִגְדָּל וְרֹאשׁוֹ
בַשָּׁמַיִם וְנַעֲשֶׂה־לָּנוּ שֵׁם פֶּן־נָפוּץ עַל־פְּנֵי
כָל־הָאָרֶץ

They said, "Come, let us build ourselves a
city and a tower with its top in Heaven.
We will make a name for ourselves, in
case we are scattered over the face of
the earth."

〉 A tower with its top in Heaven

The Tower of Babel was built for self-aggrandizement. Its build-
ers wanted to serve themselves and separate from God. They were
not fools who thought they could ascend to Heaven and "fight"
God. Rather, they wanted to use philosophies and evil intentions to
produce atheism. The same applies to those who build synagogues
and other types of religious institutions with selfish intent: they
distance people from God (*Likutey Halakhot* I, p. 248a).

11:26   וַיְחִי־תֶרַח שִׁבְעִים שָׁנָה וַיּוֹלֶד אֶת־אַבְרָם אֶת־
נָחוֹר וְאֶת־הָרָן

Terach lived seventy years and begat
Abram, Nachor and Haran.

〉 Abram

Abraham was one (Ezekiel 33:24).

Abraham was "one" in the sense that he was alone in his quest
for God. Though he was born into a family of idolaters and his

entire generation consisted of idolaters, he sought God regardless of the opposition that he faced.

So too, whoever wishes to serve God must not fear the opposition that he encounters. Even if he faces difficulties from his parents, in-laws, spouse, friends, and so forth, he must continue seeking God until, like Abraham, he will come to Him (*Likutey Moharan* II, Preface).

〉 *Abram*

Our Sages teach that Abraham had no spiritual teacher. From whence did he learn about God? His kidneys became two fountains that flowed with Godly wisdom (*Bereishit Rabbah* 95:3).

Sometimes a person has a deep yearning to serve God and study Torah, but is unable to do so, for whatever reason. This powerful desire reaches the Supernal Heart, upon which Torah teachings are inscribed. The Supernal Heart makes it possible for him to serve God despite his lack of knowledge. Then, like Abraham, he will be energized from within himself to draw close to God (*Likutey Moharan* I, 142).

11:28 וַיָּמָת הָרָן עַל־פְּנֵי תֶּרַח אָבִיו בְּאֶרֶץ מוֹלַדְתּוֹ בְּאוּר כַּשְׂדִּים

Haran died in the lifetime of his father Terach, in the land of his birth, in Ur Kasdim.

〉 *Haran died...in Ur Kasdim*

Terach accused his son Abraham before Nimrod of destroying his idols, and Nimrod had Abraham thrown into a fiery furnace. Haran thought to himself, "If Abraham triumphs, I will be on his side, and if Nimrod triumphs, I will be on his side." When Abraham triumphed [by being saved from death in the furnace], they said to Haran, "Whose side are you on?" Haran replied, "I'm on Abraham's side." They threw him into the fiery furnace and he was incinerated (Rashi).

Abraham was harassed and persecuted by the entire world. They threw him into a fire (*Ur Kasdim* literally means "the fire of Kasdim" [Chaldea]) and claimed he was an atheist, for he denied idolatry. Yet he stood up to everyone in his quest for the truth and managed to find God (*Likutey Halakhot* IV, p. 400).

⟩ Abraham and Nimrod

Abraham, the only one who believed in the true God, was called an atheist by Nimrod. This lie could only have its roots in the Chambers of Exchanges, where good and evil get mixed up and present obstacles to seeing the truth (*Likutey Halakhot* I, p. 210).

⟩ Ur Kasdim

The Torah states: "God, your Lord, is fire" (Deuteronomy 4:24). Those who waver in their faith will find this "fire" difficult for survival. But one who is truly attached to God can not only live with this "fire," but can draw vitality from it. Thus, we see that when God appeared to Moses at the burning bush, the bush was not consumed by the fire, reflecting Moses' firm faith in God (*Likutey Halakhot* III, p. 494). Devotion and attachment to God determine a person's ability to survive and weather the "elements"—the obstacles and tests that confront him throughout his life.

11:29   וַיִּקַּח אַבְרָם וְנָחוֹר לָהֶם נָשִׁים שֵׁם אֵשֶׁת־אַבְרָם
שָׂרָי וְשֵׁם אֵשֶׁת־נָחוֹר מִלְכָּה בַּת־הָרָן אֲבִי־מִלְכָּה
וַאֲבִי יִסְכָּה

Abram and Nachor took wives for themselves. The name of Abram's wife was Sarai, and the name of Nachor's wife was Milkah, the daughter of Haran, the father of Milkah and Yiskah.

⟩ Sarai

SaRai (later, Sarah) was so called because she was a *SaR* (ruler or authority) over the entire world (*Berakhot* 13a).

Her authority was apparent in her ability to reveal God's kingship (see *Likutey Moharan* I, 74).

The name *SaRai* (שרי) is similar to the word *ShiR* (שיר, song). This indicates that with Sarah's "authority," the Kingdom of Holiness—which is holy song—is brought into the world (ibid., I, 49:1).

11:32 וַיִּהְיוּ יְמֵי־תֶרַח חָמֵשׁ שָׁנִים וּמָאתַיִם שָׁנָה
וַיָּמָת תֶּרַח בְּחָרָן

**The days of Terach were two hundred
and five years. Terach died in Charan.**

〉 *Terach died in Charan...God said to Abram, "Go...to the Land"*

"Terach died in *ChaRaN*" alludes to the end of the *ChaRoN af*,
the Divine anger that indicates impatience. When one conquers
impatience, he immediately merits to "go to the Holy Land" (*Likutey
Halakhot* I, p. 67a). This is because the Holy Land represents the aspect
of patience (*Likutey Moharan* I, 155:2).

Parashat Lekh Lekha

12:1 וַיֹּאמֶר יְיָ אֶל־אַבְרָם לֶךְ־לְךָ מֵאַרְצְךָ וּמִמּוֹלַדְתְּךָ
וּמִבֵּית אָבִיךָ אֶל־הָאָרֶץ אֲשֶׁר אַרְאֶךָּ

**God said to Abram, "Go from your land,
from your birthplace, and from your father's
house, to the Land that I will show you."**

❭ Go…to the Land that I will show you

God commanded Abraham: "Go…to the Land that I will show
you," without telling him which land it was. How, then, did
Abraham know? He evaluated the spiritual nature of each land that
he passed through until, in the Holy Land, he was able to experience God's Providence directly (see *Zohar* I, 78a; *Likutey Moharan* I, 44).

❭ Go…to the Land

God sent Abraham to the Holy Land because its merit is
beneficial for having children. The Holy Land is also a locus for
prayer. However, prayer anywhere is also beneficial for having
children (*Likutey Moharan* I, 48).

❭ Go from your land, from your birthplace, and from your father's house

Abraham represents the soul of a person who wishes to serve
God. Such a person must leave behind his "land" (his materialism),
his "birthplace" (his sensual pleasures and depression), and
even his "father's house" (his family who tries to stop him from
serving God). Freed from those handicaps, he can travel to the
Holy Land—to holiness, the place where joy reigns supreme. In
that place, "I will make you a great nation" (for you will be able
to reveal Godliness even to others), "I will bless you" (for then you
will be able to draw and receive all the blessings), "I will make
your name great" (your vitality will increase), and "you will be a
blessing" (for the blessings will remain with you). Furthermore, by
leaving behind your past and embracing spirituality, even though
you may later descend to "Egypt" (the challenges and difficulties

of life), you will have the fortitude to ascend from there and even take with you many sparks of holiness *(Likutey Halakhot* II, p. 145a).

⟩ Go...to the Land

God did not reveal the Land immediately to Abraham, in order to build up his desire for the Holy Land *(Likutey Halakhot* II, p. 45a).

God did not reveal to Abraham *which* land; he had to discover for himself which land God meant. When Heaven tests a person, his knowledge of what he must do is constricted and hidden from him. Only through his desire to do God's will can he find the right path to follow. If he seeks the truth—that is, if he seeks where God is—he will come upon the right path. The same was true of the Binding of Isaac. God told Abraham to sacrifice Isaac on one of the mountains, without specifying which one (Genesis 22:2). This was calculated to intensify Abraham's test, and to increase his reward when he passed that test *(Likutey Halakhot* I, p. 212a-424).

⟩ Go from your land, from your birthplace, and from your father's house...I will make you a great nation, I will bless you, and I will make your name great

God did not tell Abraham the name of the Land immediately, in order to make it beloved to him (Rashi).

The challenges facing Abraham also face each of his descendants. *Lekh lekha* literally means "Go to yourself"—go to your soul, which is your real self. Let all your travels and searching focus on discovering your soul and its source.

How can you accomplish this? By going "from your land"—removing yourself from materialism, from the physical attractions of this world. No matter how deeply you think you have descended into a material existence, know that you can leave it behind. "From your birthplace"—from wherever you were born and raised. "From your father's house"—from your family, friends and neighbors. Even if yours were lowly beginnings, you can strive for greater heights. You need not carry around your background like excess baggage.

"Go...to the Land that I will show you" is the main test of a person in this world. God holds back from immediately showing a person what he has accomplished, for if he knew the reward for his efforts, he would no longer have free will. Therefore God holds back from showing a person direction, letting him seek it on his own. One who strengthens himself will eventually find "the Land"—the goal he is intended to reach—and especially the ultimate goal, the World to Come.

"I will make you a great nation"—you will overcome your enemies. "I will bless you"—you will draw all the blessings to benefit mankind. "I will make your name great"—you will merit an unprecedented knowledge of God. "You will be a blessing"— because one who strives to serve God remains steadfast in his devotions despite all the obstacles he faces. Thus, he will always be blessed and feel blessed.

So Abraham went and took Lot with him. Lot represents the evil inclination (see below, p. 165). Even if a person masters his evil inclination to fulfill the word of God, the forces of evil are always at the ready, ensuring the continued existence of free will. As soon as Abraham entered the Land, a famine struck and he had to descend to Egypt. This, too, was a test, forcing him to leave the realm of holiness he had so recently achieved. The same happens to every individual, but upon re-entering the realm of holiness, one brings back "cattle, silver and gold" (Genesis 13:2)—the sparks of holiness that were entrapped in the realm of evil. When one raises himself back into holiness, he merits to raise the fallen sparks as well (*Likutey Halakhot* III, p. 98-100).

⟩ Lekh lekha from your land, from your birthplace, and from your father's house, to the Land that I will show you

Lekh lekha (literally, "Go to yourself") means that wherever you go, you must always look "to yourself"—to the point of truth within you. Each individual has his own point of truth. To find it, he must leave behind his "land"—these are his material desires, for each land has its own material pursuits, some for money, others for immorality, and the like. He must leave behind his "birthplace"—these are his physical desires. And he must leave behind his ancestry—his thoughts of receiving honor and respect from others. All these deter a person from finding the truth. Then he will merit to the "Land"—to holiness (*Likutey Halakhot* VIII, p. 207a-207b).

⟩ Abraham was the first to go to the Holy Land

Abraham is called "the volunteering heart" because he *offered* his heart to God. Though Abraham did not receive the Torah, he was able to perfect his Divine service through his immense will and longing for God. His strong will enabled him to stand up to the entire world, which was completely populated by idolaters at that time. Because of his will, Abraham merited to be the first to reveal the sanctity of the Holy Land. And he merited a son, *YitZChaK* (יצחק), so named because of the *tZChoK* (צחוק, joy) that results from great longing and desire for God, which causes God to reveal His pride in us (*Likutey Halakhot* II, p. 82a).

12:2   וְאֶעֶשְׂךָ לְגוֹי גָּדוֹל וַאֲבָרֶכְךָ וַאֲגַדְּלָה שְׁמֶךָ
וֶהְיֵה בְּרָכָה

"I will make you a great nation, I will bless you, and I will make your name great. You will be a blessing."

⟩ I will make you a great nation, I will bless you...Lot went with him...Abram continued traveling, moving steadily towards the south

"I will make you a great nation"—This is why we say in the *Shemoneh Esrei* prayer "the God of Abraham" (Rashi).

Rebbe Nachman taught: Faith, prayer, miracles and the Holy Land are conceptually one. However, a person cannot attain faith, prayer, miracles or the Holy Land without truth. One who tries to pray, for example, is beset by darkness, by foreign thoughts that confuse him. To overcome these thoughts, he must seek the truth—i.e., he should recite the words of prayer as honestly as he can (*Likutey Moharan* I, 9).

Because Abraham was a man of truth, he merited to faith, prayer and the Holy Land. We say "the God of Abraham" because through his truth, Abraham revealed God to the world. He merited to the Holy Land because that is the place of prayer, and there he ascended to even greater levels of prayer and faith.

Despite Abraham's efforts, Lot accompanied him. *LoT* (לוט) implies *LaTuta* (לטותא, Aramaic for "curse"), representing the darkness that envelops one who seeks to pray, even in the Holy Land, for these confusions attack a person constantly. Anticipating this, Abraham always faced south. Using the metaphorical orientation of a person facing east (as the Talmud often describes [cf. *Bava Batra* 25b]), south refers to the right side, the side of truth. By always seeking truth, we can overcome the darkness and foreign thoughts (*Likutey Halakhot* VIII, p. 206a-206b).

〉 *I will make you a great nation, I will bless you, and I will make your name great*

"I will bless you"—with money (Rashi).

Wealth adds many friends (Proverbs 19:4).

Because Abraham would become wealthy, many people would try to befriend him. This, in turn, would "make his name great," as his fame would spread. Subsequently, he would become "a great nation," for he would be able to spread teachings about God far and wide and inspire others to serve Him (*Likutey Halakhot* III, p. 478). Rebbe Nachman adds that by giving charity to the tzaddik, one also "adds many friends" (*Likutey Moharan* I, 17:5).

〉 *I will bless you, and I will make your name great*

God blessed Abraham with wealth. Wealth makes a person's name great (making him famous) as well as increases the greatness of his soul, making it possible for him to accomplish great things. As a result, people are attracted to and befriend those who are wealthy. A wealthy person must act for the benefit of mankind by influencing those close to him to turn to God, as Abraham did (*Likutey Moharan* I, 59:5).

〉 *I will bless you, and I will make your name great. You will be a blessing*

God promised Abraham that he would merit children, wealth and a good name (Rashi).

All these rewards depend on *da'at*, which corresponds to the letter *hei* (ה) (*Likutey Moharan* I, 53). Therefore God changed his name from *Avram* (אברם, Abram) to *AvraHam* (אברהם, Abraham) (*Likutey Halakhot* II, p. 45a).

12:5   וַיִּקַּח אַבְרָם אֶת־שָׂרַי אִשְׁתּוֹ וְאֶת־לוֹט בֶּן־אָחִיו וְאֶת־
כָּל־רְכוּשָׁם אֲשֶׁר רָכָשׁוּ וְאֶת־הַנֶּפֶשׁ אֲשֶׁר־עָשׂוּ בְחָרָן
וַיֵּצְאוּ לָלֶכֶת אַרְצָה כְּנַעַן וַיָּבֹאוּ אַרְצָה כְּנָעַן

So Abram took his wife Sarai and Lot, his
brother's son, and all their possessions that
they had acquired, and the souls that they
had made in Charan, and they left to go to
the land of Canaan. They came to the land
of Canaan.

❯ The souls that they had made in Charan

One who draws others close to God, as Abraham did, creates
an environment in which God's glory is revealed—and that
environment is referred to as a holy palace for God (*Likutey Moharan* I,
59:1).

❯ The souls that they had made in Charan

"The souls that they had made"—this refers to people whom
Abraham and Sarah converted to serve God (Rashi).

Abraham continuously strove to attain greater knowledge
of God, and whatever knowledge he attained, he immediately
disseminated to others. Because all of his learning had the goal
of teaching others, Abraham exemplifies the attribute of *chesed*
(kindness) (*Likutey Moharan* I, 58:5).

❯ The souls that they had made in Charan

Though Abraham and Sarah were barren, they sanctified their
thoughts and desires to such a degree that with their union, they
were able to create the souls of converts (*Zohar* III, 168a).

Indeed, all the souls of converts are created through the union
of holy couples. This teaches us that the souls of converts are very
lofty (*Likutey Moharan* II, 72).

❯ Charan

The place name *ChaRaN* (חרן) is similar to *ChoRiN* (חורין, a free
man).

Abraham was free of evil desires, and therefore could teach others about God and influence their spiritual growth. His servant Eliezer was also able to teach others about God; however, Eliezer lacked the ability to make converts (*Likutey Moharan* I, 31:5).

〕 *The souls that they had made in Charan*

Abraham suffered terrible opposition during his proselytizing activities. He would come into the city and run about crying, "Woe! Woe!" and people would run after him the way they chase a madman. He would argue with them at length, trying to show them that they were all caught up in a profoundly mistaken way of thinking. He was quite familiar with all the arguments and rationalizations they used to justify their idolatrous practices. The idolatry of the ancients was bound up with all kinds of spurious beliefs, and Abraham was fully conversant with all of them. He used to demonstrate the falsity of their ideas and reveal the truths upon which our own holy faith is founded.

Some of the young people were attracted to him. As far as older people were concerned, he never even tried to draw them close because they were already firmly entrenched in their false beliefs and it would have been very hard to get them to change. But the younger people were drawn to him. He would go from city to city and they would run after him. But the parents and wives of these young people were strongly opposed to their newfound faith, saying they had fallen victim to evil influences and had been ruined. They put up such a front of hostility that some of these young people reverted to their old ways under the weight of domestic pressure from their parents, wives and in-laws. However, a few remained firm in their attachment to Abraham.

Abraham put great effort into spreading the true faith. He wrote books—thousands of books. He had numerous sons, and we may assume that if they were his children, they all followed the path of righteousness. Even Ishmael repented. Later on, however, when Abraham thought about how he could ensure that his legacy of books and teachings would endure in the world, he pondered deeply as to which of his sons he should bequeath them to. In the end, he decided to leave everything to Isaac (see Genesis 25:5), and so he did (*Tzaddik* #395).

12:6   וַיַּעֲבֹר אַבְרָם בָּאָרֶץ עַד מְקוֹם שְׁכֶם עַד אֵלוֹן מוֹרֶה וְהַכְּנַעֲנִי אָז בָּאָרֶץ

Abram passed through the Land as far as the place of Shekhem, up to Alon Moreh. The Canaanites were then in the Land.

〉 *Abram passed through the Land...he built an altar*

Primarily in the Holy Land, one can merit to see the revelation of God (*Likutey Halakhot* II, p. 50a).

12:9   וַיִּסַּע אַבְרָם הָלוֹךְ וְנָסוֹעַ הַנֶּגְבָּה

Abram continued traveling, moving steadily towards the south.

〉 *Abram continued traveling, moving steadily towards the south...There was a famine in the Land. Abram went down to Egypt*

Abraham went to the south but a famine set in, so from there he descended to Egypt. *NeGeV* (נגב, south) may be associated with *NeGiVah* (נגיבה, dryness). Abraham, who represents Chesed (Kindness), which is associated with water, traveled to bring humidity and wetness to the dry, barren places. *Mitzrayim* (Egypt) literally means "narrowness."

When a person sins, he arouses God's judgments, which create restrictions and constraints—i.e., "narrowness." The famine represents the fasting that a person undertakes as part of the repentance process. He goes to the "Negev"—the realm of supernal compassion and kindness—and draws the energy of that kindness into the "narrow" difficulties themselves, until the difficulties are overcome (*Likutey Moharan* I, 62:5).

12:10 וַיְהִי רָעָב בָּאָרֶץ וַיֵּרֶד אַבְרָם מִצְרַיְמָה לָגוּר שָׁם
כִּי־כָבֵד הָרָעָב בָּאָרֶץ

There was a famine in the Land. Abram went down to Egypt to stay there a while, because the famine was heavy in the Land.

There was a famine in the Land

This famine refers to a person's main test, that of earning a livelihood. As soon as "Abraham"—the spiritual seeker—attempts to enter the realm of holiness, he is beset by trials and tribulations surrounding his livelihood. This "forces" him to descend into "Egypt," where he is surrounded by material entrapments. He must strengthen himself, and then he will merit to ascend from there (*Likutey Halakhot* III, p. 98-100).

Go...to the Land...famine...Abram went down to Egypt

Since the Holy Land is so great, and God Himself told Abraham to go there, why would God bring a famine that forced Abraham to leave the Land as soon as he arrived?

Sparks of holiness are scattered throughout the world, but the main rectification for them takes place in the Holy Land. Therefore God sent Abraham to the Holy Land. But in order for Abraham to retrieve the sparks of holiness that lay outside the Land, God brought a famine that forced him to descend to Egypt and thereby elevate those sparks as well.

Each of Abraham's descendants is given the same task. Every Jew should strive to live in the Holy Land, but sometimes one who wishes to live in the Land is unable to do so at the moment. In actuality, his task is to elevate those sparks found outside the Land which are part of his soul. This explains why many people travel continually to and from the Holy Land. There are also people who wish to travel to the Holy Land yet face enormous obstacles. By yearning deeply for the Land, one can draw its sanctity upon himself and gain the strength to overcome all the challenges he faces. Then he will merit to enter the Land, rectifying the sparks that will accompany him.

What if someone experiences obstacles to serving God even after a visit to the Holy Land? His difficulties stem from the fact that he inadvertently entered a holy place, which represents a *bitul* (nullification) to God. Now he must draw that sanctity with him and bring it to places outside the Land. This effort produces the obstructions in his Divine service. Perseverance in serving God and longing for the Holy Land will eventually bring rectification in all these cases (*Likutey Halakhot* II, p. 490).

12:15 וַיִּרְאוּ אֹתָהּ שָׂרֵי פַרְעֹה וַיְהַלְלוּ אֹתָהּ אֶל־פַּרְעֹה וַתֻּקַּח הָאִשָּׁה בֵּית פַּרְעֹה

Pharaoh's officers saw her and praised her to Pharaoh, and the woman was taken to Pharaoh's house.

》 *The woman was taken to Pharaoh's house*

Sarah was taken to the depths of impurity to find the sparks of holiness hidden there. She succeeded in her task, for Pharaoh gave Abraham and Sarah many gifts (Genesis 12:16)—i.e., she extricated the sparks of holiness from that place. She also set into motion the future salvation of the Jewish people after they would be enslaved in Egypt (*Likutey Halakhot* I, p. 424).

》 *The woman was taken to Pharaoh's house*

When the Egyptian authorities saw Sarah's beauty, they took her to Pharaoh's palace. Pharaoh and his servants were punished until they released Sarah and gave Abraham generous gifts.

Sarah represents holy speech. The name *SaRah* (שרה) is related to the word *SaR* (שר, authority), and it is with one's mouth that one issues edicts. Thus, the *Zohar* teaches that the *sefirah* of Malkhut (Kingship) corresponds to the mouth (see *Tikkuney Zohar*, Introduction, p. 17a).

The Egyptians represent the forces of evil. The descent of Abraham and Sarah to Egypt symbolizes a person succumbing to and descending into the realm of evil. There the beauty of Sarah—holy speech—is captured and brought to Pharaoh. The letters of the word *PhaRaOH* (פרעה) can be rearranged to spell *HaORePh* (הערף, the nape of the neck). This indicates that the forces of evil seek to trap holy speech deep in the throat, preventing its articulation. Many times these forces succeed, to the extent that a person may forget about his holy origins altogether.

But holy speech never loses its connection to its source. Even in the realm of evil, it binds itself to other sparks of holiness. Then, when it eventually emerges, it brings with it all the other sparks of holiness to which it is bound. This is the meaning of the "gifts" which Pharaoh gave Abraham. Not only did Abraham leave the realm of evil, but he took out many sparks of holiness and goodness that had been trapped there by the forces of evil (*Likutey Moharan* I, 62:5; ibid, I, 163).

We learn from this never to despair. Even if we do wrong, we can still escape. When we strengthen ourselves with faith and prayer, we redeem ourselves. We also bind ourselves to others who require rectification and help them improve their lives as well.

》 *The woman was taken to Pharaoh's house*

SaRah (שרה), from *SaR* (שר, authority), represents the Kingdom of Holiness. The Other Side always seeks to take possession of the Kingdom of Holiness. Yet even if it takes possession, it will not be to its benefit. Ultimately, God smote Pharaoh and the Egyptians with a plague because of Sarah, and they were also forced to pay monetary compensation to Abraham. This episode set the stage for Moses to later smite the Egyptians with plagues (*Likutey Halakhot* I, p. 182). (The same occurred with Esther, who was taken to the house of Achashveirosh, and so it always is and will continue to be until Mashiach comes).

13:1 וַיַּעַל אַבְרָם מִמִּצְרַיִם הוּא וְאִשְׁתּוֹ וְכָל־אֲשֶׁר־לוֹ
וְלוֹט עִמּוֹ הַנֶּגְבָּה

**Abram went up from Egypt—he and his wife
and all that he had, and Lot with him—to
the south.**

⟩ *Abram went up from Egypt*

Because Adam ate from the Tree of Knowledge of Good and
Evil, now everything in the world is comprised of both good and
evil. Sometimes the two are balanced, sometimes there is more
good than evil, and sometimes evil predominates.

The tzaddikim of every generation are engaged in a war
between good and evil, and this war will continue until Mashiach
comes. When we see that a tzaddik is involved with the wicked,
we must understand that his intent is to remove all the good and
sparks of holiness from the realm of evil (*Likutey Moharan* I, 8:5). When
Abraham's job was complete in Egypt, he was able to leave.

Great empires and powerful ideologies have come to the
world and influenced many people, yet they are found today only
in history books. Their function was to entice people away from
God. When the good that existed within them was removed, their
power came to an end. Every generation has its temptations. But
ultimately, these run their course, and the good is liberated as the
evil dies out.

13:3 וַיֵּלֶךְ לְמַסָּעָיו מִנֶּגֶב וְעַד־בֵּית־אֵל עַד־הַמָּקוֹם אֲשֶׁר
הָיָה שָׁם אָהֳלֹה בַּתְּחִלָּה בֵּין בֵּית־אֵל וּבֵין הָעָי

**He went on his travels from the south as far
as Beit El, up to the place where his tent had
originally been, between Beit El and Ai.**

⟩ *He went on his travels*

Some say that he repaid his debts. Others opine that he returned
to the inns where he had originally lodged on his way to Egypt
(Rashi).

Debts accumulate when one allows evil to pervade his life (this is explained at length in *Likutey Halakhot, Halva'ah* 5). Abraham, who always sought Godliness, never gave evil a chance to enter his life, though it pursued him at all times. For example, right after Abraham arrived in the Holy Land, he was forced to leave it and descend to Egypt. He was penniless and had to borrow money for his trip. Yet he never gave up and continually sought God and Godliness. He was successful in that he amassed great wealth in Egypt and was able to repay his debts. This also applied to his lodgings. Wherever he went, Abraham drew Godliness into his life. Therefore, wherever he traveled, he was able to "return" to his place—a place of Godliness (*Likutey Halakhot* VII, p. 66-34a).

13:7   וַיְהִי־רִיב בֵּין רֹעֵי מִקְנֵה־אַבְרָם וּבֵין רֹעֵי מִקְנֵה־לוֹט
וְהַכְּנַעֲנִי וְהַפְּרִזִּי אָז יֹשֵׁב בָּאָרֶץ

There was a dispute between the shepherds of Abram's flocks and the shepherds of Lot's flocks. The Canaanites and the Peruzzites were then dwelling in the Land.

〉 *There was a dispute...The Canaanites...were then dwelling in the Land*

KeNaANI (כנעני, Canaanites) is similar to the phrase *KaN ANI* (כאן עני, here is poverty). When there is strife, there is poverty. But peace brings abundance (*Likutey Moharan* I, 277).

〉 *There was a dispute...the Canaanites and the Perizzites were then dwelling in the Land*

Because other nations still had some authority in the Land, a dispute came about. To free the Land from dispute, we must subdue the Other Side. The more a person stays away from disputes and strife, the more he subdues the Other Side (*Likutey Halakhot* VII, p. 292).

〉 *The Canaanites and the Peruzzites were then dwelling in the Land*

The time had not yet come for Abraham or his descendants to possess the Land (Rashi).

When God first created the world, He gave possession of the

Holy Land to the Canaanites. Only afterwards did He give the Holy Land to the Jewish people. Why didn't He give the Land to the Jews first?

A similar question could be asked about the Torah. God did not give the Torah to the first people he created, but allowed twenty-six generations to pass before He gave the Torah to the Jews. Why did He wait? One answer is that had the Torah been given right away, Torah law would have gone into effect every time a person sinned. The earlier generations were terrible sinners, so God had mercy on them and instead sustained the world through His Treasury of Unearned Gifts. This Treasury sustains those who are far from God and who lack merit to receive blessing.

The Torah and the Holy Land are synonymous, for the only place the Torah can be fulfilled in its entirety is the Land of Israel. Had God given the Land to the Jews right from the start, then Torah law would have gone into effect every time the Jews sinned, and they would have been quickly expelled from the Land. Even worse, had they lost possession, they would never have been able to extract it from the Other Side—from Canaan, the forces of evil. To preclude this from happening, God first gave the Land to idolaters and sustained its hidden sanctity through His Treasury of Unearned Gifts. When the Jews later claimed the Land, they were in a better position to keep its *mitzvot* and guard its possession.

Abraham was the one who first began to reveal the sanctity of the Land, even in its concealment. Following his example, we can strengthen our faith that we, too, will soon return to the Holy Land. Even today, God sustains the sanctity of the Land in a concealed manner, and He will eventually give it back to us as He promised (*Likutey Halakhot* V, p. 70a-140-71a).

13:9   הֲלֹא כָל־הָאָרֶץ לְפָנֶיךָ הִפָּרֶד נָא מֵעָלָי אִם־
הַשְּׂמֹאל וְאֵימִנָה וְאִם־הַיָּמִין וְאַשְׂמְאִילָה

"Isn't the whole land before you? Please
separate from me. If you go to the left,
I will go to the right, and if to the right,
I will go left."

If you go to the left, I will go to the right, and if to the right, I will go left

Abraham said to Lot, "If you go to the left, I will go to the south.
If I go south, you will be at my left. Whichever way you choose,
I will keep you to my left" (Bereishit Rabbah 41:6).

The verse states that Abraham gave Lot a choice, to go right
or left. But the Midrash says that Abraham made his choice and
gave Lot the sole option of going to the left. Is this the way to make
peace, to deny the other side a choice?

Abraham represents truth. Lot represents falsehood. Truth
was saying to Falsehood, "Separate from me. Whichever way
you choose for yourself, I will go in the opposite direction. If you
try to confront me with the 'left side'—i.e., with evil desires and
thoughts that are brought on by the Other Side—I will choose the
'right side'—the side of Torah and prayer. And if you choose the
'right side'—meaning, if the evil inclination masks itself with false
Torah teachings and self-made *mitzvot*—then I will go to the 'left
side'—I will do the exact opposite. Either way, I will choose the
path of truth."

In either case, Lot, the symbol of falsehood, would always
remain on the left side, the side of evil. As long as Abraham sought
only the truth, then no matter what choices were presented by the
left side, the side of falsehood, Abraham made sure that it would
stay on the opposite side (*Likutey Halakhot* VIII, p. 206b-207a).

14:15 וַיֵּחָלֵק עֲלֵיהֶם לַיְלָה הוּא וַעֲבָדָיו וַיַּכֵּם וַיִּרְדְּפֵם
עַד־חוֹבָה אֲשֶׁר מִשְּׂמֹאל לְדַמָּשֶׂק

**He and his servants deployed against them
at night and struck them. They pursued
them as far as Hobah, which is to the left
of Damascus.**

❯ *He and his servants deployed against them at night*

Even though Lot was wicked, Abraham pursued the Four Kings
to rescue him, because he knew that Lot had some good points in
him, even in his "night"—his darkest moments (*Likutey Halakhot* I,
p. 5a). That is, Abraham, the "man of *chesed* (kindness)," always
looks for the good points even in the "Lots," the most evil people.

14:18 וּמַלְכִּי־צֶדֶק מֶלֶךְ שָׁלֵם הוֹצִיא לֶחֶם וָיָיִן וְהוּא
כֹהֵן לְאֵל עֶלְיוֹן

**Malki-tzedek, king of Shalem, took out
bread and wine. He was a Kohen of the
Supernal One.**

❯ *Malki-tzedek… took out bread and wine*

One must be strong-minded and resolute to draw sustenance.
By conquering the Four Kings, Abraham proved himself to be a
powerful and decisive leader. Therefore Malki-tzedek gave Abraham
gifts—bread and wine—hinting to Abraham about the sacrifices
and wine libations which would be offered in the Temple. The
sacrifices in the Temple reveal Godliness, and through that
revelation, Abraham was able to draw sustenance and blessing for
all (*Likutey Halakhot* V, p. 438).

❯ *Malki-tzedek… was a Kohen of the Supernal One*

Malki-tzedek is another name for Shem, one of Noah's three sons.
He was the king of Jerusalem (Rashi; *Bereishit Rabbah* 43:6).

Our Sages teach that God originally intended to give the priest-
hood to Shem so that his descendants would perform the Temple

service. But because Malki-tzedek blessed Abraham prior to blessing God, he and his descendants lost that privilege (*Nedarim* 32b).

A person should fill his mouth with praise for God. Malki-tzedek's intention in praising Abraham was good, but he should have borne in mind that God always comes first (*Likutey Moharan* I, 34:7).

15:5 וַיּוֹצֵא אֹתוֹ הַחוּצָה וַיֹּאמֶר הַבֶּט־נָא הַשָּׁמַיְמָה וּסְפֹר הַכּוֹכָבִים אִם־תּוּכַל לִסְפֹּר אֹתָם וַיֹּאמֶר לוֹ כֹּה יִהְיֶה זַרְעֶךָ

He took him outside and said, "Look to the heavens and count the stars, if you are able to count them." Then He said to him, "Thus will your descendants be."

❱ *He took him outside and said, "Look to the heavens... Thus will your descendants be"*

God took Abraham out of this world and placed him above the stars (Rashi).

The blessing of children that Abraham received when God elevated him above the heavens teaches that the Jews, Abraham's descendants, supersede natural forces; therefore they can always accomplish things that seem beyond their reach (*Likutey Halakhot* I, p. 20a). God showed Abraham that his descendants would transcend the laws of the stellar system. They could attain levels beyond time and space (*Likutey Halakhot* V, p. 158).

15:6 וְהֶאֱמִן בַּיי וַיַּחְשְׁבֶהָ לוֹ צְדָקָה

He believed in God, and He considered it as charity.

❱ *He believed in God, and He considered it as charity*

With his faith, a person can destroy idolatry (including, in a broader sense, false beliefs). Abraham was the first person to truly believe in God. Thus, he was able to counter the idolatry of his generation (*Likutey Moharan* I, 28:2). One who suffers from doubts can overcome them by strengthening his faith. This reveals Abraham's attribute of kindness, which strengthens faith.

》 *He believed in God, and He considered it as charity*

Faith and sexual morality are interrelated. Faith corresponds to the *sefirah* of Malkhut (Kingship) and sexual morality to the *sefirah* of Yesod (Foundation), which is directly above Malkhut. Above them both is the *sefirah* of Chesed (Kindness) (see Charts, p. 344). A person who attains faith and sexual morality creates a vessel with which to draw down and receive God's kindness.

Abraham possessed both these attributes. He "believed" in God, and that was "considered as charity." The word "charity" corresponds to the *sefirah* of Yesod (which "gives"). Abraham was the first person to spread belief in God, and also the first to be circumcised (a sign of sexual purity) (*Likutey Moharan* I, 31:6). Therefore he is the paradigm of kindness.

》 *He believed in God, and He considered it as charity*

Charity reaches its perfection when one gives because God commanded him to—even if he is left with little money. Thus, we may read this verse as "He believed in God; the charity that he gave was considered as true charity."

This is the same concept as refraining from work on Shabbat. One who refrains from working solely because God has forbidden him to, and who believes that God will provide, demonstrates his faith in God (*Likutey Moharan* I, 31:2).

15:8   וַיֹּאמַר אֲדֹנָי יֱהֹוִה בַּמָּה אֵדַע כִּי אִירָשֶׁנָּה

"My Lord God, how will I know that I will inherit it?" he said.

》 *How will I know*

When Abraham questioned God's promise that he would inherit the Holy Land, he blemished faith, prayer and the Holy Land. This brought about a decree of 400 years of exile upon his descendants in Egypt—an idolatrous, materially-oriented nation that was distant from God, prayer and miracles.

When they descended to Egypt, Jacob and his sons intended to rectify this blemish. Jacob represents an all-encompassing gate through which prayers may ascend. There are also twelve gates of prayer, corresponding to the Twelve Tribes. Because Jacob and his sons represent perfected prayer, they were able to descend into the exile that had been brought about through Abraham's blemished prayer, and rectify it.

When this blemish was rectified and the time for the Exodus arrived, open miracles occurred. The Jews were redeemed and set out for the Holy Land, the inheritance of Abraham (*Likutey Moharan* I, 7:1; ibid., I, 9:6).

How will I know

This doubt and blemish of faith, which is a blemish of Divine Providence and *da'at* (cf. Abraham's words, "How will I *know*?") brought about the exile in Egypt. Furthermore, "a deep sleep fell upon Abram"—this also implies a fall from *da'at*, from awareness. This fall from *da'at* blemishes the Holy Land and causes exile and suffering (*Likutey Halakhot* I, p. 20a).

How will I know

Abraham's question displayed a blemish of *da'at*: "How will I *know*?" *Da'at* is represented by the Holy Land, which corresponds to holy intellect. To rectify this blemish in Abraham's descendants, God told him, "Your children will be strangers in a land that is not theirs" (Genesis 15:13). They would be exiled from the Holy Land, from *da'at*, from a tranquil state of mind, into "a land that is not theirs"—a turbulent state of mind (*Likutey Halakhot* V, p. 72).

How will I know

At the time of the Covenant Between the Pieces (see Genesis 15:9-21), Abraham had to decide which punishment his descendants would suffer should they sin. He chose exile as opposed to Gehinnom.

Nevertheless, there is one exception. Those who brazenly oppose people devoted to serving God are punished not with exile, but with Gehinnom (*Likutey Moharan* I, 22:12).

15:13   וַיֹּאמֶר לְאַבְרָם יָדֹעַ תֵּדַע כִּי־גֵר יִהְיֶה זַרְעֲךָ
בְּאֶרֶץ לֹא לָהֶם וַעֲבָדוּם וְעִנּוּ אֹתָם אַרְבַּע
מֵאוֹת שָׁנָה

**He said to Abram, "You will surely know
that your children will be strangers in
a land that is not theirs. They will serve
them and they will oppress them for four
hundred years."**

〉 *Your children will be strangers in a land that is not theirs*

Here God hinted to Abraham about all the future exiles the
Jews would have to endure in order to rectify the sparks of holiness
scattered throughout the world (*Likutey Halakhot* II, p. 130a).

15:14   וְגַם אֶת־הַגּוֹי אֲשֶׁר יַעֲבֹדוּ דָּן אָנֹכִי וְאַחֲרֵי־כֵן
יֵצְאוּ בִּרְכֻשׁ גָּדוֹל

**"I will also judge the nation that they will
serve, and afterwards they will leave with
great wealth."**

〉 *They will leave with great wealth*

This refers to *pidyonot* (redemption-money). When a *pidyon*
comes to the hands of a tzaddik, it can effect a redemption from
suffering and judgments. Thus, the Egyptian wealth that came into
the hands of the Jews mitigated the decree of exile from Abraham's
time (*Likutey Halakhot* I, p. 238).

16:8   וַיֹּאמַר הָגָר שִׁפְחַת שָׂרַי אֵי־מִזֶּה בָאת וְאָנָה
       תֵלֵכִי וַתֹּאמֶר מִפְּנֵי שָׂרַי גְּבִרְתִּי אָנֹכִי בֹּרַחַת

**"Hagar, maidservant of Sarai, where
are you coming from and where are you
going?" he said. "I am running away
from my mistress Sarai," she replied.**

❭ *I am running away from my mistress Sarai*

When Sarah, who represents the Kingdom of Holiness, becomes
manifest, then the maidservant Hagar, who represents the forces
of the Other Side, must flee (*Likutey Moharan* I, 36:3). This means that
when we draw the yoke of Heaven onto ourselves, we can gain
relief from the forces of evil.

16:11   וַיֹּאמֶר לָהּ מַלְאַךְ יְיָ הִנָּךְ הָרָה וְיֹלַדְתְּ בֵּן
       וְקָרָאת שְׁמוֹ יִשְׁמָעֵאל כִּי־שָׁמַע יְיָ אֶל־עָנְיֵךְ

**The angel of God said to her, "Behold!
You will conceive and give birth to a son,
and you will name him Ishmael, for God
has heard your prayer."**

❭ *God has heard your prayer*

The name *YiShMAEL* (ישמעאל, Ishmael) is composed of the
words *YiShMA EL* (ישמע אל, God will hear). *Yishmael* may also
be translated as "merchant," and the standard Hebrew word for
merchant, *socher* (סחר), has a related meaning of "encircling."

The Kabbalah speaks of a transcendental wisdom—an increased
revelation of Godliness—that encircles a person's intellect. When
he prays and God hears his prayer, he can attain that wisdom
(*Likutey Moharan* I, 7:9, ibid., I, 9:4).

17:1 וַיְהִי אַבְרָם בֶּן־תִּשְׁעִים שָׁנָה וְתֵשַׁע שָׁנִים וַיֵּרָא
יְיָ אֶל־אַבְרָם וַיֹּאמֶר אֵלָיו אֲנִי־אֵל שַׁדַּי הִתְהַלֵּךְ
לְפָנַי וֶהְיֵה תָמִים

**Abram was ninety-nine years old. God
appeared to Abram and said to him, "I am
El Shadai. Walk before me and be perfect."**

》 Walk before Me and be perfect

TaMiM (תמים, perfection) is simplicity. Because Abraham had simplicity, he attained perfection (*Likutey Halakhot* I, p. 246a).

》 Walk before Me and be perfect

The foreskin is a blemish (Rashi).

The foreskin represents falsehood; it is a blemish that does not belong where it is and must be removed. Just as the foreskin removes the Godly image from a person, falsehood removes a person from Godliness. Thus, the main means for perfection and attainment of a Godly image is through circumcision, the mark of truth (*Likutey Halakhot* V, p. 190).

》 Hit-halekh Lifanai

The word *hit-halekh* (התהלך, walk) represents the feet, symbolizing the lower, mundane levels of reality such as eating and earning a livelihood—i.e., the means that enable a person to stand on his feet. *Lifanai* (לפני, before Me) can also be translated as "to My Face." Abraham was so pure that he was able to elevate the mundane—the "feet"—to the level of God's Face, Divine Providence, which is associated with the Showbread (*Lechem HaPanim*—literally, "Bread of the Face"). A person who attains this level does not have to work for a living. Rather, all of nature will work on his behalf (*Likutey Moharan* I, 31:9).

17:5 וְלֹא־יִקָּרֵא עוֹד אֶת־שִׁמְךָ אַבְרָם וְהָיָה שִׁמְךָ
אַבְרָהָם כִּי אַב־הֲמוֹן גּוֹיִם נְתַתִּיךָ

**"No longer will you be called Abram. Your
name will be Abraham, for I have made you a
father of a multitude of nations."**

❱ Abram...Abraham...I will establish My covenant

The covenant is purity, the emblem of the tzaddik. When
the covenant is made, it reveals the name and greatness of the
tzaddik. Therefore Abraham's name was "enlarged" from Abram to
Abraham when he accepted the covenant (*Likutey Halakhot* I, p. 101a).

❱ Abram...Abraham...Sarai...Sarah

With the names Abram and Sarai, our first Patriarch and
Matriarch could not bear children. Before they could become
parents, both required the addition of the letter *hei* (ה) to their
names. This letter represents *da'at* (knowledge). (The letter
hei functions as the definite article—"the"—implying specific
knowledge.) A person can perfect his knowledge by teaching
others to serve God, for as he does so, their questions to him
sharpen his mind. Thus, by instructing others to serve God,
Abraham and Sarah attained this *hei* and were able to bear children
(*Likutey Moharan* I, 53).

The word *da'at* also implies a union that bears fruit (see above,
p. 117). A person can attain a level of knowledge so great that
God's knowledge is greater in only five areas (*Likutey Moharan* I, 53).
Abraham and Sarah attained that level, and were then able to bear
children.

17:10 זֹאת בְּרִיתִי אֲשֶׁר תִּשְׁמְרוּ בֵּינִי וּבֵינֵיכֶם וּבֵין
זַרְעֲךָ אַחֲרֶיךָ הִמּוֹל לָכֶם כָּל־זָכָר

"This is My covenant that you will keep between Me and you and your children after you: Every male must be circumcised."

⟩ Milah–The Covenant

Milah is exalted, for thirteen covenants were made over it (*Nedarim* 31b).

The number 13 represents the exalted level of Atik, the Keter, which also represents Length of Days and the Thirteen Attributes of Compassion. By performing the *milah*, we draw upon ourselves the sanctity of the Length of Days, or long life. Furthermore, by performing the circumcision, a person can attain a level of transcending time! (*Likutey Halakhot* V, p. 76a). Thus, *milah* is exalted, for these covenants can "lengthen a person's days." We can add that each person's day seems limited; it is, after all, only twenty-four hours long and contains its own distractions. But by guarding the covenant, one feels a decrease in time's pressure and can make the most out of his day.

17:14 וְעָרֵל זָכָר אֲשֶׁר לֹא־יִמּוֹל אֶת־בְּשַׂר עָרְלָתוֹ
וְנִכְרְתָה הַנֶּפֶשׁ הַהִוא מֵעַמֶּיהָ אֶת־בְּרִיתִי הֵפַר

"An uncircumcised male whose foreskin has not been circumcised—that soul will be cut off from its people; he has broken my covenant."

⟩ An uncircumcised male

From this verse, we learn that the *milah* is performed at the place where one can differentiate between male and female (Rashi).

ZaKhaR (זכר, male) is like *ZiKaRon* (זכרון, remembrance). *NaShim* (נשים, women) is like *NiShyon* (נשיון, forgetfulness). These are two distinct levels. One must strive to remember God and recall the World to Come. One must also forget the vanities, lusts and immorality of this world. And one must remove the foreskin—i.e., he must remove the foolishness that clouds the mind and blemishes the ability to remember and differentiate (*Likutey Halakhot* V, p. 150).

Parashat Vayeira

18:1   וַיֵּרָא אֵלָיו יְיָ בְּאֵלֹנֵי מַמְרֵא וְהוּא יֹשֵׁב פֶּתַח־הָאֹהֶל
כְּחֹם הַיּוֹם

**God appeared to him at the Trees of Mamre
while he was sitting at the opening to the
tent in the heat of the day.**

〕 *God appeared to him*

When Abraham was sick and weak (after his *milah*), specifically
then did he merit a revelation of God. The same applies to anyone
who is sick and weak—he merits the Divine Presence resting
upon him (*Nedarim* 40a). Similarly, on Chanukah and Purim, festivals
that fall on week (weak) days, one merits God's Presence (*Likutey
Halakhot* I, p. 24).

〕 *God appeared to him at the Trees of Mamre*

Mamre advised Abraham to perform the circumcision (Rashi).

The Trees of Mamre allude to the two Trees in the Garden of
Eden: the Tree of Life and the Tree of Knowledge of Good and Evil.
MaMRe (ממרא) is similar to *teMuRah* (תמורה, exchange), for there
is a path that leads to the Tree of Life and there is a Chambers
of Exchanges in which good and evil are mixed up, distorting a
person's path. Abraham represents the person who seeks God; by
virtue of his efforts, he finds the correct path and God appears
to him. Moreover, because of his great desire for Godliness, the
"Mamre" or Chambers of Exchanges itself gives Abraham the
advice to guard his covenant, to strive for holiness.

The Torah describes the extent of Abraham's desire for
Godliness: "He was sitting at the opening to the tent in the heat of
the day." When a person seeks spirituality, he must learn to wait
for an opening and never give up. He must wait patiently, despite
the "heat"—despite his burning desires. If he holds out, he merits
that God will appear to him. "He saw three wayfarers"—for the
ascent to holiness demands several efforts; one cannot enter on
the first try. "He ran"—because Abraham performed the *mitzvot*
with joy and zeal (*Likutey Halakhot* VI, p. 40a-80).

18:4   יִקַּח־נָא מְעַט־מַיִם וְרַחֲצוּ רַגְלֵיכֶם וְהִשָּׁעֲנוּ
תַּחַת הָעֵץ

**"Let a little water be brought, and wash
your feet. Recline beneath the tree."**

⟩ *Wash your feet*

Abraham thought they were Arabs who worship the dust of their
feet, and he was careful that idolatry should not enter his house
(Rashi).

Haughtiness and anger are akin to idolatry (*Sotah* 4b; cf. *Nedarim* 22a).

The "feet" correspond to a person's prayers. In order to attain
the mysteries of Torah, one must overcome haughtiness and anger,
and rectify his prayers (*Likutey Moharan* I, 10:6).

18:8   וַיִּקַּח חֶמְאָה וְחָלָב וּבֶן־הַבָּקָר אֲשֶׁר עָשָׂה וַיִּתֵּן
לִפְנֵיהֶם וְהוּא־עֹמֵד עֲלֵיהֶם תַּחַת הָעֵץ וַיֹּאכֵלוּ

**He took butter, milk, and the calf that he
had prepared and set it before them. He
stood over them beneath the tree, and
they ate.**

⟩ *The angels ate by Abraham*

Why did Abraham feel it was necessary to feed the angels? The
effort to purify one's eating is a major battle, one that angels do not
have to fight. Yet Abraham knew that one day the angels would try
to prevent God from giving the Torah to his children, the Jewish
people. The angels would claim that the Jews would be unable to
withstand all the tests to purify their eating and their souls in order
to merit the great gift of Torah.

When Moses ascended to Heaven to receive the Torah, the
angels indeed tried to push him away. God turned Moses' features
into those of Abraham and asked the angels, "Isn't he the one you
ate by?" The angels were silenced (*Shemot Rabbah* 28:1).

The angels visited Abraham after he had performed the mitzvah
of circumcision, which is categorically equivalent to accepting the

entire Torah. Therefore Abraham gave the angels something to eat, showing them the challenges that human beings must endure in the material world before they can ascend to true spirituality (*Likutey Halakhot* II, p. 136).

18:19 כִּי יְדַעְתִּיו לְמַעַן אֲשֶׁר יְצַוֶּה אֶת־בָּנָיו וְאֶת־בֵּיתוֹ אַחֲרָיו וְשָׁמְרוּ דֶּרֶךְ יְיָ לַעֲשׂוֹת צְדָקָה וּמִשְׁפָּט לְמַעַן הָבִיא יְיָ עַל־אַבְרָהָם אֵת אֲשֶׁר־דִּבֶּר עָלָיו

"For I have known him, that he will command his children and his household after him. They will observe the path of God, doing righteousness and justice, so that God will bring upon Abraham what He has told him."

⟩ *He will command his children*

The main devotion of the tzaddikim lies in drawing knowledge of God into the world for all generations (*Likutey Halakhot* II, p. 23a).

⟩ *He will command his children and his household after him. They will observe the path of God, doing righteousness and justice...Abraham prayed for the people of Sodom*

In our world, compassion and justice are not really compatible, but they are unified in God's system of reward and punishment. Even so, one must do his part to arouse Divine compassion during times of Divine judgment. Abraham knew this. Although an angel had already been sent to destroy Sodom, and although Abraham knew the people were sinners, he prayed for Sodom to be saved. While Abraham's prayers did not save the people of Sodom, he accomplished his objective. He managed to arouse Divine compassion towards Lot and his daughters, and through them, the soul of Mashiach was channeled to the world (Lot's older daughter gave birth to Moab, the ancestor of Ruth, the great-grandmother of King David, the ancestor of Mashiach). Abraham's example teaches us that we, too, must engage in prayer to arouse Divine compassion, even in times of justice and judgment (*Likutey Halakhot* VIII, p. 28b-29a).

⟩ *Doing righteousness and justice*

How can one do *tZeDaKaH* (צדקה, righteousness) and *mishpat* (judgment and/or justice) at the same time? By giving *tZeDaKaH* (צדקה, charity) to Torah scholars, one allows these scholars to pursue their Torah studies and draw *halakhic* conclusions—legal and binding judgments which bring forth *mishpat* (*Likutey Halakhot* VIII, p. 72b).

⟩ *He will command his children and his household after him. They will observe the path of God, doing righteousness and justice*

Rebbe Nachman testified that he was greatly motivated to serve God because of the stories about tzaddikim that he heard in his parent's home (*Rabbi Nachman's Wisdom* #138). This is the principal legacy that Abraham gave to us, his descendants, so that we should be able to "observe the path of God, doing righteousness and justice."

18:22   וַיִּפְנוּ מִשָּׁם הָאֲנָשִׁים וַיֵּלְכוּ סְדֹמָה וְאַבְרָהָם עוֹדֶנּוּ עֹמֵד לִפְנֵי יְיָ

The men turned away from there and went towards Sodom. Abraham was still standing before God.

⟩ *Abraham was still standing before God*

"Standing" represents prayer. When a person prays in a *makom kavua* (מקום קבוע, regular place), the God of Abraham will help him (*Berakhot* 6b).

Kavua (קבוע, regular) can also be translated as "persistently." Abraham represents the *sefirah* of Chesed, as in "The world is built on kindness (*chesed*)" (Psalms 89:3). When a person prays persistently, he can attain the equivalent of a new world—i.e., the manifestation of miracles (*Likutey Moharan* I, 44).

> *Abraham was still standing before God...Abraham drew near*

He drew near to pray (Rashi).

Abraham established the Morning Prayer (*Berakhot* 26b).

The Four Sons mentioned in the Pesach Haggadah allude to Isaac (the wise son), Esau (the wicked son), Jacob (the simple son), and Ishmael (the son who does not know how to ask). They are the children of Abraham.

Our Sages teach that Abraham established *Shacharit* (the Morning Prayer), which can perfect and rectify every type of person. The word *ShaChaRIT* (שחרית) is an acronym for *She'eino Yodei'a* (שאינו יודע, one who does not know), *Chakham* (חכם, the wise son), *Rasha* (רשע, the wicked son) and *Tam* (תם, the simple son) (*Likutey Moharan* I, 30:6).

18:27   וַיַּעַן אַבְרָהָם וַיֹּאמַר הִנֵּה־נָא הוֹאַלְתִּי לְדַבֵּר
אֶל־אֲדֹנָי וְאָנֹכִי עָפָר וָאֵפֶר

**Abraham answered and said, "Behold!
I desired to speak to my Lord, though
I am dust and ashes."**

> *I am dust and ashes*

To pray properly, one needs the qualities of both "dust" and "ashes." "Dust" refers to humility and to connecting oneself to tzaddikim who have died and are resting in the dust. "Ashes" corresponds to overcoming one's evil traits (*Likutey Moharan* I, 55:5).

> *I am dust*

Because the tzaddik is humble, he is comparable to the element of earth. And just as the earth draws objects to itself, so too, the tzaddik draws people to himself. However, some people resist that pull, because there exists a counterforce—the power of evil speech (*Likutey Moharan* I, 70).

⟩ *I am dust and ashes*

Because Abraham said, "I am dust (earth) and ashes," his descendants merited to two *mitzvot*: the earth of the *sotah* and the ashes of the Red Heifer (*Chullin* 88b).

Dust, or earth, represents a means of purification, an ability to "sift" through various ideas and viewpoints to see what is true and what is not. That is the function of the earth used in testing the *sotah*, the wanton woman (see Numbers 5:16-28). However, the ashes of the Red Heifer go one step further, purifying the impure while at the same time making the pure, impure (ibid., 19:1-10). These powers of purification stem from their source Above, which is extremely lofty. Abraham, who wanted very much to save Sodom and its inhabitants, pleaded with God that he was but "earth and ashes"—he tried to reveal the inherent good in the Sodomites by nullifying himself as "earth and ashes" in order to reach their root, from whence he could draw salvation and purification for them (*Likutey Halakhot* IV, p. 55a-110).

19:11   וְאֶת־הָאֲנָשִׁים אֲשֶׁר־פֶּתַח הַבַּיִת הִכּוּ בַּסַּנְוֵרִים מִקָּטֹן וְעַד־גָּדוֹל וַיִּלְאוּ לִמְצֹא הַפָּתַח

They struck the men who were at the door of the house with blindness, from the small to the great, and they tried in vain to find the door.

⟩ *They struck the men who were at the door of the house with blindness*

Petach (door) literally means "opening." A person must always search for the opening to holiness in order to enter through it. However, not everyone is worthy of entering. Those who are unworthy are misled by many problems and confusions that lead them away from the opening. Thus, "They struck the men who were at the door...with blindness"—they were prevented from finding the opening to holiness (*Likutey Halakhot* VII, p. 176a).

19:17 וַיְהִי כְהוֹצִיאָם אֹתָם הַחוּצָה וַיֹּאמֶר הִמָּלֵט עַל־
נַפְשֶׁךָ אַל־תַּבִּיט אַחֲרֶיךָ וְאַל־תַּעֲמֹד בְּכָל־הַכִּכָּר
הָהָרָה הִמָּלֵט פֶּן־תִּסָּפֶה

As they took them outside, one said, "Flee
for your life! Do not look back or stop
anywhere in the plain. Flee to the mountain
or else you will be swept away!"

》 Flee to the mountain

Flee to the "mountain"—to Abraham (Rashi).

A mountain is a place of refuge. The Torah is compared to a
"mountain," as is Abraham, the paradigm of kindness. When a
person faces difficulties, he can find refuge in the Torah and in
acts of kindness (*Likutey Moharan* I, 38:7).

19:30 וַיַּעַל לוֹט מִצּוֹעַר וַיֵּשֶׁב בָּהָר וּשְׁתֵּי בְנֹתָיו עִמּוֹ כִּי
יָרֵא לָשֶׁבֶת בְּצוֹעַר וַיֵּשֶׁב בַּמְּעָרָה הוּא וּשְׁתֵּי בְנֹתָיו

Lot went up from Tzoar and settled on the
mountain together with his two daughters,
since he was afraid to stay in Tzoar. He dwelt
in a cave, he and his two daughters.

》 He dwelt in a cave, he and his two daughters

I found My servant David. Where? In Sodom (*Bereishit Rabbah* 41:4).

From the time of Creation, King David's precious soul was
trapped in the clutches of the Other Side. In order to extricate such
a precious soul, God brought about a series of incidents. First Lot
slept with his own daughter, who gave birth to Moab. Then Judah
visited his daughter-in-law Tamar, who gave birth to Peretz. Ruth,
a descendant of Moab, converted to Judaism and married Boaz,
a descendant of Peretz. Eventually, King David was born of their
union. The reason King David suffered so much during his lifetime
was due to the depths in which his soul was trapped in the Other
Side, for the Other Side tried desperately to hang on to him (*Likutey
Halakhot* I, p. 104a-208).

20:5   הֲלֹא הוּא אָמַר־לִי אֲחֹתִי הִוא וְהִיא־גַם־הִוא
אָמְרָה אָחִי הוּא בְּתָם־לְבָבִי וּבְנִקְיֹן כַּפַּי
עָשִׂיתִי זֹאת

**"Didn't he say to me, 'She is my sister'?
And she also said, 'He is my brother.' In the
innocence of my heart and the purity of my
hands, I did this."**

》 *Didn't he say to me, "She is my sister"*

Abimelekh was surprised when God accused him of immorality
with Sarah; he thought he was innocent of any wrongdoing.
According to Abimelekh's perception of truth, Abraham was the
guilty party because he had led Abimelekh to believe that Sarah
was his sister and was not married. Therefore God told Abimelekh,
"I know you did what you did thinking you are innocent. But you
are not clean of immorality. Were you clean of immorality, you
would never have asked Abraham about Sarah in the first place.
Because you are so steeped in immorality, your perception of truth
is skewed and you think of yourself as innocent when you are not"
(*Likutey Halakhot* IV, p. 412-207a).

20:7   וְעַתָּה הָשֵׁב אֵשֶׁת־הָאִישׁ כִּי־נָבִיא הוּא וְיִתְפַּלֵּל
בַּעַדְךָ וֶחְיֵה וְאִם־אֵינְךָ מֵשִׁיב דַּע כִּי־מוֹת תָּמוּת
אַתָּה וְכָל־אֲשֶׁר־לָךְ

**"Now, return the man's wife, because he is a
prophet. He will pray for you, and you will live.
But if you do not return her, know that you
will surely die—you and all that is yours."**

》 *Return the man's wife*

The Patriarchs revealed God to the entire world through the
power of their prayer. In this regard, each of them referred
to the place of prayer by a different title. Abraham called it a
"mountain," Isaac called it a "field," and Jacob called it a "house"
(*Pesachim* 88a).

Abraham was the first to reveal God. Since very few people

were attuned to God at that time, this manifestation was called a "mountain" (cf. Genesis 22:2), which is not generally accessible.

Isaac further revealed God's presence in the world. When he established the Afternoon Prayer, he referred to the place of prayer as a "field" (cf. ibid., 24:63). A field is more accessible than a mountain. However, not everyone has a use for it.

Then, when Jacob prayed, he called the place of prayer a "house" (cf. ibid., 28:17), which is something that everyone needs.

Our mission is to elevate prayer from the conceptual levels of "mountain" and "field" to that of "house," so that everyone will recognize the power of prayer. In addition, while we must always pray to God, we must also acknowledge that only the tzaddikim know the true path of prayer. Thus, we must travel to a tzaddik and ask him to pray on our behalf and show us how to pray properly.

All of this is alluded to in the narrative of Abimelekh taking Abraham's wife Sarah and then being forced to return her.

The name *AVIMeLeKh* (אבימלך, Abimelekh) is comprised of two words, *AVI* (אבי, my desire) and *MeLeKh* (מלך, king), connoting a person who wishes to rule. Some people unjustifiably believe themselves to be tzaddikim and tell people to come to them for their prayers. They are compared to Abimelekh, who forcibly took Sarah (who represents both authority and prayer) for himself.

Such a false leader must rectify himself by returning prayer to the tzaddik, who can elevate prayers to their proper level. Therefore God told Abimelekh, "Return the man's wife, because he is a prophet." *HaSheiV* (השב, return) is an acronym for *Har* (הר, mountain), *Sadeh* (שדה, field) and *Bayit* (בית, house). Because Abimelekh damaged prayer, he now had to bring his prayers to the tzaddik, Abraham. In this way, he elevated prayer (*eishet*) through three levels until it became universally known. The word *EiSheT* (אשת, wife of) is an acronym for the phrase *Adonoy Sefatai Tiftach* (אדני שפתי תפתח, God, open my lips) (Psalms 51:17), connoting prayer.

Furthermore, Abraham is described as a prophet because the word *NaVI* (נביא, prophet) is related to the phrase *NiV sefatayim* (ניב שפתיים, movement of the lips), which also connotes prayer (*Likutey Moharan* I, 10:4). We learn from this that when a person's prayers reach perfection, he can attain prophecy (ibid., II, 1:8).

20:16   וּלְשָׂרָה אָמַר הִנֵּה נָתַתִּי אֶלֶף כֶּסֶף לְאָחִיךְ הִנֵּה
הוּא־לָךְ כְּסוּת עֵינַיִם לְכֹל אֲשֶׁר אִתָּךְ וְאֵת
כֹּל וְנֹכָחַת

To Sarah, he said, "Behold! I have given a thousand pieces of silver to your brother. Behold! Let it be a covering for the eyes for all who are with you, and to all the others."

⟩ *A covering for the eyes*

The eyes correspond to the four Supernal Colors associated with the *sefirot* of Chesed, Gevurah, Tiferet and Malkhut. Gold and silver represent the Supernal Colors. When a Jew gives his "gold and silver" (i.e., money) to charity, God's eyes look upon him with favor. In addition, this Jew makes it possible for other people's eyes to see these beautiful, Godly colors.

As long as a Jew is in possession of his money, which he will use to perform *mitzvot*, the money glows with supernal beauty. As a result, the nations desire it. But as soon as the money leaves the hands of the Jew, it no longer reveals the Supernal Colors and loses its luster.

The phrase "a covering for the eyes" can refer to a beautiful object that everyone gazes at. Everyone gazed at the money that Abimelekh gave to Abraham, for when it came into the latter's possession, it shone with supernal beauty (*Likutey Moharan* I, 25:4).

21:2   וַתַּהַר וַתֵּלֶד שָׂרָה לְאַבְרָהָם בֵּן לִזְקֻנָיו לַמּוֹעֵד
אֲשֶׁר־דִּבֶּר אֹתוֹ אֱלֹהִים

Sarah conceived and bore a son to Abraham in his old age, at the exact time at which God had told him.

⟩ *Sarah conceived and bore a son to Abraham in his old age*

Sarah conceived on Rosh HaShanah, the Day of Judgment (*Rosh HaShanah* 11a).

Isaac represents the *sefirah* of Gevurah, which is known as the Divine attribute of judgment and which represents fear and awe. King Solomon teaches: "The fear of God adds to one's days" (Proverbs 10:27). Thus, the birth of Isaac—who represents the fear of God—led to the state of "old age" (*Likutey Moharan* I, 60:5).

21:5   וְאַבְרָהָם בֶּן־מְאַת שָׁנָה בְּהִוָּלֶד לוֹ אֵת יִצְחָק בְּנוֹ

Abraham was one hundred years old when his son Isaac was born to him.

⟩ Isaac was born to Abraham

Many times a person wishes to enter the Gates of Holiness, but difficulties surround him and bar his way. This happens because he still has some impurities within himself that he might be unaware of, which must surface before he can expunge them.

Thus, at the beginning of his devotions, a person might experience a nocturnal emission or something similar. Similarly, Abraham first fathered the corrupt Ishmael. Only afterwards was he able to father Isaac, a son born in holiness (*Likutey Moharan* II, 117).

21:6   וַתֹּאמֶר שָׂרָה צְחֹק עָשָׂה לִי אֱלֹהִים כָּל־הַשֹּׁמֵעַ יִצְחַק־לִי

Sarah said, "God has made me rejoice. Whoever hears will laugh for me."

⟩ Yitzchak...God has made me rejoice

Isaac was the first child to be born Jewish. He was called *Yitzchak* because the holiness of the Jewish nation depends on their joy when doing *mitzvot* and in their service of God (*Likutey Halakhot* II, p. 146a).

⟩ The birth of Isaac...laughter

YitZChaK (יצחק, Isaac) is like *tZChoK* (צחק, laughter and joy). What is this joy? That from a seemingly mundane act, a union between a man and a woman, a holy tzaddik can be born. Why do we rejoice at a wedding? Because from this couple can come forth great tzaddikim who will rectify the world (*Likutey Halakhot* III, p. 52).

21:12 וַיֹּאמֶר אֱלֹהִים אֶל־אַבְרָהָם אַל־יֵרַע בְּעֵינֶיךָ עַל־
הַנַּעַר וְעַל־אֲמָתֶךָ כֹּל אֲשֶׁר תֹּאמַר אֵלֶיךָ שָׂרָה
שְׁמַע בְּקֹלָהּ כִּי בְיִצְחָק יִקָּרֵא לְךָ זָרַע

**God said to Abraham, "Do not be troubled
because of the boy and your maidservant.
All that Sarah tells you, listen to her voice,
for in Isaac will your offspring be called."**

》 For in Isaac will your offspring be called

Only some of Isaac's offspring would be holy and thus maintain
a link to Abraham (Rashi on Genesis 17:19).

These would be the children of Jacob, who would eventually
inherit the Holy Land. Esau is not considered a descendant of Isaac,
and therefore has no place in the Holy Land (*Likutey Moharan* I, 9:5).

21:23 וְעַתָּה הִשָּׁבְעָה לִּי בֵאלֹהִים הֵנָּה אִם־תִּשְׁקֹר לִי
וּלְנִינִי וּלְנֶכְדִּי כַּחֶסֶד אֲשֶׁר־עָשִׂיתִי עִמְּךָ תַּעֲשֶׂה
עִמָּדִי וְעִם־הָאָרֶץ אֲשֶׁר־גַּרְתָּה בָּהּ

**"Now, swear to me here by God that you
will not deal falsely with me, my children,
or my grandchildren. Show to me and to
the land in which you have been living the
same kindness that I have shown to you."**

》 Me, my children, or my grandchildren

Abraham mentioned three generations, because that is the extent
of a person's natural compassion for his descendants (Rashi).

This idea may be applied to the creation of the world. God
wished to reveal His compassion, and therefore created human
beings who would be able to appreciate it. But our ability to
appreciate God's compassion extends only from the moment of
Creation and onward—the flow of events that can be poetically
referred to as "me, my children, and my grandchildren" (*Likutey
Moharan* I, 64:6).

21:25 וְהוֹכֵחַ אַבְרָהָם אֶת־אֲבִימֶלֶךְ עַל־אֹדוֹת בְּאֵר
הַמַּיִם אֲשֶׁר גָּזְלוּ עַבְדֵי אֲבִימֶלֶךְ

**Abraham complained to Abimelekh
about the well of water that Abimelekh's
servants had stolen.**

Abraham dug wells

Abraham dug supernal wells, drawing down whatever knowledge of Godliness he could attain in order to teach the world about God (*Likutey Halakhot* II, p. 52a).

21:33 וַיִּטַּע אֶשֶׁל בִּבְאֵר שָׁבַע וַיִּקְרָא־שָׁם בְּשֵׁם יְיָ
אֵל עוֹלָם

**He planted a tree in Beersheba, and
there he called in the Name of God,
Master of the World.**

He planted a tree

He planted a tree to give its fruits to his guests, and afterwards to teach them to bless the One who feeds them (Rashi).

Through rectified eating, the act of eating for spiritual strength, one merits to call out to himself and others to seek God's Name (*Likutey Halakhot* II, p. 138).

Eating in holiness causes an elevation of God's Name, allowing It to become much more manifest in the world (ibid., III, p. 22).

21:34 וַיָּגָר אַבְרָהָם בְּאֶרֶץ פְּלִשְׁתִּים יָמִים רַבִּים

**Abraham stayed in the land of the
Philistines many days.**

Abraham stayed in the land of the Philistines many days

The fear of God adds to one's days (Proverbs 10:27).

When Abraham made his first trip to the territory of the Philistines, they did not fear God, as exemplified by Abimelekh's kidnapping of Sarah. Abraham was able to reveal the fear of God even in that land, and therefore he was able to stay there "many days"—corresponding to "adding to one's days."

The same thing occurred when Isaac entered the Philistine territory of Gerar (Genesis 26). Initially, their king, Abimelekh, lacked fear of God and forcibly took Rebecca to his home (until God told him to return her to Isaac). Isaac succeeded in bringing the fear of God to Gerar, and thus, "Isaac was there a long time" (Genesis 26:8)—corresponding to "adding to one's days" (*Likutey Moharan* I, 60:3).

22:2   וַיֹּאמֶר קַח־נָא אֶת־בִּנְךָ אֶת־יְחִידְךָ אֲשֶׁר־אָהַבְתָּ
אֶת־יִצְחָק וְלֶךְ־לְךָ אֶל־אֶרֶץ הַמֹּרִיָּה וְהַעֲלֵהוּ
שָׁם לְעֹלָה עַל אַחַד הֶהָרִים אֲשֶׁר אֹמַר אֵלֶיךָ

"Take your son, your only one, the one you love—Isaac—and go to the land of Moriah," He said. "Offer him there as a sacrifice on one of the mountains that I will tell you."

》 *On one of the mountains*

God did not tell Abraham immediately which mountain he should ascend. This is God's way: He momentarily withholds information from tzaddikim and afterwards reveals it to them. This increases their reward (Rashi).

God works the same way with us. He hides Himself to encourage us to seek and search for Him. Then, after we find God through our own efforts, we discover what He really wants from us (*Likutey Halakhot* VII, p. 110).

22:3   וַיַּשְׁכֵּם אַבְרָהָם בַּבֹּקֶר וַיַּחֲבֹשׁ אֶת־חֲמֹרוֹ וַיִּקַּח
אֶת־שְׁנֵי נְעָרָיו אִתּוֹ וְאֵת יִצְחָק בְּנוֹ וַיְבַקַּע עֲצֵי
עֹלָה וַיָּקָם וַיֵּלֶךְ אֶל־הַמָּקוֹם אֲשֶׁר־אָמַר־
לוֹ הָאֱלֹהִים

**Abraham woke up early in the morning
and saddled his donkey. He took his two
young men with him and his son Isaac.
He split the wood for the sacrifice and
got up and went to the place that God
had told him.**

》 *Abraham woke up early in the morning*

Abraham represents the morning, which is the quality of *chesed*
(kindness). One can act like Abraham and reveal God's kindness by
finding the "light" and good in other people.

22:4   בַּיּוֹם הַשְּׁלִישִׁי וַיִּשָּׂא אַבְרָהָם אֶת־עֵינָיו וַיַּרְא
אֶת־הַמָּקוֹם מֵרָחֹק

**On the third day, Abraham lifted his eyes
and saw the place from a distance.**

》 *He saw the place from a distance*

Abraham saw the place of the Temple, where his descendants
would serve God (*Yalkut Reuveini*).

But what he saw was at a distance, for at that moment he was
going to that very place to slaughter Isaac. Slaughtering Isaac
meant that he would not have any descendants. Yet in his prophetic
vision, Abraham saw his descendants serving in the Temple.

After God told him not to slaughter Isaac, Abraham set about
finding a wife for his son. This marriage, too, was distant, for Isaac
was thirty-seven years old and Rebecca had just been born. And
despite God's promise that the Land would be given to him and his
descendants, Abraham had to pay a fortune for a burial place for
Sarah. Then Rebecca was barren, and there were many trials and

tribulations yet to come with Esau and Jacob. Still, Abraham saw and knew that the salvation would come; it is just at a distance. Abraham teaches us never to give up hope, for the salvation, though in the distance, will come. In fact, if we look, we will see it coming. But we must have the patience to wait (*Likutey Halakhot* V, p. 136a-272).

22:5   וַיֹּאמֶר אַבְרָהָם אֶל־נְעָרָיו שְׁבוּ־לָכֶם פֹּה עִם־
הַחֲמוֹר וַאֲנִי וְהַנַּעַר נֵלְכָה עַד־כֹּה וְנִשְׁתַּחֲוֶה
וְנָשׁוּבָה אֲלֵיכֶם

Abraham said to his young men, "Stay here with the donkey, and the boy and I will go over there. We will worship and we will return to you."

》 *Stay here with the donkey*

IM ha-chamor (עם החמור, with the donkey) can also be read as *AM ha-chamor* (עם החמור, people of the donkey). This refers to people who remain saddled to their material desires and are thus compared to donkeys (*Ketuvot* 111a). But Abraham and Isaac went on from there to serve God (*Likutey Halakhot* I, p. 110a).

22:6   וַיִּקַּח אַבְרָהָם אֶת־עֲצֵי הָעֹלָה וַיָּשֶׂם עַל־יִצְחָק
בְּנוֹ וַיִּקַּח בְּיָדוֹ אֶת־הָאֵשׁ וְאֶת־הַמַּאֲכֶלֶת וַיֵּלְכוּ
שְׁנֵיהֶם יַחְדָּו

Abraham took the wood for the offering and put it on his son Isaac. He took the fire and the knife in his hand. The two of them went together.

》 *He took…the ma'akhelet*

All that the Jews receive in this world is due to the merit that Abraham earned by taking the *ma'akhelet* [to slaughter Isaac] (*Bereishit Rabbah* 56:3).

Ma'akhelet (knife) literally means "feeding." When a slaughterer is worthy, he causes people to be fed, insofar as the merit of his mitzvah brings bounty to the entire world. Conversely, an unworthy slaughterer causes poverty *(Likutey Moharan* I, 37:5).

22:9   וַיָּבֹאוּ אֶל־הַמָּקוֹם אֲשֶׁר אָמַר־לוֹ הָאֱלֹהִים וַיִּבֶן
שָׁם אַבְרָהָם אֶת־הַמִּזְבֵּחַ וַיַּעֲרֹךְ אֶת־הָעֵצִים
וַיַּעֲקֹד אֶת־יִצְחָק בְּנוֹ וַיָּשֶׂם אֹתוֹ עַל־הַמִּזְבֵּחַ
מִמַּעַל לָעֵצִים

They came to the place that God had told him. Abraham built the altar there and arranged the wood. He bound his son Isaac and put him on the altar, on top of the wood.

⟩ *He bound his son Isaac*

This was the most difficult of all of Abraham's ten tests *(Sanhedrin 89b).*

Judging by Abraham's righteousness, the Binding of Isaac does not really constitute a test. Even a simple person would be able to withstand such a test if God appeared to him. Abraham's real test was not to question God at all, though the messages he had received from Him seemed contradictory. First God had promised that the Jewish people would be born through Isaac. Now He was calling for the sacrifice of Isaac. Yet Abraham did not dwell on this contradiction. He knew that God's ways are not man's ways; God transcends all and therefore can do opposing things that are incomprehensible to man.

Thus, Abraham named the mountain "The Mountain That God Sees" (Genesis 22:14). Though man cannot see or understand God's ways, "God sees." In fact, the very mountaintop upon which Isaac was to be sacrificed was the Temple Mount, where Abraham's descendants would ultimately serve God *(Likutey Halakhot* VIII, p. 34b-35a).

⟩ *He bound his son Isaac*

In the end, Abraham did not sacrifice Isaac. But the two of them gained tremendous merit from their immense desire to perform God's will. This great desire for self-sacrifice for God was implanted in the Jewish nation, which explains why we see so many, many Jews throughout the generations who have willingly sacrificed themselves for God (*Likutey Halakhot* VIII, p. 163b).

22:12 וַיֹּאמֶר אַל־תִּשְׁלַח יָדְךָ אֶל־הַנַּעַר וְאַל־תַּעַשׂ לוֹ
מְאוּמָה כִּי עַתָּה יָדַעְתִּי כִּי־יְרֵא אֱלֹהִים אַתָּה
וְלֹא חָשַׂכְתָּ אֶת־בִּנְךָ אֶת־יְחִידְךָ מִמֶּנִּי

"Do not lay your hand against the boy or make a mark on him," he said. "For now I know that you are a God-fearing person; you did not withhold your son, your only one, from Me."

〉 *You did not withhold*

ChaSaKhta (חשכת, withheld) is similar to *ChoSheKh* (חשך, darkness). The "darkness" of doubts holds a person back from holiness. However, even within the "darkness," one can find the light of Godliness (*Likutey Moharan* I, 115).

Parashat Chayei Sarah

23:1   וַיִּהְיוּ חַיֵּי שָׂרָה מֵאָה שָׁנָה וְעֶשְׂרִים שָׁנָה וְשֶׁבַע
שָׁנִים שְׁנֵי חַיֵּי שָׂרָה

**Sarah's lifetime was one hundred years
and twenty years and seven years, the
years of Sarah's life.**

❯ *One hundred years and twenty years and seven years,
the years of Sarah's life*

They were all equal in goodness (Rashi).

One hundred years represent the one hundred blessings we
should recite daily. All these blessings are drawn through our
prayers—i.e., "the words of our mouths"—which are formed from
the twenty-seven letters of the Hebrew alphabet (there are twenty-
two letters plus five final consonants). Thus, the one hundred
blessings and twenty-seven letters combine to make "Sarah's
life"—a good life, a life of Godliness (*Likutey Halakhot* V, p. 458).

❯ *One hundred years and twenty years and seven years*

At one hundred, she was like a twenty-year-old, who is without
sin. At twenty, she was as beautiful as a girl of seven. And all her
years were equal in goodness (Rashi).

There are four levels of humility: to be more humble than those
who are greater than you, to be more humble than your equals, to
be more humble than those who are lesser than you, and, if you
are the most humble person, to become even more humble (*Likutey
Moharan* I, 14:4). The essence of life, especially in the World to Come,
is one's humility (see *Likutey Moharan* II, 72).

Sarah reflects the fourth level of humility, that of being the most
humble person. Whether she was one hundred, twenty or seven,
she kept humbling herself more. And "all her days were good," for
in this way, she attained true humility, which is the essence of life
(*Likutey Halakhot* V, p. 180a).

》 *One hundred years and twenty years and seven years, the years of Sarah's life*

At one hundred, she was like a twenty-year-old, who is without sin. At twenty, she was as beautiful as a girl of seven. And all her years were equal in goodness (Rashi).

The word *shanah* (year) appears four times in this verse, corresponding to the four passages included in the *tefilin*, which brings life. Just as each phase of Sarah's life was full of goodness and self-renewal—one hundred was like twenty was like seven—and Sarah always renewed her life with fresh vitality, so too, the *tefilin* empower us to renew our lives (*Likutey Halakhot* I, p. 79a).

23:3   וַיָּקָם אַבְרָהָם מֵעַל פְּנֵי מֵתוֹ וַיְדַבֵּר אֶל־בְּנֵי־חֵת לֵאמֹר

Abraham got up from before his dead and spoke to the children of Heth, saying.

》 *He spoke to the children of Heth*

"The children of Heth" are mentioned ten times in this passage. This teaches that when one helps a tzaddik acquire his possession, it is as if he fulfills the Ten Commandments (*Bereishit Rabbah* 58:8).

The sanctity of the Holy Land was established at the time of Creation but was not revealed until Abraham bought the property containing the Cave of Makhpeilah from Ephron. Abraham had to struggle with Ephron to buy the property, because this purchase represented the establishment of faith, which corresponds to the Holy Land (see above, p. 37). By revealing the sanctity of the Land that had been established at Creation, Abraham also invoked the Ten Commandments, which are rooted in the Ten Sayings of Creation (*Likutey Halakhot* V, p. 238).

23:8 וַיְדַבֵּר אִתָּם לֵאמֹר אִם־יֵשׁ אֶת־נַפְשְׁכֶם לִקְבֹּר אֶת־
מֵתִי מִלְּפָנַי שְׁמָעוּנִי וּפִגְעוּ־לִי בְּעֶפְרוֹן בֶּן־צֹחַר

He spoke with them, saying, "If it is your desire to bury my dead from before me, hear me and intercede for me with Ephron the son of Tzochar."

⟩ If it is your desire

NaFShekhem (נפשכם, your desire) comes from the same root as NeFeSh (נפש, soul). The extent of one's desire is seen in the devotions of his soul. If his RatZon (רצון, will) to serve God is great, he will RatZ (רץ, run) to serve God (Likutey Halakhot II, p. 262).

⟩ Ephron

The name EFRon (עפרון) shares the same Hebrew root as AFaR (עפר, earth), indicating laziness and depression, a lack of faith. Faith, in contrast, is compared to sprouting and growth (Likutey Moharan I, 155). Thus, the life and renewed vitality that tefilin engenders is concealed by Ephron, by laziness. Abraham, the man of faith, can remove the life force from Ephron and add light to it (Likutey Halakhot I, p. 156-158).

23:9 וְיִתֶּן־לִי אֶת־מְעָרַת הַמַּכְפֵּלָה אֲשֶׁר־לוֹ אֲשֶׁר
בִּקְצֵה שָׂדֵהוּ בְּכֶסֶף מָלֵא יִתְּנֶנָּה לִי בְּתוֹכְכֶם
לַאֲחֻזַּת־קָבֶר

"Let him give me the Cave of Makhpeilah, which is his, in the corner of his field. Let him give it to me for the full price, in your presence, for a burial ground."

⟩ The Cave of Makhpeilah

A great light existed in the Cave of Makhpeilah, shining out from the Garden of Eden. But Ephron did not see this light, and so he was eager to sell the cave. Abraham did see the light, and he knew that it marked the gateway to the Garden of Eden. Thus, he was eager to purchase the cave.

Similarly, both the common person and the tzaddik are exposed to awesome levels of Godliness that abound in the world, but only the tzaddik appreciates them. A wise person strives to overcome his foolishness and material desires in order to come close to the tzaddik, who can then reveal to him that awesome Divine beauty (*Likutey Moharan* I, 17:2).

〉 The Cave of Makhpeilah

Makhpeilah (literally, "double") indicates the four couples that were buried there: Adam and Eve, Abraham and Sarah, Isaac and Rebecca, and Jacob and Leah (Rashi).

These four couples are symbolized by the *tefilin*, in the four passages of the hand *tefilin* and the four passages of the head *tefilin*. One can "enter the cave" by putting on *tefilin* (*Likutey Halakhot* I, p. 156).

23:16 וַיִּשְׁמַע אַבְרָהָם אֶל־עֶפְרוֹן וַיִּשְׁקֹל אַבְרָהָם לְעֶפְרֹן אֶת־הַכֶּסֶף אֲשֶׁר דִּבֶּר בְּאָזְנֵי בְנֵי־חֵת אַרְבַּע מֵאוֹת שֶׁקֶל כֶּסֶף עֹבֵר לַסֹּחֵר

Abraham heard Ephron, and Abraham weighed out to Ephron the silver that he had mentioned in the hearing of the children of Heth—four hundred silver shekels in negotiable currency.

〉 Four hundred silver shekels in negotiable currency

For something as holy as the Cave of Makhpeilah, which is the portal to the Garden of Eden and the gateway through which all souls pass after death, Abraham was willing to pay top dollar rather than receive it as a gift. This is because Jewish money that is used for the performance of *mitzvot* and Torah study is itself very holy, and has the power to subdue the *kelipot*. By purchasing the cave, Abraham indicated that he was willing to give of his wealth to subdue the *kelipot* that would surround this holy place. In this way, he revealed the spirituality and Godliness that lay within (*Likutey Halakhot* VIII, p. 10b).

❊ *Four hundred silver shekels*

Kesef (כסף, silver) is related to *KiSuFin* (כסופין, yearning). The 400 silver shekels represent the 400 worlds of yearning that the tzaddikim will attain in the World to Come (*Zohar* I, 123b).

The greater a person's spiritual thirst, the greater his pleasure when he quenches it. The reward of the tzaddikim in the World to Come will be the quenching of their great thirst for God (*Rabbi Nachman's Wisdom* #259).

❊ *Abraham bought the Cave of Makhpeilah*

The purchase of the Cave of Makhpeilah constituted the beginning of the conquest of the Holy Land. Abraham bought it from the children of Heth, the first of the seven nations. *CheT* (חת) represents *ChaYaT* (חית, wild beast) (Psalms 68:31). The Holy Land cannot be conquered unless we "break the beast" within us (*Likutey Halakhot* II, p. 94).

24:1   וְאַבְרָהָם זָקֵן בָּא בַּיָּמִים וַי״ בֵּרַךְ אֶת־אַבְרָהָם בַּכֹּל

Abraham was old, advanced in years, and God blessed Abraham with everything.

❊ *Abraham was old*

Until Abraham prayed for it, people didn't age. Abraham and Isaac looked alike and no one could tell them apart. So Abraham prayed that he would appear old (*Bava Metzia* 87a).

The word *zaken* (old) also refers to wisdom (*Kiddushin* 32b). The idea of becoming "old" is rooted in the supernal wisdom, and from wisdom devolves a person's imagination and faith.

Abraham was the first to reveal faith in God. Revealing faith represents both a clarification of one's imagination (of which faith is an integral part) and an eventual attainment of intellect (which represents the truth—i.e., true knowledge of what one's faith is). Because Abraham engaged in searching for faith and truth, he merited to become a *zaken*, an elder (*Likutey Halakhot* V, p. 92).

⟩ Abraham was old...and God blessed Abraham with everything

"Old" represents wisdom. Through wisdom, Abraham was blessed with everything—which is to say, he attained peace (*Likutey Moharan* I, 27:7).

When a person attains the level of being "old"—i.e., a wise elder—he is blessed with great wealth. This wealth enables him to delve deeply into Torah mysteries and deepen his understanding of Godliness (see ibid., I, 60:2).

⟩ Ba be-yamim

Ba be-yamim (advanced in years) can also be translated as "he came with his days." Abraham infused each day with his attribute of kindness (*Likutey Moharan* I, 84).

⟩ Ba be-yamim

There are a number of principal levels of holiness, with interim levels between them. One must strive to ascend from level to level, taking care not to skip any of the interim levels.

Ba be-yamim (advanced in years) may also be translated as "he entered into many days." Abraham utilized every day and every moment of every day. Thus, he attained awesome levels of holiness, including the holiness found within the interim levels.

Even if a person does not utilize his days properly, he must at least strive to attain the principal levels of holiness, running quickly from one to the other (*Likutey Moharan* II, 59).

⟩ Bakol

Abraham had a daughter whose name was Bakol (*Bava Batra* 16b).

Abraham's "daughter" corresponds to faith (*Likutey Moharan* I, 57:4). Just as a person nurtures his daughter, so must he nurture his faith.

Abraham's "daughter" also corresponds to blessings and prayer (ibid., II, 83).

⟩ Bakol

The numerical value of the word *bakol* (בכל, with everything) is equivalent to that of the word *bayam* (בים, in the sea).

Abraham represents the *sefirah* of Chesed (Kindness), which is the first of the lower seven *sefirot*. The first six of the lower seven *sefirot* comprise the *partzuf* of Ze'er Anpin, and the last is the *sefirah* of Malkhut (Kingship). Abraham's "daughter" is Malkhut, which corresponds to holy speech and to the sea. Malkhut is a product of Chesed (*Likutey Moharan* I, 38:8).

24:2 וַיֹּאמֶר אַבְרָהָם אֶל־עַבְדּוֹ זְקַן בֵּיתוֹ הַמֹּשֵׁל בְּכָל־ אֲשֶׁר־לוֹ שִׂים־נָא יָדְךָ תַּחַת יְרֵכִי

Abraham said to his servant, the elder of his household, who was in charge of everything he owned, "Place your hand under my thigh."

〉 *His servant, the elder of his household, who was in charge of everything he owned*

> This servant was Eliezer, who possessed his master's Torah and was an authority of his master's studies (*Yoma* 28b).

The firmament, which was made on the Second Day of Creation, serves as a partition and implies the presence of a covenant between two sides. There are two types of firmament. The upper firmament, which divides between the upper waters and the lower waters (i.e., between Heaven and earth, or between Ze'er Anpin and Malkhut), corresponds to sexual morality, which is represented by the *sefirah* of Yesod that differentiates Ze'er Anpin from Malkhut and joins them as well. The lower firmament, which divides between the pure and the impure, corresponds to Torah knowledge, which explicates the differences between the two.

Abraham corresponds to the upper firmament and sexual morality. Eliezer, Abraham's servant, corresponds to the lower firmament and Torah knowledge (Eliezer mastered all of Abraham's teachings [ibid.]). A person must strive to attain a high level of sexual morality (like Abraham) and Torah knowledge (like Eliezer) in order to be as perfected as possible, and to enable God's kindness to devolve from the highest point of Ze'er Anpin to the realms of the impure so that it may purify them (see *Likutey Moharan* I, 31:5-6).

24:8 וְאִם־לֹא תֹאבֶה הָאִשָּׁה לָלֶכֶת אַחֲרֶיךָ וְנִקִּיתָ
מִשְּׁבֻעָתִי זֹאת רַק אֶת־בְּנִי לֹא תָשֵׁב שָׁמָּה

"But if the woman does not want to follow
you, you will be absolved from this oath of
mine. Only do not bring my son there."

》 *If the woman does not want to follow you*

If a wife does not comply with her husband's wishes, it is
because he does not guard his covenant properly. The husband
represents the *sefirah* of Yesod, through which bounty from Above
is channeled to Malkhut, which represents the wife. If a man's
foundation of sexual morality is misdirected, then the bounty
he channels is also misdirected. Since his wife does not receive
a direct flow of bounty from him, she naturally turns elsewhere
for it. A man can always strive to better himself and rectify his
covenant; the most propitious time to do this is during the Hebrew
month of Elul, the time of introspection and repentance before
Rosh HaShanah.

Abraham transmitted this knowledge to Eliezer when he told
him to seek a wife for Isaac. This is alluded to in Abraham's words
Ve-im Lo toveh ha-isha Lalekhet Acharekha (ואם לא תאבה האשה ללכת
אחריך, if the woman does not want to follow you). The initial
letters of the first two and last two words of this phrase spell
ELUL (אלול). The two middle words, *toveh ha-isha*, literally mean
"the woman will desire." In other words, after a man actualizes the
meaning of Elul—i.e., repentance—his wife will follow his lead
(*Likutey Moharan* II, 87).

24:14 וְהָיָה הַנַּעֲרָ אֲשֶׁר אֹמַר אֵלֶיהָ הַטִּי־נָא כַדֵּךְ וְאֶשְׁתֶּה
וְאָמְרָה שְׁתֵה וְגַם־גְּמַלֶּיךָ אַשְׁקֶה אֹתָהּ הֹכַחְתָּ
לְעַבְדְּךָ לְיִצְחָק וּבָהּ אֵדַע כִּי־עָשִׂיתָ חֶסֶד עִם־אֲדֹנִי

**"If I say to a girl, 'Please tip your jug and I
will drink,' and she says, 'Drink, and I will also
water your camels'—she is the one that You
have designated for your servant Isaac. In this
I will know that You have done kindness with
my master."**

⟫ Eliezer seeks Isaac's mate

Isaac represents strict judgments that must be mitigated. Strict
judgments are generally caused by sin, which removes the sparks
of holiness from a person and forces him to work hard in his
devotions in order to recover them. Similarly, our Sages teach
that one's mate is considered "lost" until he marries (*Kiddushin*
2b), indicating that until one marries, he is under strict judgment
(because of his "lost" mate). The story of Isaac seeking his mate
alludes to both concepts. The Torah goes into great detail about
Eliezer's travels to find Rebecca, and even repeats the story, all
because Isaac (i.e., judgments) had "lost" his mate and had to seek
her (*Likutey Halakhot* II, p. 95a).

24:15 וַיְהִי־הוּא טֶרֶם כִּלָּה לְדַבֵּר וְהִנֵּה רִבְקָה יֹצֵאת
אֲשֶׁר יֻלְּדָה לִבְתוּאֵל בֶּן־מִלְכָּה אֵשֶׁת נָחוֹר אֲחִי
אַבְרָהָם וְכַדָּהּ עַל־שִׁכְמָהּ

**He had not yet finished speaking when—
behold!—Rebecca came out, she who had
been born to Bethuel the son of Milkah, the
wife of Nachor, the brother of Abraham—
with a jug on her shoulder.**

⟫ He had not yet finished speaking

One who guards his covenant merits to perfected prayer
(*Likutey Moharan* I, 50). Eliezer represents a guarded covenant (see

Likutey Moharan I, 31:5). Eliezer's prayers were secure in his mouth. Therefore his prayers were accepted immediately, even before he finished speaking (*Likutey Halakhot* I, p. 430).

24:63 וַיֵּצֵא יִצְחָק לָשׂוּחַ בַּשָּׂדֶה לִפְנוֹת עָרֶב וַיִּשָּׂא
עֵינָיו וַיַּרְא וְהִנֵּה גְמַלִּים בָּאִים

**Isaac went out to pray in the field
towards evening. He lifted his eyes and
saw—behold!— camels were coming.**

〉 *Isaac went out to pray in the field*

It is propitious to pray in fields surrounded by nature. Then all of the grasses and other forces of nature, which continuously sing God's praises, lend their strength to one's prayers (*Likutey Moharan* II, 1:11).

Parashat Toldot

25:19 וְאֵלֶּה תּוֹלְדֹת יִצְחָק בֶּן־אַבְרָהָם אַבְרָהָם הוֹלִיד
אֶת־יִצְחָק

**These are the generations of Isaac, the son
of Abraham: Abraham gave birth to Isaac.**

❧ Isaac, the son of Abraham

Isaac represents awe and fear of God. Abraham was the first to
seek God; he is the father of all converts. Abraham had not received
the Torah, just a burning desire to serve God. His desire, longing
and love brought about the revelation of God and the ability to fear
Him and stand in awe of Him. Thus, Isaac is the son of Abraham
(*Likutey Halakhot* VII, p. 234).

❧ Abraham gave birth to Isaac

The verse teaches us that Abraham gave birth to Isaac, because
people refused to accept that Sarah became pregnant from
Abraham (Rashi).

AVRaHaM (אברהם, Abraham) has the same letters as *AiVeR MaH*
(אבר מה), which the *Zohar* explains as a "sealed organ," unable to
have children (see *Likutey Moharan* I, 53). When Isaac was born, the
Philistines rejected the notion that a great tzaddik like Abraham
could actually engage in the mundane act of marital relations.
Therefore they claimed that Sarah conceived from Abimelekh. The
Torah testifies that it was indeed Abraham who, though he totally
negated his materialistic desires, was able to have children (*Likutey
Halakhot* III, p. 52).

❧ Abraham gave birth to Isaac

Even though it is written, "Isaac, the son of Abraham," it was
necessary to state that "Abraham gave birth to Isaac" because
cynics of that generation were claiming that Sarah had become
pregnant by Abimelekh. She and Abraham had been together
for many years and she had not conceived by him. Therefore
God made Isaac's facial features so similar to Abraham's that
everyone had to admit that "Abraham gave birth to Isaac" (Rashi).

The *sefirah* of Chesed precedes the *sefirah* of Gevurah. When a person's acts of kindness (*chesed*) are pure, then the judgments (*gevurot*) that may issue forth afterwards are holy and serve to direct him towards God. But if his acts of kindness are impure, then the judgments that follow are tainted as well, and bring suffering that distances him from God.

Abraham represents the *sefirah* of Chesed and Isaac, the *sefirah* of Gevurah. Holy and pure Chesed leads to holy and pure Gevurah. Because Abraham was a holy source, Isaac, too, was holy, and even sacrificed himself completely for God's sake. This could not have happened had Isaac come from a blemished source such as Abimelekh (*Likutey Moharan* I, 74).

25:21 וַיֶּעְתַּר יִצְחָק לַיי לְנֹכַח אִשְׁתּוֹ כִּי עֲקָרָה הִוא
וַיֵּעָתֶר לוֹ יְיָ וַתַּהַר רִבְקָה אִשְׁתּוֹ

Isaac prayed to God opposite his wife, since she was barren. God acceded to him and his wife Rebecca conceived.

》 *Isaac prayed to God opposite his wife*

Isaac represents the attribute of judgment (Gevurah), and the "Torah was given from the mouth of *gevurah*" (see *Eruvin* 54b); therefore Isaac represents the Torah. Yet the fact that he represents Torah was insufficient for him to break the decree of childlessness. He had to attain prayer and persist in his prayers in order to mitigate the decree. This prayer also required the prayers of Rebecca to mitigate the decree. The combined numerical value of the names *YitZChaK* (יצחק) and *RiVKaH* (רבקה) is the same as the numerical value of the word *TeFiLaH* (תפלה, prayer), for both of them had to invoke the power of prayer (*Likutey Halakhot* VIII, p. 33a-33b).

25:22 וַיִּתְרֹצֲצ֤וּ הַבָּנִים֙ בְּקִרְבָּ֔הּ וַתֹּ֣אמֶר אִם־כֵּ֔ן לָ֥מָּה
זֶּ֖ה אָנֹ֑כִי וַתֵּ֖לֶךְ לִדְרֹ֥שׁ אֶת־יְהֹוָֽה

**The children struggled within her. "Why
is this happening to me?" she said, and
went to ask of God.**

She went to ask of God

She went to the house of study of Shem and Eber (Rashi).

The main strength of the house of study is its leaders, the
tzaddikim by whose name it is known (*Likutey Halakhot* II, p. 61a).

25:23 וַיֹּ֨אמֶר יְהֹוָ֜ה לָ֗הּ שְׁנֵ֤י גֹיִים֙ בְּבִטְנֵ֔ךְ וּשְׁנֵ֣י לְאֻמִּ֔ים מִמֵּעַ֖יִךְ
יִפָּרֵ֑דוּ וּלְאֹם֙ מִלְאֹ֣ם יֶֽאֱמָ֔ץ וְרַ֖ב יַעֲבֹ֥ד צָעִֽיר

**God said to her, "Two nations are in your
womb, and two governments will be
separated from your insides. Rulership will
pass from one government to the other,
and the greater will serve the younger."**

Two nations are in your womb…Rulership will pass from one government to the other

When one ascends, the other descends (Rashi).

Rashi explains the phrase "Rulership will pass from one
government to the other" to mean that Jacob and Esau would
battle constantly, and that the ascent of one would result in the
descent of the other. This dynamic applies to every individual's
life as well. A person cannot seek spirituality while at the same
time indulging in materialism, for the ascent of one must mean
the descent of the other. A person must exert himself to engage
in spiritual endeavors, for only in this way can he maintain and
intensify his connection to God (*Likutey Moharan* I, 1:2).

❭ Two nations are in your womb…Rulership will pass from one government to the other

Even in the womb, Jacob strove for Godliness and Esau sought idolatry. Rebecca was told that she was not pregnant with one son who would serve both God and idols, but with twins, one of whom possessed faith in God and the other, faith in idols.

As we learn from Rashi, a person cannot have it both ways— either he believes in God or he is an idolater. By strengthening our faith, we can defeat those traits that correspond to idolatry— haughtiness, anger and misplaced faith (*Likutey Moharan* I, 35:8). In addition, when we strengthen our faith, we weaken and defeat false faiths (ibid., I, 57:8).

Rashi's comments apply as well to our power of imagination, as opposed to our intellectual wisdom. Only when we subdue our illusory thoughts will we attain true wisdom (ibid., I, 25:1).

❭ Rulership will pass from one government to the other

When one ascends, the other descends (Rashi).

When holy writings are revealed, the false wisdom of atheism can be subdued (*Likutey Halakhot* III, p. 118a).

25:25 וַיֵּצֵא הָרִאשׁוֹן אַדְמוֹנִי כֻּלּוֹ כְּאַדֶּרֶת שֵׂעָר וַיִּקְרְאוּ
שְׁמוֹ עֵשָׂו

The first one came out red, like a hairy garment all over. They named him Esau.

❭ The first one came out red, like a hairy garment all over

"Red"—a sign that he would be a spiller of blood. "Like a hairy garment all over"—full of hair like a woolen *talit* that is full of hair (Rashi).

The color red refers to a blemish of one's garments (i.e., *talit*). If one blemishes his garments—i.e., he blemishes his covenant—it is akin to shedding blood (*Likutey Halakhot* I, p. 72).

25:26 וְאַחֲרֵי־כֵן יָצָא אָחִיו וְיָדוֹ אֹחֶזֶת בַּעֲקֵב עֵשָׂו
וַיִּקְרָא שְׁמוֹ יַעֲקֹב וְיִצְחָק בֶּן־שִׁשִּׁים שָׁנָה
בְּלֶדֶת אֹתָם

Afterwards his brother came out, his hand grasping onto Esau's heel. He named him Jacob. Isaac was sixty years old when she gave birth to them.

⟩ His hand grasping onto Esau's heel

Jacob will never let Esau be victorious and trap forever the souls waiting for rectification. He will grab hold of Esau and eventually remove those souls from his grip. Thus, he is called *YaAKoV* (יעקב), alluding to the *EiKeV* (עקב, heel); he is also called *YiSRaEL* (ישראל), which has the same letters as *LY RoSh* (לי ראש, I have a head—i.e., intellect), indicating that all souls will eventually be elevated to the highest levels (*Likutey Halakhot* II, p. 450 -226a).

25:27 וַיִּגְדְּלוּ הַנְּעָרִים וַיְהִי עֵשָׂו אִישׁ יֹדֵעַ צַיִד אִישׁ שָׂדֶה
וְיַעֲקֹב אִישׁ תָּם יֹשֵׁב אֹהָלִים

The boys grew up. Esau became a man who knows hunting, a man of the field, but Jacob was a wholesome man, dwelling in tents.

⟩ Jacob was a wholesome man, dwelling in tents

I am God, your Lord, since the Land of Egypt; the time will come when I will cause you to dwell in tents as in days of old (Hosea 12:10).

As in the days of Jacob when he studied in the tents of Shem and Eber (Rashi, loc. cit.).

Prior to the Giving of the Torah, the Patriarchs and other righteous individuals gathered in tents of learning where faith—how to attain it and how to reveal it to the world—was the main subject. As proof, in Talmudic times, the version of Tractate *Avodah Zarah* (which deals with idolatry) had 400 chapters, compared to our present-day edition which has only five chapters (*Avodah Zarah* 14b), for the ancients had developed extensive and profound teachings about spreading faith. These houses of study will again sprout in the Future, in the time of Mashiach (*Likutey Halakhot* VIII, p. 94a).

⟩ Jacob was a wholesome man

"Jacob" alludes to intellect and wisdom. One who seeks true wisdom—the knowledge of the Divine—is said to be *tamim* (whole and complete) (*Likutey Moharan* I:end).

25:28   וַיֶּאֱהַב יִצְחָק אֶת־עֵשָׂו כִּי־צַיִד בְּפִיו וְרִבְקָה אֹהֶבֶת אֶת־יַעֲקֹב

Isaac loved Esau because he was a trapper with his mouth, but Rebecca loved Jacob.

⟩ Isaac loved Esau because he was a trapper with his mouth

Esau would "trap" his father with false piety, asking how one should tithe salt and straw (Rashi).

Isaac knew that Esau was the "red one," representing blood and judgments. Yet because Esau fooled Isaac with his false piety, Isaac read Esau's "redness" as an attribute of holy boldness that would allow him to observe the Torah even in difficult times or when facing opposition. Even great tzaddikim can err and misread a situation, confusing who is righteous and who is not (*Likutey Halakhot* VIII, p. 39a).

⟩ Isaac loved Esau because he was a trapper with his mouth... so my soul will bless you

"A trapper with his mouth"—Esau would feed Isaac from his game. Another interpretation: He was a smooth talker. Esau would "trap" his father with false piety, asking how one should tithe salt and straw (Rashi).

How could Isaac have chosen Esau over Jacob to receive the blessings? Even if Esau appeared to be righteous, it was known to all that Jacob, who continually studied and served God, was the greater tzaddik!

Isaac well knew that Jacob was a tzaddik, just as he knew that Esau was a trapper. But since Esau presented himself as a sincere person interesting in tithing his wealth, Isaac wanted to help him serve God in the manner he could best, by supporting Torah and the tzaddikim. For this, Esau needed the blessings to garner sufficient wealth to distribute to charity. Conversely, Isaac did not think that Jacob required material blessings, as his portion was in the spiritual realm.

In reality, Esau had no desire at all to serve God, nor to be charitable to those who did. Not only did he not intend to support Jacob, the tzaddik, but he demanded that Jacob feed him from his broth when he returned home "tired" from the field. (Our Sages say that "tired" refers to idolatry, murder and adultery, as Esau drew upon himself the desire for the material world [see *Bava Batra* 16b].) Esau would even dip into Jacob's pocket to support his immoral desires. When Isaac heard that Esau had sold his birthright, he immediately recognized that Esau had no desire at all for Godliness or to support those who wished to serve Him. Then he willingly gave the blessings to Jacob (*Likutey Halakhot* VII, p. 117a *ff*).

25:29   וַיָּזֶד יַעֲקֹב נָזִיד וַיָּבֹא עֵשָׂו מִן־הַשָּׂדֶה וְהוּא עָיֵף

Jacob simmered a stew. Esau came in from the field, and he was exhausted.

❩ *Jacob simmered a stew...Esau said, "Behold! I am going to die"*

One should always strive to attain *da'at* (knowledge of God) and transmit it to future generations. When Abraham passed away, Jacob prepared the required mourner's meal to feed his father Isaac, indicating that he would continue to draw the *da'at* of Abraham. Jacob also desired the birthright, which represents wisdom—as in "The first is wisdom" (Psalms 111:10)—in order to increase his knowledge of God.

In contrast, Esau shunned *da'at*. On the day that Abraham passed away, Esau committed idolatry, adultery and murder, showing that he did not want to inherit Abraham's *da'at*. He also did not believe that with something as mundane as food, a person could display his desire to draw Godliness. He said, "I am going to die," meaning, "There is no means of transmitting one's intellect after death. There is no reason to leave behind one's *da'at*." Therefore Jacob bought the birthright—*da'at*—from him.

Later, Isaac tried to show Esau how a person *could* reach a level of desire to serve God even through the mundane act of eating. He told Esau to bring him something to eat so that he could bless him. But here, too, Jacob merited to receive Isaac's blessings—for the blessings and the birthright are the same idea (*Likutey Halakhot* V, p. 213a-426).

25:30 וַיֹּאמֶר עֵשָׂו אֶל־יַעֲקֹב הַלְעִיטֵנִי נָא מִן־הָאָדֹם הָאָדֹם הַזֶּה כִּי עָיֵף אָנֹכִי עַל־כֵּן קָרָא־שְׁמוֹ אֱדוֹם

Esau said to Jacob, "Feed me some of that red, red stuff, for I am exhausted." Therefore he was called Edom.

⟩ Feed me

Esau's eating is gluttonous: "Feed me." In contrast, a Jew must practice patience in his eating habits. First he arises in the morning and recites his prayers. Then he washes his hands and recites the blessing over food. Only then can he begin to eat. Likewise, before partaking of meat, he must slaughter the ox, remove its blood and fats, and so on. All of these preliminaries teach patience, helping us ascend beyond the level of Esau, the level of "Feed me" (*Likutey Halakhot* III, p. 15a).

Now we can understand the Talmudic account of the eating habits of Hillel and Shammai. The Talmud relates that Shammai would always eat to honor Shabbat. Whenever he found a nice cut of meat, he would set it aside to eat on Shabbat. But if the following day he found a piece of meat that was even nicer, he would eat the first piece and set aside the second piece for Shabbat. In this way, he always drew the honor of Shabbat into his weekday meals. Hillel, on the other hand, ate every day according to the blessing God bestowed on that particular day (*Beitzah* 16a).

Why didn't Hillel choose to eat daily a portion set aside for Shabbat? And why didn't Shammai eat according to the blessing of that day? The answer is that Shammai was known to be severe and short-tempered. His personality type was reminiscent of Esau, who was impatient. In order for Shammai to overcome his impatience, he had to draw the sanctity of Shabbat—the day of rest—into his weekdays to help him overcome his impatience. But Hillel was a man of patience. Therefore he was able to draw blessing every day—and blessing represents Shabbat (*Likutey Halakhot* III, p. 30).

25:31 וַיֹּאמֶר יַעֲקֹב מִכְרָה כַיּוֹם אֶת־בְּכֹרָתְךָ לִי

Jacob said, "Sell, as the day, your birthright to me."

〉 *Jacob, Esau and the birthright*

One must always seek the hidden wisdom in every thing in order to find the Godliness within it. Doing so constitutes true wisdom, which is compared to sunlight—a light that illumines a person's path so that he may know the way to travel. As the verse states: "A man's wisdom illumines his face" (Ecclesiastes 8:1). Indeed, "Wisdom gives life" (ibid., 7:12). One who does not seek the Godliness in every thing has closed his mind to wisdom and to life. And whether or not a person applies his mind to this wisdom represents the principal battle between his good and evil inclinations.

This idea is reflected in Jacob and Esau's battle for the birthright. The birthright is generally intended for the "firstborn," which connotes wisdom, as in the verse "The first is wisdom" (Psalms 111:10). The name *YaAKoV* (יעקב, Jacob) also connotes wisdom, as in the phrase *vaYaAKVeini* (ויעקבני, he outwitted me) (Genesis 27:36). Jacob sought the birthright of wisdom and so spent his days in the "tents of study" (Rashi on Genesis 25:27). Esau, on the other hand, sought material gratification and despised the birthright of wisdom and the knowledge of God.

When we seek the spiritual root within everything and study Torah, as Jacob did, we draw close to God (*Likutey Moharan* I, 1:2).

25:32 וַיֹּאמֶר עֵשָׂו הִנֵּה אָנֹכִי הוֹלֵךְ לָמוּת וְלָמָּה־זֶּה
לִי בְּכֹרָה

**Esau said, "Behold! I am going to die.
What good is a birthright to me?"**

》 *I am going to die*

One must use his intellect to seek the Godliness in every thing.
The birthright—which represents intellect and wisdom—would
aid Jacob in that quest, helping him understand the inner meaning
of every material thing and attach it to Godliness. But Esau viewed
the birthright solely as the firstborn's responsibility to serve God (a
role which the Kohanim later assumed). He rejected that role along
with any belief in the World to Come. By selling the birthright to
Jacob, Esau thought he was free and clear of God.

Nevertheless, when Jacob received the blessings, Esau was
furious. Though Esau just wanted this world, a person cannot attain
the blessings of this world without seeking the Godliness in every
thing. Upon his return to the Holy Land, Jacob sent a message to
Esau: "I have oxen and donkeys" (Genesis 32:6). In this way, he told
Esau that he had attained the ability to bind the material—the oxen
and the donkeys—to the spiritual, as he himself had attained great
spiritual levels and thus merited the blessings. Consequently, Esau
would not be able to defeat him (*Likutey Halakhot* VIII, p. 132b-133a).

25:33 וַיֹּאמֶר יַעֲקֹב הִשָּׁבְעָה לִּי כַּיּוֹם וַיִּשָּׁבַע לוֹ וַיִּמְכֹּר
אֶת־בְּכֹרָתוֹ לְיַעֲקֹב

**Jacob said, "Swear to me as this day." He
swore to him, and he sold his birthright
to Jacob.**

》 *He sold his birthright to Jacob*

Jacob took the birthright from Esau, for he was the true prince
and deserved that title (*Likutey Halakhot* I, p. 210). Furthermore, despite
what it demands and takes as its due (i.e., by force), the Other Side
will eventually be compelled to give up and return everything it

has removed from the realm of holiness, and at the full price of the damage it caused. This explains why it was insufficient for Esau to simply give away the birthright; he had to actually sell it. Jacob, the first twin to be formed (see Rashi on Genesis 25:26), should rightfully have been born first, but Esau usurped him. Eventually, Esau returned the birthright. And so it will be in the future: Esau and the Other Side will return everything they ever took and stole from the Jewish nation, at full price (*Likutey Halakhot* VIII, p. 205a).

25:34 וְיַעֲקֹב נָתַן לְעֵשָׂו לֶחֶם וּנְזִיד עֲדָשִׁים וַיֹּאכַל
וַיֵּשְׁתְּ וַיָּקָם וַיֵּלַךְ וַיִּבֶז עֵשָׂו אֶת־הַבְּכֹרָה

Jacob gave Esau bread and lentil stew.
He ate and drank and got up and left.
Thus, Esau rejected the birthright.

▶ Jacob and Esau

The main conflict between Jacob and Esau centers on joy versus depression. Originally, the sacrifices in the Temple—which represent joy, as in "You will rejoice before God [when you bring your sacrifices]" (Deuteronomy 12:12)—were to be brought by the firstborn sons, such as Esau. By partaking of the sacrifices and eating in holiness, a person could attain true joy. However, the type of eating that interested Esau was "Feed me some of that red, red stuff." He ate like a glutton, not in a state of holiness—a type of eating which represents depression. Thus, Esau despised the birthright and the service of God, while Jacob merited both the birthright and the blessings because he sought true joy (*Likutey Halakhot* II, p. 146a).

▶ Jacob and Esau

The birthright refers to intellect. Desiring this world, Esau was willing to sell even his birthright—his intellect—for porridge—for materialism. Jacob took advantage of Esau's gross lusts and gluttony to persuade him to sell the birthright. Thus, Jacob, who subdued his material desires, acquired the intellect and left Esau the material world (*Likutey Halakhot* III, p. 290).

⟩ *Jacob gave Esau...Esau rejected the birthright*

Esau was a firstborn, but he represents the Other Side. He sold his birthright for gluttony, the opposite of eating in holiness. Jacob represents holiness. He bought the birthright by giving away his food. In effect, Jacob "gave Esau" his desire—gluttony—and took the portion of holiness for himself.

The firstborn of Israel fast on the day before Pesach in remembrance of the killing of the firstborn of Egypt on that first Pesach night. When God smote the Egyptian firstborn, He subdued the firstborn of evil and elevated the firstborn of holiness, of the Jewish nation. Therefore fasting represents the subjugation of evil, of Esau and of evil empires, which is the reverse of eating in holiness (*Likutey Halakhot* IV, p. 35a-70).

⟩ *The birthright and the blessings*

A person's table is compared to the Altar (cf. *Chagigah* 27a).

The concept of the Rectification of the Altar refers to eating in holiness and presenting a complete and perfected sacrifice to God. When a person eats in holiness, he is able to reveal Godliness, so that even those who are very distant can draw close to God. And through a perfected sacrifice, not only the Jews but all the nations can accept the service of God (see *Likutey Moharan* I, 17).

Isaac asked Esau to prepare him a meal so that Esau would have a part in Isaac's holy eating and, through it, be drawn close to God. But Esau cared nothing for holy eating: he had sold his birthright in order to "swallow the red, red stuff." Afterwards, when Esau bemoaned his loss of the blessings to Jacob, he confessed to Isaac that he had sold his birthright—the means of devotion and sacrifice to God. When Isaac heard that, he said, "Let the blessings remain with Jacob," for he realized that Jacob alone was worthy of performing the Rectification of the Altar (*Likutey Halakhot* VII, p. 40a-80).

⟩ *He left*

Esau left, and didn't kiss the mezuzah (*Otzrot Efraim*).

When Jacob, the person who seeks God, must leave his abode to go out into the marketplace, he places his hand on the mezuzah to make sure he takes the Name of God with him. When Esau, the wicked person who does not seek God, "left," he neglected to place his hand on the mezuzah. Esau's house, which has the potential to be a place of Godliness, lacks spirituality because of his neglect of the mezuzah (*Likutey Halakhot* V, p. 242-244).

26:3　גּוּר בָּאָרֶץ הַזֹּאת וְאֶהְיֶה עִמְּךָ וַאֲבָרְכֶךָּ כִּי־לְךָ וּלְזַרְעֲךָ
אֶתֵּן אֶת־כָּל־הָאֲרָצֹת הָאֵל וַהֲקִמֹתִי אֶת־הַשְּׁבֻעָה
אֲשֶׁר נִשְׁבַּעְתִּי לְאַבְרָהָם אָבִיךָ

"Stay in this Land and I will be with you and bless you. For I will give all these lands to you and your offspring, and I will uphold My oath that I swore to your father Abraham."

❯ I will be with you

Eheyeh (אהיה, I will be) may also be read as a Divine Name (cf. Exodus 3:14), corresponding to the *sefirah* of Keter—and Keter corresponds to wisdom and is the source of all blessing. When a person attains the level of Keter—which is also associated with faith and repentance—he can draw down blessings continuously (*Likutey Moharan* I, 24:7).

26:5　עֵקֶב אֲשֶׁר־שָׁמַע אַבְרָהָם בְּקֹלִי וַיִּשְׁמֹר מִשְׁמַרְתִּי
מִצְוֹתַי חֻקּוֹתַי וְתוֹרֹתָי

"Because Abraham listened to My voice and kept My observances, My commandments, My decrees and My laws."

❯ Abraham kept My observances, My commandments, My decrees and My laws

How? He had no rabbi and no Torah to learn from! Rather, his kidneys became like fountains from which flowed forth the wisdom of Torah (*Bereishit Rabbah* 95:3).

The kidneys advise (*Berakhot* 61a).

Because of Abraham's purity, the advice his "kidneys" provided helped him attain knowledge of Torah even before it was given at Mount Sinai. His kidneys gave good advice, enabling him to counter the bad advice given by the Serpent to Adam, which brought about man's downfall (*Likutey Halakhot* III, p. 193a).

❱ *Abraham fulfilled the Torah*

Before the Torah was given, very great tzaddikim were able to perceive its truth and understand how to serve God even though they had not actually received the Torah. Therefore God said of Abraham, "He observed My Torah." But we—who are unable to perceive on our own what is right, who is righteous and who is wicked—received the Torah at Mount Sinai, and now even we can discern the truth (*Likutey Halakhot* IV, p. 51a).

26:12   וַיִּזְרַע יִצְחָק בָּאָרֶץ הַהִוא וַיִּמְצָא בַּשָּׁנָה הַהִוא מֵאָה שְׁעָרִים וַיְבָרְכֵהוּ יְיָ

Isaac planted in that land and reaped a hundredfold in that year, for God had blessed him.

❱ *Isaac planted in that land and reaped a hundredfold*

Because Isaac possessed the fear of God and guarded his covenant even while residing in an immoral land, he attained abundant blessing (*Likutey Moharan* I, 60:3).

26:18   וַיָּשָׁב יִצְחָק וַיַּחְפֹּר אֶת־בְּאֵרֹת הַמַּיִם אֲשֶׁר חָפְרוּ בִּימֵי אַבְרָהָם אָבִיו וַיְסַתְּמוּם פְּלִשְׁתִּים אַחֲרֵי מוֹת אַבְרָהָם וַיִּקְרָא לָהֶן שֵׁמוֹת כַּשֵּׁמֹת אֲשֶׁר־קָרָא לָהֶן אָבִיו

Isaac returned and re-dug the wells of water that were dug in the days of his father Abraham, which the Philistines had plugged up after Abraham's death. He called them by the same names that his father had called them.

❱ *Isaac returned and re-dug the wells*

The wells represent the "wellsprings of advice" that were blemished when Adam ate from the Tree of Knowledge. Ever since, the

correct path is concealed from us and we must strive to reveal it.
Many arguments, conflicts and wars arise in each generation as
a result of each person claiming that his is the right path. This
state of affairs reflects a blemish in faith in the tzaddikim. Though
Abimelekh challenged Isaac again and again, Isaac kept digging
until he was finally able to reveal the proper advice for all to see
(*Likutey Halakhot* III, p. 480).

❳ Isaac returned and re-dug the wells

The Torah records this episode specifically about Isaac because
Isaac represents Gevurah (Restraint), a reference to darkness and
concealment. Isaac strove to reveal that which was hidden, to
bring forth the light concealed in the darkness (*Likutey Halakhot* III,
p. 478-240a).

27:1 וַיְהִי כִּי־זָקֵן יִצְחָק וַתִּכְהֶיןָ עֵינָיו מֵרְאֹת וַיִּקְרָא אֶת־
עֵשָׂו בְּנוֹ הַגָּדֹל וַיֹּאמֶר אֵלָיו בְּנִי וַיֹּאמֶר אֵלָיו הִנֵּנִי

**When Isaac was old and his eyesight had
dimmed, he called his elder son Esau and
said to him, "My son." "Here I am," he
answered him.**

❳ Isaac was old

This expression refers to a person who ages with holiness.
There are those who age without holiness and whose long life
gives strength to the Other Side. Isaac represents judgments and
thus, while Isaac aged, Esau—who embodies the evil of those who
age without holiness and who is also rooted in judgment—was
aroused. To counter this evil, Jacob—the God-fearing Jew—must
bring a gift to Isaac in order to mitigate the judgments and decrees.
That gift is charity, since charity counteracts the effects of evil and
reveals Divine Favor.

Therefore Isaac asked Jacob, "How did you find it so quickly?"
and Jacob replied, "God caused it to happen." Then Isaac said,
"The voice is the voice of Jacob"—for Jacob reveals Divine Favor.
This was why Jacob merited the blessings which state: "May God
grant you from the Heaven and the earth" (cf. Genesis 27:28). That is,

God will provide everything through Divine Favor and man will not have to work for his livelihood (*Likutey Halakhot* II, p. 185a). It follows, then, that by giving charity, one merits to work less and receive greater blessings! (see *Likutey Moharan* II, 4:3).

⟩ *His eyesight had dimmed*

> At the moment that Isaac was bound upon the altar and his father was about to slaughter him, the heavens opened and the ministering angels saw and wept. Their tears fell upon Isaac's eyes, and therefore his eyes were dimmed (Rashi).

Sometimes people come very close to God in the sense that they achieve the blessings they desire, such as wealth, power and vibrant health. Yet this leads to a complacency that dims their spiritual sight (*Likutey Moharan* II, 82).

⟩ *His eyesight had dimmed*

The force of evil called Lilith draws its strength from diminished sight (*Likutey Moharan* I, 205; see above, p. 56). Thus, when Isaac's eyesight was dimmed, he was led to believe that he should bless Esau, which would have added to the strength of the Other Side. To subdue this evil force, a person must strive to rectify his sight. He must look at the goodness—the Godliness—in the world.

27:3   וְעַתָּה שָׂא־נָא כֵלֶיךָ תֶּלְיְךָ וְקַשְׁתֶּךָ וְצֵא הַשָּׂדֶה
וְצוּדָה לִּי צֵידה (צָיִד)

"Now, take your weapons, your sword and your bow, and go out to the field and trap game for me."

⟩ *Take your weapons, your sword and your bow, and go out to the field*

Isaac sent Esau "out to the field"—a place outside the realm of holiness—to bring his material food into the house—into the realm of holiness. "Weapons" refers to faith, the "sword" and "bow" to morality. *TeLYekhah* (תליך, your sword) also alludes to Torah learning, as it is similar to *TaLuY* (תלוי, doubts), which are clarified through one's studies. With these armaments, one can tame the unholy and bring it into holiness.

But Esau was wicked, as Scripture testifies: "Esau went" (Genesis 27:5). He did not have to go far—he was a man of the field, an impure person, who did not have to exert himself to be in the realm of impurity. In the end, Jacob received the blessings, because Jacob had faith, morality and Torah study (*Likutey Halakhot* VIII, p. 171b).

⟫ *Take your weapons*

Check your slaughtering knife carefully so as not to feed me something unkosher (Rashi).

Many, many souls are reincarnated in animals. When one is careful with the slaughtering, using an unblemished knife and reciting the blessing properly, he elevates those souls. Since Esau sought materialism, Isaac wanted him to be active in elevating those souls and thereby elevate his own soul as well. Isaac told Esau to be careful with his slaughtering knife so that his soul, too, would be elevated (*Likutey Halakhot* V, p. 152a).

⟫ *Take your weapons*

Check your slaughtering knife carefully so as not to feed me something unkosher (Rashi).

Keilekha (your weapons) literally means "your vessels." To prepare kosher food, one must first prepare proper vessels to absorb the holiness found in that food (*Likutey Halakhot* IV, p. 136a). It is insufficient to think that all one must do is eat kosher food. The way to become elevated by eating is to make one's self a proper vessel within which to receive the sanctity of kosher food.

27:9 לֶךְ־נָא אֶל־הַצֹּאן וְקַח־לִי מִשָּׁם שְׁנֵי גְּדָיֵי עִזִּים
טֹבִים וְאֶעֱשֶׂה אֹתָם מַטְעַמִּים לְאָבִיךָ כַּאֲשֶׁר אָהֵב

"Go to the flock and take for me two choice kid goats from there. I will make from them delicacies for your father, as he loves."

⟫ *Two choice kid goats*

This took place on Pesach night. One goat was for the Pesach sacrifice, the other for the Festival sacrifice (Rashi).

The sacrifices represent oaths taken for the sake of God. One who takes such an oath merits to the delight of God. Therefore Jacob was blessed with "May God grant you from the Heaven and the earth" (cf. Genesis 27:28). Moreover, because Jacob was able to wrest the blessings from Esau, he prepared the way for the Pesach night of the Exodus. On that night, the Jews took away the abundant wealth of the Egyptians, since it was rightfully theirs (*Likutey Halakhot* III, p. 292).

27:10 הֵבֵאתָ לְאָבִיךָ וְאָכָל בַּעֲבֻר אֲשֶׁר יְבָרֶכְךָ לִפְנֵי מוֹתוֹ

"You will bring it to your father and he will eat, so that he may bless you before his death."

﴿ *The blessings*

There is a body, there is a soul. There is matter, there is form. There is death, there is life. The first of each of these pairs are all one concept, as are the latter. One must strive to subjugate the material to the spiritual (*Likutey Moharan* I, 37:2).

Jacob sought a spiritual life. Esau sought a material life. Isaac thought that Esau, too, desired a spiritual life, so he wanted to bless him with material blessings that would support the spiritual. But Rebecca knew that Esau wanted only the material. She sent Jacob to get the blessings in order that the material—Esau—would be subjugated to the spiritual—Jacob (*Likutey Halakhot* V, p. 302-152a).

27:11 וַיֹּאמֶר יַעֲקֹב אֶל־רִבְקָה אִמּוֹ הֵן עֵשָׂו אָחִי אִישׁ שָׂעִר וְאָנֹכִי אִישׁ חָלָק

Jacob said to his mother Rebecca, "But my brother Esau is a hairy man and I am a smooth-skinned man."

﴿ *My brother Esau is a hairy man*

Sa'IR (שער, hairy) is similar to *Se'ARah* (שערה, storm wind) (*Likutey Moharan* I, 8:3). Just as a storm wind is momentary, so too, the influence of Esau, the evil inclination, is fleeting. If one has patience and can wait him out, he can attain all the physical and spiritual blessings.

27:12 אוּלַ֣י יְמֻשֵּׁ֣נִי אָבִ֗י וְהָיִ֧יתִי בְעֵינָ֛יו כִּמְתַעְתֵּ֖עַ וְהֵבֵאתִ֥י עָלַ֛י קְלָלָ֖ה וְלֹ֥א בְרָכָֽה

"Perhaps my father will feel me. I will be like a mocker in his eyes, and I will bring upon myself a curse rather than a blessing."

〕 *Perhaps my father will feel me...and I will bring upon myself a curse rather than a blessing*

"My father" is Isaac, the attribute of judgment. Jacob was worthy of receiving the blessings, but because he had to obtain them in a stealthy manner, he was afraid that the attribute of judgment might "feel" him and detect a minor flaw that would make him unworthy. Rebecca, who represents prayer (see above, p. 204), assured Jacob that with prayer, one can overcome even the strictest judgment. Thus, she was willing to accept upon herself any curse that Isaac might pronounce (*Likutey Halakhot* VIII, p. 34b).

27:19 וַיֹּ֨אמֶר יַעֲקֹ֜ב אֶל־אָבִ֗יו אָנֹכִי֙ עֵשָׂ֣ו בְּכֹרֶ֔ךָ עָשִׂ֕יתִי כַּאֲשֶׁ֥ר דִּבַּ֖רְתָּ אֵלָ֑י קֽוּם־נָ֣א שְׁבָ֗ה וְאָכְלָה֙ מִצֵּידִ֔י בַּעֲב֖וּר תְּבָרְכַ֥נִּי נַפְשֶֽׁךָ

Jacob said to his father, "I am Esau, your firstborn. I have done as you have told me. Please arise, be seated, and eat of my game so that your soul may bless me."

〕 *Jacob brought food to Isaac...Esau brought food*

When Jacob entered Isaac's presence, an aroma from the Garden of Eden accompanied him. When Esau entered, a whiff of Gehinnom accompanied him (Rashi).

This happened specifically when they brought food to Isaac. Jacob's intention in serving the food highlighted the spirituality of the food; therefore the Garden of Eden was present in his work. Esau's preparation highlighted the material properties of the food; therefore Gehinnom could be sensed in it (*Likutey Halakhot* IV, p. 254-128a).

Later, it is written, "The voice is the voice of Jacob, but the hands are the hands of Esau" (Genesis 27:22). The "voice" represents the spiritual; the hands, the material. This explains why kosher wine is rendered non-kosher when a non-Jew touches it, for "Esau's hands" lower the wine from a spiritual realm to a material one and bring with it the sufferings of the alcoholic (*Likutey Halakhot* IV, p. 130).

27:22 וַיִּגַּשׁ יַעֲקֹב אֶל־יִצְחָק אָבִיו וַיְמֻשֵּׁהוּ וַיֹּאמֶר הַקֹּל
קוֹל יַעֲקֹב וְהַיָּדַיִם יְדֵי עֵשָׂו

Jacob came closer to his father Isaac, and he felt him. He said, "The voice is the voice of Jacob, but the hands are the hands of Esau."

〉 *The voice is the voice of Jacob, but the hands are the hands of Esau*

There is a prayer of compassion and supplication, and a prayer which is demanding, which forces an issue with God.

Isaac knew that Jacob was a man of compassion and truth who would always beseech God for compassion. Isaac also knew that Esau was wicked, a demanding person who would use force to attain his desires. Isaac wanted Esau to repent and therefore he tried to draw him close. By blessing Esau with material wealth, Isaac felt that Esau would become a better person.

But Rebecca knew the full extent of Esau's wickedness. She knew that he would sin even more with abundant wealth. So she instructed Jacob to take the blessings for himself. When Jacob came before his father and Isaac heard his voice, he knew which son stood before him. Thus, Isaac remarked, "The voice is the voice of Jacob"—the one who is righteous, the one who prays, the one who always arouses compassion from God. "But the hands are the hands of Esau"—for he understood that Jacob appeared in Esau's "clothing," in the position of demanding the blessings.

Moreover, Isaac understood from this ploy that Jacob was truly deserving of the blessings. He realized that in order for the righteous to exist, they must subdue "Esau"—the realm of the Other Side—by adopting his methods of demanding and forcing an issue. Although tzaddikim must pray with supplications before God, there are times when they must demand a reply from God—because with those prayers they are attempting to subdue evil and ultimately remove the blessings from the Other Side, returning them to their rightful place in the realm of holiness (*Likutey Halakhot* IV, p. 20a).

⟩ The voice is the voice of Jacob

The "voice of Jacob" corresponds to the voice of rebuke, which gives off a good smell to draw people close to God. Thus, when Jacob entered Isaac's presence, Isaac said, "The smell of my son is like the Garden of Eden"—the good "smell" of rebuke (*Likutey Halakhot* I, p. 46a).

To complete his disguise, Jacob wore Esau's clothes, which were actually the garments that God had made for Adam after he sinned. All clothing has its source in those first garments and correspond to *tzitzit*, which are a rectification for the garments that Adam blemished by eating from the Tree. By choosing physical nourishment over spiritual nourishment, Adam weakened his sense of smell—his ability to receive rebuke. Jacob rectified Adam's sin (ibid., p. 46a-92). Jacob also brought wine with him, for wine arouses *da'at* (ibid., I, p. 48a).

⟩ The voice is the voice of Jacob

There are two types of "voice"—one that reflects weeping and begging for salvation, and one that reflects joy and happiness (*Likutey Halakhot* II, p. 296). The name *YaAKoV* (יעקב, Jacob) is similar to *EiKeV* (עקב, heel), which is at the lowest extremity of the body. When we are conceptually "Jacob"—at a very low level—we must use our voice to cry out to God (*Likutey Moharan* I, 21:8).

⟩ The voice is the voice of Jacob

Jacob guarded his covenant, his sexual morality. Even though he did not marry until the age of eighty-four, he had never wasted seed (Rashi on Genesis 49:3). Guarding one's covenant leads to a clear and pure voice. Therefore Jacob is described in that context: "The voice is the voice of Jacob" (*Likutey Moharan* I, 27:6).

〗 The hands are the hands of Esau

One who believes that "his hands" provide his livelihood has the "hands of Esau," who represents idolatry, for he lacks belief that God is the One Who provides (*Likutey Halakhot* I, p. 23a).

27:30   וַיְהִי כַּאֲשֶׁר כִּלָּה יִצְחָק לְבָרֵךְ אֶת־יַעֲקֹב וַיְהִי אַךְ יָצֹא יָצָא יַעֲקֹב מֵאֵת פְּנֵי יִצְחָק אָבִיו וְעֵשָׂו אָחִיו בָּא מִצֵּידוֹ

When Isaac finished blessing Jacob, and Jacob had just left his father Isaac's presence, his brother Esau came back from his hunt.

〗 Jacob, Esau and the blessings

Jacob represents the tzaddik who studies Torah for its own sake. Esau represents the charlatan who presents a pious face to the public, asking questions that make him seem very religious, like "How does one tithe salt?" Yet in his private life, he commits murder, idolatry and adultery. Still, Esau's chicanery fools his father, who believes that Esau will support the Torah and its scholars. But Rebecca is not fooled by Esau. She understands that Esau will just use the blessings to indulge in material lusts, so she sends Jacob to take the blessings instead.

Jacob then enters Isaac's presence wearing Esau's clothing and goatskins to simulate Esau's hairy flesh. There are times when Jacob, the tzaddik, must take on the appearance of an Esau in order to draw blessing. Yet his appearance as one who seeks material benefit is only for the moment; without some type of sustenance, he could not exist. In the same way, Jacob is characterized by "the voice of Jacob"—the voice of Torah and prayer—while Esau is personified by his "hands"—brute strength. Still, there were times when "Jacobs" also grasped the sword and used it to defeat their enemies (*Likutey Halakhot* V, p. 271a-544).

❱ Jacob received the blessings

You have done justice and charity with Jacob (Psalms 99:4).

Because he perfected both the attributes of charity or compassion (*chesed*) and justice (*gevurah*), Jacob merited to have a "full couch"—all his children were righteous. Not so Abraham, who represents the attribute of compassion. Though Abraham attained perfection on the level of compassion, he was not able to blend it properly with justice, and thus fathered the evil Ishmael. *YiShMaEL* (ישמעאל, Ishmael) was so named because he represents the person who receives charity and compassion but is not worthy of it. Such a person says, "*YiShMa EL* (ישמע אל, God has heard)"—that is, he prays for something once and does not pray again and again until he sees his prayers answered. Thus, he is not really worthy of blessing.

Similarly, Isaac, who attained perfection on the level of justice, was not able to blend it properly with compassion and fathered the evil Esau. *ESaV* (עשו, Esau) was so named because he represents *ASiYah* (עשיה, doing) (cf. Rashi on Genesis 25:25)—he displays piety as if he is acting strictly according to the law, when in fact he is performing the worst sins. Only Jacob was able to blend compassion and justice properly, making him worthy of receiving the blessings and fathering twelve tzaddikim (*Likutey Halakhot* VIII, p. 32a).

27:34 כִּשְׁמֹעַ עֵשָׂו אֶת־דִּבְרֵי אָבִיו וַיִּצְעַק צְעָקָה גְּדֹלָה
וּמָרָה עַד־מְאֹד וַיֹּאמֶר לְאָבִיו בָּרֲכֵנִי גַם־אָנִי אָבִי

When Esau heard his father's words, he cried an exceedingly loud and bitter cry. He said to his father, "Bless me, too, Father!"

❱ Bless me, too, Father

R' Yonah Lebel (d. 1961), a leading Breslover chassid of Jerusalem, was well-known for his heartfelt prayers. Once he came to Rabbi Zvi Aryeh Rosenfeld (1922-1978) with a broad smile after a night of *hitbodedut*. "Last night I hit upon a great prayer," he said. "It worked for Esau, so it should work for me, too!" This prayer was "Bless me, too, Father!" (*R' Gedaliah Fleer*).

27:35 וַיֹּאמֶר בָּא אָחִיךָ בְּמִרְמָה וַיִּקַּח בִּרְכָתֶךָ

"Your brother came with stealth and took your blessing," he said.

》 *With stealth*

The Torah specifically states: "Do not steal" (Exodus 20:13). Yet we find that Jacob had to take away the blessings from Esau with stealth, and when he later fled from Laban, he "stole Laban's heart" (Genesis 31:20). Why did Jacob resort to a *modus operandi* at odds with his righteous nature?

When God created the world, He intended that the Torah would illumine the path of each person so that he would recognize his Creator. But when Adam and Eve ate from the Tree of Knowledge, they blemished man's ability to receive from the Torah directly. Since then, the Torah's message is hidden and must come to us through many "cloaks" and concealments. This is especially true of the stories and parables found in the Torah, Talmud and Midrash, which conceal deep mysteries. These stories convey the hidden message of the Torah in a manner that can be received by all, for when Torah is revealed, great wealth and blessings abound.

Jacob represents the Torah, to which blessings are attached. But because of Adam's sin, Jacob had to be concealed in order to receive those blessings. Therefore he resorted to subterfuge by going to Isaac dressed up in Esau's clothes. According to the Midrash, these clothes actually belonged to Adam, so this scene symbolizes the Torah being cloaked in "other garments" so that it can be received properly and invoke blessing.

So it is throughout the generations. Jacob had to resort to subterfuge to escape Laban, and Joseph acted with subterfuge towards his brothers in Egypt (Genesis 42). The brothers had blemished by selling Joseph, so the only way Joseph could reach out to them and help them receive from him properly was by "cloaking" and concealing himself (*Likutey Halakhot* VIII, p. 200a-201a).

27:38 וַיֹּאמֶר עֵשָׂו אֶל־אָבִיו הַבְרָכָה אַחַת הִוא־לְךָ אָבִי
בָּרֲכֵנִי גַם־אָנִי אָבִי וַיִּשָּׂא עֵשָׂו קֹלוֹ וַיֵּבְךְּ׃

**Esau said to his father, "Do you have
only one blessing, Father? Bless me, too,
Father!" Esau lifted his voice and cried.**

❩ *Esau lifted his voice and cried*

Esau's ability to harm the Jewish people comes from the tears
he shed when he lost the blessing. We, in turn, must cry to negate
the power of those tears (*Likutey Moharan* II, 30).

❩ *Esau cried*

There is a power that attracts and a power that repels. God
is the power of drawing close, as in "Draw me after You" (Song
of Songs 1:4). The forces of evil are the power that repels, keeping
people away from God. When Esau cried, he drew the power of
God, the "power of the draw," to himself, and Isaac blessed him.
Then Esau turned around and drew that power into evil, causing
the destruction of the Temple and the suffering of the Jews in exile
(see *Likutey Moharan* I, 70) (*Likutey Halakhot* III, p. 360).

❩ *Esau cried... when your complaints mount, you will throw his
yoke off your neck*

Esau's crying represents depression, for tears are a bodily
excess, and excess parallels depression. In the second verse (Genesis
27:40), Rashi translates *tarid* as anguish—i.e., depression. These
two verses are connected, implying that Esau will be able to throw
off Jacob's yoke and gain ascendancy when he brings depression
into the lives of the Jewish people. The Jews can counter the tears
of Esau through their own crying for God's closeness. Therefore
we must cry over the destruction of the Temple, for this expression
of our willingness to serve God in His House arouses Divine
compassion and favor, and draws God's Providence and blessings
upon us (*Likutey Halakhot* VII, p. 238-120a-240).

27:40 וְעַל־חַרְבְּךָ תִחְיֶה וְאֶת־אָחִיךָ תַּעֲבֹד וְהָיָה
כַּאֲשֶׁר תָּרִיד וּפָרַקְתָּ עֻלּוֹ מֵעַל צַוָּארֶךָ

"You will live by your sword and serve your brother. But when your complaints mount, you will throw his yoke off your neck."

⟩ You will live by your sword

Those who attack the Holy Land with the "sword" of slander prevent other Jews from reaching the Land. Such people draw from the power of the sword bequeathed to Esau in Isaac's blessing (*Likutey Moharan* I, 20:6).

28:9 וַיֵּלֶךְ עֵשָׂו אֶל־יִשְׁמָעֵאל וַיִּקַּח אֶת־מָחֲלַת בַּת־
יִשְׁמָעֵאל בֶּן־אַבְרָהָם אֲחוֹת נְבָיוֹת עַל־נָשָׁיו
לוֹ לְאִשָּׁה

Esau went to Ishmael and took Machalath the daughter of Ishmael, Abraham's son, the sister of Nebayoth, as a wife in addition to his other wives.

⟩ Esau took Machalath the daughter of Ishmael...Jacob took from the stones of the place

Jacob took stones and placed them under his head. The stones united and formed a single stone (Rashi on Genesis 28:11).

Immediately after Jacob fled, Esau took Ishmael's daughter as his wife. Esau and Ishmael represent the forces of evil that are now uniting to try to destroy Jacob. To fortify himself against them, Jacob fled to the yeshivah of Shem and Eber and strengthened himself with Torah study. After his years of study, he slept at Mount Moriah, where the different stones united under his head. As long as Esau and Ishmael were individuals, Jacob knew he could overcome either of them. But when they united, it would be very difficult to overcome them. He had to effect a unity, to ascend to a level where all the "stones"—i.e., all things—are rooted in their source. Armed with this intellect and intelligence, he could overcome the forces of evil (*Likutey Halakhot* V, p. 378).

Parashat Vayeitzei

28:10 וַיֵּצֵא יַעֲקֹב מִבְּאֵר שָׁבַע וַיֵּלֶךְ חָרָנָה

Jacob left Beersheba and went to Charan.

⟫ *Jacob left Beersheba and went to Charan*

When a Jew wishes to ascend from one level to the next, obstacles spring up to confront him. These obstacles are mainly in his imagination and illusions, and stem from God's anger. Thus, when Jacob wished to ascend from the "seventh" level—i.e., *Be'er Sheva* (literally, "well of seven")—to a higher spiritual plane, he left for *ChaRaN* (חרן), which is similar to *ChaRoN af* (חרון אף, Divine anger), signifying the obstacles he would face before attaining his goal.

Nevertheless, Jacob was resolute in his determination to serve God, and came upon *HaMakom* (the Place). He could identify it as such because he knew he was not experiencing a descent (as he had already embarked on his spiritual journey), yet he faced obstacles which prevented his continuing on that journey. Every person has a "place," a point in life where he finds difficulties going forward. "The sun had set"—alluding to the obstruction of the intellect, when a person must rely upon faith. Jacob gathered twelve stones—corresponding to the Twelve Tribes and the collective good points of the Jewish nation—and placed his head (with its obstructed intellect) upon those stones, as if to assert that he was not giving up.

He dreamt of a ladder with angels ascending and descending, hinting that this is man's mission in this world, to ascend from level to level and not allow obstacles to sidetrack him. One who accepts this mission can recognize which is an ascent and which is an obstacle that causes descents. Despite the obstacles he faced, Jacob surged forward and merited to a vision of God, Who promised to be with him always (for such is the reward of one who seeks God). Then Jacob promised to tithe his income, for the main means of overcoming obstacles is by giving charity.

Then Jacob "lifted his legs"—alluding to elevating the lower levels—and "went towards the land of the people of *KeDeM* (קדם)"—a reference to God, Who preceded (קדם, *KaDaM*) everything. Jacob traveled to those who are created by God, yet who find themselves trapped in the "land" and materialism of this world. The "well" represents the wellsprings of Torah that can bring life to all, but there is a "big stone" upon the well—a "heart of stone" (Ezekiel 36:26) that represents the Evil One and the obstacles to spiritual living. The "three flocks" allude to three types of people: righteous, average and wicked. When they gather together, they can remove the stone for a short period while they "water the flocks" and draw spiritual sustenance. But this is only temporary and the "stone" is returned to its place.

Jacob asks them, "Where are you from?" and the shepherds answer, "From *ChaRaN* (חרן)"—from the *ChaRoN af* (חרון אף)— meaning, we suffer from all the obstacles. Jacob asks, "Do you know Laban?" since Laban is the chief obstacle, the archetype of all the false leaders who deflect a Jew's sincere desire to serve God. They answer, "We know him"—that is, we are familiar with the illusions the Evil One presents, and we cannot break them.

"Here is his daughter Rachel coming with the flock"—Rachel represents the Torah that can lead the flock, except that Laban's presence obscures its truth. Jacob says, "The day is still long"—the battle is not yet over and the exile will take its toll—"water your flocks." When the shepherds protest that they cannot do it alone, Jacob rolls off the stone himself, demonstrating that the true tzaddik has the power to counter all the obstacles, evil approaches and false leaders (*Likutey Halakhot* VIII, p. 11a-15b).

28:11 וַיִּפְגַּע בַּמָּקוֹם וַיָּלֶן שָׁם כִּי־בָא הַשֶּׁמֶשׁ וַיִּקַּח מֵאַבְנֵי הַמָּקוֹם וַיָּשֶׂם מְרַאֲשֹׁתָיו וַיִּשְׁכַּב בַּמָּקוֹם הַהוּא

He came to the place and slept there, for the sun had set. He took from the stones of the place and put them under his head, and he lay down in that place.

He came to the place

Vayifga (he came) refers to prayer. Jacob established the Evening Prayer (*Berakhot* 26b).

Jacob passed by the place and then returned to it. Why didn't Heaven stop him when he first passed by? If he didn't think of stopping, why should they? (see *Chullin* 91b).

Foreseeing the long night of exile facing his children, Jacob established the Evening Prayer. Through this, he taught us that even in absolute darkness, one can find hope by turning to God (*Likutey Halakhot* II, p. 446).

The fact that Jacob initially passed by the place indicates that at first he didn't think of praying during the dark exile. But he realized he was wrong—a person must arouse himself to God, even in the darkest moments. Therefore he returned to the place and established the Evening Prayer.

As he retraced his steps, the Temple Mount came to greet him (Rashi on Genesis 28:17), since his "arousal from below" caused an "arousal from Above." He gathered the stones from the place and put them under his head, implying that all the sparks of holiness to be found there could be rectified when placed "under his head"—under the control of a mind free from evil thoughts. Then Jacob dreamed of a ladder with angels ascending and descending, alluding to the "arousal from Above" and the "arousal from below." It was at that time that Jacob grasped the greatness of the place. He realized that with an "arousal from below," one can evoke great sanctity and inspire all Israel to return to God even in the darkest night. By establishing the Evening Prayer, Jacob established the ability to make an "arousal from below" (*Likutey Halakhot* II, p. 224a-450).

⟩ *He came to the place*

The entire account of Jacob's dream alludes to the steps one must take to ascend the spiritual ladder in order to experience higher and higher levels of Godliness.

"He came to the place"—Jacob arrived at the barrier that separates between the Keter, the highest level of intellect, and the levels beneath it.

"He slept there, for the sun had set"—not being able to attain all the intellects in serving God at once, one must rest.

"He took from the stones of the place"—he gathered the sparks of holiness that were there—"and put them beneath his head"—he tied them to his intellect.

"He slept"—after studying Torah (i.e., after gathering the sparks of holiness).

"He dreamt"—this alludes to a person having to come down to this material world where good and evil exist, and choosing good in order to ascend the spiritual ladder.

"A ladder"—this refers to Jacob's ability to call out to God, for *SULaM* (סולם, ladder) has the same numerical value as *KOL* (קול, voice). This "voice" refers to both types of cries: those of joy and those of beseeching for salvation from difficulties.

"Angels of God were ascending and descending"—the tzaddikim teach a person how to serve God.

Having merited all these levels, "God appeared above him"—Jacob merited astounding levels of holiness, the Holy Land! This leads to the spread of Godliness throughout the entire world, as God promises Jacob, "You will spread out to the west, east, north and south."

"All the families of the earth will be blessed through you and your offspring"—for one who descends into the material world and ascends from it on his spiritual journey causes the blessings to be effected.

"Jacob awoke...God is in this place and I didn't know it"—when one delves into his spiritual devotions, tying his Torah to his intellect and striving for the barriers, yet not extending beyond his capabilities, he merits to attain the zenith of knowledge, of

Godliness. Yet despite having reached Godliness, he knows that he has still not begun to fully comprehend God's greatness. Thus, "God is in this place and I didn't know it"—I am still not aware of God's true greatness (*Likutey Halakhot* II, p. 148a-296-149a).

⟩ *He came to the place and slept there, for the sun had set*

> There he slept. But he did not sleep during the fourteen years that he resided in the house of study of Shem and Eber (Rashi).
>
> Neither did he sleep during the nights that he guarded Laban's flocks; he recited Psalms (*Bereishit Rabbah* 74:11).

Prior to Creation, only God existed. In order to create our world, God constricted His Presence (the *Tzimtzum*) to make a Vacated Space, within which He formed the rest of Creation. This Vacated Space is a paradox: If God vacated the Space, it must be devoid of Godliness. But no place can exist without Godliness to sustain it. Therefore God must be in that void! According to the Ari, the Vacated Space is meant to give man free will. Certainly God is there, but one cannot see or experience Him. To enter into the Vacated Space (i.e., to seek God in this world where He does not appear to be), one must have faith that God is there, despite his inability to understand this intellectually.

"He came to the place"—this represents the Vacated Space.

"He slept there, for the sun had set"—the sun represents the intellect, which illumines a person's path in life. Sleep represents faith, when one's intellect cannot function or absorb the concepts he encounters (i.e., the Vacated Space). Thus, Jacob, who had arrived at the level of understanding the roots of Creation, set aside his intellect and relied solely on faith.

"He took from the stones of the place"—these represent the heresies that are found within the Vacated Space—"and put them under his head"—subjugating his intellect to faith.

When he awoke, Jacob pledged to make the stone into an altar for God—for the main way to defeat heresies is by giving charity and elevating all of one's property to the realm of holiness (i.e., to God). Encouraged, Jacob proceeded to Laban's house, where he married two God-fearing women, Rachel and Leah—who represent Malkhut/faith, indicating that Jacob had attained perfected faith.

Afterwards, Jacob recited Psalms while guarding Laban's flocks—prayers and praises of God also represent Malkhut/faith. Because of his great faith, Jacob also merited to great wealth, hinted at by the "ringed, spotted and flecked" sheep (Genesis 31:10). The Ari explains that these three descriptions correspond to the awesome supernal worlds found within the origin of the Vacated Space (*Likutey Halakhot* VIII, p. 123b-124b).

⟫ He slept there, for the sun had set...angels of God ascending and descending

There are times when a person begins to serve God and experiences a very sweet feeling from his devotions. He thinks that finally—finally!—he will merit to be a God-fearing person. Suddenly, "the sun sets." He is forced to "lie down"—to reduce his spiritual activity. In Jacob's dream, the angels ascended and descended, just like a person who tries to serve God experiences many highs and lows. But if one is stubborn in his desire to draw close to God, he will eventually see his efforts rewarded (*Likutey Halakhot* V, p. 276).

⟫ He took from the stones

The stones began to argue among themselves, each one saying, "Upon me the tzaddik will rest his head!" Immediately God made one large stone out of them, as it is written, "He took the *stone* that he had placed under his head" (Genesis 28:18) (Rashi).

When Jacob stopped at the place, he established the Evening Prayer. Each stone that he collected to put under his head represented an individual letter in that prayer. Each stone began to claim, "Upon me the tzaddik will rest!" meaning, "Let the tzaddik meditate upon me and not proceed with the rest of the prayer!" But Jacob knew that a person cannot stand still—he must proceed with his prayer. Therefore all the stones joined together—the letters united in Jacob's mind and concentration, enabling him to complete his prayer (*Likutey Halakhot* II, p. 248a-496).

⟫ He took from the stones of the place and put them under his head

Stones represent stumbling blocks created by opposing opinions. Jacob, the man of truth, can unite opposing sides, for everyone is joined together by the truth (*Likutey Halakhot* VIII, p. 209a).

❯ He took from the stones of the place...vayifga, vayalen, ufaratzta

He took twelve stones, which coalesced into a single stone (Rashi).

Jacob transcended the concept of space and thus covered great distances in a short span of time. The coalescing of the stones into one stone represents the *Even Shetiyah* (Foundation Stone) which God created first and from which He drew the rest of Creation, which also transcended space (*Likutey Halakhot* I, p. 76-39a).

Each of the concepts mentioned in this passage—*vayifga* (he came), *vayalen* (he slept), *ufaratzta* (you will spread out)—allude to how Jacob transcended space. He merited an "inheritance without borders or restraints" (*Shabbat* 118b) (*Likutey Halakhot* I, p. 41a). This inheritance is seen in Shabbat, which mirrors the eternal world, an infinite world beyond borders and restraints.

❯ Stones...tithes

He took twelve stones, which coalesced into a single stone (Rashi).

Because Jacob represents truth, he was able to unite all the stones (i.e., the people) and do away with all arguments and differences between them. He then made an oath to give tithes, because to draw unity, one requires the great mitzvah of charity (*Likutey Halakhot* II, p. 390).

❯ He lay down in that place...He dreamt...a ladder...Angels of God were ascending and descending

Jacob foresaw the difficulties of the exile, especially the fact that prayer would be neglected. Therefore "he lay down"—this refers to prayers that lack vitality, prayers without *kavanah* (proper intentions). Jacob placed himself into such a situation in order to see how it could be rectified, and perceived that there must be a ladder that stretches from earth to Heaven. *SULaM* (סולם, ladder) has the same numerical value as *KOL* (קול, voice). That is, one must arouse his voice to pray to God, and the only way to do this is when he stands firmly upon the earth, for "Truth will sprout from the earth" (Psalms 85:12). When a person tries to utter his prayers as truthfully and sincerely as possible, he, too, will see "angels ascending and descending"—his prayers will be elevated to God and the answers to his prayers will be sent down (*Likutey Halakhot* III, p. 498).

28:12 וַיַּחֲלֹם וְהִנֵּה סֻלָּם מֻצָּב אַרְצָה וְרֹאשׁוֹ מַגִּיעַ
הַשָּׁמָיְמָה וְהִנֵּה מַלְאֲכֵי אֱלֹהִים עֹלִים וְיֹרְדִים בּוֹ

**He dreamt. Behold! A ladder was standing
on earth with its top reaching to the heavens.
Behold! Angels of God were ascending and
descending on it.**

》 *Jacob's dream*

Jacob passed by the place and didn't realize that this was
Heaven's gate. He returned and lay down to sleep. He did not
sleep the entire fourteen years that he studied at the yeshivah of
Shem and Eber, but he slept at Heaven's gate! (Rashi).

Jacob dreamt about a ladder, which represents the ability to
combine the upper levels with the lower levels. The ladder was
"standing on earth"—signifying that one must realize God is with
him even on the lowest levels of this material world—"with its
top reaching to the heavens"—indicating that at the same time,
one knows nothing about God's greatness, since He is Infinite. This
is the essence of a person's devotions all the days of his life: to
combine "knowing" with "not knowing" God.

Why did Jacob lie down to sleep in such a holy place? "Sleep"
indicates a lowering of consciousness, a decision to set aside one's
intellect and place oneself totally in God's hands. It represents the
lofty level of "not knowing" God—i.e., recognizing Him as Infinite
(*Likutey Halakhot* V, p. 15a-30).

》 *A ladder was standing on earth with its top reaching to the heavens*

When one practices humility and considers himself as lowly as
the earth, he merits to attain heights as high as the heavens (*Likutey
Halakhot* 5, p. 352).

》 *A ladder was standing on earth with its top reaching to the heavens*

The ladder in Jacob's dream alludes to three concepts. The
lower point is the student, who must be firmly grounded in order
to receive his master's teachings. The upper point is the master,

whose lofty teachings can inspire even those who are mired in earthly, materialistic pursuits. The ladder itself, stretching between the two, reflects the teachings of the master and the channel through which the student can draw down those teachings (*Likutey Halakhot* III, p. 56).

》 *Angels of God were ascending and descending*

Jacob dreamt that three angels ascended and descended the ladder to Heaven. The fourth angel, corresponding to the fourth and current exile, ascended but did not descend (*Midrash Tanchuma, Vayeitzei* 2).

Jacob was on his way to Laban, the foremost double-dealer, who would trick him in every way possible. Jacob understood that this would be the challenge of the fourth and final exile, too: the chicanery and lies that would be presented before the Jews to distance them from God. He was very much afraid, but was strengthened by God's promise: "I will be with you…I will not leave you." That is, God will always be with us, no matter what we endure (*Likutey Halakhot* IV, p. 51a).

28:17 וַיִּירָא וַיֹּאמַר מַה־נּוֹרָא הַמָּקוֹם הַזֶּה אֵין זֶה כִּי אִם־בֵּית אֱלֹהִים וְזֶה שַׁעַר הַשָּׁמָיִם

He became frightened and said, "How awesome is this place! It must be the House of God, and this is the gate of Heaven!"

》 *This is the gate of Heaven*

All prayers ascend to Heaven through the Holy Land, so prayer is associated with the Holy Land (*Likutey Moharan* I, 7:1).

28:20 וַיִּדַּר יַעֲקֹב נֶדֶר לֵאמֹר אִם־יִהְיֶה אֱלֹהִים עִמָּדִי
וּשְׁמָרַנִי בַּדֶּרֶךְ הַזֶּה אֲשֶׁר אָנֹכִי הוֹלֵךְ וְנָתַן־לִי
לֶחֶם לֶאֱכֹל וּבֶגֶד לִלְבֹּשׁ

Jacob made a vow, saying, "If God will be with me and guard me on this journey that I am taking, and will give me bread to eat and clothes to wear."

》 *Jacob made a vow*

Making and fulfilling a vow rectifies a person's fallen faith. This applies not only to faith in God, the Torah and the tzaddikim, but also to faith in oneself. A person must believe that he, too, is important in God's eyes.

Jacob made a vow not because he doubted God's promise to him, but because he doubted his own worthiness. Realizing that his faith in himself was flawed, he made a vow to rectify it (*Likutey Moharan* I, 57:2; see *Parparaot LeChokhmah*, ad loc.).

》 *Bread to eat and clothes to wear*

Jacob asked for clothes, which represent a clean garment for his soul. Similarly, he asked for bread that would provide nourishment for his soul more than his body. Conceptually, this type of food is the manna, which was completely absorbed in the body, producing no waste matter (*Avodah Zarah* 5b). This type of eating also alludes to receiving the Torah, for Moses did not eat or drink for forty days and forty nights while he received the Torah in Heaven (*Likutey Halakhot* II, p. 58a).

》 *Bread to eat and clothes to wear*

BeGeD (בגד, clothes) is similar to *GiDim* (גידים, sinews), which represent the organ of the covenant. When a person guards his covenant and also guards his clothes from becoming soiled, he attains an easy livelihood—i.e., "bread to eat" (*Likutey Moharan* I, 29:5).

29:1   וַיִּשָּׂא יַעֲקֹב רַגְלָיו וַיֵּלֶךְ אַרְצָה בְנֵי־קֶדֶם

Jacob lifted his legs and went towards the land of the people of the East.

⟩ Jacob lifted his legs

He rejoiced in God's promise of protection and drew that joy into his heart, which then lifted up his legs to walk effortlessly (Rashi).

A person must draw his joy into his heart in order to infuse his lower extremities with joy —so that, for instance, he can lift his legs in dance (*Likutey Moharan* I, 10:6; see ibid., I, 32).

29:10   וַיְהִי כַּאֲשֶׁר רָאָה יַעֲקֹב אֶת־רָחֵל בַּת־לָבָן אֲחִי אִמּוֹ
וְאֶת־צֹאן לָבָן אֲחִי אִמּוֹ וַיִּגַּשׁ יַעֲקֹב וַיָּגֶל אֶת־הָאֶבֶן
מֵעַל פִּי הַבְּאֵר וַיַּשְׁקְ אֶת־צֹאן לָבָן אֲחִי אִמּוֹ

When Jacob saw Rachel the daughter of Laban, his mother's brother, and the flock of Laban, his mother's brother, Jacob came closer and rolled the stone off the mouth of the well and watered the flock of Laban, his mother's brother.

⟩ Jacob came closer and rolled the stone off the mouth of the well and watered the flock

There are times when the "stone" upon one's heart is very heavy and cannot be moved easily in order to reveal the wellsprings of Torah that lie hidden underneath. The way to get the stone moving is to long and desire to serve God (*Likutey Halakhot* IV, p. 80).

⟩ He rolled the stone off the mouth of the well

"The stone covering the mouth of the well" refers to the clouded vision that prevents people from perceiving the beauty of Torah. Jacob, the tzaddik, can reveal the life-giving waters and water his "flock"—the people who follow him—with refreshing insights and soul-satisfying inspiration (*Likutey Halakhot* VIII, p. 49b-50a).

》 *He rolled the stone off the mouth of the well*

He removed the stone as easily as a person removes a cork from a bottle (Rashi).

The waters of the well represent the faith that nourishes and sustains a person. The stone represents the obstacles to faith. During the days of Abraham and Isaac, there was a limited amount of faith in the world. Though Abraham began to reveal faith and Isaac continued this effort, the response was negligible. By the time Jacob began revealing faith, however, there was a greater chance of attaining it. Thus, Jacob was able to roll the stone off the well as if he were uncorking a bottle, because by then, faith was becoming more accessible (*Likutey Halakhot* V, p. 226a-452). In other words, Jacob was the third generation of those working to install faith in people. The combined efforts of all those who revealed faith wore down the resistance of those who opposed it.

29:11 וַיִּשַּׁק יַעֲקֹב לְרָחֵל וַיִּשָּׂא אֶת־קֹלוֹ וַיֵּבְךְּ

Then Jacob kissed Rachel, and he lifted his voice and cried.

》 *Jacob kissed Rachel…He stayed with him for a month*

Rachel represents the Oral Law. The name *RaCheL* (רחל) means "sheep," as in "two hundred sheep (רחלים, *ReCheiLim*)" (Genesis 32:15). Just as a shepherd continuously shears the wool from his sheep, so do Talmudic scholars continuously "shear" laws from the Oral Law (*Tikkuney Zohar* #21, p. 46b).

When Jacob—the tzaddik—kissed Rachel, he became united with the Oral Law. Similarly, when a student studies a tzaddik's teachings, he "kisses" the tzaddik in the sense that he is attaching himself to the tzaddik and to his teachings.

If a student is unworthy, however—if he is on the level of Laban—then the tzaddik's teachings may mislead him. Such a student may recognize his unworthiness and desire to repent. To do so, he must exercise patience and wait *ChoDeSh yamim* (חדש ימים, a month of days). This phrase may also be read as *meChaDeSh yamim* (ימים מחדש, renew one's days). This student must renew his days with sincerity (*Likutey Moharan* I, 12).

29:13 וַיְהִי כִשְׁמֹעַ לָבָן אֶת־שֵׁמַע יַעֲקֹב בֶּן־אֲחֹתוֹ וַיָּרָץ לִקְרָאתוֹ וַיְחַבֶּק־לוֹ וַיְנַשֶּׁק־לוֹ וַיְבִיאֵהוּ אֶל־בֵּיתוֹ וַיְסַפֵּר לְלָבָן אֵת כָּל־הַדְּבָרִים הָאֵלֶּה

When Laban heard the news of Jacob, his sister's son, he ran to greet him. He hugged him, kissed him, and brought him to his house. He told Laban all that had happened.

❩ Jacob and Laban

Jacob was a tzaddik who generated original Torah thoughts. Laban was a "scholar-demon," a tricky and haughty charlatan (*Likutey Moharan* I, 12). One who wishes to learn Torah must choose as a mentor someone who corresponds to "Jacob"—someone who knows the value of Torah and who encourages others to seek Godliness. He must avoid a person who corresponds to "Laban"—someone who seems wise and knowledgeable, but who uses his Torah to lead people away from—and conceals—God.

29:17 וְעֵינֵי לֵאָה רַכּוֹת וְרָחֵל הָיְתָה יְפַת־תֹּאַר וִיפַת מַרְאֶה

Leah's eyes were weak, while Rachel was beautiful of form and beautiful of appearance.

❩ Leah's eyes were weak, while Rachel was beautiful

Leah cried because she was afraid she would have to marry Esau (Rashi).

Together Leah and Rachel represent the Jewish nation. Leah was afraid to fall victim to Esau, so she cried profusely to be saved from him. Her tears led to Rachel's being beautiful, for the Jews were saved from Esau and were able to blossom (*Likutey Halakhot* III, p. 221a).

⟩ Leah's eyes were weak

Leah was destined to marry Esau, for she is rooted in strict judgments, like Esau. But she overcame her handicap with tears and sweetened those harsh judgments. Therefore she merited to marry Jacob (*Likutey Halakhot* I, p. 56a).

⟩ Jacob, Leah and Rachel

Jacob corresponds to Ze'er Anpin, the Written Law (see Charts, p. 346). Rachel and Leah correspond to Malkhut, with Leah corresponding to prayer and Rachel to the Oral Law. Leah is connected to prayer because she cried profusely to avoid marrying Esau. Rachel (whose name means "sheep" in Hebrew) refers to the Oral Law, for just as a shepherd continuously shears the wool from his sheep, so do Talmudic scholars continuously "shear" laws from the Oral Law (*Tikkuney Zohar* #21, p. 46b).

Jacob wanted to marry Rachel first, because to truly understand and fulfill the Written Law, one must first study the Oral Law. Only afterwards can one attain the great level of prayer (Leah) to come close to God. However, Laban also saw the beauty of Rachel (for the Oral Law is quite impressive) and tried to prevent Jacob from getting it right away. Laban thought that by giving Leah to Jacob first, it would delay Jacob's connection to the Oral Law.

Rachel saw this happening. To spare her sister from embarrassment, she revealed to Leah the secret signals that she had made up with Jacob. That is, the Torah itself will show a person how to pray before God to attain that level of closeness with Him. And we see from this story that to truly attain the Oral Law, one must first shed many tears and prayers before God to help him achieve that level. Although a person may not know where to begin, whether from Torah or from prayer, he should begin his devotions to God through both. He should both study Torah and pray to God to be able to fulfill the Torah (*Likutey Halakhot* III, p. 102a-206).

Jacob also married the maidservants, Bilhah and Zilpah, who represent the Mishnah, which is Torah study that is not perfected. Because Jacob merited to both Torah and prayer, he was able to elevate even the maidservants into the realm of holiness (*Likutey Halakhot* III, p. 103a).

29:18 וַיֶּאֱהַב יַעֲקֹב אֶת־רָחֵל וַיֹּאמֶר אֶעֱבָדְךָ שֶׁבַע שָׁנִים
בְּרָחֵל בִּתְּךָ הַקְּטַנָּה

Jacob loved Rachel. He said, "I will work for you seven years for Rachel, your younger daughter."

❩ *I will work for you seven years for Rachel, your younger daughter*

Jacob knew that Laban represented the Chambers of Exchanges, and that he was liable to switch Rachel with her sister Leah. In order to overcome Laban, Jacob agreed to descend into servitude—into the animal kingdom—and become Laban's shepherd. That is, he entered into a realm other than his own in order to assure the elevation of animalistic tendencies to the human level and protect himself from any damage the Chambers of Exchanges might cause.

But Laban tricked him anyway and gave him Leah instead of Rachel. This switch led to the jealousy of the brothers against Joseph (for had Rachel been Jacob's first wife and Joseph the firstborn, the brothers would not have complained about Jacob's extra attention to Joseph). It also led to the exile in Egypt, for because of their jealousy, the brothers sold Joseph, and it further resulted in the split between the Ten Tribes and the Kingdom of Judah (*Likutey Halakhot* I, p. 111a).

29:20 וַיַּעֲבֹד יַעֲקֹב בְּרָחֵל שֶׁבַע שָׁנִים וַיִּהְיוּ בְעֵינָיו כְּיָמִים
אֲחָדִים בְּאַהֲבָתוֹ אֹתָהּ

Jacob worked seven years for Rachel; they seemed to him like a few days because he loved her so much.

❩ *They seemed to him like a few days*

When a person serves God out of love, the amount of time he spends on his devotions is of no consequence to him (*Likutey Moharan* II, 79).

29:25 וַיְהִי בַבֹּקֶר וְהִנֵּה־הִוא לֵאָה וַיֹּאמֶר אֶל־לָבָן מַה־זֹּאת עָשִׂיתָ לִּי הֲלֹא בְרָחֵל עָבַדְתִּי עִמָּךְ וְלָמָּה רִמִּיתָנִי

In the morning, behold! It was Leah. "How could you do this to me?" he said to Laban. "Didn't I work for you for Rachel? Why did you deceive me?"

》 *In the morning, behold! It was Leah*

"Leah" represents the hidden level of the *sefirah* of Binah. Through the joy of dancing at his wedding, Jacob attained the hidden mysteries of the Torah (*Likutey Moharan* I, 32).

》 *In the morning, behold! It was Leah*

"The morning" represents the Resurrection of the Dead. Kabbalistically, "Leah" corresponds to the *luz* bone, from which the body will be reconstructed at that time (*Likutey Moharan* II, 85).

29:34 וַתַּהַר עוֹד וַתֵּלֶד בֵּן וַתֹּאמֶר עַתָּה הַפַּעַם יִלָּוֶה אִישִׁי אֵלַי כִּי־יָלַדְתִּי לוֹ שְׁלֹשָׁה בָנִים עַל־כֵּן קָרָא־שְׁמוֹ לֵוִי

She conceived again and gave birth to a son. "This time my husband will accompany me, because I have borne him three sons," she said. Therefore he named him Levi.

》 *Leah's eyes were weak… This time my husband will accompany me… therefore he named him Levi*

Diminished sight is associated with the evil force of *LYLYt* (לילית, Lilith), which is given that name because it is always whining (מיללת, *meYaLeLet*) and brings *YeLaLah* (יללה, wailing) into the world. Wicked people generate an abundance of sad and mournful melodies, for their music is associated with the wailing of the Other Side.

Music in general attracts people. Music comes from the same root as the Tribe of Levi, who played musical instruments in the Temple. The name *LeVi* (לוי) comes from the word *meLaVeh* (מלוה, accompany)—i.e., people wish to be in his company.

When we sing melodies on Shabbat in a heartfelt manner, we elevate the fallen, sad melodies to the realm of holiness. This is because Shabbat represents rectified sight. Thus, it overcomes the power of Lilith (*Likutey Moharan* I, 226; see also ibid., I, 237).

29:35 וַתַּהַר עוֹד וַתֵּלֶד בֵּן וַתֹּאמֶר הַפַּעַם אוֹדֶה אֶת־
יְהֹוָה עַל־כֵּן קָרְאָה שְׁמוֹ יְהוּדָה וַתַּעֲמֹד מִלֶּדֶת

She conceived again and gave birth to a son. "This time, I will thank God," she said. Therefore she named him Judah. Then she stopped having children.

》 *This time, I will thank God*

In the Future, all the sacrifices will be abolished other than the thanksgiving-offering (*Vayikra Rabbah* 9:7).

ODeH (אודה, I will thank) refers to the *Korban TODaH* (קרבן תודה, thanksgiving-offering). As Judah symbolizes Mashiach, his descendant, and the concept of always giving thanks to God, the thanksgiving-offering will remain in place even after Mashiach comes (*Likutey Halakhot* I, p. 242).

30:8 וַתֹּאמֶר רָחֵל נַפְתּוּלֵי אֱלֹהִים נִפְתַּלְתִּי עִם־אֲחֹתִי
גַּם־יָכֹלְתִּי וַתִּקְרָא שְׁמוֹ נַפְתָּלִי

Rachel said, "I have struggled with my sister with divine struggles, and I have succeeded." She named him Naphtali.

》 *Naphtali*

Menachem ben Seruk teaches that the name *NaPhTaLI* (נפתלי) comes from the same root as the word *PeTIL* (פתיל, cord), rendering this verse as "By bonds from God have I been joined to my sister" (Rashi).

The letters of the name *naFTaLI* (נפתלי, Naphtali) contain many of the same letters as the word *TeFILah* (תפילה, prayer). When we consider that "the name *NaPhTaLI* comes from the same root as the word *PeTIL* (cord)," we can understand that prayer is the principal devotion that binds a person to God (*Likutey Moharan* II, 84).

⟩⟩ Naphtali

NaFTaLi (נפתלי, Naphtali) comes from the same root as *NiFTaLti* (נפתלתי, I wrestled or I struggled) (Rashi).

This concept is similar to *TeFiLah* (תפילה, prayer), for one must struggle and be persistent in praying to God when he has not yet received the answers to his petition. Eventually, his prayers will be answered, as were Rachel's (*Likutey Halakhot* I, p. 80a-160-81a).

30:23 וַתַּהַר וַתֵּלֶד בֵּן וַתֹּאמֶר אָסַף אֱלֹהִים אֶת־חֶרְפָּתִי

She conceived and gave birth to a son. "God has gathered in my shame," she said.

⟩⟩ God has gathered in my shame...She named him Joseph

As long as a woman doesn't have a child, she is blamed for anything that goes wrong in the house; but when she has a child, she can blame the child (Rashi).

Not only does Joseph (יוסף, *YoSeF*) gather in (אסף, *aSaF*) his mother's embarrassment, he also gathers in the humiliation of sinners. *YoSeF* also represents the tzaddik who draws others close to God and therefore increases (מוסיף, *mOSiF*) holiness. (For example, Joseph would spend time with the children of the maidservants [i.e., those who are distant from God]). Later, Joseph is called the *ben zekunim*, the "wise son" (Genesis 37:3). This wisdom refers to the great compassion Joseph displayed for all those who were distant from God (*Likutey Halakhot* I, p. 14a, 26).

⟩⟩ God has gathered in my shame...She named him Joseph

Joseph is the paradigm of the tzaddik, one who guards the covenant. Should a man blemish his covenant, he feels shame. Therefore Joseph's birth, which is the revelation of the tzaddik, indicates the removal of shame (*Likutey Moharan* I, 19:3, 34:8, 82). The tzaddik mitigates the humiliation that comes as a result of a damaged covenant (ibid., I, 54:6).

30:24 וַתִּקְרָא אֶת־שְׁמוֹ יוֹסֵף לֵאמֹר יֹסֵף יְיָ לִי בֵּן אַחֵר

She named him Joseph, saying, "May God
add to me another son."

❩ *She named him Joseph, saying, "May God add to me another son"*

Joseph (יוסף, *YoSeF*) earns the title of "tzaddik" because he
continually adds (מוסיף, *mOSiF*) freshness to his devotions. Every
day he wants God to see him as a "new" son. This verse also implies
that the tzaddik constantly works to bring new souls back to God
(*Likutey Halakhot* II, p. 77a-154).

30:25 וַיְהִי כַּאֲשֶׁר יָלְדָה רָחֵל אֶת־יוֹסֵף וַיֹּאמֶר יַעֲקֹב
אֶל־לָבָן שַׁלְּחֵנִי וְאֵלְכָה אֶל־מְקוֹמִי וּלְאַרְצִי

After Rachel had given birth to Joseph,
Jacob said to Laban, "Let me leave. I will
go to my place and my land."

❩ *Let me leave. I will go to my place and my land*

Jacob wanted to make sure that at least his last child, Benjamin,
would be born in the Holy Land. Otherwise, the Jews might never
be able to leave the exile (*Zohar* I, 158b).

Benjamin's birth completed the holiness of the Twelve Tribes,
and thus represents the joy of holiness. Had Benjamin been born
outside the Holy Land, this joy would have been drawn to the
forces outside the realm of holiness, canceling its positive effects,
as it is written, "With joy you will leave [the exile]" (Isaiah 55:12)
(*Likutey Halakhot* II, p. 157a).

30:28 וַיֹּאמַר נָקְבָה שְׂכָרְךָ עָלַי וְאֶתֵּנָה

"Tell me your wage and I will provide it,"
he said.

❩ *Tell me your wage*

Until Joseph was born, Jacob worked for Laban in order to pay
off the "debt" of marrying his daughters. After Joseph was born,

Laban asked Jacob to work for him for wages. Jacob agreed only because of Joseph's birth. Joseph represents the paradigm of the tzaddik, a guarded covenant. Only when one is moral and pure, the wealth he gains will be pure and without blemish (*Likutey Halakhot* V, p. 478).

⟩ *Jacob and Laban*

Jacob, who merited to the Holy Tongue, fought his main battle with Laban, who represents *Targum*, the translation of the Torah. (Therefore we find that Jacob gave a Hebrew name to the monument, *Gal-eid*, while Laban gave it the same name in Aramaic, *Yegar Sahaduta* [see Genesis 31:47]).

The Holy Tongue generates great levels of holiness. Opposite it stands total impurity (represented by Esau or the seventy nations). *Targum* is a bridge between the two extremes: it can help a person ascend the spiritual ladder into holiness, or it can drag him down from purity to impurity. Jacob took his wives from Laban's house in order to elevate them into the realm of holiness. Conversely, when Esau sought to murder Jacob, Jacob understood that in order to subdue the totally evil Esau, he must first subdue Laban—the *Targum* or bridge between them.

Thus, Jacob served Laban for seven years, corresponding to the seventy impure nations (in the Kabbalah, each level is comprised of ten *sefirot*; seven years multiplied by ten *sefirot* equals seventy). Then Jacob waited until the birth of Joseph to leave Laban's house. Joseph represents the purity of the guarded covenant; in order to attain the Holy Tongue, one requires sexual purity (*Likutey Halakhot* II, p. 464).

30:30 כִּי מְעַט אֲשֶׁר־הָיָה לְךָ לְפָנַי וַיִּפְרֹץ לָרֹב וַיְבָרֶךְ יְיָ
אֹתְךָ לְרַגְלִי וְעַתָּה מָתַי אֶעֱשֶׂה גַם־אָנֹכִי לְבֵיתִי

**"For the little you had before I came has
expanded greatly. God blessed you because
of me. Now, when will I also do something
for my own house?"**

⟩ God blessed you because of me

Vayevarekh YHVH otkha le-ragli (God blessed you because of
me) literally means "God blessed you at my feet." Jacob elevated
the "feet," the lower levels of reality, to serve God, and so he
attained blessing (*Likutey Moharan* I, 24:4).

30:32 אֶעֱבֹר בְּכָל־צֹאנְךָ הַיּוֹם הָסֵר מִשָּׁם כָּל־שֶׂה נָקֹד
וְטָלוּא וְכָל־שֶׂה־חוּם בַּכְּשָׂבִים וְטָלוּא וְנָקֹד בָּעִזִּים
וְהָיָה שְׂכָרִי

**"I will go through all your flocks today.
Remove from there every lamb that is
spotted or streaked, and every lamb among
the sheep that has brown markings, and
those that are spotted and streaked among
the goats—that will be my wage."**

⟩ Jacob and Laban...the flock

Jacob represents the tzaddik who transmits the Torah in its pure
form for the benefit of others. Laban represents the charlatan who
studies Torah in order to gain honor, wealth and other material
benefits for himself. The battle between Jacob and Laban is the
prototype for all future battles between the true tzaddikim and
false leaders who present themselves as paradigms of Torah, yet
are lacking in all the necessary qualities. This explains why Jacob's
main battle with Laban was over the sheep. The sheep—Laban's
wealth—were taken away from him and given over to Jacob, for
a person's lust for wealth and personal gain cause him to fall in
stature (*Likutey Halakhot* V, p. 269a).

〉 *Jacob and Laban*

Jacob represents truth, as in "Give truth to Jacob" (Micah 7:20). As the paradigm of truth, Jacob was able to successfully battle Esau and Laban, the archetypes of falsehood and evil. From Laban, Jacob extracted his four wives and twelve sons. His twelve sons represent the parameters of holiness—the twelve hours of the day, twelve hours of the night, twelve months of the year, twelve signs of the zodiac—that sustain the entire world. Evil—Laban—tries to swallow whatever it can of holiness. But one who merits to truth can extract a heavy price from the side of evil (*Likutey Halakhot* VIII, p. 207b-208a).

30:33 וְעָנְתָה־בִּי צִדְקָתִי בְּיוֹם מָחָר כִּי־תָבוֹא עַל־שְׂכָרִי לְפָנֶיךָ כֹּל אֲשֶׁר־אֵינֶנּוּ נָקֹד וְטָלוּא בָּעִזִּים וְחוּם בַּכְּשָׂבִים גָּנוּב הוּא אִתִּי

"My righteousness will answer for me in the future, when I let you inspect all that I have taken as my pay. Any goat that is not spotted or streaked, or any sheep that does not have brown markings, is stolen if it is found with me."

〉 *My righteousness*

Tzidkati (my righteousness) can also mean "my charity." A person must direct his charity to worthy causes, so that its power can subdue evil (*Likutey Moharan* I, 251; see *More Blessed to Give: Rebbe Nachman on Charity*, published by the Breslov Research Institute).

〉 *My righteousness will answer for me in the future*

Our world is comparable to the Vacated Space, where a person cannot find answers to deep questions regarding reward and punishment, and must rely on faith. When one strengthens his faith in this world, then, in the Messianic future, we will attain the answers regarding our "righteousness" (*Likutey Moharan* I, 64:6).

30:37 וַיִּקַּח־לוֹ יַעֲקֹב מַקַּל לִבְנֶה לַח וְלוּז וְעַרְמוֹן וַיְפַצֵּל
בָּהֵן פְּצָלוֹת לְבָנוֹת מַחְשֹׂף הַלָּבָן אֲשֶׁר
עַל־הַמַּקְלוֹת

**Jacob took for himself fresh rods of white
poplar, hazel and chestnut. He peeled white
stripes in them, uncovering the white of the
rods.**

》 *He peeled white stripes in them*

This refers to the "whiteness"—i.e., the purity—of the covenant. Jacob was able to draw down the purity of the covenant not
only for himself, but for others, too (*Likutey Moharan* I, 29:5).

31:1 וַיִּשְׁמַע אֶת־דִּבְרֵי בְנֵי־לָבָן לֵאמֹר לָקַח יַעֲקֹב אֵת
כָּל־אֲשֶׁר לְאָבִינוּ וּמֵאֲשֶׁר לְאָבִינוּ עָשָׂה אֵת כָּל־
הַכָּבֹד הַזֶּה

**He heard the words of Laban's sons, saying,
"Jacob took everything that belonged to
our father. He made all this wealth from our
father's property."**

》 *He made all this wealth from our father's property*

Why did Jacob work so hard to increase his flocks and garner
wealth from Laban? Because the root of the soul and the root of
wealth are the same (*Likutey Moharan* I, 69).

The entire time that they lived together, Laban tried to trick
Jacob and build his own wealth, thereby trapping both the souls of
the Jewish nation and its wealth in his domain. But Jacob was able
to outsmart Laban and take back control of the Jewish souls and
their wealth (*Likutey Halakhot* VIII, p. 191b).

31:10 וַיְהִי בְּעֵת יַחֵם הַצֹּאן וָאֶשָּׂא עֵינַי וָאֵרֶא בַּחֲלוֹם
וְהִנֵּה הָעַתֻּדִים הָעֹלִים עַל־הַצֹּאן עֲקֻדִּים נְקֻדִּים
וּבְרֻדִּים

"During the mating time of the flocks, I
lifted my eyes and saw in a dream, behold!
The he-goats that were mounting the flock
were ringed, spotted and flecked."

》 *Ringed, spotted and flecked*

These three descriptions of Jacob's sheep are inclusive of
all the holy intellects and correspond to Chokhmah, Binah and
Da'at. The "trough" represents the intellect, where the "waters"
of holiness are stored. Jacob placed a striped staff in front of the
trough—that is, he revealed beautiful Torah teachings, causing
the "sheep"—i.e., his flock—that came to drink from his waters
to become "warm" and enflamed with a desire to serve God with
fervor. Jacob mainly worked with the "young" sheep—for the main
battles with the Evil One take place in one's youth. Though these
battles can be overwhelming, a young person has the strength to
overcome his desires.

Still, Jacob had to flee from Laban—for the Evil One attacks a
person's spiritual devotions ceaselessly. Thus, Jacob told Laban, "If
the God of my fathers...had not been with me...and seen the work
of my hands" (Genesis 31:42)—meaning, Jacob worked continually to
counter evil, which otherwise takes hold of weak people even as
they try to serve God. Were it not for Jacob's labors, others who are
affected by the Evil One might not remain steadfast. Jacob's main
strength was *hitbodedut*, his prayers out in the fields—as he was
stricken "by scorching heat by day and frost at night" (ibid., 31:40)
(*Likutey Halakhot* VIII, p. 14a-15b).

》 *Ringed, spotted and flecked*

There are three levels of awe: awe of God, awe of one's teacher,
and awe of one's parents. Jacob, who said after his dream, "How
awesome is this place!" (Genesis 28:17), understood awe. As he tended
Laban's sheep, he endeavored to draw down the different levels of
awe for everyone to experience.

"Ringed" sheep represent the level of awe of God, since the *akudim* (rings) represent the very origins of Creation, prior to the devolvement of even the *sefirot* (which are definable). "Spotted" sheep allude to the student, who is a "spot" compared to his teacher's knowledge and stature. "Flecked" sheep represent awe of parents, since the flecked markings appeared on the feet of the sheep (Rashi) and children are called "the knees of the parents" (cf. *Eruvin* 70b). Thus, Jacob drew all types of awe of God while tending the sheep (*Likutey Halakhot* V, p. 480-241a).

31:45 וַיִּקַּח יַעֲקֹב אָבֶן וַיְרִימֶהָ מַצֵּבָה

Jacob took a stone and raised it as a monument.

❯ *He raised it as a monument*

Jacob represents the Jew who wants to be pure. He is relentlessly pursued by *LaVaN* (לבן, Laban, whose name literally means "white"), who whitewashes his evil deeds in order to bring a person to his downfall. Jacob must flee from Laban and not look back. Yet should Laban find him, he must build a monument, a testament to his persistence in wanting to serve God (*Likutey Halakhot* I, p. 192).

Also, one must "steal away" from Laban. If attacked by evil thoughts, he must engage in side issues or even silliness to rest his mind and divert it from evil. Then God Himself will warn "Laban" not to harm Jacob. This is what is meant by Jacob fleeing without telling Laban (Genesis 31:20). Had he told Laban he was leaving, he would be begging for Laban to pursue him. Often we say we do not want evil to follow us, but we manage to leave an opening for it to follow. Furthermore, Jacob puts himself to the task of gathering stones—that is, each and every good thought and deed, even if it seems minuscule—and building with it his testament to God and goodness (*Likutey Halakhot* I, p. 192-97a).

31:46   וַיֹּאמֶר יַעֲקֹב לְאֶחָיו לִקְטוּ אֲבָנִים וַיִּקְחוּ אֲבָנִים
וַיַּעֲשׂוּ־גָל וַיֹּאכְלוּ שָׁם עַל־הַגָּל

**Jacob said to his brothers, "Gather stones."
They took stones and made a monument,
and they ate there by the monument.**

⟩ *They ate there by the monument*

The *GaL* (גל, monument) represents *LaG* BaOmer (ל"ג בעומר) (Ari).

GaL (גל, monument) is also related to *GiLah* (גילה, joy). Eating with joy brings holiness and positive strength into one's nourishment (*Likutey Halakhot* III, p. 218).

31:47   וַיִּקְרָא־לוֹ לָבָן יְגַר שָׂהֲדוּתָא וְיַעֲקֹב קָרָא לוֹ גַּלְעֵד

**Laban called it Yegar Sahaduta, but Jacob
called it Gal-eid.**

⟩ *Laban called it Yegar Sahaduta, but Jacob called it Gal-eid*

Laban and Jacob both gave the monument the same name, "Monument of Witness," but Laban named it in Aramaic while Jacob named it in Hebrew.

Laban represents *Targum* (the Aramaic translation of the Torah), which acts as an intermediary between the Holy Tongue and evil speech. Laban's intention was to bring impurity into the covenant he made with Jacob and thereby damage the Jewish people. Jacob was aware of Laban's intention. Therefore he invoked the Holy Tongue, bringing purity to those who would be members of the covenant with God (*Likutey Moharan* I, 19:4; see above, p. 248).

Parashat Vayishlach

32:4   וַיִּשְׁלַח יַעֲקֹב מַלְאָכִים לְפָנָיו אֶל־עֵשָׂו אָחִיו אַרְצָה שֵׂעִיר שְׂדֵה אֱדוֹם

Jacob sent messengers before him to his brother Esau, to the field of Edom in the land of Seir.

》 *Jacob sent messengers...to Esau...I stayed with Laban*

The messengers were real angels (Rashi).

Though Jacob stayed (גרתי, *GaRTY*) with Laban, he kept all 613 (תרי"ג, *TaRYaG*) *mitzvot*. Since he was totally immersed in Godliness, he merited to have real angels do his bidding (*Likutey Halakhot* VII, p. 197a).

32:5   וַיְצַו אֹתָם לֵאמֹר כֹּה תֹאמְרוּן לַאדֹנִי לְעֵשָׂו כֹּה אָמַר עַבְדְּךָ יַעֲקֹב עִם־לָבָן גַּרְתִּי וָאֵחַר עַד־עָתָּה

He instructed them, saying, "This is what you should say: 'To my lord Esau. So says your servant Jacob: "I stayed with Laban and have delayed my return until now."'"

》 *I stayed with Laban*

Despite the fact that I stayed (גרתי, *GaRTY*) with Laban, I kept the 613 (תרי"ג, *TaRYaG*) *mitzvot* (Rashi).

Specifically because I stayed with Laban and knew that he was trying to cause me to fall from my devotions, I strengthened myself and attained the knowledge and ability to observe the 613 *mitzvot*. I attained this level specifically because of my adversary, Laban (i.e., I used the adversity I faced to bring me closer to Torah) (*Likutey Halakhot* III, p. 250-126a).

⟩ I stayed with Laban and have delayed my return until now… I have cattle and donkeys

Despite the fact that I stayed (גרתי, *GaRTY*) with Laban, I kept the 613 (תרי"ג, *TaRYaG*) *mitzvot* (Rashi).

By preparing to attack Jacob, Esau showed that he had reached the zenith of impure audacity: the desire to combat everything holy. Therefore Jacob sent this message to Esau: "I stayed with Laban"—despite having lived with evil, I managed to remain steadfast in serving God. Having observed the Torah, I attained the levels of holy boldness with which to counter your impure audacity. Moreover, "I have delayed my return until now"—"now" represents the power of prayer. That is, I built up my desire to serve God and transformed my Torah studies into prayers to achieve even greater levels. Now that I have attained those greater levels, I am ready to match and even overcome you. The "cattle and donkeys" represent the two Mashiachs who will eventually conquer all the forces of evil (*Likutey Halakhot* VIII, p. 40a).

⟩ I stayed with Laban

And kept the 613 *mitzvot* (Rashi).

Esau hated Jacob because he had received the blessings. When Esau decided to kill him, Jacob fled. En route to Laban's house, Jacob studied Torah in the yeshivah of Shem and Eber for fourteen years (Rashi on Genesis 28:9). Fortified by that Torah learning, Jacob was able to draw the light of God into everything he did.

Thus, he was able to draw down blessing, removing Leah and Rachel from the realm of evil of Laban and bringing them into his realm of holiness. He was also able to draw great wealth, as nearly all of Laban's wealth was transferred to him through his cultivation of Laban's flocks. When Jacob met Esau again, he said, "I stayed with Laban and I observed the 613 *mitzvot*." That is, "I studied Torah and fortified myself with it. The 613 *mitzvot* of the Torah gave me the strength and ability to overcome Laban. Therefore I will be able to overcome you, too" (*Likutey Halakhot* IV, p. 136a-272).

⟩ I stayed with Laban

While Esau represents atheists who are wild beasts and lustful people, Laban represents atheists who are cunning and devious—

the "root" of other atheists, concealing Divine Favor. Jacob represents the one who tries to reveal Divine Favor.

Esau was jealous of Jacob for receiving the blessings from
Isaac, since those blessings included bounty from the dew and
plentiful produce, all blessings of a natural order. As an atheist,
Esau preferred to believe in a natural order rather than Divine
Providence. Threatened by his brother, Jacob realized that in order
to overcome Esau, he must overcome Esau's "root," which is Laban.
So when Jacob returned from Charan, he sent word to Esau: "I
stayed with Laban"—meaning, "I was able to subdue your source.
Therefore I can defeat you, too." When they finally met again, Esau
conceded the blessings to Jacob, recognizing that if Jacob was able
to subdue Laban and reveal Divine Favor, then Jacob truly deserved
the blessings (*Likutey Halakhot* I, p. 154a).

32:8   וַיִּירָא יַעֲקֹב מְאֹד וַיֵּצֶר לוֹ וַיַּחַץ אֶת־הָעָם אֲשֶׁר־אִתּוֹ
וְאֶת־הַצֹּאן וְאֶת־הַבָּקָר וְהַגְּמַלִּים לִשְׁנֵי מַחֲנוֹת

**Jacob became very frightened and distressed.
He divided the people who were with him into
two camps, along with the sheep, cattle and
camels.**

》 *Jacob became very frightened*

Although God had promised to protect Jacob with His Providence,
Jacob was afraid in case he had sinned (*Berakhot* 4a).

When a person perceives God's will—when he sees that
everything happening to him is a result of Divine Providence—he
comes to fear God. But if he believes that nature is a force unto
itself, he cannot attain the fear of God. Jacob was afraid that he
had not appreciated Divine Providence and therefore had lost the
fear of God and allowed himself to sin, in which case he no longer
deserved God's Providence (*Likutey Moharan* II, 4:5).

32:9   וַיֹּאמֶר אִם־יָבוֹא עֵשָׂו אֶל־הַמַּחֲנֶה הָאַחַת וְהִכָּהוּ
וְהָיָה הַמַּחֲנֶה הַנִּשְׁאָר לִפְלֵיטָה

**He said, "If Esau will come to one camp and
strike it, the remaining camp will survive."**

⟩ The remaining camp will survive

Jacob prepared himself to meet Esau in three ways: with a gift,
with prayer, and with readiness for battle (Rashi).

Jacob's meeting with Esau represents the confrontation of every
Jew with the forces of evil. A "gift" represents certain devotions
that are given over to the Other Side (e.g., the goat to Azazel on
Yom Kippur, the *mayim achronim* before the Grace After Meals,
etc.). "Prayer" refers to one's supplications to God to be protected
from the Evil One. "Battle" represents one's constant preparedness
to repel "Esau" and his cohorts, together with the determination
never to fall into despair: "Even if I cannot fully win this battle, at
least I will salvage some of my devotions, some of my preparedness
to serve God" (*Likutey Halakhot* III, p. 254-128a).

32:14   וַיָּלֶן שָׁם בַּלַּיְלָה הַהוּא וַיִּקַּח מִן־הַבָּא בְיָדוֹ מִנְחָה
לְעֵשָׂו אָחִיו

**He slept there that night. He took from what
he had with him a gift for his brother Esau.**

⟩ A gift for his brother Esau

Since Esau was an angry person, why did Jacob send him a
present that showed off his wealth? Wouldn't Esau be jealous of
that wealth, making him even angrier and desirous of harming
Jacob even more?

Jacob planted a telling message in his choice of a gift for
Esau, whose whole being and power stemmed from anger and
thus represents the paradigm of anger. One who controls his
anger can merit to great wealth (see *Likutey Moharan* I, 68). By sending
Esau the fruits of his twenty-year relationship with Laban, Jacob
demonstrated that he had never succumbed to the frustrations of

Laban's constant attempts to deceive him. Rather, he had controlled his anger all that time, thereby meriting to great wealth. More importantly, Jacob was able to control anger—i.e., Esau—itself (*Likutey Halakhot* VIII, p. 191b).

32:17 וַיִּתֵּן בְּיַד־עֲבָדָיו עֵדֶר עֵדֶר לְבַדּוֹ וַיֹּאמֶר אֶל־עֲבָדָיו
עִבְרוּ לְפָנַי וְרֶוַח תָּשִׂימוּ בֵּין עֵדֶר וּבֵין עֵדֶר

He put his servants in charge of each herd separately. He said to his servants, "Go ahead of me and leave space between one herd and the next."

❩ *Leave space between one herd and the next*

Foreseeing the future exiles, Jacob prayed that when the Jews were in exile and beset by troubles, there should be some "breathing space" between their sufferings (*Bereishit Rabbah* 76:8).

Jacob foresaw the long exile and its suffering, and understood the despair that would befall his descendants. He prayed for them to have the wisdom to perceive the brief respites amid the suffering. He prayed that they would recognize the respites even while enduring their individual sufferings, and always find the few comforts between difficulties that give a person the strength to continue (*Likutey Halakhot* V, p. 388).

32:23 וַיָּקָם בַּלַּיְלָה הוּא וַיִּקַּח אֶת־שְׁתֵּי נָשָׁיו וְאֶת־
שְׁתֵּי שִׁפְחֹתָיו וְאֶת־אַחַד עָשָׂר יְלָדָיו וַיַּעֲבֹר אֵת
מַעֲבַר יַבֹּק

He got up that night and took his two wives, his two maidservants and his eleven children, and he crossed Ma'avar Yabok.

❩ *He crossed Ma'avar Yabok*

He made himself into a bridge, taking his animals and his movable property from one side of the river to the other (Rashi).

Jacob, the epitome of truth, taught his descendants that with truth, one can pass across the very narrow bridge of life. By making himself into a bridge, Jacob demonstrated that one needs truth to overcome Esau and all the vicissitudes of life (*Likutey Halakhot* I, p. 158).

⟩ *He crossed Ma'avar Yabok*

He made himself into a bridge, taking his animals and his movable property from one side of the river to the other (Rashi).

Rebbe Nachman once said, "The whole world is a very narrow bridge. The main thing is not to be afraid" (*Likutey Moharan* II, 48).

32:25 וַיִּוָּתֵר יַעֲקֹב לְבַדּוֹ וַיֵּאָבֵק אִישׁ עִמּוֹ עַד עֲלוֹת הַשָּׁחַר

Jacob was left alone. A man wrestled with him until the break of dawn.

⟩ *Jacob fought the angel...the sciatic nerve*

The battle they fought was over the exile. Esau's angel sought to defeat Jacob so that the Jews in exile would succumb to Esau's dominion. However, Jacob was a great tzaddik and was able to defeat the angel. The angel was able only to touch Jacob's thigh—that is, he managed to damage Jacob's future generations, those "who descend from his thighs." The thigh also corresponds to the Ninth of Av when the Temple was destroyed (*Zohar* I, 170b). Throughout the generations, Esau wields the weapon of depression and sadness against the Jewish people.

After losing the battle, the angel claimed that he had to leave, since it was his turn to "sing before God" (Rashi). He felt somewhat victorious in that he would be able to fill the Jews with depression in the future. But Jacob protested, "Not until you bless me"—meaning, even the depression will be transformed into joy! The angel was forced to concede that he would indeed contribute to the blessings and joy of the Jewish nation at the end of the long exile.

After the angel departed, God shone the sun of the Future Redemption for Jacob (*Bereishit Rabbah* 78:5). Jacob gathered up the small vessels that he had retrieved from the other side of the river (Rashi) and returned to his family. The "small vessels" refer to lost souls. By defeating the angel of Esau and bringing joy to his descendants, Jacob the tzaddik will also be able to breathe new life into lost souls (*Likutey Halakhot* II, p. 150a-151a).

32:26 וַיַּרְא כִּי לֹא יָכֹל לוֹ וַיִּגַּע בְּכַף־יְרֵכוֹ וַתֵּקַע כַּף־יֶרֶךְ יַעֲקֹב בְּהֵאָבְקוֹ עִמּוֹ

He saw that he couldn't overcome him, so he struck the socket of his thigh. Jacob's hip joint became dislocated as he wrestled with him.

❯ *He struck the socket of his thigh…the sun shone for him*

The thigh represents those who support Torah. That day, the hours that the sun shone were extended (Rashi on Genesis 32:32).

The angel wanted to cripple the Jewish people's ability to understand the Torah's laws. The best way to accomplish this, he decided, would be to hinder the support given to Torah scholars. But the sun shone for Jacob in order to heal his wound. In other words, Jacob was able to draw the sun of the Future, the "extended sun," the light and support of the Future, to keep the Torah study of his descendants strong (*Likutey Halakhot* V, p. 199a).

32:29 וַיֹּאמֶר לֹא יַעֲקֹב יֵאָמֵר עוֹד שִׁמְךָ כִּי אִם־יִשְׂרָאֵל כִּי־שָׂרִיתָ עִם־אֱלֹהִים וְעִם־אֲנָשִׁים וַתּוּכָל

"No longer will your name be said to be Jacob, but Israel," he said. "For you have battled with angels and with men and have been victorious."

❯ *No longer will your name be said to be Jacob, but Israel*

There is an immanent intellect and a transcendental intellect. In order to attain Godliness, a person must transform the transcendental intellect into immanent intellect, so that he will possess both levels of Godliness.

The name *YaAKoV* (יעקב, Jacob) represents the lower level of intellect, the *EiKeV* (עקב, heel). The letters of the name *YiSRaEL* (ישראל, Israel) may be rearranged to form the phrase *LY ROSh* (לי ראש, I have a head), indicating the higher level of intellect. When a person feels that he is on a low level and not growing spiritually, he must cry out to God. Then he attains transcendental intellect, and he incorporates the qualities found in the names *Yaakov* and *Yisrael* (*Likutey Moharan* I, 21:8).

⟩ *Jacob...Israel...you have battled with angels*

YaAKoV (יעקב, Jacob) represents a lower devotion to God, as represented in the word *EiKeV* (עקב, heel—the lowest part of the body). *YiSRael* (ישראל, Israel) represents a higher devotion, as in "You have battled (שרית, *SaRita*) with angels." That is, you took your devotions seriously and can overcome even angels in order to serve God (*Likutey Halakhot* II, p. 258).

32:30   וַיִּשְׁאַל יַעֲקֹב וַיֹּאמֶר הַגִּידָה־נָּא שְׁמֶךָ וַיֹּאמֶר לָמָּה זֶּה תִּשְׁאַל לִשְׁמִי וַיְבָרֶךְ אֹתוֹ שָׁם

Jacob returned the question. "Tell your name," he said. "Why do you ask my name?" he replied. Then he blessed him there.

⟩ *Why do you ask my name*

Angels are given names according to their missions, and these missions change constantly. Therefore the angel said to Jacob, "Why do you ask my name?" Jacob, on the other hand, represents truth and stability—i.e., an unchanging mission to serve God. This truth equipped him with the ability to withstand the attacks of the angels and always choose the right path. Thus, the angel said to Jacob, "for you have battled with angels...and have been victorious" (*Likutey Halakhot* VIII, p. 211a).

32:32 וַיִּזְרַח־לֹו הַשֶּׁמֶשׁ כַּאֲשֶׁר עָבַר אֶת־פְּנוּאֵל וְהוּא
צֹלֵעַ עַל־יְרֵכֹו

**The sun shone for him as he passed Penuel.
He was limping on his hip.**

The sun shone for him

The sun shone in order to heal him (Rashi).

Jacob is compared to the sun, which brings healing. Similarly, charity is compared to the sun—as in the phrase "A sun of charity" (Malakhi 3:20). Like the sun, charity brings healing (*Likutey Moharan* I, 86; ibid., I, 251).

The sun shone for him

Jacob is compared to the sun. Just as the sun illumines a person's physical path, so does his intellect illumine his path in life. The name *YaAKoV* (יעקב, Jacob) itself implies intellect, as in the phrase *vaYaAKVeini* (ויעקבני, he outwitted me) (Genesis 27:36) (*Likutey Moharan* I, 1; ibid., I, 74).

32:33 עַל־כֵּן לֹא־יֹאכְלוּ בְנֵי־יִשְׂרָאֵל אֶת־גִּיד הַנָּשֶׁה
אֲשֶׁר עַל־כַּף הַיָּרֵךְ עַד הַיֹּום הַזֶּה כִּי נָגַע בְּכַף־
יֶרֶךְ יַעֲקֹב בְּגִיד הַנָּשֶׁה

**Therefore the Jewish people do not eat the
sciatic nerve which is on the thigh socket to
this very day, because he touched Jacob's
thigh on the sciatic nerve.**

He touched Jacob's thigh on the sciatic nerve

YaAKoV (יעקב, Jacob) was so named because of the *EiKeV* (עקב, heel) which he grasped (Genesis 25:26). Advice and counsel are the "feet" (or legs) upon which one stands. Therefore the angel tried to damage Jacob's legs, in order to blemish his advice and counsel for survival in life (*Likutey Halakhot* III, p. 196a).

〗 He touched Jacob's thigh on the sciatic nerve

The angel fought Jacob to prevent him from establishing a nation that would serve God. By touching Jacob's sciatic nerve (גיד הנשה, *gid haNaSheH*), the angel tried to instill forgetfulness (נשיון, *NiShyon*) of one's goal in the Jewish nation. When Jacob defeated the angel, "the sun shone for him." The sun represents truth. In order to overcome forgetfulness, one must strive for truth (*Likutey Halakhot* II, p. 346).

〗 He touched Jacob's thigh on the gid ha-nasheh

There are three explanations for the word *haNaSheh* (הנשה, sciatic): *NaShu ve-kaftzu* (נשו וקפצו, moved away from); *NaShani* (נשני, forgot or became removed from); *NaShu gevuratam* (נשו גבורתם, lost their strength) (Rashi).

These three interpretations may be applied to those who have lost the courage to approach and serve God. *Nashu ve-kaftzu*—there are some people who at one time recognized God, but who have moved away from Him. *Nashani*—others have, over time, forgotten their connection to God. *Nashu gevuratam*—still others want to serve God, but feel too weak to do so.

The angel who wrestled with Jacob intended to create situations that would induce people to leave God. But Jacob and the tzaddikim in general are always seeking ways to help people who are far from God to draw close to Him (*Likutey Moharan* I, 56:3).

33:1 וַיִּשָּׂא יַעֲקֹב עֵינָיו וַיַּרְא וְהִנֵּה עֵשָׂו בָּא וְעִמּוֹ אַרְבַּע מֵאוֹת אִישׁ וַיַּחַץ אֶת־הַיְלָדִים עַל־לֵאָה וְעַל־רָחֵל וְעַל שְׁתֵּי הַשְּׁפָחוֹת

Jacob lifted his eyes and saw—behold! Esau was coming with four hundred men. He divided the children among Leah, Rachel, and the two maidservants.

〗 Esau was coming with four hundred men

The phrase *RA AYiN* (רע עין, Evil Eye) has the numerical value of 400. Esau intended to cast an evil eye upon Jacob by finding fault with him (*Rabbi Nachman's Wisdom* #242).

33:3 וְהוּא עָבַר לִפְנֵיהֶם וַיִּשְׁתַּחוּ אַרְצָה שֶׁבַע
פְּעָמִים עַד־גִּשְׁתּוֹ עַד־אָחִיו

He went ahead of them and bowed to
the ground seven times until he reached
his brother.

❭ *He bowed to the ground seven times until he reached
his brother*

This was an error on Jacob's part. Though Jacob was humble,
one should not always "bow" to an Esau. This act led to the Jews
bowing to Haman, Esau's descendant (*Likutey Halakhot* I, p. 178), and to
other subservience throughout the exiles.

33:9 וַיֹּאמֶר עֵשָׂו יֶשׁ־לִי רָב אָחִי יְהִי לְךָ אֲשֶׁר־לָךְ

"I have a lot," Esau said. "Keep what you
have, brother."

❭ *I have a lot*

Yesh li rav (יש לי רב, I have a lot) may also be read as "I have a
Rav." That is to say, Esau is the leader of the Other Side, and he
presents himself as a Torah authority. This same idea may be seen
in the phrase *Alufei bnei Esav* (אלופי בני עשו, the chieftains of the
sons of Esau) (Genesis 36:15), which the *Targum* renders as *Rabbanei
bnei Esav* (רבני בני עשו), a phrase that connotes both "multitudes"
and "rabbis."

In general, we must realize that there are some Torah scholars
whose learning does not come from holiness, but from the Other
Side (*Likutey Moharan* I, 8:3).

❭ *Yesh li rav*

Esau was an evil person. His problem stemmed from *Yesh li rav*
(יש לי רב, literally, "I have a Rav"). That is, Esau chooses an adviser
who is good in *his* eyes, who parrots Esau's thoughts and desires
rather than brings him closer to truth (*Likutey Halakhot* VII, p. 174).

33:10   וַיֹּאמֶר יַעֲקֹב אַל־נָא אִם־נָא מָצָאתִי חֵן בְּעֵינֶיךָ
וְלָקַחְתָּ מִנְחָתִי מִיָּדִי כִּי עַל־כֵּן רָאִיתִי פָנֶיךָ
כִּרְאֹת פְּנֵי אֱלֹהִים וַתִּרְצֵנִי

"No, please, if I have found favor in your
eyes, take my gift from my hand," Jacob said.
"For seeing your face is like seeing God's
Face, and you have shown me favor."

》 *Take my gift from my hand…For seeing your face is like seeing
God's Face*

When a person gives charity, he manifests Godliness in the
world. If a person is unfairly taxed, it is considered as if he gave
that money to charity (*Bava Batra* 9a). Thus, Jacob, who felt forced to
present a gift to Esau, said, "In seeing your face and giving you a
gift, it is as if I gave to charity, and so merited to see God's Face"
(*Likutey Moharan* II, 4:10).

》 *Take my gift*

Esau draws his essential strength from Isaac, who represents
Gevurah (strict judgments). To neutralize Esau's evil effect, Jacob
gave him a *MiNChaH* (gift), which also represents judgments (for
Isaac established the Afternoon Prayer called *MiNChaH*). Jacob
himself represents Divine Favor, which can also counteract Esau.
Since Divine Favor is aroused through charity, Jacob hinted to
Esau that he could overcome him because he gives gifts (*Likutey
Halakhot* II, p. 185a).

33:11   קַח־נָא אֶת־בִּרְכָתִי אֲשֶׁר הֻבָאת לָךְ כִּי־חַנַּנִי
אֱלֹהִים וְכִי יֶשׁ־לִי־כֹל וַיִּפְצַר־בּוֹ וַיִּקָּח

"Please take my blessing as it was brought
to you, since God has been gracious to me
and I have everything." He urged him, and
he took it.

》 *God has been gracious to me*

Initially, Esau wanted to destroy Jacob and his children. But when

Jacob said, "God has been gracious to me," he imbued himself and his children with the blessing of gaining grace or favor (*Bereishit Rabbah* 78:10).

The letter *CheT* (ח) alludes to intellect, as it suggests the words *ChiyuT* (חיות, vitality) and *Chokhmah* (חכמה, Godly wisdom). To attain *Chokhmah*, a person requires the faith that it exists, so that he may seek it. This faith is alluded to by the letter *nun* (נ). Together, *Chet* and *Nun* form the word *CheN* (חן, grace or favor).

Jacob had faith and sought wisdom. Thus, he attained *CheN*, and as a result, found favor in Esau's eyes. In general, a person who has Godly intellect attains grace and favor (*Likutey Moharan* I, 1:4).

❯ God has been gracious to me and I have everything

A person dies without reaching half his desires (*Kohelet Rabbah* 1:34).

By nature, a person is never satisfied. No matter how much he has, he always wants more. Therefore the Midrash teaches: "A person dies without reaching half his desires." Nevertheless, there is a blessing of God that contains a "double portion." One who receives this blessing earns "double" of what he was supposed to get, thereby satisfying his desire for more. Jacob, who was graced and blessed by God in this way, therefore said, "I have everything" (*Likutey Halakhot* VIII, p. 196b).

33:14 יַעֲבָר־נָא אֲדֹנִי לִפְנֵי עַבְדּוֹ וַאֲנִי אֶתְנָהֲלָה לְאִטִּי לְרֶגֶל הַמְּלָאכָה אֲשֶׁר־לְפָנַי וּלְרֶגֶל הַיְלָדִים עַד אֲשֶׁר־אָבֹא אֶל־אֲדֹנִי שֵׂעִירָה

"Let my lord go ahead of his servant. I will make my way slowly, according to the pace of the herds before me and the pace of the children, until I come to my lord at Seir."

❯ I will make my way slowly

He who wants to purify himself must be patient. The Talmud offers the analogy of one who enters a spice shop wishing to purchase a sweet-smelling fragrance. He is told by the proprietor,

"Wait! Absorb the smells, see what is attractive, and then you will buy" (*Yoma* 39a).

This was Jacob's attitude: "I have much to do. My children are young and not tempered." Only by being patient can one attain his goal (*Likutey Halakhot* VIII, p. 226a).

33:17 וַיַּעֲקֹב נָסַע סֻכֹּתָה וַיִּבֶן לוֹ בָּיִת וּלְמִקְנֵהוּ עָשָׂה סֻכֹּת עַל־כֵּן קָרָא שֵׁם־הַמָּקוֹם סֻכּוֹת

Jacob traveled to Sukkot. He built himself a house and made sukkahs for his flocks. Therefore he named the place Sukkot.

》 *Jacob traveled to Sukkot. He built himself a house...therefore he named the place Sukkot*

Jacob worked his entire life to reveal faith in God. Even his house was built with this goal in mind. For faith is mainly revealed through the idea of *SuKkaH* (סוכה), which is similar to *SoKheH* (סוכה, oversee). The tzaddik oversees faith and nurtures it, using every means available to him to reveal it to others. Thus, "He made sukkahs for his flocks"—for those people whom he was able to influence, he illumined true faith (*Likutey Halakhot* VIII, p. 257b).

33:18 וַיָּבֹא יַעֲקֹב שָׁלֵם עִיר שְׁכֶם אֲשֶׁר בְּאֶרֶץ כְּנַעַן בְּבֹאוֹ מִפַּדַּן אֲרָם וַיִּחַן אֶת־פְּנֵי הָעִיר

Jacob came whole to the city of Shekhem, which is in the land of Canaan, when he arrived from Padan Aram. He camped facing the city.

》 *Jacob came whole to the city of Shekhem*

Shalem (שלם, whole or complete) applies to health, wealth and Torah studies (*Shabbat* 33b).

Despite the efforts of Laban and Esau to destroy him, Jacob came *shalem* (whole or complete) to Shekhem. Jacob was complete in health—the four elements of his constitution were in harmony, since he had mastered his desires. He was complete in wealth—not lacking any possessions, despite having given Esau a massive gift. And he was complete in his Torah study—he had no questions and was able to study without any barriers to understanding (*Likutey Moharan* I, 27:8). Also, Jacob was found to be complete in his guarding of the covenant (see Rashi on Genesis 49:3).

❧ Jacob came whole to the city of Shekhem

Jacob represents the attribute of truth, as the verse states: "Give truth to Jacob" (Micah 7:20). When a person reveals truth, he draws people to God, "to serve Him with one accord" (Zephaniah 3:9). The Hebrew word for "accord" is *shekhem* (שכם). Thus, Jacob's truth leads to peace and accord (*Likutey Moharan* I, 27:2).

❧ He camped facing the city

Vayichan et pnei ha-ir (he camped facing the city) can also be translated as "he graced the city's countenance." Our Sages explain this to mean that Jacob minted coins and built bathhouses (*Shabbat* 33b).

Jacob personifies truth and an illumined spiritual countenance. Conversely, avarice and idolatry represent a dark countenance. When Jacob entered Shekhem, he struggled to cleanse its inhabitants from avarice by minting coins, and he purified them from idolatry by building bathhouses (to cleanse them from their idol-worship) (*Likutey Moharan* I, 23:1-3).

33:20 וַיַּצֶּב־שָׁם מִזְבֵּחַ וַיִּקְרָא־לוֹ אֵל אֱלֹהֵי יִשְׂרָאֵל

He erected an altar there and called it "God is the Lord of Israel."

❧ He called it "God is the Lord of Israel"

Vayikra lo El Elohei Yisrael (He called it "God is the Lord of Israel") can also be read as "The Lord of Israel called him (i.e., Jacob) 'El.'" In other words, God called Jacob a divine being (*Megillah* 18a).

The Jews—represented by Jacob—possess, as it were, power over God. Their prayers can mitigate His decrees and even change nature (*Likutey Moharan* II, 2:4).

34:14 וַיֹּאמְרוּ אֲלֵיהֶם לֹא נוּכַל לַעֲשׂוֹת הַדָּבָר הַזֶּה
לָתֵת אֶת־אֲחֹתֵנוּ לְאִישׁ אֲשֶׁר־לוֹ עָרְלָה כִּי־
חֶרְפָּה הִוא לָנוּ

They said to them, "We cannot do such a thing, to give our sister to an uncircumcised man. That would be a disgrace for us."

》 *Uncircumcised*

A blemished covenant, such as when the foreskin is not removed, results in humiliation. Removing the foreskin brings peace. So too, when a person removes the "foreskin of his heart," he reveals the covenant of peace. Moreover, guarding one's covenant increases one's livelihood (*Likutey Moharan* I, 39).

》 *We cannot do such a thing, to give our sister to an uncircumcised man. That would be a disgrace for us*

A blemished covenant causes shame and disgrace. Therefore Shekhem's deed humiliated Jacob and his children (*Likutey Moharan* I, 19:3; ibid., I, 82).

A blemished covenant leads to a broken heart. A broken heart represents the broken Tablets of the Law, and corresponds to the Shattering of the Vessels that occurred when the world was created (ibid., I, 34:7).

35:2 וַיֹּאמֶר יַעֲקֹב אֶל־בֵּיתוֹ וְאֶל כָּל־אֲשֶׁר עִמּוֹ הָסִרוּ
אֶת־אֱלֹהֵי הַנֵּכָר אֲשֶׁר בְּתֹכְכֶם וְהִטַּהֲרוּ וְהַחֲלִיפוּ
שִׂמְלֹתֵיכֶם

Jacob said to his household and everyone with him, "Remove the foreign gods that are in your midst. Purify yourselves and change your clothes."

》 *Remove the foreign gods that are in your midst*

By virtue of influencing people to become converts, Jacob subdued idolatry (*Likutey Moharan* I, 59:5).

35:11 וַיֹּאמֶר לוֹ אֱלֹהִים אֲנִי אֵל שַׁדַּי פְּרֵה וּרְבֵה גּוֹי
וּקְהַל גּוֹיִם יִהְיֶה מִמֶּךָּ וּמְלָכִים מֵחֲלָצֶיךָ יֵצֵאוּ

God said to him, "I am El Shadai. Be fruitful and multiply. A nation and a congregation of nations will come into existence from you. Kings will emerge from your loins."

El Shadai

The Holy Name *ShaDaI* (שדי) can be understood as meaning *She-yeish DaI* (יש די, there is enough). This may be understood in several ways:

There is enough Godliness for everyone; each individual can experience God on his own level. Furthermore, each person's knowledge of God is within his own parameters of understanding, which he must not exceed (*Likutey Moharan* II, 5:7).

He Who said to His world, "*Dai* (Enough)!" should say, "*Dai!*" to my suffering (*Bereishit Rabbah* 92:1). This also refers to the constriction of one's ability to understand God's ways when he is suffering (ibid., II, 5:3).

There is enough Godly blessing in the world for each person to have his own livelihood. Consequently, one should be satisfied with what he has and believe that God is giving him what is best for him (cf. *Avot* 4:1). Blessing and joy abound when one is satisfied with his lot (*Likutey Moharan* I, 23:4).

"There is enough" refers to Shabbat. A person need not slave away his entire life. God "worked six days" and then said, "Enough!" Our work, too, should be limited so that we may focus on Shabbat, which is the ultimate reason for Creation (cf. ibid., I, 11:4).

A person should guard himself from arrogance and consider what he has to be "enough." Our Sages teach that arrogance leads to adultery and immorality (*Sotah* 4b), because one who is never satisfied will seek sensual pleasures outside of his marriage. When a person guards himself from arrogance, he guards his covenant; similarly, by guarding the covenant, he foregoes arrogance and attains humility. He attains the blessings of "*El Shadai*" because he has "enough" and appreciates his blessings (*Likutey Moharan* I, 11:3).

35:18   וַיְהִי בְּצֵאת נַפְשָׁהּ כִּי מֵתָה וַתִּקְרָא שְׁמוֹ בֶּן־אוֹנִי וְאָבִיו קָרָא־לוֹ בִנְיָמִין

As her soul was departing—for she died— she named him Ben Oni. But his father named him Benjamin.

❱ Ben Oni

Rachel called her newborn son *Ben Oni* (son of my mourning) before she died in childbirth and was buried alongside the road over which the Jews would travel into exile; they would stop at her grave to weep and lament over the destruction of the Temple and their bitter fate (see Rashi on Genesis 48:7). But Jacob called his son *Binyamin* (son of the right), referring to his birth in the Holy Land which is situated to the right of Aram Naharayim, from whence Jacob had just come. Unlike Rachel who was caught up in her suffering, Jacob foresaw the joy and happiness that the Jews would experience when the Redemption takes place and the exile ends (*Likutey Halakhot* II, p. 312).

36:1   וְאֵלֶּה תֹּלְדוֹת עֵשָׂו הוּא אֱדוֹם

These are the generations of Esau—he is Edom.

❱ Esau—he is Edom

Esau is associated with the liver, which contains much blood, for Esau is called *EDoM* (אדום), which is similar to *DaM* (דם, blood) (*Zohar* III, 232b).

The liver is a hardworking organ that continuously filters blood. Thus, the Talmud teaches: "The liver is angry" (*Berakhot* 58b) because of its bloody work.

Though the function of liver is to filter and purify blood, Esau sought only bloodshed and did not care about purity at all. Therefore Esau is an angry person, and before the Heavenly Court, Esau's angel is the "Great Accuser" who grows angry at those who make mistakes, and denounces them before God (*Likutey Moharan* I, 57:6).

Parashat Vayeishev

37:1 וַיֵּשֶׁב יַעֲקֹב בְּאֶרֶץ מְגוּרֵי אָבִיו בְּאֶרֶץ כְּנָעַן

Jacob dwelt in the area where his fathers had stayed, in the land of Canaan.

⟩ *Jacob dwelt in the area where his fathers had stayed*

Jacob represents truth, as the verse states: "Give truth to Jacob" (Micah 7:20). A person who attains truth attains the Holy Land—he gets to live there or in its atmosphere, and he is able to reveal the sanctity of the Land to others (*Likutey Moharan* I, 47).

⟩ *Jacob dwelt in the area where his fathers had stayed, in the land of Canaan*

The place name *KeNaAn* (כנען, Canaan) is similar to the word *haKhNaAh* (הכנעה, submission), indicating humility. A humble person can dwell in the Holy Land (see *Rabbi Nachman's Wisdom* #261).

⟩ *Jacob dwelt in the area where his fathers had stayed*

The words *MeGuRei Aviv* (מגורי אביו, in the area where his fathers had stayed) allude to *MeGiyuRei Aviv* (מגיורי אביו, where his fathers made converts). Just as Abraham and Isaac made converts to God, so did Jacob (*Bereishit Rabbah* 84:4).

Jacob wished to dwell in tranquility. Immediately the troubles with Joseph and his brothers began (Rashi).

Jacob was unable to dwell in tranquility because one who works to spread the word of God cannot sit in peace. The dynamic of a convert is one of struggle—of struggling with his lifelong beliefs and accepting God through faith. (Our Sages teach that in the Messianic era, converts will no longer be accepted, since then there will be no more struggle, for Godliness will be revealed for all to see [*Yevamot* 24b]). Thus, the effort to make *ba'alei teshuvah* and converts precludes dwelling in peace (*Likutey Moharan* I, 228).

〉 *Jacob dwelt in the area where his fathers had stayed... These are the generations of Jacob: Joseph*

> Jacob made converts, as did his fathers (*Bereishit Rabbah* 84:4).
>
> Jacob wondered how he could overcome Esau—until he recognized the power of Joseph. Jacob is compared to the "fire," but Joseph is the "burning flame and smoke" that consumes (Rashi).
>
> Jacob wished to dwell in tranquility. Immediately, the troubles with Joseph and his brothers began (Rashi).

It is impossible to dwell in tranquility when one tries to make converts and draw people close to God. One must confront opposition, for this allows the other person to draw close to God out of choice, despite there not being a clear path. Then the convert's service of God will be in truth (*Likutey Moharan* I, 228).

This applies to every person who sincerely attempts to draw close to God, for he must realize that he faces difficulties. He can overcome these difficulties through the strength of the tzaddik (represented by Joseph), who possesses the power to overcome the opposition (Esau). Joseph gained this strength because, despite his descent into slavery, he remained steadfast in his devotion to God and overcame all the obstacles to His service. For these reasons he was called *YoSeF* (יוסף): "God has gathered in (אסף, *aSaF*) my shame [of sin]" (Genesis 30:23), and "May God add (יסף, *YoSeF*) to me another son" (ibid., 30:24); Joseph, the tzaddik, will be able to bring others close to God.

Thus, "Jacob"—the intellect—when it "dwells" and delves into God's service, will face opposition. But when "Joseph"—the flame—is kindled to serve God, then the opposition can be confronted and defeated (*Likutey Halakhot* II, p. 153a-155a).

〉 *Jacob dwelt*

> Jacob wished to dwell in tranquility. Immediately, the troubles with Joseph and his brothers began (Rashi).

Jacob—representing the Jew who wishes to serve God—felt that his troubles were over. After all, he had overcome his difficulties with the wicked Laban and Esau (conceptually, the different types of evil inclinations) and defeated their influence over him. However, there are many levels to serving God. Though it is relatively easy to overcome the opposition of evil, it is far more difficult to overcome the strife and conflicts generated between righteous people and those who oppose them. Thus, "Jacob wished to dwell in tranquility. Immediately, the troubles with Joseph and his brothers began" (*Likutey Halakhot* III, p. 126a).

37:2 אֵלֶּה תֹּלְדוֹת יַעֲקֹב יוֹסֵף בֶּן־שְׁבַע־עֶשְׂרֵה שָׁנָה הָיָה רֹעֶה אֶת־אֶחָיו בַּצֹּאן וְהוּא נַעַר אֶת־בְּנֵי בִלְהָה וְאֶת־בְּנֵי זִלְפָּה נְשֵׁי אָבִיו וַיָּבֵא יוֹסֵף אֶת־דִּבָּתָם רָעָה אֶל־אֲבִיהֶם

These are the generations of Jacob: Joseph, at the age of seventeen, was a shepherd with his brothers by the flock, but he was a lad with the sons of Bilhah and Zilpah, his fathers' wives. Joseph brought evil reports about them to their father.

❱ *These are the generations of Jacob: Joseph*

In the previous chapter, Jacob saw the *ALuFei bnei Esav* (אלופי בני עשו, the chieftains of the sons of Esau) (Genesis 36:15)—which can also be read as the "thousands (אלפים, *ALaFim*) of descendants of Esau"—and wondered, "How can anyone overcome them?" Therefore the Torah testifies: "These are the generations of Jacob: Joseph." An analogy is made to a blacksmith who sees a camel laden with a huge bundle of flax. "Where can all this flax go?" asks the blacksmith. A wise man replies, "One spark from your bellows will burn the entire load." So too, Jacob wondered how he could overcome Esau's thousands of descendants. A spark— Joseph—will come forth from Jacob and destroy them all (Rashi on Genesis 37:1).

ALuFei bnei Esav refers to the false leaders (*ALuF* means "learned one" in Hebrew and Aramaic) who lead the Jewish nation astray. Who can defeat them? The answer is that there will always be a Joseph—a tzaddik—who can ignite Jewish hearts with a burning desire for God and His truth. This will overcome the false leaders (*Likutey Halakhot* VIII, p. 212a-212b).

⟩ *These are the generations of Jacob: Joseph*

Jacob and Joseph are considered as one (Rashi).

This means that Joseph comprised the essence of Jacob more than did any of Joseph's brothers (*Likutey Moharan* I, 1:5).The Kabbalah describes Jacob as Tiferet and Joseph as Yesod. Thus, Jacob and Joseph are considered to be inseparable.

In greater detail, the letter *vav* (ו) has the numerical value of 6. The Kabbalah describes the letter *vav* as containing two *vavs* (for one cannot pronounce "*vav*" without pronouncing the *V* sound twice). The first *vav* represents the *sefirah* of Tiferet (as Tiferet is the principal *sefirah* of the *partzuf* of Ze'er Anpin, which contains six *sefirot*), corresponding to Jacob. The second *vav* represents the *sefirah* of Yesod (which is the sixth and last *sefirah* in the *partzuf* of Ze'er Anpin), corresponding to Joseph (see Charts, p. 346). Thus, Jacob and Joseph are considered as one (see *Likutey Moharan* I, 80).

⟩ *These are the generations of Jacob: Joseph*

There is a state of spiritual reality called the *Noam HaElyon* (Divine Pleasantness), through which all bounty (such as children, livelihood and good health) come into being. One can arouse the Divine Pleasantness by giving charity.

This idea is alluded to in the verse "These are the *toldot* (generations or descendants) of Jacob: Joseph." The descendants are the bounty. Jacob corresponds to charity, as in the verse "You have done justice and charity with Jacob" (Psalms 99:4). And Joseph corresponds to the Divine Pleasantness (as reflected in his handsome physical appearance) (*Likutey Moharan* II, 71). Thus, this verse can be read as meaning that bounty results when one gives charity and arouses the Divine Pleasantness.

37:3 וְיִשְׂרָאֵל אָהַב אֶת־יוֹסֵף מִכָּל־בָּנָיו כִּי־בֶן־זְקֻנִים
הוּא לוֹ וְעָשָׂה לוֹ כְּתֹנֶת פַּסִּים

Israel loved Joseph more than any of his sons since he was a child of his elder years. He made him a multicolored coat.

❩ *Ben zekunim*

Zekunim (elder years) refers to an "elder of holiness" and an "elder of the Other Side." Jacob always tried to give strength to the side of holiness, to add fear of God which "adds to one's days" (Proverbs 10:27). One should always endeavor to start anew each day, taking a fresh approach to his devotions, lest he "grow old" with "the same old devotions" and give strength to the Other Side. Joseph (*Yosef*) was the *ben zekunim*, the son of the elder years, since *YoSeF* means "he will add [to the realm of holiness]" (*Likutey Halakhot* II, p. 154a).

❩ *A multicolored coat*

After Joseph mastered Jacob's teachings, he believed he had merited "clean clothes" (a garment for the soul), so Jacob gave him the multicolored coat. But this garment was given prematurely, for Joseph had not yet been tested in spiritual or moral integrity. Because the brothers knew that Joseph was not yet tested, they stripped him of his multicolored coat and presented the garment to Jacob, who cried, "A wild beast consumed him!" (Genesis 37:33)—referring to the tests Joseph would still have to undergo.

Later, when Joseph fled from Potiphar's wife, "he left his garment in her hand" (ibid., 39:12), because he knew this had been a test of his integrity. Having passed his test (leaving the garment behind indicates he had "clean clothes" and that he had no further use of that garment), Joseph became viceroy of Egypt and gave his brothers "garments" (ibid., 45:22) to allude to his meriting "clean clothes" (*Likutey Halakhot* II, p. 132).

❩ *A multicolored coat*

Because Joseph would interact with so many different types of people, from tzaddikim to wicked people, he needed to be able to cloak the light of God in various ways, colors, etc. (*Likutey Halakhot* I, p. 14a).

37:4 וַיִּרְאוּ אֶחָיו כִּי־אֹתוֹ אָהַב אֲבִיהֶם מִכָּל־אֶחָיו
וַיִּשְׂנְאוּ אֹתוֹ וְלֹא יָכְלוּ דַּבְּרוֹ לְשָׁלֹם

**His brothers saw that their father loved
him more than all his brothers, and they
hated him. They were not able to speak
with him peaceably.**

)) *They were not able to speak with him peaceably*

All arguments stem from the Chambers of Exchanges, where
things become confused to the point of "selling" the true tzaddik,
Joseph, as a slave (*Likutey Halakhot* II, p. 312).

Joseph and his brothers were all very great tzaddikim. Yet they
sold him into slavery thinking that he deserved it, for they thought
that his dreams were lies. This false impression stemmed from
the Chambers of Exchanges. Thus, we understand that they were
sincere in their actions against him (ibid., I, p. 214). This teaches us
that not every sincere deed or devotion is acceptable. One must
scrutinize his intentions and deeds most carefully.

37:7 וְהִנֵּה אֲנַחְנוּ מְאַלְּמִים אֲלֻמִּים בְּתוֹךְ הַשָּׂדֶה
וְהִנֵּה קָמָה אֲלֻמָּתִי וְגַם־נִצָּבָה וְהִנֵּה תְסֻבֶּינָה
אֲלֻמֹּתֵיכֶם וַתִּשְׁתַּחֲוֶיןָ לַאֲלֻמָּתִי

**"Behold! We were binding sheaves in the
middle of the field. Behold! My sheaf rose
up and remained standing. Behold! Your
sheaves gathered around and bowed to
my sheaf."**

)) *Joseph's dreams*

In the first dream, Joseph saw sheaves bowing to him; in the
second, he saw the sun, the moon and the stars bowing to him.
These dreams represent the two types of stories that clothe Torah
teachings: stories that relate to the Revealed Torah, and stories that
convey the deepest mysteries of the Torah. The first dream, which

depicted the brothers working in the field, alludes to the lower level, our material world. The second dream, which depicted the solar system, alludes to the higher level, which is beyond this world.

Joseph's understanding of both types of Torah helped him to interpret the dreams of Pharaoh and his advisors, for he perceived the deeper meaning of those dreams and could foresee the famine. Therefore he merited to become the viceroy, collecting all the wealth of this world and directing it towards attaining even greater levels of intellect (*Likutey Halakhot* V, p. 46-24a).

Joseph's dreams

Joseph's dream of his sheaf standing above the others implies that he elevated his level of eating to the point that he could rectify the sin of Adam, who had eaten from the Tree. Through this dream, Joseph was telling his brothers that he had attained some of the levels of their father, Jacob. His second dream speaks of the stellar system, implying the mystery of intercalation, a deep wisdom of which only very great souls are aware (see Deuteronomy 4:6; *Shabbat* 75a). Though Jacob took note of the dreams, the brothers refused to accept that Joseph was greater than they. Their opposition to Joseph was rooted in the strife found between the tzaddikim, who are always confronted by the difficult test of discerning the real truth: Who is the greater tzaddik? (*Likutey Halakhot* III, p. 252).

Joseph's dreams

The bundles of sheaves in Joseph's first dream represent knots with which the tzaddik binds and draws close those who are distant from God. Joseph's "knots" were superior to those of the other tzaddikim—his brothers—in that they remained firm. The sun and moon in his second dream represent the benefactor and beneficiary, the Rav and his closest disciple. The Rav draws his great intellect from Above and illumines his student, who receives directly from him. The stars represent those who are distant from God (*Likutey Halakhot* I, p. 14a-28).

Your sheaves gathered around and bowed to my sheaf

Although the brothers were great tzaddikim in their own right, Joseph was even greater. Joseph represents the true tzaddik whose directives guide everyone towards true service of God. Therefore Joseph told his brothers, "Your sheaves bowed to my sheaf," implying that they must still come to him for direction.

But the brothers misinterpreted Joseph's intentions, assuming they arose not from holiness but from a desire to rule over others. This they rejected, and distanced themselves from Joseph to the point of selling him into slavery. The "selling" of the tzaddik represents their own blemish, the desire for wealth, which blinds a person to the tzaddik (*Likutey Halakhot* VII, p. 466-234a).

37:8 וַיֹּאמְרוּ לוֹ אֶחָיו הֲמָלֹךְ תִּמְלֹךְ עָלֵינוּ אִם־מָשׁוֹל תִּמְשֹׁל בָּנוּ וַיּוֹסִפוּ עוֹד שְׂנֹא אֹתוֹ עַל־חֲלֹמֹתָיו וְעַל־דְּבָרָיו

His brothers said to him, "Will you rule over us? Will you dominate us?" They hated him even more for his dreams and for his words.

》 *Joseph and his brothers*

Joseph represents the true tzaddik, while the brothers— tzaddikim in their own right—still lacked perfection. Despite their purity, they were misled into arguing against Joseph and eventually selling him into slavery. This story of strife between the tzaddikim repeats itself in each generation, as each tzaddik claims the truth that conceals the true tzaddik.

When the brothers were caught in possession of Joseph's goblet after their second trip to Egypt, they began to realize their error in selling him and said, "God has found us guilty" (Genesis 44:16). Joseph made them feel like thieves because they had thought that Joseph, the true tzaddik, acted in stealth and was not really greater than they. Only after they admitted the truth did Joseph reveal himself to his brothers (*Likutey Halakhot* III, p. 386-194a).

37:13 וַיֹּאמֶר יִשְׂרָאֵל אֶל־יוֹסֵף הֲלוֹא אַחֶיךָ רֹעִים בִּשְׁכֶם לְכָה וְאֶשְׁלָחֲךָ אֲלֵיהֶם וַיֹּאמֶר לוֹ הִנֵּנִי

Israel said to Joseph, "Aren't your brothers shepherding in Shekhem? Come, I will send you to them." "Here I am," he answered him.

❱ Aren't your brothers shepherding in Shekhem

The place name *SheKheM* (שכם) connotes a garment with *tzitzit*, as in the verse "Shem and Japheth took the garment [i.e., with the *tzitzit* (*Tikkuney Zohar* #18, p. 37a)] and placed it on both their shoulders (שכם, *SheKheM*)" (Genesis 9:23). *Tzitzit* are associated with guarding the covenant, so they are associated with Joseph, the guardian of the covenant par excellence.

Why did Jacob send Joseph to his brothers, knowing of their enmity towards him? The answer is that Jacob had no qualms about sending Joseph to them since he thought they were in Shekhem—which, conceptually speaking, was Joseph's domain, a guarded covenant (*Likutey Moharan* I, 7:end). But the brothers were actually in Dothan, and when Joseph came to them, they sold him into slavery. Yet this occurred because God had decreed that it was Joseph's destiny to precede his family into Egypt in order to provide them with sustenance (see Genesis 45:7).

37:14 וַיֹּאמֶר לוֹ לֶךְ־נָא רְאֵה אֶת־שְׁלוֹם אַחֶיךָ וְאֶת־ שְׁלוֹם הַצֹּאן וַהֲשִׁבֵנִי דָּבָר וַיִּשְׁלָחֵהוּ מֵעֵמֶק חֶבְרוֹן וַיָּבֹא שְׁכֶמָה

He said to him, "Go see how your brothers are doing and how the sheep are doing, and bring me back word." He sent him from the valley of Hebron, and he came to Shekhem.

❱ He sent him from the valley of Hebron

Mei'EMeK (מעמק, from the valley) can also be translated as *Mei'AMoK* (מעמוק, from the depth). Jacob sent Joseph from the deep advice of the tzaddik who was buried in Hebron, Abraham, to fulfill what was said to Abraham at the Covenant Between the Pieces: "For your offspring will be aliens [i.e., in the Egyptian exile]" (Genesis 15:13) (Rashi).

Notwithstanding the brothers' deliberations, Joseph was actually sent to Egypt through the counsel of Abraham. When Abraham asked, "How will I know that I will inherit [the Land]?" (Genesis 15:8), this precipitated the exile. Divine Providence developed the scenario for several generations and now it was being carried out (*Likutey Halakhot* III, p. 386-194a).

37:24 וַיִּקָּחֻהוּ וַיַּשְׁלִכוּ אֹתוֹ הַבֹּרָה וְהַבּוֹר רֵק אֵין בּוֹ מָיִם

They took him and threw him into the pit. The pit was empty; there was no water in it.

⟩ *The pit was empty; there was no water in it*

It was empty of water, but it contained snakes and scorpions (Rashi).

It is better for a person to fall into a pit filled with snakes and scorpions than to fall into the hands of his enemies (*Zohar* I, 185).

The *Zohar's* comment is difficult to understand, since snakes and scorpions are more likely to harm a person! This teaching can be explained as follows: There are two types of suffering. The first type—symbolized by the snakes and scorpions—is suffering sent by Heaven. Though it is hard to endure, a person can look beyond this type of suffering and come to recognize God's message and His Kindness that transcend the suffering. The second type is that caused by human beings. When a person suffers due to human beings, it is harder to look beyond the suffering, because his enemies are bent on deflecting him from thinking about God altogether. Thus, suffering caused by human beings is far greater than suffering sent directly from God (*Likutey Halakhot* V, p. 92a).

37:28 וַיַּעַבְרוּ אֲנָשִׁים מִדְיָנִים סֹחֲרִים וַיִּמְשְׁכוּ וַיַּעֲלוּ
אֶת־יוֹסֵף מִן־הַבּוֹר וַיִּמְכְּרוּ אֶת־יוֹסֵף לַיִּשְׁמְעֵאלִים
בְּעֶשְׂרִים כָּסֶף וַיָּבִיאוּ אֶת־יוֹסֵף מִצְרָיְמָה

**Midianite traders passed by. They pulled
Joseph up out of the pit and sold Joseph
to the Ishmaelites for twenty pieces of
silver. They brought Joseph to Egypt.**

⟫ Joseph is sold to Egypt

Joseph slandered his brothers with three accusations: that they
ate a limb from a live animal, that they treated the children of the
maidservants as slaves, and that they were guilty of immorality.
He was punished for all three accusations. After selling Joseph,
the brothers slaughtered a goat, disproving the charge that they
ate limbs from live animals. Regarding their behavior towards
their half-brothers, Joseph was sold as a slave. Countering the
accusation of immorality, Joseph was tested with Potiphar's wife
(Rashi on Genesis 37:2).

All slander stems from a blemished mind, for slander generally
results from a distorted perception of another person's intentions.
Eating the limb of a live animal represents eating unfit food, which
blemishes the mind; so too, immorality blemishes the mind. The
brothers suspected that Joseph possessed a flawed intellect. Their
theory was reinforced by his dreams, which they interpreted as
delusions.

But Joseph, who remained steadfast throughout all his tests,
proved that he possessed an unblemished mind. His dreams were
correct and reflected the reality of the situation. Furthermore, he
demonstrated that his memory was sound. When the brothers
came before him, it is written, "Joseph remembered the dreams
that he had dreamt" (Genesis 42:9)—for he recalled that their enmity
towards him stemmed from what they perceived as his blemished
intellect, which was not the case.

In his dealings with Pharaoh's three officers—the Wine Steward,
the Baker and the Chief Butcher—Joseph was able to attain mastery
over each one. He was also able to interpret the dreams of Pharaoh,
who represents a blemished mind (PhaRAoH [פרעה] comes from
the same root as le-haPhRiA [להפריע, to confuse]). Joseph was pure

and his mind was pure, and so he was able to subjugate the impure to the pure (*Likutey Halakhot* IV, p. 18a-36).

❭ Joseph is sold into slavery... Er and Onan

Joseph represents the guarded covenant. Despite being sold into an immoral land, and as a slave no less, Joseph guarded his covenant and drew Divine Providence into the place he found himself. In contrast, Er and Onan blemished their covenant by spilling their seed. Their actions repelled Divine Providence: "Er, Judah's firstborn, was evil in God's eyes" (Genesis 38:7)—namely, wasted seed negatively affects sight (*Likutey Halakhot* VII, p. 408).

37:31   וַיִּקְחוּ אֶת־כְּתֹנֶת יוֹסֵף וַיִּשְׁחֲטוּ שְׂעִיר עִזִּים
וַיִּטְבְּלוּ אֶת־הַכֻּתֹּנֶת בַּדָּם

They took Joseph's coat, slaughtered a goat, and dipped the coat in the blood.

❭ Joseph and his brothers

The brothers opposed Joseph, believing that his desire to rule over them was based on brazenness (he was, after all, the younger brother). After he was sold, they slaughtered a *seir iZim* (שעיר עזים, kid goat) to counteract his perceived *aZut* (עזות, brazenness) and affirm their own, holy boldness. Meanwhile, Joseph was tested by Potiphar's wife; by withstanding that test, he turned his brazenness into holy boldness.

Judah sent a *gedi iZim* (גדי עזים, kid goat) to Tamar, for he, too, had to oppose brazenness (in this case, the brazenness of immorality and harlotry) with holy boldness. By purifying his boldness, Judah merited to be the ancestor of Mashiach (*Likutey Halakhot* IV, p. 202).

❭ They dipped the coat in the blood

When the Chozeh of Lublin (Rabbi Yaakov Yitzchak Horowitz, 1745-1815) passed away, in order to raise money for his widow, people bid on his belongings. One man bid several hundred rubles for the yarmulke (head covering) of the Chozeh. Intending to honor the man, the Chozeh's widow washed the yarmulke thoroughly before handing it to him. Upon seeing the freshly-laundered yarmulke, the man exclaimed, "*Gevalt!* It was the sweat of the Chozeh that I was looking for!" (*Rabbi Levi Yitzchok Bender*).

The brothers were not aware of Joseph's great devotions; rather, they viewed him as not such a great devotee. This is the meaning of "They dipped the coat in the blood"—they were looking for evidence of sweat, blood and other efforts to determine Joseph's level of devotion. Because they were unable to discern Joseph's efforts, they felt it necessary to dip his coat in blood.

38:1 וַיְהִי בָּעֵת הַהִוא וַיֵּרֶד יְהוּדָה מֵאֵת אֶחָיו וַיֵּט עַד־אִישׁ עֲדֻלָּמִי וּשְׁמוֹ חִירָה

At that time, Judah went down from his brothers. He became friends with an Adullamite man named Hirah.

Judah went down

He Who says in the beginning what will be in the end (Isaiah 66:7).

Even before the first exile, the Final Redeemer was made (*Bereishit Rabbah* 85:2).

Even before the Jews descended into their first exile in Egypt, Judah fathered Peretz, the progenitor of King David and Mashiach, showing that every miracle or redemption in this world is drawn from the Future Redemption. Thus, the miracles of the Exodus and those of the Red Sea were all drawn from the power of the Divine Providence, which will manifest with the coming of Mashiach (*Likutey Halakhot* I, p. 121a).

38:7 וַיְהִי עֵר בְּכוֹר יְהוּדָה רַע בְּעֵינֵי יְיָ וַיְמִתֵהוּ יְיָ

Er, Judah's firstborn, was evil in God's eyes, and God made him die.

Er, Judah's firstborn, was evil in God's eyes...what he did was evil in God's eyes

The spark of holiness can remain steadfast only in the realm of holiness, in Yesod, which is represented by the covenant of

circumcision. One who defiles the covenant removes that spark
of holiness and allows it to enter the realm of impurity. Thus, the
sins of Er and Onan are considered the worst transgressions of
all. Only by revealing *chesed* (kindness) can one merit to gather
in the lost spark of holiness, for in doing so, one makes a vessel
of *chesed* within which the spark can be repaired. Kabbalistically
speaking, the Shattered Vessels of Yesod of Atzilut fell into the
realm of Chesed of Beriah, the lower universe (see Charts, p. 347).
Thus, when one performs acts of *chesed*, he can also rectify the
vessels of Yesod which have fallen there and rectify his blemished
covenant (*Likutey Halakhot* I, p. 112).

⟩ *Er, Judah's firstborn, was evil*

Er's sin was masturbation. The *Zohar* (I, 57a) teaches that whoever commits this sin is "evil" in the sense that he harms others
as well as himself. One who masturbates is always bad-tempered
and disagreeable, and thus upsets others (*Rabbi Nachman's Wisdom*
#249). In contrast, a tzaddik who guards his covenant is always
pleasant and agreeable to others, as alluded to in the verse "God
saw that the light [of the tzaddik] was good" (Genesis 1:4) (*Likutey
Moharan* I, 23:3).

38:18 וַיֹּאמֶר מָה הָעֵרָבוֹן אֲשֶׁר אֶתֶּן־לָךְ וַתֹּאמֶר חֹתָמְךָ
וּפְתִילֶךָ וּמַטְּךָ אֲשֶׁר בְּיָדֶךָ וַיִּתֶּן־לָהּ וַיָּבֹא אֵלֶיהָ
וַתַּהַר לוֹ

**"What guarantee should I give you?" he
asked. "Your seal, your cloak, and your
staff which is in your hand," she replied.
He gave them to her and came to her, and
she conceived by him.**

⟩ *What guarantee should I give you…Your seal, your cloak, and your staff*

With three things the world was created: With a *sefer* (ספר,
book—i.e., the Torah), a *sofer* (סופר, scribe—i.e., God), and a *sippur*
(סיפור, story—i.e., the history of mankind) (*Sefer Yetzirah* 1:1). In the
holy writings, these three things are referred to as the parchment

upon which the book is written, the ink that is inscribed in the book, and the quill that writes the book.

These three things correspond to the three items that Judah gave Tamar as collateral. The cloak corresponds to the *sefer*—i.e., the "skins" upon which a book is written. The seal represents the *sofer*, the medium of the ink. The staff is the *sippur*, the quill that writes the book.

The Torah is written on parchment with ink from a quill. The tongue is also said to be the quill that inscribes the story upon one's heart. When a person is willing to accept the sanctity of the Torah, he draws the Godliness that is present in creation and tells his own *sippur*—his deeds that proclaim Godliness (*Likutey Halakhot* VII, p. 252).

What guarantee should I give you...Your seal, your cloak, and your staff

The meeting between Judah and Tamar was the prelude to the birth of Mashiach. Mashiach himself is the guarantor for the entire world, the assurance that everyone will reach perfection. Therefore Tamar insisted on collateral for their union, in order to invoke the collateral that Mashiach would represent.

The three guarantees that she requested combat the three characteristics that deter a person from reaching perfection. These characteristics are: one who degrades others (which is similar to murder), one who is immoral, and one who lacks faith. The seal represents the "seal of holiness"—the covenant, morality. The cloak represents one's "cloak of honor"—his pledge to honor others and not degrade them. The staff represents faith—as represented by the staff of Moses which was used to perform miracles that spread faith in God. These three items represent the characteristics that lead to perfection and to Mashiach, who will bring the world to perfection (*Likutey Halakhot* VII, p. 74a-148).

What guarantee should I give you...Your seal, your cloak, and your staff

When God wished to create man, the angels opposed Him, claiming that man would sin. God then took counsel with the souls of the righteous, since they are the ones who take responsibility for the world. The main tzaddik who accepts this responsibility is the soul of Mashiach, since he must make sure to rectify every person. Thus, the first mention of a guarantor in the Torah appears in the story of Judah and Tamar, as their union led to the birth of Mashiach, who will bring the world to perfection.

Tamar asked for Judah's seal, cloak and staff as guarantees. The seal represents *tefilin*, the cloak represents the *talit/tzitzit*, and the staff is the "quill"—namely, the many books of Torah that spread Godliness. At times the tzaddikim become very zealous in fulfilling their mission; indeed, Tamar's life was threatened when Judah took issue with what he viewed as her promiscuity. These guarantees represent *mitzvot* that demonstrate the acceptance and fulfillment of Torah, which the tzaddikim can use to rectify the world (*Likutey Halakhot* VII, p. 126a).

The concept of Mashiach as a guarantor for mankind is also reflected in Judah's pledge to take responsibility for Benjamin when the brothers descended to Egypt (Genesis 43:9). Here Judah represents the soul of Mashiach. A further allusion lies in the juxtaposition of the story of Joseph being sold into slavery and the story of Judah's meeting with Tamar. As the Midrash states: "The tribes were busy selling Joseph; Joseph was busy with his sackcloth and fasting [over his tribulations]; Reuben was busy with his sackcloth and fasting [over his efforts to repent]; Jacob was busy with his sackcloth and fasting [over the loss of Joseph]; Judah was busy finding himself a wife; and God was busy creating the light of Mashiach" (*Bereishit Rabbah* 85:1). Because of Joseph's sanctity and morality, he ascended from slavery to become the second-in-command of Egypt. When Joseph began drawing upon himself the sanctity of Mashiach, God "busied Himself" with the birth of Mashiach (*Likutey Halakhot* VII, p. 126a-127a).

39:6 וַיַּעֲזֹב כָּל־אֲשֶׁר־לוֹ בְּיַד־יוֹסֵף וְלֹא־יָדַע אִתּוֹ מְאוּמָה
כִּי אִם־הַלֶּחֶם אֲשֶׁר־הוּא אוֹכֵל וַיְהִי יוֹסֵף יְפֵה־תֹאַר
וִיפֵה מַרְאֶה

**He left all his affairs in Joseph's hands,
and with him around, concerned himself
with nothing but the bread he ate. Joseph
was handsome of form and handsome of
appearance.**

》 Joseph was handsome

Joseph is the paradigm of the tzaddik—the true spiritual beauty
and grace of the world—because he withstood sexual temptation
(*Likutey Moharan* II, 67).

39:8 וַיְמָאֵן וַיֹּאמֶר אֶל־אֵשֶׁת אֲדֹנָיו הֵן אֲדֹנִי לֹא־יָדַע
אִתִּי מַה־בַּבָּיִת וְכֹל אֲשֶׁר־יֶשׁ־לוֹ נָתַן בְּיָדִי

**He adamantly refused. He said to his
master's wife, "Look, with me here, my
master doesn't even know what's going
on in the house. He has put me in charge
of everything he owns."**

》 He adamantly refused

Joseph withstood the test of Potiphar's wife's attempts to
seduce him. Yet the fact that the Torah considers this a test is a
mystery. Rationally speaking, since Joseph was wise, this should
not have presented any difficulties for him. For anyone with even
a bit of intellect can overcome immoral thoughts and deeds (*Likutey
Moharan* I, 72).

》 He adamantly refused

The cantillation note on the word *vayema'ein* (he adamantly
refused) is called the *shalshelet*, which is a long, drawn-out note.
Rabbi Yitzchok Breiter (d. 1943) was wont to say that this is
because, when tempted by sin, one must remain steadfast and
refuse again and again.

39:10   וַיְהִי כְּדַבְּרָהּ אֶל־יוֹסֵף יוֹם יוֹם וְלֹא־שָׁמַע אֵלֶיהָ
לִשְׁכַּב אֶצְלָהּ לִהְיוֹת עִמָּהּ

**She spoke to Joseph day after day but he
would not listen to her, to lie beside her
or to be with her.**

❱ *She spoke to Joseph day after day*

YoSeF (יוסף, Joseph) represents the additional (נוסף, *noSaF*) sanctity that a person can gain when he withstands a test. Each person can become a *Yosef* on a daily basis, by adding holiness into his day (*Likutey Halakhot* I, p. 268).

39:11   וַיְהִי כְּהַיּוֹם הַזֶּה וַיָּבֹא הַבַּיְתָה לַעֲשׂוֹת מְלַאכְתּוֹ
וְאֵין אִישׁ מֵאַנְשֵׁי הַבַּיִת שָׁם בַּבָּיִת

**On one such day, he came to the house to
do his work. No one from the household
staff was there.**

❱ *No one from the household staff was there*

Although no one from the household was present, Joseph did see Jacob's image appear (*Sotah* 36b).

The fact that Joseph was able to see this image was something wondrous, especially since Jacob himself was unaware of it (*Likutey Moharan* I, 150).

39:12   וַתִּתְפְּשֵׂהוּ בְּבִגְדוֹ לֵאמֹר שִׁכְבָה עִמִּי וַיַּעֲזֹב בִּגְדוֹ
בְּיָדָהּ וַיָּנָס וַיֵּצֵא הַחוּצָה

**She grabbed him by his garment, saying,
"Lie with me." He left his garment in her
hand and fled, going outside.**

❱ *She grabbed him by his garment... He left his garment in her
hand and fled*

Joseph's test was "humble" compared to the test that Boaz endured when Ruth lay down at his feet. And Boaz's test was "humble" compared to the test that Palti ben Layish endured: he had to remain celibate while sharing a bed with Michal, who was married to David but was forced to live with Palti by King Saul (*Sanhedrin* 19b).

Our Sages' use of the word "humbled" when speaking about overcoming sexual temptation shows that humility protects a person from immorality and, conversely, that arrogance leads to immorality (*Likutey Moharan* I, 130).

She grabbed him by his garment

The forces of the Other Side and the Evil One grab a man by his garment. The necessity of obtaining garments and clothing can disturb a person greatly and prevent him from serving God. Thus, "she grabbed him by his garment."

If you are a master of your soul and have your heart strongly bound to God, you will pay no attention to this. You may have no clothing to wear, but it will not disturb you, for you do not allow yourself to be distracted by such things. It is written, "He left his garment in her hand and fled." You must leave your worries of garments and clothing behind and flee from the forces of evil. Pay no attention to what you lack. Do what God requires of you and serve Him to the best of your ability (*Rabbi Nachman's Wisdom* #100).

The implication is that the Evil One catches a person "by his garment," causing him to pursue the material cloaks of this world. On a deeper level, this alludes to man's tendency to assume that appearance equals essence. Defying this impression is the tzaddik, who seems like an ordinary person but is actually someone far greater and loftier. The tzaddik's "cloak" of normalcy conceals his true essence.

"Garments" (as well as property) represent the area in which man falls victim to jealousies. We see this in the rebellion of Korach against Moses (Numbers 16). Korach was jealous of Aaron who, as High Priest, dressed in royal robes. Therefore Korach dressed himself and his followers in garments that were pure *tekheilet* as a way of showing that he, too, had attained purity of soul and was worthy of a high position. He failed to understand that Moses and Aaron possessed great depth, which their appearances concealed (*Likutey Halakhot* VII, p. 139a-278-140a).

⟩ *He fled*

The sea saw and fled (Psalms 114:3).

The sea split for the Jews in Joseph's merit (*Bereishit Rabbah* 87:8).

In the merit of the tzaddik, the sea splits. The "sea" refers to the Sea of Wisdom, which opens to one who is attached to the tzaddik (*Likutey Halakhot* II, p. 68a).

Parashat Mikeitz

41:1 וַיְהִי מִקֵּץ שְׁנָתַיִם יָמִים וּפַרְעֹה חֹלֵם וְהִנֵּה עֹמֵד
עַל־הַיְאֹר

**Two years later, Pharaoh was dreaming.
Behold! He was standing on the river.**

❯ *Two years*

Shenatayim yamim (two years) literally means "two years of
days." When a person is searching for God, each day is as valuable
as a year (*Likutey Moharan* II, 2:6).

❯ *Two years later, Pharaoh was dreaming. Behold! He was
standing on the river…The bad-looking, scrawny cows ate
the seven handsome and healthy cows*

The letters of the word *MiKeitZ* (מקץ, at the end) may be rearranged to form the word *KaMatZ* (קמץ, withhold)—in particular, to
withhold blessing.

The term *shenatayim yamim* (literally, "two years of days") refers
specifically to slander. (Slander misleads the person who talks evil
of others into thinking of things not as they actually were; hence,
"days are years"—what actually happened is viewed through the
lens of imagination rather than reality.) As punishment for the sin
of the spies who slandered the Holy Land, the Jews were forced
to spend a *year* in the desert for every *day* of the spies' mission
(Numbers 14:34). More broadly, because the slanderer is unsure of
the facts or of people's motivations for their actions, slander is
associated with the power of unbridled imagination.

In his dream, Pharaoh was "standing on the river." This river is
the Nile, which is also called the Pishon River (Rashi on Genesis 2:11).
PIShON (פישון) alludes to the phrase *PI ShONeh Halakhot* (פי שונה
הלכות, a mouth that speaks Torah law). True Torah teachings bring
blessing (Leviticus 26), whereas imaginary Torah teachings result
in famine (for they create a delusory, "false Heaven" that cannot
give rain).

"Pharaoh" refers to a person who is not steeped in or steadfast in Torah law, yet who seeks to create novel Torah teachings based on his imagination. These imaginary Torah thoughts are harmful to the world, for they prevent God's blessing from descending. Thus, in Pharaoh's dream, the seven fat cows of blessing are swallowed up by the seven scrawny cows of imaginary teachings.

In summation, the verse "Two years later, Pharaoh was dreaming. Behold! He was standing on the river" may be interpreted to mean "Blessings are withheld due to the power of deluded imagination, which leads a person to create unfounded Torah insights." These false teachings are rectified by Joseph, the tzaddik, who elevates a person beyond his imagination, so that with a rectified imagination (the opposite of slander), one can find good even in bad situations (see *Likutey Moharan* I, 54:6).

⟩ *Pharaoh was dreaming*

Pharaoh dreamt about seven fat cows that were swallowed up by seven scrawny cows. Pharaoh represents one who has great wealth yet always craves more, as if he is always hungry. His name, *PhaRaOh* (פרעה), resembles *PeiRaOn* (פרעון, repayment). Pharaoh always *must* make payments, whether he is buying material goods for his comfort or paying off his debts. Joseph, the tzaddik, advises him to "tax" the bounty at twenty percent. In other words, Joseph advises the wealthy to "tax their wealth" by giving to charity, an act that will protect their wealth (*Likutey Halakhot* II, p. 79a).

Pharaoh's dreams occurred after *shenatayim yamim* (literally, "two years of days"). This phrase, alluding to "years" which are connected to "days," recalls the spies who slandered the Holy Land and were punished with a *year* in the desert for every *day* they had toured the Land (Numbers 14:34). Just as Pharaoh desired untold wealth, the blemish of the spies was avarice. God wanted the Jews to conquer the Land of Israel in a supernatural and miraculous way, and the Land itself was primed to yield its bounty in a miraculous manner, which defies avarice. But the spies wanted to conquer the Land in a "natural" manner, implying that their desire for wealth was great. The Hebrew word *meRaGLim* (מרגלים, spies) comes from the root word *ReGeL* (רגל, foot), since those with avarice travel about constantly looking for a deal, always seeking more wealth and never relying on God to provide for them where they live (*Likutey Halakhot* II, p. 158-80a).

》 *Pharaoh was dreaming*

The seven lower *sefirot* correspond to all the good and evil attributes and characteristics in the world. In order to come close to good and give oneself over to God, one must undergo a process of self-nullification. Conceptually, this process is represented by sleep.

When Pharaoh slept, he saw good cows at first, as he moved towards self-nullification. But then he pulled back to the side of evil and saw bad cows swallow up the good ones. For that is how it is—at first one draws close to God, but then he is overcome by the Other Side. So Pharaoh went to sleep again, attempting self-nullification once more. Yet again, despite seeing good, he again saw evil and was overpowered by it. In contrast, Joseph, the tzaddik, is one who can nullify himself completely. In particular, he can perceive the good and teach others how to overcome the evil (*Likutey Halakhot* I, p. 28a).

41:2   וְהִנֵּה מִן־הַיְאֹר עֹלֹת שֶׁבַע פָּרוֹת יְפוֹת מַרְאֶה
וּבְרִיאֹת בָּשָׂר וַתִּרְעֶינָה בָּאָחוּ

Behold! Seven cows, beautiful of appearance and of healthy flesh, emerged from the river and grazed in the marshland.

》 *Seven healthy cows*

The seven healthy cows represent the tzaddikim. They are called "healthy" because "A tzaddik eats to satisfy his soul" (Proverbs 13:25). By acquiring and disseminating faith, the tzaddik teaches other people how to satisfy their souls. Later, Joseph told Pharaoh, "Ration the produce of Egypt" (Genesis 41:34). *VeChiMeish* (וחמש, ration) is similar to *ChaMeiSh* (חמש, five), which represents the Five Books of the Torah. The rations of one's spiritual food are the Torah. The tzaddik shows us how to store up spiritual energy for the lean years (*Likutey Halakhot* V, p. 50a).

⟩ *Seven healthy cows...seven scrawny cows*

The seven healthy cows in Pharaoh's dream represent prayer, as in "Seven times a day I have praised You" (Psalms 119:164). The seven scrawny cows represent the thoughts that overcome a person during his prayers, causing him to think that his prayers are worthless. The person then strengthens himself and begins to pray another time, but again evil thoughts rise up and disturb his prayers. Pharaoh found the solution to his dream by relying on Joseph, the tzaddik. Joseph teaches us to grab hold of the good when it is present and store it up, so that we can face the hardships that come later (*Likutey Halakhot* III, p. 20a-40).

41:8   וַיְהִי בַבֹּקֶר וַתִּפָּעֶם רוּחוֹ וַיִּשְׁלַח וַיִּקְרָא אֶת־כָּל־חַרְטֻמֵּי מִצְרַיִם וְאֶת־כָּל־חֲכָמֶיהָ וַיְסַפֵּר פַּרְעֹה לָהֶם אֶת־חֲלֹמוֹ וְאֵין־פּוֹתֵר אוֹתָם לְפַרְעֹה

In the morning, his spirit was troubled. He sent for and summoned all the magicians of Egypt and all the wise men. Pharaoh told them his dream, but no one could interpret them to Pharaoh.

⟩ *No one could interpret them to Pharaoh*

Only Joseph was able to interpret Pharaoh's dream correctly. Good and evil (the healthy cows and the scrawny cows) always exist in the world, and it appears that evil always conquers the good. But the tzaddik, who is able to overcome evil, can show that there is good even within evil, even if the good has been "swallowed up" by the evil. Later, Joseph advises the Egyptians to put away food to tide them over during the forthcoming years of famine. In this way, he taught others to take advantage of the good days and good times and store up one's good deeds in this world. Then, even in the bad days, in times of evil, one will have good to fall back on (*Likutey Halakhot* III, p. 490).

❩ *Pharaoh told them his dream, but no one could interpret them*

His wise men did interpret the dreams to him, but the interpretations did not sit well with Pharaoh. For example, they said that he would beget seven daughters and bury seven daughters (Rashi).

Altogether, there were twenty-eight cows and stalks in Pharaoh's dreams (seven healthy cows, seven scrawny cows, seven fruitful stalks, seven ravished stalks). These twenty-eight items correspond to the twenty-eight types of "time" delineated in Ecclesiastes 3:1-8, which are divided into fourteen positive times and fourteen negative times. These positive and negative times represent truth and falsehood, with falsehood always trying to overcome and swallow up truth. While there are many interpretations of what takes place in a person's life, falsehood has a way of hiding the real meaning of what is taking place at any given time. Only Joseph could interpret Pharaoh's dreams correctly—for the tzaddik, the man of truth, can see through the veils that surround a person and get right to the real meaning of his life (*Likutey Halakhot* VIII, p. 211a-211b).

Furthermore, the scrawny cows and stalks represent the false leaders who swallow up the truth and rob the Jews of their knowledge, as it is written, "They [the healthy cows] came inside them [the scrawny cows], but there was no way of knowing that they had come inside them" (Genesis 41:21). Here, too, the tzaddik can show us how to overcome the false leaders (*Likutey Halakhot* VIII, p. 212b).

41:21 וַתָּבֹאנָה אֶל־קִרְבֶּנָה וְלֹא נוֹדַע כִּי־בָאוּ אֶל־
קִרְבֶּנָה וּמַרְאֵיהֶן רַע כַּאֲשֶׁר בַּתְּחִלָּה וָאִיקָץ

"They came inside them, but there was no way of knowing that they had come inside them. Their appearance was just as bad as it was at first. Then I awoke."

❩ *There was no way of knowing that they had come inside them*

The forces of evil swallow up a person's awareness of all the good he ever knew (*Likutey Moharan* I, 54:6).

41:26 שֶׁבַע פָּרֹת הַטֹּבֹת שֶׁבַע שָׁנִים הֵנָּה וְשֶׁבַע הַשִּׁבֳּלִים הַטֹּבֹת שֶׁבַע שָׁנִים הֵנָּה חֲלוֹם אֶחָד הוּא

"The seven good cows are seven years, and the seven good stalks are seven years. It is one dream."

❱ *It is one dream*

Both of Pharaoh's dreams involved food (the cows and the cornstalks) because a person's rectification and purification comes through eating. Joseph advised Pharaoh to set aside "food" (meaning spiritual food—i.e., Torah and prayer) during the good years, whenever the opportunity presented itself, in order to strengthen himself for the difficult times. Therefore Joseph said, "God has sent me ahead of you to prepare [spiritual] sustenance for you" (Genesis 45:7)—for the tzaddik teaches us how to apply every effort to remain steadfast during years of famine and exile (*Likutey Halakhot* II, p. 132).

41:35 וְיִקְבְּצוּ אֶת־כָּל־אֹכֶל הַשָּׁנִים הַטֹּבֹת הַבָּאֹת הָאֵלֶּה וְיִצְבְּרוּ־בָר תַּחַת יַד־פַּרְעֹה אֹכֶל בֶּעָרִים וְשָׁמָרוּ

"Let them collect all the food of those seven good years to come. Let them store grain under Pharaoh's control, and guard it, for food in the cities."

❱ *Let them collect all the food of those seven good years*

Joseph was successful. He was a happy person (*Bereishit Rabbah* 86:4).

Joseph represents holiness, the aspect of joy, life and vitality. In contrast to these states is death, which is experienced in a small way during sleep, as the Midrash states: "Sleep is one-sixtieth of death" (*Berakhot* 57b). But when Joseph, the tzaddik, sleeps, he rests his mind, keeping it attached to life and joy. Therefore Joseph merits not only true dreams, but even to understand the dreams of others.

Pharaoh's dream foresaw a long famine (i.e., exile), since the scrawny cows swallowed up the healthy cows, decreasing prosperity and leading to sadness and depression. But Joseph, a "man of spirit," was always joyous, and thus was able to bring happiness and overcome the effects of sadness with the idea of stockpiling Egypt's surplus (*Likutey Halakhot* II, p. 155a-310).

⟩ Let them collect all the food of those seven good years

The seven "good" years correspond to the seven species for which the Land of Israel is praised (see Deuteronomy 8:8). Pharaoh's dream indicated his desire to conquer the Jews and keep them away from their Land. Thus, he wanted the seven "bad" years to overpower the seven "good" years.

Joseph, in contrast, wanted holiness to overcome evil. By instructing the Egyptians to stock up during the "good" years, he taught that one must grab whatever holiness he can find during the "good times" to have strength to do battle with the forces of evil during the "bad times." In a similar vein, Joseph urged his brothers to bring his bones back to the Holy Land when the Exodus from Egypt would take place (see Genesis 50:25). Since he was attuned to holiness and knew the importance of every drop of holiness a person can grab, he was always attached to the Holy Land (*Likutey Halakhot* II, p. 93a-186-94a).

41:38   וַיֹּאמֶר פַּרְעֹה אֶל־עֲבָדָיו הֲנִמְצָא כָזֶה אִישׁ אֲשֶׁר
רוּחַ אֱלֹהִים בּוֹ

Pharaoh said to his servants, "Can there be another man like this who has the spirit of God in him?"

⟩ Can there be another man like this who has the spirit of God in him

Because Joseph guarded his covenant, he attained a spirit of God (*Likutey Moharan* I, 19:3).

41:39   וַיֹּאמֶר פַּרְעֹה אֶל־יוֹסֵף אַחֲרֵי הוֹדִיעַ אֱלֹהִים
אוֹתְךָ אֶת־כָּל־זֹאת אֵין־נָבוֹן וְחָכָם כָּמוֹךָ

Pharaoh said to Joseph, "Since God has informed you about all this, there is no one as perceptive and wise as you."

⟩ *There is no one as perceptive and wise as you*

Because he guarded his covenant, Joseph achieved a pure mind. He attained Torah revelations and the levels associated with the *sefirot* of Binah (Understanding) and Chokhmah (Wisdom) (*Likutey Moharan* I, 36:2).

⟩ *There is no one as perceptive and wise as you*

Once someone asked Reb Moshe Breslover (a leading student of Reb Noson) about the *tzaddik emet* (true tzaddik) that Rebbe Nachman always speaks about in his lessons. "Who can Rebbe Nachman be referring to?" the man wondered. Reb Moshe told the man that even Pharaoh was wiser than he. Pharaoh understood that because Joseph spoke of a wise man to oversee the production of food in Egypt, he was wise enough to be that person. If Rebbe Nachman always spoke of the true tzaddik, then he must have that special quality to make him a true tzaddik (*Breslov oral tradition*).

41:40   אַתָּה תִּהְיֶה עַל־בֵּיתִי וְעַל־פִּיךָ יִשַּׁק כָּל־עַמִּי רַק
הַכִּסֵּא אֶגְדַּל מִמֶּךָּ

"You will be in charge of my house, and all my people will be fed by your command. Only by the throne will I outrank you."

⟩ *You will be in charge of my house, and all my people will be fed by your command*

"House" refers to the fear of God (cf. *Shabbat* 31b). *Al pikha* (by your command) literally means "in accordance with your mouth" and refers to prayer. "All my people will be fed" indicates great bounty. Thus, when a God-fearing person prays, he brings bounty to the world (*Likutey Moharan* I, 102).

❯ Only by the throne will I outrank you

I will be called the king (Rashi).

The tzaddik always strives to attain great spiritual heights. However, he must constantly remember that God is *always* greater than he and that there are spiritual realms that are still beyond him. Thus, "I (God) will be called the King"—a person must strive for greatness, but always remember that there is a limit to how far he can go (*Likutey Halakhot* II, p. 310).

41:43 וַיַּרְכֵּב אֹתוֹ בְּמִרְכֶּבֶת הַמִּשְׁנֶה אֲשֶׁר־לוֹ וַיִּקְרְאוּ
לְפָנָיו אַבְרֵךְ וְנָתוֹן אֹתוֹ עַל כָּל־אֶרֶץ מִצְרָיִם

He had him ride in his second royal chariot and they called before him, "Avreikh!" He appointed him over the entire land of Egypt.

❯ His second royal chariot

Ha-mishnah (second) can also mean "double." This alludes to the double portion of bounty on Shabbat enjoyed in full by the tzaddik (*Likutey Moharan* I, 58:4) and by every individual on his own level.

❯ They called before him, "Avreikh!"

AVReiKh (אברך) is a composite of the words AV (אב, fatherly and wise) and RaKh (רך, young). Though Joseph was young, he was wise (Rashi).

Rakh also translates as "soft" and "bending." Despite one's level of wisdom and intelligence, he should know how to "bend" before others when implementing his will. Thus, we find that when King David was anointed, he said, "Today, I am *rakh* but anointed as king" (II Samuel 3:39). One must learn to be pliable, as our Sages teach: "Man must always be *rakh* like a reed and not unbending like a cedar tree" (*Ta'anit* 20a) (*Likutey Halakhot* III, p. 76a).

41:44 וַיֹּאמֶר פַּרְעֹה אֶל־יוֹסֵף אֲנִי פַרְעֹה וּבִלְעָדֶיךָ לֹא־
יָרִים אִישׁ אֶת־יָדוֹ וְאֶת־רַגְלוֹ בְּכָל־אֶרֶץ מִצְרָיִם

**Pharaoh said to Joseph, "I am Pharaoh.
Without you, no man may raise his hand
or foot in the entire land of Egypt."**

❭ *Without you, no man may raise his hand or foot*

Only through the tzaddik are the levels of reality called "hands"
and "feet" elevated. This creates a supernal union, which results in
the mitigation of harsh decrees.

The tzaddik is the heart of the people. When an individual
rejoices in his own heart, it causes him to elevate his hands and
feet and dance joyfully. His joy causes a sympathetic resonance in
the tzaddik, the heart of the people. Then the tzaddik makes the
people joyous and elevates them (*Likutey Moharan* I, 10:9).

41:51 וַיִּקְרָא יוֹסֵף אֶת־שֵׁם הַבְּכוֹר מְנַשֶּׁה כִּי־נַשַּׁנִי
אֱלֹהִים אֶת־כָּל־עֲמָלִי וְאֵת כָּל־בֵּית אָבִי

**Joseph named the firstborn Manasseh
"because God caused me to forget all my
hardship and all my father's house."**

❭ *Caused me to forget*

NaShani (נשני, caused me to forget) shares the same root as
NaShim (נשים, women). *ZaKhaR* (זכר, remembered) shares the same
root as *ZaKhaR* (זכר, male). The more a man pursues immoral
desires vis-à-vis women, the more he will forget his real purpose
in this world—to remember the ultimate goal (*Likutey Halakhot* VII,
p. 128a).

41:52 וְאֵת שֵׁם הַשֵּׁנִי קָרָא אֶפְרָיִם כִּי־הִפְרַנִי אֱלֹהִים
בְּאֶרֶץ עָנְיִי

He named the second one Ephraim
"because God made me fruitful in the
land of my suffering."

❭ God made me fruitful in the land of my suffering

HiFRani (הפרני, made me fruitful) is similar to *HiFRia* (הפריע,
disturbing). When a person stands before God in prayer, he must
forget any distinguished lineage he may have and concentrate on
his prayers as if he came from the most humble beginnings. If one's
prayers are to be fruitful, he must banish all such bothersome,
distracting thoughts (*Likutey Moharan* I, 97).

41:55 וַתִּרְעַב כָּל־אֶרֶץ מִצְרַיִם וַיִּצְעַק הָעָם אֶל־פַּרְעֹה
לַלָּחֶם וַיֹּאמֶר פַּרְעֹה לְכָל־מִצְרַיִם לְכוּ אֶל־יוֹסֵף
אֲשֶׁר־יֹאמַר לָכֶם תַּעֲשׂוּ

The entire land of Egypt hungered and the
people cried out to Pharaoh for bread.
Pharaoh said to all of Egypt, "Go to Joseph.
Whatever he tells you, do."

❭ Whatever he tells you, do

Joseph told them to circumcise themselves (Rashi).

All blessings come through the tzaddik. Thus, Joseph was able
to feed the Egyptians even during the famine, and when Jacob
descended to Egypt, the famine ended prematurely (Rashi on Genesis
47:19). For this reason, Pharaoh told his people to obey Joseph when
the latter told them to circumcise themselves. A guarded covenant
brings bounty (*Likutey Halakhot* II, p. 71a).

41:56 וְהָרָעָב הָיָה עַל כָּל־פְּנֵי הָאָרֶץ וַיִּפְתַּח יוֹסֵף אֶת־
כָּל־אֲשֶׁר בָּהֶם וַיִּשְׁבֹּר לְמִצְרַיִם וַיֶּחֱזַק הָרָעָב
בְּאֶרֶץ מִצְרָיִם

The famine was upon the entire face of the earth. Joseph opened all the storehouses and supplied food to Egypt. But the famine grew stronger in the land of Egypt.

❭ *The famine was upon the entire face of the earth*

"The face of the earth" refers to wealthy people (Rashi).

"Face" denotes the countenance of the Other Side, which is idolatry. The lust for money is a type of idolatry. If a person is avaricious, that will appear on his countenance as darkness (*Likutey Moharan* I, 23:end).

42:1 וַיַּרְא יַעֲקֹב כִּי יֶשׁ־שֶׁבֶר בְּמִצְרָיִם וַיֹּאמֶר יַעֲקֹב
לְבָנָיו לָמָּה תִּתְרָאוּ

Jacob saw that there were provisions in Egypt. Jacob said to his sons, "Why are you showing off?"

❭ *Jacob saw that there were provisions in Egypt*

The word *SheVer* (שבר, provisions) literally means "break"; it can also be read as *SeiVeR* (שבר, hope). Thus, the Midrash states: "Jacob saw *shever*—a famine; he saw *seiver*—the plentitude of their harvest. Jacob saw *shever*—Joseph descended to Egypt; he saw *seiver*—Joseph was the ruler. Jacob saw *shever*—the Jews would be enslaved there; he saw *seiver*—the Jews would be redeemed from there" (*Bereishit Rabbah* 91:1).

Jacob, the paradigm of a Jew, understands that there is always hope, that a person must always await salvation. Whenever one feels closed in, embattled from without and troubled from within, he must look inward, at the level he is on at that moment. He will then see that despite the *shever*, he has *seiver*, and can draw strength from the knowledge that all will be rectified (*Likutey Halakhot* V, p. 143a-286).

Rebbe Nachman presents a similar teaching on the verse "In my distress, You relieved me" (Psalms 4:2). If a person considers God's kindnesses, he will see that even when God causes him distress, within the distress itself God provides him with relief and increases His kindness towards him. Not only do we look to God to speedily save us from all distress and provide us with great good, but also even within the distress itself, we look to Him to provide us with relief (*Likutey Moharan* I, 195).

42:6 וְיוֹסֵף הוּא הַשַּׁלִּיט עַל־הָאָרֶץ הוּא הַמַּשְׁבִּיר
לְכָל־עַם הָאָרֶץ וַיָּבֹאוּ אֲחֵי יוֹסֵף וַיִּשְׁתַּחֲווּ־לוֹ
אַפַּיִם אָרְצָה

Joseph was the ruler over the land; he was the one who provided food to all the people of the land. Joseph's brothers came and bowed to him, their faces to the ground.

〉 *Joseph was the ruler…he was the one who provided food*

The word *shalit* (ruler) corresponds to Divine judgment and the *sefirah* of Gevurah. "Provided food" indicates Divine benevolence and the *sefirah* of Chesed. The tzaddik is the only one who knows how to combine these two attributes properly (*Likutey Moharan* I, 80).

42:9 וַיִּזְכֹּר יוֹסֵף אֵת הַחֲלֹמוֹת אֲשֶׁר חָלַם לָהֶם וַיֹּאמֶר
אֲלֵהֶם מְרַגְּלִים אַתֶּם לִרְאוֹת אֶת־עֶרְוַת הָאָרֶץ
בָּאתֶם

Joseph remembered the dreams that he had dreamt about them. "You are spies!" he said to them. "You have come to see the lay of the land!"

〉 *You are spies…You have come to see the lay of the land*

When Joseph's brothers wrongfully sold him out of the Land of Israel into Egypt, they blemished the concept of the tzaddik and of the Holy Land as well. For this reason, Joseph accused them of being spies who had come to see the lay of the land (*ervat ha'aretz*). *Ervat* (literally, "nakedness") implies a blemished covenant, the blemish against the tzaddik (Joseph). And "spies" alludes to the blemish of the spies who slandered the Holy Land (see Numbers 13) (*Likutey Halakhot* II, p. 158).

42:13   וַיֹּאמְרוּ שְׁנֵים עָשָׂר עֲבָדֶיךָ אַחִים אֲנַחְנוּ בְּנֵי אִישׁ־אֶחָד בְּאֶרֶץ כְּנָעַן וְהִנֵּה הַקָּטֹן אֶת־אָבִינוּ הַיּוֹם וְהָאֶחָד אֵינֶנּוּ

"We, your servants, are twelve brothers, the sons of one man in the land of Canaan," they said. "The youngest is now with our father, and one is no more."

⟩ *One is no more*

For that one brother, we fanned out through the city to search for him (Rashi).

When the brothers sold Joseph, they committed a very serious blemish of faith in the tzaddik. By the time they arrived in Egypt, they regretted their deed and sought to rectify it. Therefore they spread out through the land of Egypt to search for him. Every one of us can do likewise. If we have blemished the tzaddik or his honor, our rectification of that blemish begins with our wholehearted search for him. And the tzaddik is always present, waiting to help us. As Joseph said, "God has sent me ahead of you to prepare [spiritual] sustenance for you" (Genesis 45:7) (*Likutey Halakhot* V, p. 100).

42:24 וַיִּסֹּב מֵעֲלֵיהֶם וַיֵּבְךְּ וַיָּשָׁב אֲלֵהֶם וַיְדַבֵּר אֲלֵהֶם
וַיִּקַּח מֵאִתָּם אֶת־שִׁמְעוֹן וַיֶּאֱסֹר אֹתוֹ לְעֵינֵיהֶם

**He turned away from them and cried. He
returned to them and spoke to them, and he
took Simeon from them and imprisoned him
before their eyes.**

〕 *He took Simeon from them*

Simeon was the one who had thrown Joseph in the pit; he was
the one who said to Levi, "Here comes the dreamer" (Genesis 37:19)
(Rashi).

ShiMon (שמעון, Simeon) represents judgments; he was so named
"because God heard (שמע, *ShaMa*) that I am hated" (Genesis 29:33),
which is the concept of judgment. Simeon was the one who
proposed killing Joseph, having passed judgment on him.

When judgments abound, the test of immorality rises to the
fore. The Tribe of Simeon transgressed the ideals of immorality
when its leader, Zimri, and 24,000 of its ranks succumbed to the
enticements of the daughters of Moab and died in a plague (Numbers
25:9; see Rashi). Thus, Simeon was the one who advocated selling
Joseph, the tzaddik who represents the guarded covenant and who
opposes immorality. It was Joseph's descendant Phineas (who was
also a grandson of Aaron) whose zealousness ended the plague
(*Likutey Halakhot* V, p. 326).

42:35 וַיְהִי הֵם מְרִיקִים שַׂקֵּיהֶם וְהִנֵּה־אִישׁ צְרוֹר־כַּסְפּוֹ
בְּשַׂקּוֹ וַיִּרְאוּ אֶת־צְרֹרוֹת כַּסְפֵּיהֶם הֵמָּה וַאֲבִיהֶם
וַיִּירָאוּ

**As they were emptying their sacks, behold!
Every man's bundle of money was in his
sack. They and their father saw their bundles
of money, and they were terrified.**

〕 *As they were emptying their sacks*

Joseph had given his brothers sacks filled with grain to nourish
them. The tzaddik helps people attain the awe and love of God so
that they can feel it even in their bodies.

Similarly, when one gives charity—which corresponds to Joseph, who fed the Egyptians as well as his own family—that makes it possible for him to fear and love God. One's intellect also makes it possible for him to fear and love God. However, if he sins, his intellect becomes obstructed. Joseph's brothers were trying to shake off the lethargy of their bodies, which were empty of the awe and love of God, and thus were "empty sacks" (*Likutey Moharan* I, 17:end).

42:36 וַיֹּאמֶר אֲלֵהֶם יַעֲקֹב אֲבִיהֶם אֹתִי שִׁכַּלְתֶּם יוֹסֵף אֵינֶנּוּ וְשִׁמְעוֹן אֵינֶנּוּ וְאֶת־בִּנְיָמִן תִּקָּחוּ עָלַי הָיוּ כֻלָּנָה

Their father Jacob said to them, "You have caused me a loss! Joseph is no more, and Simeon is no more, and now you will take Benjamin? Everything is happening to me!"

〉 ***Simeon…Benjamin***

Two of the central figures in this narrative are Simeon and Benjamin. The name *ShiMON* (שמעון, Simeon) comes from the word *SheMA* (שמע, hear). This alludes to hearing the words of the tzaddik. Benjamin corresponds to the Altar, for the Temple Altar was placed in Benjamin's territory. When a person heeds the words of the tzaddik, that perfects the Altar, which in turn helps elevate all humanity to God (*Likutey Moharan* I, 17:end).

〉 ***Their father Jacob said to them, "You have caused me a loss! Joseph is no more, and Simeon is no more, and now you will take Benjamin?"***

Some people mistakenly think of themselves as worthy leaders of the Jewish nation. But when they examine themselves carefully, they see that even if they had engaged in devotions directed at "emptying their sacks"—i.e., ridding their bodies of evil desires (whether their own or those they inherited)—those desires still cling to them. Then their intellect rebukes them and they become afraid to lead.

Jacob represents the intellect (see *Likutey Moharan* 1:1). Thus, he told his sons, "You have caused me a loss." This is because an arrogant person loses his wisdom (*Pesachim* 66b).

Joseph corresponds to the rectification of error. But now "Joseph is no more." That is to say, Jacob's other sons lack the ability to be leaders and rectify people's wrongdoing. And if Joseph is no more, then "Simeon is no more"—meaning, Simeon is not despised by the people because he does not truly rebuke them. Jacob concluded, "And now you will take Benjamin?" "Benjamin" is a reference to greatness—surely, if one lacks the qualities to be a leader, he will refrain from claiming authority for himself (*Likutey Moharan* I, 10:4).

43:11 וַיֹּאמֶר אֲלֵהֶם יִשְׂרָאֵל אֲבִיהֶם אִם־כֵּן אֵפוֹא זֹאת עֲשׂוּ קְחוּ מִזִּמְרַת הָאָרֶץ בִּכְלֵיכֶם וְהוֹרִידוּ לָאִישׁ מִנְחָה מְעַט צֳרִי וּמְעַט דְּבַשׁ נְכֹאת וָלֹט בָּטְנִים וּשְׁקֵדִים

Their father Israel said to them, "If so, this is what you must do. Take from the famous products of the Land in your vessels and bring a gift down to the man—a little balsam, a little honey, wax, lotus, nuts and almonds."

❭ Zimrat ha'Aretz

Zimrat ha'Aretz (famous products of the Land) can also be translated as "melody of the Land." Every place has its own melody. Furthermore, every level of vegetation—each blade of grass—has its own melody which extends its blessing throughout the world.

Music, which is made by sifting and selecting sounds, represents separating the good from the bad. Thinking that Joseph was an Egyptian ruler, Jacob sent him a melody from the Holy Land befitting his status, and constructed it in such a way as to elicit his compassion (*Likutey Moharan* II, 63).

43:14   וְאֵל שַׁדַּי יִתֵּן לָכֶם רַחֲמִים לִפְנֵי הָאִישׁ וְשִׁלַּח לָכֶם
אֶת־אֲחִיכֶם אַחֵר וְאֶת־בִּנְיָמִין וַאֲנִי כַּאֲשֶׁר שָׁכֹלְתִּי
שָׁכָלְתִּי

**"May El Shadai grant you compassion before
the man and let you go, along with your other
brother and Benjamin. As for me, as I have lost,
so I have lost."**

⟩ *May El Shadai grant you compassion before the man*

Sometimes God makes a person suffer to induce him to repent.
In such a case, God is actually being compassionate. But Jacob
prayed, "May God grant you compassion." That is to say, may
God's compassion be the kind that we naturally understand to be
compassionate (*Likutey Moharan* II, 62).

⟩ *May El Shadai grant you compassion before the man and let
you go, along with your other brother and Benjamin*

He Who said to His world, "*Dai* (Enough)!" should say, "*Dai*!" to
my suffering (*Bereishit Rabbah* 92:1).

The word *Dai* (די) has the numerical value of 14, the same as
the name *DaViD* (דוד), the progenitor of Mashiach. Jacob prayed
that He Who said, "Enough!" should now say, "Enough!" and
send us the Mashiach, so that we will no longer suffer in exile.
We, too, pray that our "other brother"—those who have been lost
to us through the exiles and suffering—should be comforted and
consoled, and there should no longer be any suffering, not for the
general populace or for any individual (*Likutey Halakhot* I, p. 135a).

43:29 וַיִּשָּׂא עֵינָיו וַיַּרְא אֶת־בִּנְיָמִין אָחִיו בֶּן־אִמּוֹ וַיֹּאמֶר
הֲזֶה אֲחִיכֶם הַקָּטֹן אֲשֶׁר אֲמַרְתֶּם אֵלָי וַיֹּאמַר
אֱלֹהִים יָחְנְךָ בְּנִי

He lifted his eyes and saw his brother
Benjamin, his mother's son. "Is this your
little brother whom you told me about?"
he asked. "May God be gracious to you,
my son," he said.

❯ *May God be gracious to you, my son*

When Esau confronted Jacob's children, Jacob blessed them with
grace and favor. But at that time, Benjamin had not yet been
born. As the leader of a future tribe of Israel, he, too, deserved
to be blessed with grace. Therefore, when he appeared before
Joseph, Joseph blessed him (*Bereishit Rabbah* 78:10).

Of Benjamin's eleven brothers, only Joseph was able to grant
him grace, because Joseph comprised the essence of Jacob. Just as
Jacob attained grace (cf. Genesis 33:11), so did Joseph. While in Egypt,
separated from his family for twenty-two years, Joseph remained
steadfast in his faith and attained great intellect. These are the two
necessary conditions for attaining grace and favor in God's eyes
(*Likutey Moharan* I, 1:4).

44:2 וְאֶת־גְּבִיעִי גְּבִיעַ הַכֶּסֶף תָּשִׂים בְּפִי אַמְתַּחַת הַקָּטֹן
וְאֵת כֶּסֶף שִׁבְרוֹ וַיַּעַשׂ כִּדְבַר יוֹסֵף אֲשֶׁר דִּבֵּר

"And my goblet—the silver goblet—put in
the mouth of the sack of the youngest one,
together with the money for his provisions."
He did exactly as Joseph had instructed him.

❯ *Joseph's goblet*

The *gevi'a* (goblet) symbolizes awesome levels of Divine
compassion. The word *GeVi'a* (גביע) contains the letters *yod-gimmel*
(ג-י) and *ayin-vet* (ע-ב). *Yod-gimmel*, which has the numerical value
of 13, alludes to the Thirteen Attributes of Compassion; *ayin-vet*,

which has the numerical value of 72, represents the Seventy-Two-Letter Name of God which encompasses those Thirteen Attributes. Joseph's brothers experienced severe travails due to the goblet, but this goblet was also the vehicle through which Joseph was reunited with his brothers, drawing forth great compassion and love. Thus, we see how deep suffering can lead to awesome levels of Divine compassion (*Likutey Halakhot* II, p. 312).

⟫ *The goblet*

The word *GeVi'a* (גביע) contains the letters *yod-gimmel* (י-ג) and *ayin-vet* (ע-ב). *Yod-gimmel*, which has the numerical value of 13, alludes to the Thirteen Attributes of Compassion through which all salvation comes. *Ayin-vet*, which has the numerical value of 72, represents the Seventy-Two-Letter Name of God, which also corresponds to incredible compassion and mercy. Taken together, 13 multiplied by 72 equals 936, the numerical value of *ShaLOM* (when the final *mem* is counted with the value of 600 [see Charts, p. 348]), meaning peace, the ultimate salvation. Joseph tested the brothers with the goblet to arouse this great compassion and effect peace between them (*Likutey Halakhot* III, p. 195a).

44:3   הַבֹּקֶר אוֹר וְהָאֲנָשִׁים שֻׁלְּחוּ הֵמָּה וַחֲמֹרֵיהֶם

Morning dawned and the men and their donkeys were sent on their way.

⟫ *Morning dawned and the men and their donkeys were sent on their way*

"Morning" corresponds to Abraham, who is associated with the *sefirah* of Chesed (Kindness). With the appearance of Divine kindness, people are able to leave behind their evil traits, evil speech, and base material desires (*Likutey Moharan* I, 38:4).

Parashat Vayigash

44:18 וַיִּגַּשׁ אֵלָיו יְהוּדָה וַיֹּאמֶר בִּי אֲדֹנִי יְדַבֶּר־נָא עַבְדְּךָ
דָבָר בְּאָזְנֵי אֲדֹנִי וְאַל־יִחַר אַפְּךָ בְּעַבְדֶּךָ כִּי כָמוֹךָ
כְּפַרְעֹה

Judah came closer to him and said, "Please, my lord, let your servant speak a word in my lord's ears. Do not become angry at your servant, for you are like Pharaoh."

❱ *Judah came closer to him*

YeHUDah (יהודה, Judah) represents the YeHUDim (יהודים, Jews). Joseph represents the tzaddik. In order to draw close to God, the Jews must first draw close to the tzaddik, who will transform their Torah study into blessing. Otherwise, their efforts will be transformed into toil and wasted effort (*Likutey Halakhot* VII, p. 464).

❱ *Judah came closer... Let your servant speak a word in my lord's ears. Do not become angry... for you are like Pharaoh*

Let my words enter your ears (Rashi).

When the brothers realized their mistake, YeHUDah (יהודה, Judah) approached Joseph. Similarly, the Jews, who are called YeHUDim (יהודים), display faith in the tzaddikim by approaching them and repenting of their evil ways. This faith must be entrenched in the heart. Thus, "Let my words enter your ears"—for "Hearing is dependent on the heart" (see *Berakhot* 15a; *Tikkuney Zohar* #58, p. 92a). One's words must enter the heart of the tzaddik to prove that he is truly interested in serving God.

Judah also asked Joseph not to get angry. This refers to mitigating all the decrees that were issued before a person repents, and requesting kindness and compassion. The key is to follow the advice of the tzaddikim and not fall prey to extraneous advice and counsel, which is represented by PhaRAoH (פרעה, from the same root as leHaPhRiA [להפריע, to confuse]). Judah said to Joseph, "You are like Pharaoh"—for as much as Pharaoh can cause confusion, you, the tzaddik, are capable of giving counsel to counter that confusion (*Likutey Halakhot* III, p. 194a-388).

⟩ *Judah came closer to him and said, "Please, my lord, let your servant speak a word in my lord's ears...for you are like Pharaoh"*

Kings assembled, they came together (Psalms 48:5).

This refers to Judah and Joseph, who represent the Kingdoms of Judah and Israel (*Bereishit Rabbah* 93:2).

VayiGaSh (ויגש, he came closer) alludes to eating. As the verse states: "At the time of eating, come here (גשי הלם, *GoShi halom*)" (Ruth 2:14). *Halom* (הלם, here) connotes kingship (see *Shabbat* 113b). When we eat in a holy manner, we can bring about the union between "kings" (and adversaries), and then God is revealed in the world.

But this can occur only when the food is spiritually purified and fit for human consumption. In order to purify food, we must elevate the sparks of holiness within it. We do so by spreading faith to those who are distant from God. Sparks of holiness abound in the world but remain unrecognized. When we spread faith, these sparks are elevated. Thus, speech rectifies the sparks of holiness.

Judah asked to speak directly to Joseph, because in truth, there are no intermediaries between God and creation. Only Divine Providence guides the world. This faith must be revealed, and so Judah told Joseph, "You are like Pharaoh." The name *PhaRAoh* (פרעה) is similar to the word *PaRuA* (פרוע, uncovered). When a person speaks words of faith, he can bring about unity and the revelation of Godliness (*Likutey Moharan* I, 62:6).

⟩ *Let your servant speak a word in my lord's ears...for you are like Pharaoh*

Let my words enter your ears (Rashi).

Judah represents the individual Jew. Joseph represents the tzaddik. "Let your servant speak a word in my lord's ears" refers to prayer. Each person must bind his prayers to the tzaddikim, since they are the ones who teach us how to pray properly so that our prayers will ascend Above. "Let my words enter your ears" connotes a person asking the tzaddik for help in rectifying his prayers, so he can pray more intensely and with greater fervor.

Pharaoh, on the other hand, represents the power of illusion that deters a person from proper prayer. But Joseph—the tzaddik—is "like Pharaoh." Just as Pharaoh has the power to steer a person away from God by confusing him during prayer, the tzaddik has sufficient powers to help a person combat the confusions and attain proper prayer (*Likutey Halakhot* VIII, p. 213a).

44:30   וְעַתָּה כְּבֹאִי אֶל־עַבְדְּךָ אָבִי וְהַנַּעַר אֵינֶנּוּ אִתָּנוּ
וְנַפְשׁוֹ קְשׁוּרָה בְנַפְשׁוֹ

> **"Now, if I come to my father, your servant, the boy will not be with us. His soul is bound up with his soul."**

⟩ *His soul is bound up with his soul*

When a person attains great love for the tzaddik, he is bound to the tzaddik's soul (*Likutey Moharan* I, 135).

45:5   וְעַתָּה אַל־תֵּעָצְבוּ וְאַל־יִחַר בְּעֵינֵיכֶם כִּי־מְכַרְתֶּם
אֹתִי הֵנָּה כִּי לְמִחְיָה שְׁלָחַנִי אֱלֹהִים לִפְנֵיכֶם

> **"Now, don't be sad or feel guilty that you sold me here, for God sent me ahead of you to be a provider."**

⟩ *Don't be sad*

Once a person is close to the tzaddik, he has every reason to rejoice, and he can overcome depression (*Likutey Halakhot* II, p. 156a).

⟩ *For God sent me ahead of you to be a provider*

Because Joseph resisted temptation, he merited to bring inspiration and life to all those who followed him, even into the darkest exile (*Likutey Halakhot* I, p. 326).

45:12 וְהִנֵּה עֵינֵיכֶם רֹאוֹת וְעֵינֵי אָחִי בִנְיָמִין כִּי־פִי הַמְדַבֵּר אֲלֵיכֶם

"Behold! You and my brother Benjamin see with your own eyes that my mouth is speaking to you."

》 *My mouth is speaking to you*

My mouth is speaking to you in the Holy Tongue (Rashi).

Though Joseph had been in exile for twenty-two years, he still possessed a Holy Tongue, because he had guarded his covenant (*Likutey Moharan* I, 19:3).

》 *My mouth is speaking to you*

Joseph guarded the covenant and therefore was a tzaddik. He attained holy Malkhut (Kingship), particularly over his heart and emotions. And he was a ruler over others as well. Because authority is revealed through the mouth (which issues edicts), Joseph said specifically, "My mouth is speaking to you" (*Likutey Moharan* I, 34:8).

45:13 וְהִגַּדְתֶּם לְאָבִי אֶת־כָּל־כְּבוֹדִי בְּמִצְרַיִם וְאֵת כָּל־אֲשֶׁר רְאִיתֶם וּמִהַרְתֶּם וְהוֹרַדְתֶּם אֶת־אָבִי הֵנָּה

"Tell my father about all my honor in Egypt and about everything that you have seen. You must hurry and bring my father down here."

》 *Tell my father about all my honor*

Tell Jacob not to worry about coming down to Egypt, where the impurities of the exile might overwhelm us. Since I have kept my honor and not blemished my soul, I have prepared the way for the Jewish people to remain steadfast during the exile (*Likutey Halakhot* II, p. 67a).

》 *Tell my father about all my honor in Egypt*

The fact that Joseph was sent down to Egypt turned out to be a great Divine favor for the Jews. For in that land, Joseph was able to define what honor is and use it solely for God's sake. The purpose of Creation is to reveal God's honor, but when God's honor is blemished, it is taken from the worthy and given over to the brazenfaced, who usurp leadership and mislead the people. Since Joseph was a true tzaddik, he was able to return honor to God and pave the way for the Jews to remain steadfast during the Egyptian exile. He instructed his brothers, "Tell my father about all my honor in Egypt"—tell Jacob that I have prepared the way for God's honor to be revealed even in Egypt (*Likutey Halakhot* VIII, p. 279a).

45:22 לְכֻלָּם נָתַן לָאִישׁ חֲלִפוֹת שְׂמָלֹת וּלְבִנְיָמִן נָתַן
שְׁלֹשׁ מֵאוֹת כֶּסֶף וְחָמֵשׁ חֲלִפֹת שְׂמָלֹת

He gave each of them a change of clothing. But to Benjamin he gave three hundred pieces of silver and five changes of clothing.

❩ *But to Benjamin he gave three hundred pieces of silver and five changes of clothing*

In wealth lie supernal lights that illumine when a person conducts himself honestly in business and gives charity. Since Joseph charitably supported and fed the people during the Egyptian famine, he was able to bring the supernal illuminations to light (see *Likutey Moharan* I, 25:1).

Joseph's gift of five garments to his brother Benjamin hinted at the future repository of supernal illumination, the Temple, which reflected all the colors of supernal beauty and which would be built in Benjamin's territory. On Yom Kippur, the High Priest would change his garments five times, alternating between his service in the outer courtyard and his ministrations in the Holy of Holies. Through the gift of five garments, Joseph hinted to Benjamin to prepare for a great revelation of Godliness in the future, in which he would have a major portion.

Since Joseph had mastered the ability to bring forth and reveal the supernal illuminations, he merited to ascend above his imagination and attain true intellect. Therefore he also gave Benjamin 300 pieces of silver, representing the three areas of intellect—the

potential, the actual and the acquired—that transcend the imagination (*Likutey Halakhot* IV, p. 187a).

45:27 וַיְדַבְּרוּ אֵלָיו אֵת כָּל־דִּבְרֵי יוֹסֵף אֲשֶׁר דִּבֶּר אֲלֵהֶם
וַיַּרְא אֶת־הָעֲגָלוֹת אֲשֶׁר־שָׁלַח יוֹסֵף לָשֵׂאת אֹתוֹ
וַתְּחִי רוּחַ יַעֲקֹב אֲבִיהֶם

**They told him all the words that Joseph had
told them, and he saw the wagons that
Joseph had sent to carry him. Then the spirit
of their father Jacob was revived.**

⟩ *He saw the wagons... The sons of Israel carried their father Jacob*

When Jacob descended to Egypt—which represents the material
world—his children carried him just as the Tabernacle was carried
in the desert, since Jacob represented sanctity. That is, all his travels
were for the sake of God and spirituality, and thus resembled the
"travels" of the Tabernacle. When Jacob saw the wagons that Joseph
had sent him, he realized that Joseph understood the greatness
of such travel, and that Joseph also understood the value of the
"wagons" (donated by the tribes' presidents for the travels of the
Tabernacle) and the order that would apply to the travels of the
Tabernacle (*Likutey Halakhot* II, p. 52).

⟩ *The spirit of their father Jacob was revived*

The spirit of Jacob was revived as a result of his joy. When
a person is joyful, he gains life and can attain the Light of the
Face—an awesome level of radiating spiritual light that helps
subdue the face of darkness, which corresponds to idolatry and
the Other Side (*Likutey Moharan* I, 23:1).

⟩ *The spirit of their father Jacob was revived*

He regained the *ruach ha-kodesh* (Divine inspiration) that had left
him [during the years of Joseph's absence] (Rashi).

This spirit may be understood as a reference to the spirit of
Mashiach, which is a spirit of resurrection (*Likutey Moharan* I, 78).

The "speaking spirit" that God placed in man (cf. Targum Onkelos on Genesis 2:7) is holy. When a person speaks words of holiness — words of Torah and prayer — he draws his life force directly from God, and in that sense, his spirit is Divinely inspired.

46:4   אָנֹכִי אֵרֵד עִמְּךָ מִצְרַיְמָה וְאָנֹכִי אַעַלְךָ גַם־עָלֹה
וְיוֹסֵף יָשִׁית יָדוֹ עַל־עֵינֶיךָ

"I will descend with you to Egypt and I will also bring you up. Joseph will place his hand upon your eyes."

》 I will descend with you to Egypt and I will also bring you up

All descents are for the purpose of ascent. One must learn to strengthen himself during the difficult times — the times of descent — because those times are intended to forge him into a greater person. He can draw strength by contemplating that God is always with him, both when things are just beginning to look bad and when the situation starts to look much darker.

Jacob was about to descend into exile with his entire family, and he foresaw that this exile would continue for several generations. Yet he strengthened himself with the knowledge that God is with every person both in the descent and during the duration of his troubles, and He waits with the person for his salvation and ascent (*Likutey Halakhot* V, p. 286-144a-288).

》 A'alcha gam aloh

God accompanies the Jews in all their descents; He is found with them in all circumstances. In the phrase *A'alcha gam aloh* (I will also bring you up), the word *aloh* (above) seems redundant. This word teaches that when God begins to elevate us, He does so continually. He elevates us again and again, to ever higher levels (*Likutey Halakhot* III, p. 25a-50).

》 I will descend with you to Egypt and I will also bring you up

ANoKhI (I) is the same as "*ANoKhI* (I) am God your Lord, Who took you out of the land of Egypt (מצרים, *MitZRayim*)" (Exodus 20:2). As long as you remember that "I am God your Lord," I will be there to take you out of your suffering (מצר, *MeitZaR*). Not only that, but *ve-Anokhi a'alcha* (literally, "I will elevate you")—you will merit to go higher and higher, to become greater and greater (*Likutey Halakhot* III, p. 250a-500).

⟩ *Joseph will place his hand upon your eyes*

"Hand" is a reference to music, for a person moves his hands across a musical instrument to bring forth the proper notes. The description of Joseph, the tzaddik, "placing his hand" means that he chooses melodious notes. He draws forth the good points from the musical instrument of reality, as it were. In doing so, he rectifies people's imagination—the way they view reality, which was damaged by a jaundiced view that is associated with slander—and gives them clarity of mind (*Likutey Moharan* I, 54:6).

46:27 וּבְנֵי יוֹסֵף אֲשֶׁר־יֻלַּד־לוֹ בְמִצְרַיִם נֶפֶשׁ שְׁנָיִם כָּל־
הַנֶּפֶשׁ לְבֵית־יַעֲקֹב הַבָּאָה מִצְרַיְמָה שִׁבְעִים

And Joseph's sons who were born to him in Egypt, two souls. All the souls of the house of Jacob who came to Egypt were seventy.

⟩ *All the souls of the house of Jacob who came to Egypt were seventy*

The seventy souls of Jacob's household correspond to the "seventy faces of the Torah." These souls were the roots of the Jewish nation. Each one has a corresponding root in the Torah itself and thus can always connect to the Torah.

Countering these seventy souls are "seventy nations" (enumerated in Genesis 10)—i.e., evil characteristics that can distance a person from his Divine root (*Likutey Moharan* I, 36:1). When a Jew recognizes himself as a descendant of Jacob, he can draw upon the "seventy faces of the Torah" for inspiration. If he does not recognize himself as a descendant of Jacob, then he is alienated from the Torah, and he draws his inspiration from the seventy nations.

46:29 וַיֶּאְסֹר יוֹסֵף מֶרְכַּבְתּוֹ וַיַּעַל לִקְרַאת־יִשְׂרָאֵל
אָבִיו גֹּשְׁנָה וַיֵּרָא אֵלָיו וַיִּפֹּל עַל־צַוָּארָיו וַיֵּבְךְּ
עַל־צַוָּארָיו עוֹד

**Joseph harnessed his chariot and went
up to greet his father Israel in Goshen.
He appeared before him and fell upon his
neck. He cried on his neck a long time.**

》 *He cried on his neck a long time*

But Jacob did not cry on Joseph's neck, because he was reciting
the Shema (Rashi).

It was the beginning of the exile and Jacob and his descendants
were about to enter Egypt, the land of immorality. This descent
was necessary because the Jewish people had to pass a test in
the crucible of the seventy nations—a test of immorality—before
they merited the revelation of Torah. This test is mirrored in the
life of every single Jew as well, for he must endure the "exile of
the seventy nations" before he receives his personal revelation of
Torah (see *Likutey Moharan* I, 36).

The way to overcome immorality is to accept the yoke of
Heaven, thereby banishing the authority of the Other Side. A
person accomplishes this by declaring his faith in God through
the recitation of the Shema—and this is especially propitious if he
sheds tears during its recital. Tears—the body's excesses—stem
from the waste products, depression and the spleen (see *Anatomy of
the Soul*, Chapter 11). These tears have the power to banish the forces
of impurity.

Joseph, who was tested by Potiphar's wife, was able to banish
the forces of immorality with his tears. Yet he summoned the
strength to overcome temptation because of Jacob, whose face
appeared to him (*Sotah* 36b). Both are necessary: the Shema and
tears. Jacob prepared his children for exile by reciting the Shema.
Joseph prepared the Jews for exile by crying and shedding tears
(*Likutey Halakhot* I, p. 326).

46:30   וַיֹּאמֶר יִשְׂרָאֵל אֶל־יוֹסֵף אָמוּתָה הַפָּעַם אַחֲרֵי רְאוֹתִי אֶת־פָּנֶיךָ כִּי עוֹדְךָ חָי

Israel said to Joseph, "Now I can die, having seen your face, for you are still alive."

] *Now I can die, having seen your face*

I thought I would die in both worlds—this world and the next. Now that I have seen your face, I will die only in this world, but I will live in the World to Come (Rashi).

Jacob, who represents the Jewish nation ("the Children of Israel") came face to face with Joseph, who represents the tzaddik. One who draws close to the tzaddik—i.e., "sees his face"—will experience death only in this world. But he will inherit the World to Come (*Likutey Halakhot* II, p. 332).

47:12   וַיְכַלְכֵּל יוֹסֵף אֶת־אָבִיו וְאֶת־אֶחָיו וְאֵת כָּל־בֵּית אָבִיו לֶחֶם לְפִי הַטָּף

Joseph provided his father, his brothers, and his father's entire household with bread according to the children.

] *Joseph provided his father, his brothers, and his father's entire household*

Because he had defiled Jacob's couch, Reuben lost the birthright. Jacob then chose to transfer the birthright to Joseph, because Joseph sustained Jacob and his household while they were in Egypt. Joseph deserved the birthright for another reason: he guarded the covenant. In gaining the birthright, Joseph received a double portion, so each of his two children headed his own tribe (*Likutey Moharan* I, 2:2-3).

47:23 וַיֹּאמֶר יוֹסֵף אֶל־הָעָם הֵן קָנִיתִי אֶתְכֶם הַיּוֹם
וְאֶת־אַדְמַתְכֶם לְפַרְעֹה הֵא־לָכֶם זֶרַע וּזְרַעְתֶּם
אֶת־הָאֲדָמָה

**Joseph said to the people, "Look, I have
bought you and your land today for Pharaoh.
Here is seed for you. Sow the earth."**

⟩ Here is seed for you

Hei (הא, here) may also be read as the letter hei (ה). Therefore
Joseph was telling the people, "The letter hei is seed for you." The
word "seed" can refer more broadly to blessing.

What is the nature of the letter hei? Hei has the numerical value
of 5, representing the five articulations of speech (guttural, palatal,
lingual, dental and labial). Therefore this letter refers to speech.

Speech has therapeutic powers that can lead to peace. Thus,
Joseph was assisting these people simply by speaking with them.
When a person gives charity, he can accomplish a similar effect
(*Likutey Moharan* I, 57:8).

Parashat Vayechi

47:28 וַיְחִי יַעֲקֹב בְּאֶרֶץ מִצְרַיִם שְׁבַע עֶשְׂרֵה שָׁנָה וַיְהִי יְמֵי־יַעֲקֹב שְׁנֵי חַיָּיו שֶׁבַע שָׁנִים וְאַרְבָּעִים וּמְאַת שָׁנָה

Jacob lived in the land of Egypt seventeen years. Jacob's days—the years of his life—were one hundred and forty-seven years.

⟩ *Jacob lived in the land of Egypt*

The main life that Jacob experienced was in Egypt, where he lived with joy and peace (see *Zohar* I, 111b).

How is it that in the Holy Land, Jacob did not attain peace, but in Egypt, an impure land where his descendants would eventually suffer in bondage, he did attain peace?

The greatest levels of joy come about when one takes hold of his sadness and depression and transforms them into happiness. Exile corresponds to sadness and depression; Jacob's response shows us how to turn around its effects. Jacob "lived in the land of Egypt"—he knew that the exile would continue until all the sparks of holiness would be gathered up. But he was able to find peace and even attain great happiness in Egypt, for he strengthened himself and his descendants with the joyful promise of the Future Redemption (*Likutey Halakhot* II, p. 158a).

47:31 וַיֹּאמֶר הִשָּׁבְעָה לִי וַיִּשָּׁבַע לוֹ וַיִּשְׁתַּחוּ יִשְׂרָאֵל עַל־רֹאשׁ הַמִּטָּה

"Swear to me," he said. He swore to him, and Israel bowed towards the head of the bed.

⟩ *Israel bowed towards the head of the bed*

His "bed" was pure: he had twelve sons, all God-fearing, with no wicked children among them. Therefore he brought great unity

Above. He bowed towards his bed and was thankful for his good fortune.

Jacob's bowing towards his bed corresponds to prayer (see *Likutey Moharan* I, 9). Since the first three blessings of the *Shemoneh Esrei* are praises to God and the final three blessings are prayers of thanks, the central part of this prayer is the middle twelve blessings, which correspond to the Twelve Tribes (*Likutey Halakhot* I, p. 360).

48:1 וַיְהִי אַחֲרֵי הַדְּבָרִים הָאֵלֶּה וַיֹּאמֶר לְיוֹסֵף הִנֵּה אָבִיךָ
חֹלֶה וַיִּקַּח אֶת־שְׁנֵי בָנָיו עִמּוֹ אֶת־מְנַשֶּׁה וְאֶת־אֶפְרָיִם

A short time later, someone said to Joseph, "Behold, your father is ill." He took his two sons, Manasseh and Ephraim, along with him.

❯ Your father is ill

Until Jacob, there was no illness prior to death. A person would sneeze and his soul would depart. Jacob prayed for illness so that a person would have time to prepare a will for his heirs and say goodbye to his family before he passes away (*Bava Metzia* 87a).

The most important legacy one can bequeath to his children and descendants is the knowledge of serving God. Thus, when Jacob was on his deathbed and called his sons together, they all accepted his charge and recited, "Hear, Israel! God is our Lord. God is One" (*Likutey Halakhot* VIII, p. 48a).

Similarly, writes Reb Noson, the main purpose of a will is to command one's children to follow the ways of God. While Jacob was blessed with children who were all pious and God-fearing, he knew he had to instill in them a greater feeling for Godliness in order to ensure their continued allegiance to God after he was gone. Therefore he prayed for illness, which caused his family to gather around him and gave him the opportunity to transmit his knowledge of God to them (ibid., V, p. 262a).

❯ Manasseh and Ephraim

They were born in Egypt, yet they remained tzaddikim. Their names reflect Joseph's own difficulties in Egypt and how he,

too, overcame them. *MeNaSheh* (מנשה, Manasseh) was so named
"because God caused me to forget (נשני, *NaShani*) all my hardship"
(Genesis 41:51). Though Joseph found himself in very difficult
circumstances, he realized that God was with him and He was
helping him forget his travails so he could look forward to a better
life. *EFRaim* (אפרים, Ephraim) was so named "because God made
me fruitful (הפרני, *hiFRani*) in the land of my suffering" (ibid., 41:52).
Despite all the evil around him, Joseph was able to find merit and
grow (*Likutey Halakhot* III, p. 156).

48:8   וַיַּרְא יִשְׂרָאֵל אֶת־בְּנֵי יוֹסֵף וַיֹּאמֶר מִי־אֵלֶּה
**Israel saw Joseph's sons and said, "Who
are these?"**

⟩ *Who are these… They are my sons whom God gave me here*

Jacob foresaw that both Manasseh and Ephraim would have
wicked descendants. Therefore he said, "Who are these [who are
unworthy for blessing]?" and did not want to bless them. Joseph
disagreed and prayed for them. Then a Divine spirit rested upon
Jacob and he saw that tzaddikim, too, would descend from
Manasseh and Ephraim, and he blessed them (Rashi).

The disagreement between Jacob and Joseph lay in finding
merit even in the most wicked people. When Jacob foresaw these
wicked descendants, he weakened to the point where he could no
longer find any good in them and refused to bless them. Joseph, on
the other hand, was able to find merit. He said, "They are my sons
whom God gave me *here*"—here, even in the wicked, we must look
for and find some merit, some redeeming factor (*Likutey Halakhot* III,
p. 78a).

48:13 וַיִּקַּח יוֹסֵף אֶת־שְׁנֵיהֶם אֶת־אֶפְרַיִם בִּימִינוֹ
מִשְּׂמֹאל יִשְׂרָאֵל וְאֶת־מְנַשֶּׁה בִשְׂמֹאלוֹ מִימִין
יִשְׂרָאֵל וַיַּגֵּשׁ אֵלָיו

Joseph took the two of them. With his right hand, he placed Ephraim to Israel's left, and with his left hand, he placed Manasseh to Israel's right. Then he came closer to him.

〕 *Manasseh…Ephraim…Jacob*

Manasseh corresponds to the "dwellers above"—those tzaddikim who search for God on the highest of levels. *MeNaSheh* (מנשה, Manasseh) was so named "because God caused me to forget (נשני, *NaShani*) all my hardship and all my father's house" (Genesis 41:51)—implying that Manasseh transcended this physical world. Ephraim represents the "dwellers below," those who feel connected to this world. *EFRaim* (אפרים, Ephraim) was so named "because God made me fruitful (הפרני, *hiFRani*) in the land" (ibid., 41:52)—that is, despite his connection to the world, Ephraim still remembered God and knew that he could always find Him.

When Joseph brought his sons to Jacob for a blessing, he placed Manasseh next to Jacob's right hand and Ephraim next to Jacob's left hand. Since Manasseh was the eldest and the "dweller above," Joseph assumed that he would receive the stronger blessing (represented by the right hand). But Jacob crossed his hands, placing his right hand on Ephraim's head to give him the greater blessing. For the world is sustained through those who are distant from God yet who still wish to draw close to Him (*Likutey Halakhot* VII, p. 332-167a).

48:14 וַיִּשְׁלַח יִשְׂרָאֵל אֶת־יְמִינוֹ וַיָּשֶׁת עַל־רֹאשׁ אֶפְרַיִם
וְהוּא הַצָּעִיר וְאֶת־שְׂמֹאלוֹ עַל־רֹאשׁ מְנַשֶּׁה שִׂכֵּל
אֶת־יָדָיו כִּי מְנַשֶּׁה הַבְּכוֹר

Israel extended his right hand and placed it
on Ephraim's head—he was the younger one.
He placed his left hand on Manasseh's head.
He crossed his hands, for Manasseh was the
firstborn.

》 *He crossed his hands*

SiKheiL (שכל, crossed) is similar to *SeiKheL* (שכל, intellect).
Intellect is the principal blessing that a person can bestow. Therefore Jacob channeled intellect into the blessings that he gave to his
grandchildren (*Likutey Moharan* I, 24:5).

48:16 הַמַּלְאָךְ הַגֹּאֵל אֹתִי מִכָּל־רָע יְבָרֵךְ אֶת־הַנְּעָרִים
וְיִקָּרֵא בָהֶם שְׁמִי וְשֵׁם אֲבֹתַי אַבְרָהָם וְיִצְחָק
וְיִדְגּוּ לָרֹב בְּקֶרֶב הָאָרֶץ

"May the angel who redeems me from all
evil bless the young children, and may
my name and the name of my fathers,
Abraham and Isaac, be called upon them.
May they increase in the land like fish."

》 *May the angel who redeems me from all evil bless the young children*

"The young children" can be understood as a reference to the
cherubim engraved on the Ark in the Temple, through which an
angel would deliver God's prophecy. So too, Jacob blessed all Jews
that they should have the potential to be like the cherubim and
receive Divine inspiration (*Likutey Moharan* II, 1:6).

48:22 וַאֲנִי נָתַתִּי לְךָ שְׁכֶם אַחַד עַל־אַחֶיךָ אֲשֶׁר
לָקַחְתִּי מִיַּד הָאֱמֹרִי בְּחַרְבִּי וּבְקַשְׁתִּי

"I have designated for you one portion more than your brothers, which I took from the Emorite with my sword and my bow."

》 *I have designated for you one portion more than your brothers*

The Twelve Tribes correspond to the twelve manifestations of prayer. As their patriarch, Jacob represents all-inclusive prayer, and as such he is able to bring life and sustenance to all levels of creation. Thus, Jacob had the power to give an extra portion to Joseph.

SheKheM (שכם, portion) is an acronym for *Shafal* (שפל, earthly), *Kokhav* (כוכב, stellar) and *Malakh* (מלאך, angelic), indicating all levels of existence (*Likutey Moharan* I, 9:2). Jacob was able to give Joseph the power and ability to rule over all that exists!

》 **With my sword and my bow**

With my prayer and my request (Targum Onkeles).

Prayer is comparable to a double-edged sword because it contains two elements: praise and requests. Just as prayer was Jacob's principal weapon, so will it be the principal weapon of Mashiach.

Jacob represents judgment and charity. Thus, the verse speaks of "*mishpat* (justice or judgment) and *tzedakah* (charity) in Jacob" (Psalms 99:4). Both are conducive to prayer. A person requires judgment in order to speak and pray wisely. Being charitable also gives him the ability to weigh his words and pray properly (*Likutey Moharan* I, 2:1-2).

》 **With my bow**

Keshet (bow) also means "rainbow." The rainbow is composed of three primary colors. These three colors correspond to the elements of fire, air and water, which combine to bring forth song (via the "fire" or warmth of the throat, the "water" or fluids of the mouth, and the "air" expelled from the lungs). Throughout the Kabbalah, any grouping of three is said to parallel the Patriarchs.

When we sing to God in prayer, we arouse the merit of the Patriarchs and thus mitigate Divine decrees (*Likutey Moharan* I, 42). In this way, our prayer corresponds to the bow with which Jacob defeated his enemies.

49:1 וַיִּקְרָא יַעֲקֹב אֶל־בָּנָיו וַיֹּאמֶר הֵאָסְפוּ וְאַגִּידָה לָכֶם אֵת אֲשֶׁר־יִקְרָא אֶתְכֶם בְּאַחֲרִית הַיָּמִים

Jacob called for his sons. "Come together and I will tell you what will happen to you at the End of Days," he said.

⟫ *Jacob called for his sons*

Jacob wanted to reveal the time of the Future Redemption, but the Divine Presence left him (Rashi). He became afraid that perhaps his sons were unworthy. They said to him, "*Shema Yisrael Adonoy Eloheinu Adonoy Echad*—Hear, Israel! God is our Lord. God is One." Gratified that his lapse in prophecy was not due to his children's shortcomings, Jacob responded, "*Barukh Shem Kevod Malkhuto LeOlam VaEd*—Blessed is the Name of His glorious kingdom forever and ever." Later, however, when Moses said the Shema (Deuteronomy 6:4), he did not include "*Barukh Shem…*" To honor Jacob, we say it, but to honor Moses, we recite it quietly (*Pesachim* 56a).

Jacob saw that the Final Redemption would not take place until even those who were farthest from God would return to Him. Therefore he said, "*Barukh Shem…*," knowing that God's kingship is everywhere but the time had not yet come for it to be manifest. Moses also knew this, but he did not reveal it in the Torah expressly because the time had not yet come and many pitfalls could delay it. As an example, Moses himself drew the mixed multitude close to God before the appointed time, thereby causing the sin of the golden calf. Despite the importance of "*Barukh Shem…*," we must recite it quietly, until such time as the sparks of holiness will be rectified and it can be recited aloud (*Likutey Halakhot* I, p. 244).

❯ *Jacob called for his sons... Come together... Gather together*

> Jacob wanted to reveal the End of Days, but the Divine Presence left him. He began saying other things (Rashi).

If the prophecy Jacob wanted to reveal is not recorded in the Torah because the Divine Presence left him, why does the Torah record his opening statement? The answer is that Jacob's intention, albeit thwarted, also contains a message which helps draw blessing. Rebbe Nachman teaches that the tzaddik strives to gather Jews together. The more they unite, the greater the Torah he can reveal to them. In order to effect this revelation, he must perform two devotions. The first is to gather the souls together. The second is to elevate those souls to a higher level; this ascent allows the tzaddik to draw Torah from a higher level (see *Likutey Moharan* I, 13).

Using the first devotion, Jacob called to his sons, urging them to unite. When he saw that he was forbidden to reveal the End of Days, he admonished them to gather a second time, alluding to the second devotion of ascending together in unity to draw Torah. For mainly by means of the Torah will we merit to the Messianic era. As all his sons were elevated to greater heights, Jacob was able, to an extent, to bring down the message of the End of Days and hide it in his blessings (many Midrashim explain how these blessings refer to the Messianic era) (*Likutey Halakhot* VIII, p. 56a).

❯ *Jacob called for his sons*

Jacob gave these blessings primarily to illumine his sons with his *da'at* (knowledge of God)—this is the main heritage one must bequeath to his children in this world. Moses had the same intention when he blessed the Twelve Tribes. Their blessings are similar in that where Jacob's left off, Moses' began (*Devarim Rabbah* 11:1). The outcome of Jacob's *da'at* was the ability to conquer the Holy Land. Thus, we find in most of Moses' blessings (according to Rashi) that the tribes were blessed with the wherewithal to conquer the Land (*Likutey Halakhot* VII, p. 332).

) *Come together...Gather together and listen*

Jacob wanted to reveal the End of Days, but the Divine Presence left him (Rashi).

At first Jacob called together his sons with the term *hei'asfu* (come together), which connotes a gathering of those who are nearby. This assemblage was meant to be one of tzaddikim. Jacob thought that a gathering of tzaddikim would be sufficient to bring a conclusion to the exile. But when the Divine Presence left him, he realized that more was needed: one must make sure to include even those who are distant from God. Therefore he added *hi-kavtzu* (gather together), referring to those who are distant from God.

God's compassion is unending and He wants everyone to be rectified and redeemed. The Redemption will come because the Community of Israel will grow and more and more people will join it in its service of God. Therefore Jacob said to Simeon and Levi, "Let my soul not enter into their conspiracy" (Genesis 49:6) (referring to the rebellions of Korach and Zimri). Each soul that joins the holy community enhances it, but strife and rebellion demean the community and lessen its chances for redemption (*Likutey Halakhot* VI, p. 54-28a). In contrast, the blessing Jacob gave to Judah alludes to the battles that Judah will wage to spread Godliness "until the coming of Shiloh" (Genesis 49:10)—for Judah's teachings will cause those who are distant from God to draw near, even converts (*Likutey Halakhot* VI, p. 29a-58).

) *Jacob called for his sons...Reuben...Simeon...Levi...Judah*

Every blemish that we find in the very great tzaddikim in the Torah stemmed from their forcing an issue rather than waiting patiently for God to answer them. Adam erred on the same day he was created—he should have waited until Shabbat began to engage in marital relations with Eve. Abraham demanded of God, "How will I know that I will inherit [the Land]?" (Genesis 15:8). Isaac wanted to give Esau the blessings so that Esau could be subservient to Jacob and support his Torah efforts—however, this result could not occur before the coming of Mashiach. Jacob wanted to reveal the End of Days, and the Divine Presence left him (see Rashi on Genesis 49:1).

When he began to bless his sons, Jacob actually rebuked the first three tribes, Reuben, Simeon and Levi, to impress upon them the importance of patience. Reuben forced the issue by moving Jacob's couch (see Rashi on Genesis 35:22). Simeon and Levi attacked Shekhem without consulting their father (Genesis 34:25). In Judah, however, Jacob saw the progenitor of Mashiach, who would exemplify true patience and master the power of supplication and prayer (*Likutey Halakhot* VIII, p. 223a-223b-224a).

A person should never force an issue, especially when he is praying to God. Instead, he should appeal constantly to God with various supplications and requests in order to draw close to Him and to draw upon himself the sanctity of Torah. One must endure many tests in order to properly attain Torah; being patient in prayer is the main way he can exercise his free will and learn to direct his will towards serving God (ibid., p. 228a).

49:2   הִקָּבְצוּ וְשִׁמְעוּ בְּנֵי יַעֲקֹב וְשִׁמְעוּ אֶל־יִשְׂרָאֵל אֲבִיכֶם

**"Gather together and listen, sons of Jacob.
Listen to your father Israel."**

❩ *Gather together and listen, sons of Jacob*

Unity among Jews will bring the Redemption. Thus, Jacob indicated to his children that they must be "together." He continued, "Gather together and listen, sons of Jacob"—for the way to attain this unity is by guarding your counsel. Seek only good advice from the true tzaddikim, and beware of faulty and improper counsel. This is hinted at in the name *YaAKoV* (יעקב, Jacob), from *EiKeV* (עקב, heel), since advice is the "feet" upon which a person stands.

Jacob rebuked the first three tribes for following improper advice. Reuben moved his father's couch and Simeon and Levi attacked Shekhem, each without seeking proper counsel. Jacob gave his blessing to Judah, however, because Judah confessed his sin (Targum Onkelos on Genesis 49:8). Confessing one's sins is the best advice, as it helps one to recognize his shortcomings and rectify them (*Likutey Halakhot* III, p. 390-196a-392).

❩ *Gather together...Reuben...Simeon...Levi*

Rebbe Nachman teaches that the tzaddik strives to gather Jews together. The more they unite, the greater the Torah he can reveal to them. In order to effect this revelation, he must perform two devotions. The first is to gather the souls together. The second is to elevate those souls to a higher level; this ascent allows the tzaddik to draw Torah from a higher level (see *Likutey Moharan* I, 13).

Jacob did not actually bless his first three sons, but rebuked them. They were the elder brothers, very great tzaddikim in their own right, but they were admonished because they represent the first, more difficult devotion of uniting the souls together. The "gathering" they require represents a constriction which must be widened and mitigated. Thus, Jacob rebuked them. The remainder of the tribes were blessed, for by then, the judgment was mitigated (*Likutey Halakhot* VIII, p. 56a-57a).

Reb Noson continues that this is why, even though they were rebuked, the first three tribes are enumerated in a special genealogy in Exodus 6:14-25. Rashi explains there (loc. cit. 6:14) that these three tribes are named by themselves because Jacob had rebuked them and Scripture wishes to show that they are important and not to be belittled. Within our context, the Egyptian exile refers to a constriction, which incurs difficulties and arouses wrath—similar to the rebuke Jacob gave his three eldest sons because he was trying to unite the souls. The time when all the Jews were getting ready to leave Egypt corresponds to the ascent of the souls from their constrictions. Thus, the Torah includes these three tribes in the ascent of the souls to attain the revelations of Torah (*Likutey Halakhot* VIII, p. 56a-56b).

49:3   רְאוּבֵן בְּכֹרִי אַתָּה כֹּחִי וְרֵאשִׁית אוֹנִי יֶתֶר שְׂאֵת וְיֶתֶר עָז

"Reuben, you are my firstborn, my might and the first of my manhood; foremost in rank and foremost in power."

⟩ My might and the first of my manhood

When a person heeds the teachings of the tzaddikim, his own speech gains power, to the extent that it can enable those who were barren—including the person himself—to bear children.

This is alluded to in Jacob's words "My might and the first of my manhood." Because Jacob's speech was powerful, he was able at the age of eighty-four to father children (*Likutey Moharan* I, 60:8).

49:6 בְּסֹדָם אַל־תָּבֹא נַפְשִׁי בִּקְהָלָם אַל־תֵּחַד כְּבֹדִי כִּי בְאַפָּם הָרְגוּ אִישׁ וּבִרְצֹנָם עִקְּרוּ־שׁוֹר

"Let my soul not enter into their conspiracy! Let my honor not join with their congregation! For they have killed a man in their anger, and maimed an ox with their will."

› *Let my honor not join with their congregation*

This refers to the congregation of Korach, a descendant of Levi, who gathered all the people against Moses and Aaron (Numbers 16) (Rashi).

There is a tzaddik who is so great that although many people oppose him, his greatness overcomes them. If all these people would band together, however, the sum total of the goodness that they possess might outweigh his greatness.

This is alluded to in Jacob's blessing, which may also be read: "Let 'honor' not band together in their congregation." Jacob prayed that when Korach and his band would rise up against Moses, the "honor" and goodness within each one of the participants would not join together with that of the others—for if that were to happen, they might overcome Moses (*Likutey Moharan* I, 181).

› *Let my soul not enter into their conspiracy! Let my honor not join with their congregation…I will divide them…I will disperse them*

The Tribe of Simeon rebelled during the incident of Pe'or (Numbers 25:6-9). Korach, a Levite, rebelled against Moses (ibid., 16:1), who continued the heritage of the Patriarchs by revealing Divine Favor. Jacob prayed that his name not be mentioned or included in these rebellions, since they tried to conceal Divine Favor while Jacob tried to reveal it. Instead, Jacob mandated that the Tribe of Simeon would be poor and that the Tribe of Levi would have to collect tithes as their due. Charity reveals Divine Favor and counters the effects of those who conceal it. By being involved in charity, albeit on the receiving end, Simeon's and Levi's rebellions would be mitigated (*Likutey Halakhot* I, p. 138a).

49:10 לֹא־יָסוּר שֵׁבֶט מִיהוּדָה וּמְחֹקֵק מִבֵּין רַגְלָיו עַד
כִּי־יָבֹא שִׁילֹה וְלוֹ יִקְהַת עַמִּים

"The scepter will not be removed from Judah, nor authority from between his feet, until the coming of Shiloh; then his will be a gathering of nations."

⟩ *Nor authority from between his feet*

Even though Judah—who represents the Jewish nation— descends to the "feet" (i.e., the lowest levels), still, authority (*mechokek*) will not be removed from him. The *mechokek* (literally, an inscribing or engraving pen) represents all the good that was ever done by the Jews, and serves as an indelible record of the good points that can always be found in them (*Likutey Halakhot* III, p. 156).

⟩ *Until the coming of Shiloh*

Shiloh is another name for Mashiach; it is also a reference to Moses, since the numerical value of both *ShILoH* (שילה) and *MoSheH* (משה) is the same (*Likutey Moharan* I, 118). Just as Moses is compared to Mashiach, so too, every tzaddik partakes of the nature of Mashiach (ibid., I, 2:6). Thus, a Messianic presence exists in every generation.

God considered Moses a possible candidate for Mashiach because he devoted himself to the point of self-sacrifice on behalf of the Jewish people (ibid., I, 79).

⟩ *The mechokek will not be removed...until the coming of Shiloh; then his will be a gathering of nations...He will tie his foal to the vine*

Mechokek (inscribing or engraving pen) refers to printed volumes of Torah. Foreseeing the long exile, Jacob prophesied that the Jewish people would be able to endure through Torah study. This verse tells us that the Torah that is recorded and published will remain with us until Mashiach comes, at which time even the nations of the world will turn to God and join in serving Him.

Yet Torah alone is not enough to bring Mashiach—we also need prayer. Therefore Mashiach incorporates the concepts of both Moses (*MoSheH*, whose name has the same numerical value as *ShILoH*, and who is connected with Torah) and King David (the progenitor of *Mashiach ben David*, who is connected with prayer). When Torah and prayer are combined, one can draw the salvation of Mashiach. Then "he will tie his foal to the vine," for the fruit of the vine—wine—represents the abundant joy that will prevail during the Messianic era (*Likutey Halakhot* IV, p. 320).

49:13 זְבוּלֻן לְחוֹף יַמִּים יִשְׁכֹּן וְהוּא לְחוֹף אֱנִיֹּת וְיַרְכָתוֹ עַל־צִידֹן

"Zebulun will settle the seashores. He will be a harbor for ships, and his border will reach Tzidon."

〕 *Zebulun will settle the seashores*

The Tribe of Zebulun provided a livelihood for the Tribe of Issachar, whose members dedicated their days to the study of Torah. Because Zebulun broke his avarice and shared his wealth with the righteous, he merited to "settle the seashores" and receive territory on the northernmost border of the Land of Israel, in Tzidon. In other words, his territory represents the gateway to the Holy Land, which is attained by breaking one's avarice. A person who breaks his desire for wealth (i.e., Zebulun) and gives charity to the tzaddikim (i.e., Issachar) merits to the Holy Land, because "Tzaddikim will inherit the Land" (Psalms 37:29) (*Likutey Halakhot* II, p. 254).

49:14 יִשָּׂשכָר חֲמֹר גָּרֶם רֹבֵץ בֵּין הַמִּשְׁפְּתָיִם

"Issachar is a strong-boned donkey, crouching between the borders."

⟩ *Issachar is a strong-boned donkey*

Issachar represents deep Torah learning and wisdom (*Likutey Moharan* I, 30:9). Thus, the leading members of the Sanhedrin generally came from the Tribe of Issachar. For this reason, Jacob blessed Issachar with great wealth (see Targum Onkelos). For just as a person requires a basic livelihood in order to attain general levels of Torah understanding, he requires great wealth in order to attain a profound understanding of Torah (ibid., I, 60:1, 9).

⟩ *Issachar is a strong-boned donkey, crouching between the borders*

Issachar took upon himself the yoke of Torah like a *ChaMoR* (חמור, donkey) takes on a yoke. In a deeper sense, this refers to the way that the tzaddik dedicates himself to reveal Godliness even to those who are steeped in *ChuMRiyut* (חומריות, materialism), thereby elevating materialism into holiness. "He crouches between the borders"—because the tzaddik goes down to the lowest borders in order to reach those distant from God and draw them near (*Likutey Halakhot* III, p. 160a-320).

49:18 לִישׁוּעָתְךָ קִוִּיתִי יְיָ

"I await Your salvation, O God!"

⟩ *I await Your salvation, O God!*

Jacob foresaw the deeds of Samson and the salvation that he would bring to the Jewish nation during his lifetime (Rashi). But he also foresaw that the Final Redemption would not take place at that time. Nevertheless, he exclaimed, "I await Your salvation, O God!" for tzaddikim never despair of God's salvation. Even if it doesn't come at the moment we seek it, it will come. We must await it (*Likutey Halakhot* III, p. 154).

49:20 מֵאָשֵׁר שְׁמֵנָה לַחְמוֹ וְהוּא יִתֵּן מַעֲדַנֵּי־מֶלֶךְ

"**From Asher will come rich foods; he will provide delicacies fit for a king.**"

》 *From Asher will come rich foods... Naphtali... delivers words of beauty*

When a person realizes that his income ("rich foods") comes to him through Divine Providence, he can pray and praise God ("words of beauty") (*Likutey Moharan* II, 16).

49:21 נַפְתָּלִי אַיָּלָה שְׁלֻחָה הַנֹּתֵן אִמְרֵי־שָׁפֶר

"**Naphtali is a hind let loose, who delivers words of beauty.**"

》 *Naphtali... delivers words of beauty*

The Talmud teaches that one can attain a good life when he wears *tefilin* (*Menachot* 44a).

King Solomon writes that one can attain a good life when he marries, as the verse states: "See life with the woman you love" (Ecclesiastes 9:9).

The concepts of *tefilin* and marriage combine in Jacob's blessing to Naphtali. The letters of the name *NaFTaLi* (נפתלי) are contained in the word *TeFiLiN* (תפילין). The word *IShaH* (אשה, woman) in King Solomon's verse is an acronym for *Ha-notein Imrei Shefer* (הנותן אמרי שפר, delivers words of beauty) in Jacob's blessing. Additionally, Jacob's blessing evokes the concept of the Holy Land. For Naphtali is associated with "words of beauty," and "beauty" refers to the Holy Land (*Likutey Moharan* I, 47).

49:22 בֵּן פֹּרָת יוֹסֵף בֵּן פֹּרָת עֲלֵי־עָיִן בָּנוֹת צָעֲדָה עֲלֵי־שׁוּר

"Joseph is a fruitful bough, a fruitful bough upon the well. Girls stepped out to see him."

⟩ *Joseph is a fruitful bough, a fruitful bough upon the well*

Ayin (well) also means "eye." Because Joseph guarded his covenant, he attained the attribute of judgment, which is associated with the eyes—as in the place name *Ein Mishpat* (Eye of Judgment) (Genesis 14:7). Therefore Joseph's eyes were blessed (*Likutey Moharan* I, 2:5).

⟩ *Aleh ayin*

Aleh ayin (upon the well) literally means "those who transcend the eye." Joseph ascends over and above what the eye sees (i.e., what there is in this world) in order to attain perceptions of God (*Likutey Halakhot* I, p. 28a-56).

Joseph transcended the "eye of lust"—the main lust of the seventy nations (the word *ayin* [eye] is homonymous with the letter *ayin* [ע], which has a numerical value of 70)—when he resisted the temptation of Potiphar's wife. Because Joseph transcended that "eye of lust," he merits to transcend the evil eye, which cannot gain power over Joseph or his descendants (*Likutey Halakhot* IV, p. 26a).

49:23 וַיְמָרֲרֻהוּ וָרֹבּוּ וַיִּשְׂטְמֻהוּ בַּעֲלֵי חִצִּים

"They embittered him and attacked him. The archers hated him."

⟩ *The archers hated him*

"Archers" are hostile people whose words are like arrows (*Likutey Moharan* I, 46; ibid., I, 145).

49:24 וַתֵּשֶׁב בְּאֵיתָן קַשְׁתּוֹ וַיָּפֹזּוּ זְרֹעֵי יָדָיו מִידֵי אֲבִיר
יַעֲקֹב מִשָּׁם רֹעֶה אֶבֶן יִשְׂרָאֵל

"His bow stayed firm and his arms were gilded. This was from the hands of the Mighty One of Jacob, and from then on, he became a shepherd of the Rock of Israel."

❭ *His bow stayed firm…he became a shepherd of the Rock of Israel*

Joseph held firm to his bow—i.e., to the purity of his covenant. As a result, he attained the Rock. The word *EVeN* (אבן, rock) comprises two words, *AV* (אב, father) and *BeN* (בן, son). These refer to Jacob and his sons, who together exemplify prayer. Thus, guarding the covenant leads to prayer (*Likutey Moharan* I, 7:end).

49:27 בִּנְיָמִין זְאֵב יִטְרָף בַּבֹּקֶר יֹאכַל עַד וְלָעֶרֶב
יְחַלֵּק שָׁלָל

"Benjamin is a predatory wolf; in the morning he eats and in the evening he divides his prey."

❭ *Benjamin is a predatory wolf; in the morning he eats and in the evening he divides his prey*

Benjamin is compared to a wolf that tears away at its enemy. *YiTRaF* (יטרף, he tears) may also be read as *TeReF* (טרף, sustenance). Through his eating, a tzaddik draws down spiritual sustenance ("in the morning he eats") and can tear apart his spiritual enemies ("in the evening he divides his prey").

The Talmud teaches that the Temple Altar was built in the territory of Benjamin (*Zevachim* 54a). As a result of the sacrifices consumed upon the Altar, spiritual sustenance was drawn down to the Jews and their enemies were defeated (*Likutey Moharan* I, 17:3).

49:28 כָּל־אֵלֶּה שִׁבְטֵי יִשְׂרָאֵל שְׁנֵים עָשָׂר וְזֹאת אֲשֶׁר־
דִּבֶּר לָהֶם אֲבִיהֶם וַיְבָרֶךְ אוֹתָם אִישׁ אֲשֶׁר כְּבִרְכָתוֹ
בֵּרַךְ אֹתָם

**All these are the tribes of Israel—twelve—and
this is what their father told them when he
blessed them. Each according to his blessing
did he bless them.**

⟫ *This is what their father told them*

> *Zot* (This) corresponds to Malkhut (see *Tikkuney Zohar*, Introduction, p. 11b).

Malkhut is associated with holy speech. After Jacob finished blessing his sons, he taught them that the greatest blessing of all is pure and holy speech. With holy speech, one can subdue evil speech (the impure mirror image of Malkhut, called the Malkhut of impurity) and defeat his adversaries (*Likutey Moharan* I, 38:2).

50:18 וַיֵּלְכוּ גַּם־אֶחָיו וַיִּפְּלוּ לְפָנָיו וַיֹּאמְרוּ הִנֶּנּוּ לְךָ לַעֲבָדִים

**Then his brothers came and threw themselves
before him. "Behold! We are your slaves!"
they said.**

⟫ *We are your slaves*

Despising others leads to servitude. Because the brothers despised Joseph, they eventually had to offer themselves as his slaves (*Likutey Moharan* II, 1:10).

50:20 וְאַתֶּם חֲשַׁבְתֶּם עָלַי רָעָה אֱלֹהִים חֲשָׁבָהּ לְטֹבָה
לְמַעַן עֲשֹׂה כַּיּוֹם הַזֶּה לְהַחֲיֹת עַם־רָב

> **"Though you intended to do me harm,**
> **God intended it for good. He made it**
> **come about, as it actually did, to sustain**
> **a great nation."**

❭ *God intended it for good*

Though the brothers' original intention to sell Joseph may have
been bad, Joseph's descent to Egypt enabled them all to survive the
famine and eventually elevate all the fallen sparks of holiness in
Egypt (*Likutey Halakhot* II, p. 306).

50:21 וְעַתָּה אַל־תִּירָאוּ אָנֹכִי אֲכַלְכֵּל אֶתְכֶם וְאֶת־
טַפְּכֶם וַיְנַחֵם אוֹתָם וַיְדַבֵּר עַל־לִבָּם

> **"Now, do not fear. I will provide for you**
> **and your children." He comforted them**
> **and spoke to their hearts.**

❭ *He spoke to their hearts*

Joseph spoke words that were soothing and acceptable to his
brothers' hearts (Rashi).

In this manner, Joseph exercised the principal power of the
tzaddik, which is to arouse people's hearts so that they may come
to serve God (*Likutey Moharan* I, 34:8).

The Order of the Ten Sefirot

כתר
Keter

חכמה
Chokhmah

בינה
Binah

[דעת]
[Da'at]

חסד
Chesed

גבורה
Gevurah

תפארת
Tiferet

נצח
Netzach

הוד
Hod

יסוד
Yesod

מלכות
Malkhut

The Structure of the Sefirot

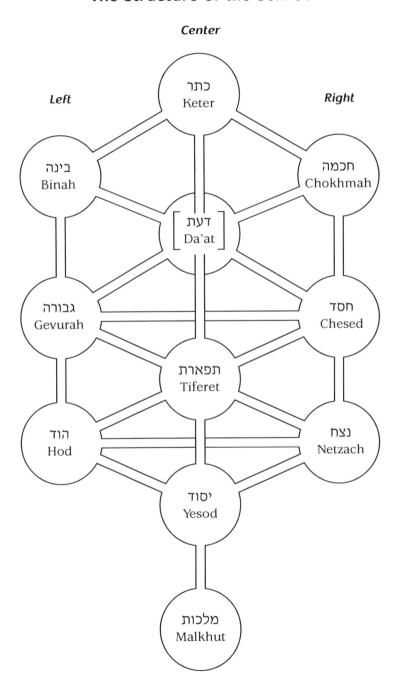

The Divine Personae (Partzufim)

Sefirah		Persona
Keter		Atik Yomin
		Arikh Anpin
Chokhmah ⌉		Abba
	Da'at	
Binah ⌋		Imma

Tiferet	⌈ Chesed	
	Gevurah	
	Tiferet	
	Netzach	Ze'er Anpin
	Hod	
	⌊ Yesod	

| Malkhut | Nukva of Ze'er Anpin |

Alternative names for Ze'er Anpin and Malkhut:
Ze'er Anpin: Yaakov, Yisrael, Yisrael Saba, Torah, Written Law,
        Holy King, the Sun
Malkhut: Leah, Rachel, Prayer, Oral Law, *Shekhinah*, the Moon

The Supernal Colors

Keter (Crown, Will)	Blinding, invisible white
Chokhmah (Wisdom)	A color that includes all color
Binah (Understanding)	Yellow and green
Chesed (Kindness)	White and silver
Gevurah (Strength, Restraint)	Red and gold
Tiferet (Beauty, Harmony)	Yellow and purple
Netzach (Victory, Endurance)	Light pink
Hod (Splendor)	Dark pink
Yesod (Foundation)	Orange
Malkhut (Kingship)	Blue

The Sefirot and Man

Keter (Crown, Will)	Skull
Chokhmah (Wisdom)	Right brain
Binah (Understanding)	Left brain
Da'at (Knowledge, Awareness)	Middle brain
Chesed (Kindness)	Right arm
Gevurah (Strength, Restraint)	Left arm
Tiferet (Beauty, Harmony)	Torso
Netzach (Victory, Endurance)	Right leg
Hod (Splendor)	Left leg
Yesod (Foundation)	Sexual organ (brit)
Malkhut (Kingship)	Feet

Alternatively: Chokhmah corresponds to brain/mind; Binah to heart
Alternatively: Malkhut corresponds to man's mate, or the mouth

Levels of Existence

World	Manifestation	Sefirah	Soul	Letter
Adam Kadmon		Keter	Yechidah	Apex of Yod
Atzilut	Nothingness	Chokhmah	Chayah	Yod
Beriah	Thought	Binah	Neshamah	Hei
Yetzirah	Speech	Tiferet (six sefirot)	Ruach	Vav
Asiyah	Action	Malkhut	Nefesh	Hei

World	Inhabitants	T–N–T–A
Adam Kadmon	The Holy Names	
Atzilut (Nearness)	Sefirot, Partzufim	Ta'amim (Cantillations)
Beriah (Creation)	The Throne, Souls	Nekudot (Vowels)
Yetzirah (Formation)	Angels	Tagim (Crowns)
Asiyah (Action)	Forms	Otiyot (Letters)

Hebrew / English Transliteration Schema

lamed	L	ל	*aleph*	silent*	א
mem	M	מ, ם	*bet*	B	בּ
nun	N	נ, ן	*vet*	V	ב
samekh	S	ס	*gimel*	G	ג
ayin	silent*	ע	*dalet*	D	ד
pei	P	פ	*hei*	H	ה
phei	Ph, F	פ, ף	*vav*	V, O, U	ו, וֹ, וּ
tzadi	tZ	צ, ץ	*zayin*	Z	ז
kuf	K	ק	*chet*	Ch	ח
reish	R	ר	*tet*	T	ט
shin	Sh	שׁ	*yod*	Y	י
sin	S	שׂ	*kaf*	K	כ
tav	T	ת	*khaf*	Kh	כ, ך

* The letters א and ע are "silent" consonants (with no English letter-equivalents) and are transliterated based on their accompanying vowel-point as A (Æ), E, I, O (Œ), or U

Hebrew Letter Numerology (Gematria)

300 = שׁ	70 = ע	20 = כ,ך	6 = ו	1 = א
400 = ת	80 = פ,ף	30 = ל	7 = ז	2 = ב
	90 = צ,ץ	40 = מ,ם	8 = ח	3 = ג
	100 = ק	50 = נ,ן	9 = ט	4 = ד
	200 = ר	60 = ס	10 = י	5 = ה

Alternate values for the five end-letters, *MaNtZPaKh*:

900 = ץ	800 = ף	700 = ן	600 = ם	500 = ך

Glossary

Achashveirosh: the Persian king during the Purim story

Ari: an acronym for Rabbi Isaac Luria (1534-1572), Jewish scholar and founder of the modern study of Kabbalah

Ba'al teshuvah (pl. *ba'alei teshuvah*): literally, "master of return"; a Jew who returns to God and Jewish religious practice

Binah: understanding; when capitalized, refers to one of the Ten Sefirot

Chassid (pl. *chassidim*): a religiously devout person; a follower of the movement to revitalize Jewish spiritual life initiated by the Baal Shem Tov, great-grandfather of Rebbe Nachman, in the 18th century

Chesed: kindness; when capitalized, refers to one of the Ten Sefirot

Chokhmah: wisdom; when capitalized, refers to one of the Ten Sefirot

Chumash: the Five Books of Moses

Da'at: higher perception; complete knowledge or awareness of God; when capitalized, refers to one of the Ten Sefirot

Gehinnom: hell

Gevurah (pl. *gevurot*): strength, restraint; when capitalized, refers to one of the Ten Sefirot

Haggadah: liturgy of the Pesach Seder

Halakhic: pertaining to Jewish law

Havdalah: literally, "separation"; ceremony marking the conclusion of Shabbat

Hitbodedut: literally, "self-seclusion"; Rebbe Nachman uses the term to refer to a daily practice in which one sets a time and place to speak to God

Kabbalah: body of esoteric Jewish wisdom

Kaddish: Jewish memorial prayer

Karpas: greens such as celery or parsley which are dipped in salt water and eaten during the Pesach Seder

Kelipah (pl. *kelipot*): literally, "husk"; in Kabbalistic thought, an unholy force that surrounds and conceals the sparks of holiness (the various aspects of holiness and spiritual vitality present in creation)

Keter: crown; when capitalized, refers to the highest of the Ten Sefirot

Kohen (pl. *Kohanim*): a member of the Jewish priestly class, a patrilineal descendant of Moses' brother Aaron

Lag BaOmer: literally, "thirty-third day of the Omer"; the *yahrtzeit* of Rabbi Shimon bar Yochai and a minor festival during the forty-nine-day Counting of the Omer

Malkhut: kingship; when capitalized, refers to the lowest of the Ten Sefirot

Manna: the Heavenly food that fell for the Jewish people during their forty-year sojourn in the desert, as described in Exodus 16:13-36

Mashiach: the Jewish Messiah

Matzah: unleavened bread eaten on Pesach

Mayim achronim: literally, "final waters"; a small amount of water poured on the fingertips after eating and prior to the recitation of the Grace After Meals. According to the Kabbalah, this small amount of water is a "gift" to the Other Side

Mezuzah: literally, "doorpost"; more commonly, the scroll containing Scriptural passages that every Jewish dwelling is required to have affixed to its doorposts and gateways, as mandated by Deuteronomy 6:9

Midrash: homiletical teachings on the Tanakh

Milah: circumcision

Mishnah: the redaction of the Oral Law that forms the first part of the Talmud, redacted by Rabbi Yehudah HaNasi, circa 200 C.E.

Mitzvah (pl. *mitzvot*): a Torah commandment; religious precept

Omer: a barley-offering brought in the Holy Temple on the second day of Pesach, inaugurating a forty-nine-day period called the Counting of the Omer which connects the festivals of Pesach and Shavuot

Other Side: the system of evil that stands opposite the force of holiness, called *Sitra Achra* in Aramaic

Parashah: weekly Torah reading

Partzuf: Aramaic for "face"; one of five unitary constellations of *sefirot*, each corresponding to a particular *sefirah* or set of *sefirot*—e.g., Arich Anpin is the *partzuf* of Keter, Abba is the *partzuf* of Chokhmah, etc.

Pesach: the Jewish Passover, a biblical festival commemorating the Exodus from Egypt, occurring in spring

Rashi: an acronym for Rabbi Shlomo Yitzchaki (1040-1110), the pre-eminent commentator on the Talmud and Tanakh whose commentary appears in all standard editions of these works

Rav: literally, "master"; a rabbi or teacher

Rosh Chodesh: the first day of each Hebrew month

Rosh HaShanah: the Jewish New Year

Sanhedrin: the Jewish Supreme Court of seventy-one Sages that presided during the Second Temple period through the fourth century C.E. in the Land of Israel

Seder: literally, "order"; the ritual meal held on the first night of Pesach, commemorating the redemption of the Jewish people from slavery in Egypt

Sefirah (pl. *sefirot*): one of ten Divine emanations through which all entities on all levels of creation came into being and are continually recreated *ex nihilo*. These emanations are: Keter, Chokhmah, Binah, [Da'at,] Chesed, Gevurah, Tiferet, Netzach, Hod, Yesod and Malkhut.

Shabbat: the Jewish Sabbath, beginning at sundown on Friday afternoon and ending on Saturday night with the appearance of three medium-sized stars in the nighttime sky

Shavuot: biblical festival commemorating the Giving of the Torah on Mount Sinai, occurring in early summer

Shema (also *Shema Yisrael*): a declaration of faith in the Oneness of God and a commitment to fulfilling His commandments, comprised of verses from Deuteronomy 6:4-9 and 11:13-21 and Numbers 15:37-41. Recited daily during morning and evening prayers, and before going to sleep.

Shemoneh Esrei: literally, "Eighteen"; the silent devotional prayer which is the focus of the three daily obligatory prayers. So named because it initially consisted of eighteen blessings; an additional blessing was added later.

Sukkah: a thatch-covered structure of three or four walls, used as a residence during the festival of Sukkot

Sukkot: biblical festival commemorating God's benevolent care of the Jewish people during their forty-year sojourn in the desert, and His continuing Providence over material blessing, occurring in autumn

Talit: prayer shawl

Talmud: the Oral Law, expounded by the rabbinical leaders between approximately 50 B.C.E. and 500 C.E. The first part of the Talmud, called the Mishnah, was codified by Rabbi Yehudah HaNasi around 188 C.E. The second part, called the Gemara, was edited by Rav Ashi and Ravina around 505 C.E.

Tanakh: an acronym for *Torah, Nevi'im, Ketuvim* (Torah, Prophets, Writings), comprising the twenty-four books of the Hebrew Bible

Targum: an Aramaic translation of the *Chumash*

Tefilin: mitzvah of wearing special leather boxes on the head and the arm during morning prayers (except on Shabbat and Festivals); the boxes themselves, which contain biblical verses declaring the Oneness of God and the miracles of the Exodus from Egypt

Tekheilet: a special blue dye used to make the clothing of the High Priest, the tapestries of Tabernacle, and the threads of *tzitzit*, obtained from the blood of a marine creature known as the *chilazon* (see *Menachot* 44a)

Tiferet: beauty; when capitalized, refers to one of the Ten Sefirot

Torah: literally, "teaching"; the Written Law given by God to Moses on Mount Sinai; in an extended sense, the entire corpus of Jewish religious thought

Tzaddik (pl. **tzaddikim**): righteous person; in Chassidic thought, one who has purified his heart of all evil, making himself a channel for Divine revelation and true compassion

Tzaddik emet: literally, "true tzaddik"; one who has completely purified himself of evil and realized the essence of being, enabling himself to relate to people on all spiritual levels in order to bring about their rectification

Tzimtzum: constriction; when capitalized, refers to God's original constriction of His Essence in order to begin the process of Creation

Tzitzit: specially spun and tied strings which Jewish men are required to affix to their four-cornered garments, as stipulated in Numbers 15:37-41 and discussed in *Menachot* 43b

Yahrtzeit: anniversary of death

Yeshivah: literally, "sitting"; a Torah academy

Yesod: foundation; when capitalized, refers to one of the Ten Sefirot

Yom Kippur: the Day of Atonement on which Jewish males aged 13 and older and Jewish females aged 12 and older are required to fast from sundown until the appearance of three medium-sized stars the following night

Zohar: the greatest classic of the Kabbalah, a mystical commentary on the Torah authored by the school of Rabbi Shimon bar Yochai, a Mishnaic Sage and leading disciple of Rabbi Akiva, during the second century C.E.

Made in the USA
Las Vegas, NV
09 September 2021

29917095R00206